Harvard Historical Studies · 138

Published under the auspices
of the Department of History
from the income of the
Paul Revere Frothingham Bequest
Robert Louis Stroock Fund
Henry Warren Torrey Fund

Slave Patrols

*Law and Violence in Virginia
and the Carolinas*

Sally E. Hadden

HARVARD UNIVERSITY PRESS
Cambridge, Massachusetts
London, England
2001

Library of Congress Cataloging-in-Publication Data

Hadden, Sally E.
　　Slave patrols : law and violence in Virginia and the Carolinas /
Sally E. Hadden.
　　　　p.　　cm. — (Harvard historical studies ; v. 138)
　　Includes bibliographical references (p.) and index.
　　ISBN 0-674-00470-1 (alk. paper)
　　1. Slaves—Government policy—Southern States—History.
2. Slaves—Southern States—Social conditions.　3. Law enforcement—
Southern States—History.　4. Police—Southern States—History.
5. Violence—Southern States—History.　6. Virginia—Race relations.
7. North Carolina—Race relations.　8. South Carolina—Race relations.
9. Afro-Americans—Southern States—History.　I. Title.　II. Series.

E443 .H33 2001
326′.09757—dc21　　　00-061336

326.097

For Doris Marguerite Ratliff Hadden

Contents

Figures

Acknowledgments

Although the act of writing is usually a solitary one, the single author's name upon a title page can be misleading. The finished product the reader holds is like a solo concert at which the audience never sees the stagehands, manager, or other loyal supporters who have made it all possible. The funding, research support, guidance, and encouragement that a writer receives along the way powerfully demonstrate the communal nature of this type of endeavor.

During the writing of this book I gratefully received financial support from many sources, including the Harry Frank Guggenheim Foundation, the Josephine de Kármán Foundation, the Andrew W. Mellon Foundation, the Virginia Historical Society, an Archie K. Davis Fellowship from the North Caroliniana Society, the Littleton-Griswold Fund of the American Historical Association, a Kate B. and Hall J. Peterson Fellowship at the American Antiquarian Society, the Mark DeWolfe Howe Fund of Harvard Law School, and the Charles Warren Center and the History Department of Harvard University. Research leave given by the University of Toledo and Florida State University made it possible for me to revise and complete this book without the distractions of other professional responsibilities.

Any historian will tell you that without librarians and archivists, our work would be virtually impossible. I am deeply indebted to the librarians and staff at Widener Library (Harvard College), Langdell Library (Harvard Law School), and Strozier Library (Florida State University). While in North Carolina, I was graciously assisted at the North Carolina Division of Archives and History by Lee Albright, Charles Morris, George Stevenson, and Pam Thoms. In Chapel Hill, Harry McKown in the North Carolina Collection aided me with his knowledge of their vast holdings, and David Moltke-Hansen, Richard Shrader, John White, and Genevieve Innes of the Southern Historical Collection and the Southern

Folklife Collection also rendered every possible assistance. The guidance of staff members at the Duke University Rare Book, Manuscript, and Special Collections Library far exceeded my expectations. Both William Ervin, Jr., and Tony Jenkins merit special praise for their kind attentions. In South Carolina, my stay was made infinitely more pleasant by the presence of Herb Hartsook and Allen Stokes at the South Caroliniana Collection. At the South Carolina Department of Archives and History, I was assisted by Bryan McKown and Carolyn Quickmire McDonnell, in addition to support given by Tricia Montgomery. In Richmond, the entire staff of the Virginia Historical Society patiently provided me with all I could ask for; Frances Pollard and Nelson Lankford deserve special commendation for their services. At the Library of Virginia, my efforts were aided by Mary Sine Clark, John Kneebone, Marianne McKee, Brent Tarter, and Minor Weisiger. The staff at the Special Collections Department of the University of Virginia Library gave me significant help as I waded through their enormous holdings.

Although the services rendered by librarians and archivists provide immediate scholarly assistance to the wandering researcher, it is often the more intangible aid and comfort given by friends and colleagues that make long-term research and writing projects even possible. I could not have completed this book without the support of my friends in the Harvard History Department, especially David Bush and Russell Martin. Chip and Rose Pate generously opened their home to me on more than one research trip. The years I spent at Harvard were notably enhanced by my association with Lowell House, its many gifted students and tutors, and its masters, Bill and Mary Lee Bossert. I wish to thank Suhnne Ahn, Rosemary Byrne, Christoph Lüthy, Ben Miller, Kevin O'Rourke, Lee (Hyung Il) Pai, Barbara Petzen, Jeff Richter, Tom Sugrue, and Lars Waldorf.

The boundary between professional advice and friendship is narrowest when a colleague makes shrewd observations about the historian's craft following a delicious meal. This work significantly improved after conversations (with or without food) that I had with other historians, who gave freely of their time and expertise. William Gienapp and Rachelle Friedman read this manuscript several times, and their suggestions improved it at every stage. Edward Ayers, Canter Brown, J. Michael Crane, Betty Dessants, Sharla Fett, Ronald Fisher, Lacy Ford, Joan Gunderson, Robinson Herrera, Peter Hoffer, Woody Holton, Neil Jumonville, John Edward Lendon, Janet Lindmann, Timothy Lockley, Michael McDonnell, Carol Bresnahan Menning and Ralph Menning, Elizabeth Meyer, Alex Moore, John Hammond Moore, Harold Moser, Michael Nicholls, Mark Pitcavage, William Powell, Kym Rice, William Warren Rogers, Jr., Darrett and Anita Rutman, Philip Schwarz, Gerald Shinn, and Alan D. Watson all offered useful advice and urged me on in this undertaking. Angelica Bernal and Andrew Thompson went above and beyond the call of duty as research assistants. In addition, many of my colleagues at Florida State University's History Department have encouraged me during this project. Two that merit special mention are Richard Greaves and William Warren Rogers, Sr., who have inspired me with their abilities to juggle teaching, family, and publishing, while gently exhorting a younger scholar along the way. I also acknowledge Aïda Donald of Harvard University Press, who believed that this book was an important story waiting to be told.

This book began as a dissertation under the direction of Bernard Bailyn, and the assistance of such an advisor is inestimable. From the beginning, Professor Bailyn had confidence in my ability to complete this task, and showed me through his own superb work what it means to be a historian. Although the flaws that remain in this work are entirely my own, he helped me weed and prune to remove infelicities of language and imprudent historical thought.

Last of all, I thank my family, who have supported my work in history through the years. My husband, Robert Berkhofer III, and his parents, Genevieve and Robert Berkhofer, Jr., have lovingly encouraged me. My sisters, Jill Hadden, Patricia Gunter, Fran Hadden, and Peggy Hadden, and my brothers, Earl Hadden and John Gunter, have listened patiently as I labored on this project. Finally, I wish to thank my parents, Doris and Earl Hadden. My one regret at the end of this particular journey is that my mother could not be here to enjoy its conclusion with me.

Of Perpetrators and Police

Historians interested in crime in the modern period have customarily concentrated on jails and the criminals thrown into them for breaking the law. The persons actually charged with capturing lawbreakers, however, known since the nineteenth century as the police, have attracted less historical study. Until recently, police and their activities were largely left to sociologists and political scientists, who principally investigated police of the twentieth century.[1] Meanwhile, prisons and punishment have been eloquently described by historians like Edward Ayers or Michael Hindus, who evoked the dehumanizing effects of chain gangs or the changing nature of incarceration.[2] The historical profession's traditional emphasis on institutional history has certainly motivated much of this prison research, while more recent scholars have no doubt been inspired by the theories of Michel Foucault about the prison or the asylum.[3] Alternatively, scholars who investigate the "deviant," the criminal, have often been stimulated by progressive, social, or Marxist history trends to search for patterns in the law or the nature of offenders that would reveal larger issues of social injustice and class bias in the criminal code.[4] But whether they looked at jails, criminals, or even briefly examined the police, most works in the history of crime have focused their attention on New England, and left the American South virtually untouched.[5]

Law enforcement groups have not received the same degree of scrutiny from Southern legal historians. Work done on Southern legal records has largely been left to the historians of slavery, who have paid great attention to slave courts, codes, and punishment in order to em-

1

phasize the marked contrast with what white criminal Southerners would have experienced under similar circumstances.[6] Few have moved beyond the statutes themselves, or the most grisly cases, when working on slave law, and historians have noted this limited perspective: Philip Schwarz has drawn attention to the fact that while scholars have studied slave laws, courts, and cases, virtually no work has been done on how slaves themselves perceived and influenced outcomes in slave courts.[7] Even the more elaborate studies of slave law often neglect to mention that people other than masters or overseers had legitimate rights, indeed, legal duties, to regulate slave behavior.

This book examines the public regulation of slavery in Virginia and the Carolinas, focusing on slave patrols during the period 1700 to 1865. By moving beyond the worlds of slave and master to include a third party—the slave patrols—we can better understand how the laws of slavery actually applied to slaves.[8] Some readers may desire to know only how slaves perceived patrollers (see Chapter 4), but my intention is to consider a broader range of historical questions. Scrutinizing patrollers will flesh out our understanding of how slave laws were actually enforced, day to day, while providing information about how the formation of Southern police forces was affected by regional influences like the presence of slavery and white conceptions of honor.[9] Some have seen patrols as merely another example of masters controlling slaves, but patrols routinely included nonowners although they did not include free blacks.[10] Nor were patrols an all-male concern: in South Carolina, women who owned slaves were required to provide a substitute for patrol service.[11] Although patrols were an integral part of both masters' and slaves' lives in the South, they have received but scant attention from scholars to this point. H. M. Henry, in his 1914 study of patrols in South Carolina, focused almost exclusively on the laws that connected patrols to the militia, ignoring patrol personnel, procedures, and differences that existed between urban and rural areas.[12] Similarly, Benjamin Callahan's fifty-three-page analysis of patrols in North Carolina followed a similar pattern: he examined most closely the creation of patrols and the brutality of slave patrollers.[13] To my knowledge, no investigation of patrols in Virginia exists.

This study explores patrols in Virginia and North and South Carolina, colonies that were among the first to contain slaves in what would eventually become the United States. This regional survey allows for comparisons of unusual sources, while compensating for the limited amount of surviving material that usually accompanies studies of militia-related groups. Owing to their earlier settlement, these eastern seaboard states had a longer tradition of employing slave patrols than did those of the Deep South, and thus they provide a stable view of how patrols functioned through multiple decades, wars, and slave revolts.

Each of the six chapters in this book is devoted to a different aspect of slave patrols. The first and last chapters proceed chronologically, on the "birth" and "death" of patrols; the four remaining chapters progress thematically. Chapter 1 focuses on the late seventeenth and eighteenth centuries and the reasons behind the formation of the original patrol groups. Chapter 2 discusses the organization and administration of slave patrols, with greater emphasis on the eighteenth and nineteenth centuries. In Chapter 3, I describe slave patrol personnel, in particular their method of appointment and their composition, to test the long-held, though unproven, view that patrols were composed of the poorest whites of Southern society. The everyday, regular functions of slave patrols are considered in Chapter 4, while the responses of patrols to times of crisis, both in slave insurrections and in wartime, is covered in Chapter 5. The impact of the Civil War on patrols and their eventual demise are explored in Chapter 6. The Epilogue briefly traces the legacy of patrols for both police groups and the Ku Klux Klan during Reconstruction.

Patrols were not created in a vacuum, but owed much to European institutions that served as the slave patrol's institutional forebears. Efforts by slave patrols to limit the movements and behavior of slaves evoke memories of the *posse comitatus,* the bands of men called out in early modern England to chase down and arrest fleeing felons. Likewise, the "hue and cry" that a constable would bellow in the wake of elusive criminals, calling upon all available men to help him capture the thief or the burglar, also provided a model for chasing down slaves in the New World. The unforced nature of service in the posse or in answering a constable's cry was altered, however, when Caribbean, and later Southern, colonists discovered the need to limit the mobility and actions of their bondsmen as well as to compel their neighbors to serve on patrols. Combining their knowledge of posses and militia groups, Spanish and English settlers devised a new law enforcement institution to supplement the authority of slave owners—the slave patrol.

The reliance upon race as a defining feature of this new colonial creation reveals the singular difference that set slave patrols apart from their European antecedents. Although slave patrols also supervised the activities of free African Americans and suspicious whites who associated with slaves, the main focus of their attention fell upon slaves. Bondsmen could easily be distinguished by their race and thus became easy and immediate targets of racial brutality. As a result, the new American innovation in law enforcement during the eighteenth and early nineteenth centuries was the creation of racially focused law enforcement groups in the American South.

The creation of patrols had other effects upon law enforcement in the region. As Southern urban areas expanded in the eighteenth and nineteenth centuries, they might have been expected to develop their own police forces, comparable to those created in Northern cities. In some cities, patrols were replaced by police groups. But in other Southern towns, patrols continued to function in many ways like police groups: breaking up nighttime gatherings, hauling in suspicious characters, trying to prevent mischief before it happened, or capturing the lawbreakers after the fact. The big difference was that in the South, the "most dangerous people" who were thought to need watching were slaves—they were the prime targets of patrol observation and capture. The history of police work in the South grows out of this early fascination, by white patrollers, with what African American slaves were doing. Most law enforcement was, by definition, white patrolmen watching, catching, or beating black slaves.

The difficulties of relying upon race and slavery to define the main contours of Southern law enforcement revealed themselves in the Civil War's aftermath. No longer permitted to use race as an explicit criteria for conviction or punishment, Southern whites discovered during Reconstruction that their system of law enforcement was flawed: they could not overtly use racial status to sanction, legally, the whipping and brutalizing of freedmen. The connection between law enforcement and racial hatred would have to evolve in Southern society. Although slave patrols officially ceased to operate at the close of the Civil War, their functions were assumed by other Southern institutions. Their law-enforcing aspects—checking suspicious persons, limiting nighttime movement—became the duties of Southern police forces, while their lawless, violent aspects were taken up by vigilante groups like the Ku Klux Klan. The Klan's reign of racial terror in the late nineteenth century emphasized the most extreme elements of earlier slave patrol behavior.

Many people I have talked with have jumped to the conclusion that patrolling violence of an earlier century explains why some modern-day policemen, today, have violent confrontations with African Americans. But while a legacy of hate-filled relations has made it difficult for many African Americans to trust the police, their maltreatment in the seventeenth, eighteenth, or nineteenth centuries should not carry all the blame. We may seek the roots of racial fears in an earlier period, but that history does not displace our responsibility to change and improve the era in which we live. After all, the complex police and racial problems that our country continues to experience in the present day are, in many cases, the results of failings and misunderstandings in our own time. To blame the 1991 beating of Rodney King by police in Los Angeles on slave patrollers dead nearly two hundred years is to miss the point. My purpose in writing this text is a historical one, an inquiry into the earliest period of both Southern law enforcement and Southern race-based violence. Although the conclusions below may provide insight into the historical reasons for the pattern of racially targeted law enforcement that persists to the current day, it remains for us to cope with our inheritance from this earlier world without overlooking our present-day obligation to create a less fearful future.

1

Colonial Beginnings and Experiments

> With us, every citizen is concerned in the maintenance of order, and in
> promoting honesty and industry among those of the lowest class who
> are our slaves; and our habitual vigilance renders standing armies,
> whether of soldiers or policemen, entirely unnecessary. Small guards
> in our cities, and occasional patrols in the country, insure us a repose
> and security known nowhere else.
>
> *1845 letter from former South Carolina governor James Henry*
> *Hammond to Thomas Clarkson*

With these words, James Henry Hammond sought to justify as well as
explain to a leading English abolitionist that all white Southerners recognized their collective responsibility for maintaining dominance over
the black slaves among them.[1] Moreover, he presumed that such collective responsibility was best achieved through slave patrols. Other Southerners grasped Hammond's meaning: everywhere across the South, in
newspapers and in the influential *DeBow's Review*, where his words were
reprinted in 1849, white editors and correspondents acknowledged his
views as an accurate reflection of their slaveholding society. They were
familiar with patrols and the need for every citizen to be concerned "in
the maintenance of order."[2]

The picture Hammond evokes of the members of Southern white society standing shoulder to shoulder as sentinels armed against their
slaves is one that modern readers understand almost implicitly. Southern whites feared their slaves and needed mastery over them; in Hammond's South Carolina they were outnumbered by their bondsmen from
nearly the beginning of the eighteenth century. And though they tried to
be vigilant, many whites lived in almost a "crisis of fear" from one rumor
of rebellion or insurrection to another.[3] Nevertheless, some recent schol-

arship on slavery in the South stresses how whites routinely took action as individuals to intimidate and control their slaves, and implies they only rarely came together in groups for that purpose.[4] Our conception of Southern society in the eighteenth and nineteenth centuries persists as one dominated by the individual figure of the slave master, set against the collective of the slave community. Who, then, were the "[s]mall guards in our cities, and occasional patrols in the country" that Hammond thought guaranteed Southerners "repose and security known nowhere else"?

This particular method of slave domination developed through a lengthy process of trial and error, experimentation and failure, and often curious digressions. The story of patrollers, both rural and urban, begins in a sixteenth- and seventeenth-century Caribbean that a nineteenth-century observer like Hammond would hardly recognize as the birthplace of the institution he knew. Nonetheless, the beginnings of a formal, organized, and public slave patrol system in the antebellum South can be traced to the private, informal, and sometimes voluntary efforts of Spanish and English colonists in the Caribbean and Latin America who sought to control their growing enslaved populations. Although the eventual nature of nineteenth-century patrols was not obvious in these colonial origins, their forebears evolved from clusters of interrelated colonial laws regulating trade, the militia, and slavery itself. The beginnings and evolution of patrolling left few tracings behind, but they can be found in the successive laws white colonial officials enacted to cope with the bondspeople in their midst. Because so little evidence survives from other sources for the early history of slave patrols, we can at best derive the outline of their creation from the laws themselves. Those laws reveal repeated beginnings, failed as well as successful experiments, and paths not taken—the very origins of formal, public slave patrols that Hammond and others thought so crucial to the security of a white Southern society that embraced the "peculiar institution."

Individual colonists in the New World had to experience difficulty controlling their slaves before the rest of the white community would intervene to help restrict slave behavior. As a result, patrolling in the earliest period was innovative but limited, and persisted as a response to fears of the white community. Fear of would-be rebellious slaves fueled the creation of slave patrols in the colonial era, but patrols also served a dual security purpose. Even into the eighteenth century, European powers like Spain and England challenged one another repeatedly, presenting a grave danger to slave-owning colonists. As rivals trying to gain any advantage in the New World contest, Spaniards might entice English colonists' slaves to freedom by giving bondsmen a safe haven as runaways, or by encouraging them to act as fifth-column forces during battle. Southern colonists needed patrols not only to enforce slave laws, but to rebuff external security threats.

The colonists' willingness to run the risks of owning slaves sprang both from their racism and from their greed.[5] Not content to market products cultivated solely by their own efforts, English colonists rapidly began using indentured servants and bondsmen to increase their productive capacity. The first settlers in Virginia and the Carolinas either arrived with their own slaves or soon bought Africans from traders visiting the colonies. In Virginia, the Jamestown colonists purchased Africans from Dutch traders in 1619, barely a decade after their own arrival in 1607. South Carolina bondsmen arrived with the first permanent colonists in 1670, slaves and colonists alike coming from Barbados. Settled sporadically in the 1650s, North Carolina had slaves by the 1690s.[6] (See Figure 1.)

Along with their slaves, colonists brought with them English law to address the myriad problems in their society; they were confident that it would resolve their conflicts. In America, bad debts, slander, and moral offenses like fornication each had corresponding legal definitions and penalties in English law.[7] Technical writs and pleadings, plus prior exposure to everyday applications of common law, merged in the legal consciousness of colonists, who adapted what they read and remembered to their new surroundings.[8] But in one area—slavery—the English common law was sparse. English law recognized the existence of slavery elsewhere, and responded to it as it impinged upon England. English law did not recognize absolute slavery within the boundaries of England, however, and so English courts were slow to create extensive case law relating to enslaved persons.[9] Thus the laws that Southern colonists created to regulate their slaves did not come exclusively from England, but were derived from their legal imagination, from their long-standing participation in the militia, and from neighboring Caribbean slaveholding colonies.[10] The first elements of colonial patrolling did not arise from conditions peculiar to the American South, but found a transplanted home there after their germination in the Caribbean. Once a Caribbean patrol system existed that could be elaborated on, colonists in the Carolinas and Virginia developed their own distinctive slave patrols in the eighteenth century, experimenting with payment, ever-expanding duties, and increased government involvement.

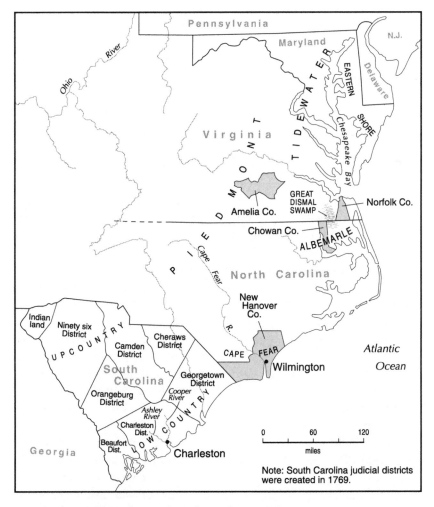

1. Virginia, North Carolina, and South Carolina, c. 1750

Caribbean Patrolling

Historians have long accepted South Carolina's heavy reliance on Barbadian slave law, so it should come as no surprise that the origins of slave patrolling also had a Caribbean connection.[11] Barbadian slave owners faced the same problems that slaveholding colonists elsewhere confronted. Virtually every colony in the Caribbean, regardless of its French, Spanish, Portuguese, or English settlement background, had difficulties controlling its slaves and placed similar restrictions on them. "Every island passed laws for the pursuit, capture, suppression and punishment of runaway slaves; and these laws were usually severe." Barbadian colonists did not invent a slave code and patrollers in a vacuum. They modeled their slavery legislation upon New World laws introduced by Spanish and Portuguese colonists, who had the longest and most extensive experience in recapturing slave runaways in the region.[12]

Fugitive bondsmen caused recurring trouble for Spanish and Portuguese settlers. By the 1520s, runaways already posed problems for Spanish authorities in colonial Mexico.[13] Fugitives had to be hunted down, lest they inspire others to flee. The earliest identifiable New World antecedents of patrols were slave-hunting groups of owners in the 1530s, the volunteer militia *hermandad,* which chased fugitives in Cuba.[14] Gradually the *hermandad* was replaced by expert slave hunters, *rancheadores,* who were paid for each individual capture.[15] Resorting to the most brutal tactics, these slave catchers used fierce dogs to apprehend fugitive slaves.[16] Indians, free blacks, and slaves in several Caribbean and South American colonies also found employment capturing fugitives, spurred on by the prospect of earning reward money or even their own freedom.[17] In Peru, enslaved and free blacks "owned by the municipality or private individuals" served with whites as *cuadrilleros* in Lima, apprehending runaways as early as the 1540s.[18] Throughout the Spanish and Portuguese empires in the New World, administrators and lawmakers formed piecemeal legislation to handle slave-related situations as they occurred, including the recovery of runaways; their preoccupation with slave control was dominated by a concern for public order.[19] Eventually, every Caribbean island and mainland colony created laws for the capture and punishment of fugitive bondsmen.[20] Spaniards and the Portuguese used a combination of former slaves, paid slave catchers, and the militia as apprehenders, all of them forerunners of patrols.

White Barbadians emulated these Spanish and Portuguese slave-hunting models once slaveholding began in Barbados in earnest in the seventeenth century. They relied first upon overseers and privately hired slave catchers, later upon all white residents, and finally upon the militia to control their bondspeople. Barbados had no slave laws in the earliest years of its settlement, and patrols were unknown at first. Controlling the movement of indentured servants, and later slaves, however, became an increasing priority by the mid-seventeenth century.[21] After an aborted rebellion in 1649, slaves were required to carry a signed pass when traveling away from their home plantations.[22] In this early period, overseers played a crucial role: the primary responsibility for enforcing the laws against slaves' possessing weapons, stealing, or moving about on Sundays was initially placed on the individual overseer. The historian Richard Dunn has written that overseers were "expected to keep the Negro cabins under close surveillance, searching twice a month for stolen goods, clubs, and wooden swords."[23] Unlike in the Spanish colonies, few indications suggest that white Barbadians used former bondsmen as slave catchers; the Barbados colonists relied more upon expert slave catchers and the militia.[24] Barbadian records from the 1640s and 1650s are spotty, but they hint that the militia and professionals were not very effective: the preamble of one 1652 law stated that individually hired slave catchers were not nearly as active in taking up runaways as they previously had been.[25]

The failures of privately paid slave catchers in the 1650s may have influenced the 1661 slave code, the first comprehensive law regulating slaves in Barbados.[26] This new law shifted the job of slave control firmly onto the shoulders of all whites, not just overseers. The preamble to the "Act for the Better ordering and governing of Negroes" reveals the motivating impulse behind that law's enactment. Slaves were a "heathenish brutish" and "dangerous kinde of people" who had to be controlled; their propensity to "wander away" from their masters' plantations, either to run away deliberately or to steal goods and then resell them for personal gain, had long been the bane of Barbadian planters' lives.[27] Constables and other white Barbadians shared responsibility for apprehending runaways who managed to flee their home plantation.[28]

Again, in the revised 1688 version of this slave law, the burden of capturing runaways was explicitly placed on all white men—"all Masters, Overseers, and other Persons whatsoever"—who were required to give wandering slaves with no ticket a sound whipping, and detain them until the owner could retrieve them. The law now mandated that bondsmen have passes when leaving their plantations "as it is absolutely necessary to the Safety of this Place."[29] The historian Hilary Beckles has observed that "[i]n this sense, the entire white community functioned under law as a collective police force."[30]

We should not, however, mistake the existence of an elaborate legal code as proof that Barbadian slaves were rigorously policed. The continued reenactment of legislation might, in fact, suggest precisely the opposite, that slaves were able to flee or engage in other acts of resistance and that only a concerted effort could restrain them. In some areas of slave control, the government was never able to eradicate completely "dangerous" slave activities. Certainly the English colony was more lax than others in the Caribbean. The historian Elsa Goveia, who has closely studied colonial slave control in the Caribbean, asserts that "[t]he English government never, until the nineteenth century, showed so careful and sustained an interest in the subject of slave regulations as did the government of Spain from earliest times."[31]

An example of failed Barbadian regulation can be found in the laws designed to eliminate slave "huckstering," or slaves trading goods, laws later copied on the mainland and enforced by slave patrols there. By the mid-seventeenth century, Barbadian slaves sold goods and food near town markets, products that planters feared might be stolen property. The legislature repeatedly tried to obliterate and, later, to regulate the sale of goods and foodstuffs by slaves around urban areas.[32] The island economy, however, needed these traders. Enforcing antihuckstering laws would have been difficult, and would have required whites to expend precious money and effort to scrutinize their slaves more closely than ever before. Only in 1708 did the legislature empower the clerk of the market to hire men to apprehend slaves who illegally peddled goods, an expensive precaution which it had delayed implementing for almost fifty years.[33] In South Carolina, efforts to eradicate slave huckstering would be repeated (with similar levels of success) and would form part of basic patrol work.

During the seventeenth century, Barbados planters came to rely upon "an increasingly powerful alliance of the local militia, Imperial troops and navy" and a tough legal code to keep their slaves in line.[34] With a decreasing number of whites and rapidly rising numbers of slaves, eventually the militia, not individual owners or overseers, held greatest responsibility for policing the Barbadian slave community.[35] A formal military structure was in place by the late 1640s, which included all able-bodied adult white males, indentured servants, and even free blacks.[36] The militia went through heavy reorganization in the 1650s, which resulted in "[i]ncreased slave policing and the expansion of militia forces . . . [as a response to] the failed [1649] insurrection."[37] After protecting the colony from foreign invasion, the militia's principal duty was to patrol slave gatherings to prevent revolts and incipient rebellions.[38] Governor Willoughby made this clear in 1667 when he said of the militia that "though there be no enemy abroad, the keeping of slaves in subjection must still be provided for."[39] Whenever a slave plot was suspected, in the 1660s, 1670s, and later, the militia was put on alert.

The militia's supervision of Barbadian slaves in the late seventeenth century was achieved in large part by providing mounted men to "petrol" each Saturday, Sunday, and holiday.[40] Slaves doubtless viewed these patrols as a hindrance, if not a threat, but some whites confidently believed that patrols kept bondsmen from revolting, as shown in some falsified papers distributed in Barbados in the 1680s. Rumors about a slave revolt circulated in November 1683, causing patrols and militiamen to go on active duty, but no plans of rebellion were subsequently discovered among the slaves.[41] Barbados patrols were ordered out whenever the government suspected plotting, as in 1686, when the lieutenant governor ordered "the Patrolls to ride more frequently and diligently" to prevent the bondsmen from assembling together.[42] Militia patrols responded to and helped suppress the 1686 rebellion in which slaves and Irish servants conspired together. In addition to searching slave houses for weapons and hunting runaways, they also attended cultural activities that attracted slaves, in order to control the bondsmen. Whether at assemblies, markets, funerals, or festivals, the militia patrol was present.[43]

Even the presence of patrols could not scare Barbadian slaves enough to forgo planning insurrections, however. Another aborted rebellion in 1675, coupled with the rising number of fugitives, caused the Barbados Assembly to enact even greater slave restrictions toward the end of the seventeenth century.[44] After an unsuccessful rebellion in 1692, the assembly offered freedom to any slave who provided information to whites concerning insurrections.[45] Fewer revolts surfaced in the last quarter of the seventeenth century, possibly because of the presence of patrols, but the number of bondsmen attempting to gain permanent freedom (known as "maroons") also increased, suggesting that flight became slaves' preferred method of resistance. The final move in policing Barbadian slaves in the seventeenth century came with the importation of two thousand professional English soldiers, who were installed on plantations as intimidating "militia tenants." Arriving between 1696 and 1702, they did not perform manual labor but instead functioned exclusively as slave control forces. Their presence served the white colonists' purposes well: throughout the eighteenth century only one slave rebellion attempt was reported in Barbados.[46]

For all its flaws and later alterations, the Barbadian slave code of 1661 provided the model for several other English slave-holding colonies. The 1664 Jamaican code and the Antiguan slave code of 1702 were patterned after it.[47] Both of these areas experienced a huge influx of Barbadian planters to their islands. Likewise, when Barbadians settled South Carolina after 1670, colonists borrowed heavily from their Barbadian experiences in designing the first slave laws and enforcement groups on the mainland.

South Carolina

Carolinians copied the Barbadian slave laws, but did not initially make use of patrollers in the seventeenth century.[48] After several ill-fated efforts to found a colony, a group of Barbadian colonists finally established themselves in South Carolina in 1670; by the following year, Barbadians constituted nearly half of South Carolina's population.[49] During the colony's first twenty years, few laws restricted slave behavior, primarily because there were not many slaves in obvious need of restraint. Blacks did not outnumber whites until 1708; before then, the population of blacks and whites together barely numbered seven thousand.[50] Thus it is hardly surprising that the first patrols in South Carolina did not appear until the early eighteenth century. But whites felt that even meager numbers of slaves still constituted a threat; Carolinians recognized, as a 1698 law stated, that "the great number of negroes which of late have been imported into this Collony" could "endanger the safety thereof."[51]

Slaves began running away almost as soon as they landed in South Carolina, and white colonists needed assistance recapturing them because of the unfamiliar terrain. The absentee proprietors, living in England but in charge of South Carolina's government, wanted colonists to use Native Americans to chase the fugitives.[52] But South Carolina's settlers wanted to sell Indians into slavery, which made it difficult to hire them as slave catchers too. Unfamiliar with the idea of militia patrols, the proprietors assumed that only Native Americans could recapture African runaways. The proprietors repeatedly insisted to the colonists that without the Indians "you can never get in the Negros that run away."[53] By the eighteenth century, the slave-catching abilities of Native Americans had finally gained the respect of many colonists, particularly because the Indians were willing to go into swamps and other desolate regions where whites were hesitant to travel.[54]

While they reluctantly used Native Americans to return runaways, white South Carolinians gradually realized they needed their own laws and means of enforcement to supervise slaves. In the late seventeenth century, South Carolina's location made slave control even more important than it would be in Virginia and North Carolina. Slaves in South Carolina were close to both the Spanish in Florida and the Native American settlements; the relative proximity of both groups meant that blacks were more likely to run away or seize the opportunity for rebellion.[55] Building on their Barbadian experiences, South Carolina colonists wrote laws to restrain their slaves even more—setting curfews, strengthening the militia, preventing slaves from bartering goods, and establishing the Charleston town watch. Portions of each of these statutes would later be fused together and form the first slave patrol law in the Carolinas.[56]

As in Barbados, white Carolinians viewed huckstering as an intractable problem lawmakers wanted to eliminate.[57] How could whites distinguish between slaves legitimately selling their masters' extra produce from slaves hawking vegetables stolen from a neighbor's garden? The problem of slaves selling stolen goods "to the impoverishing of their said masters" led the assembly to enact laws that mimicked earlier Barbadian legislation. The simplest expedient, in 1687, was to prohibit sales or transactions altogether, unless the slave had the explicit permission of his master or mistress.[58] The Barbadian practice, adopted in South Carolina, required bondsmen to carry a ticket (also called a pass) designating their destination and their business.

White South Carolinians imported another useful slave control tactic from Barbados: curfews. Near the close of the 1687 slave-trading law, lawmakers inserted a curfew for all slaves: "It shall not be lawful for any negroe or negroes, or other slave, upon any pretence whatsoever, to travel or goe abroad, from his or their master or mistresses house in the night time, between the sunsetting and the sunrising, or in the day time, without a note from his or her master or mistresse or overseer."[59] The masters re-created the pass system they knew so well from Barbados. Slaves would need such passes, for trading or travel, until 1865. Under the terms of the 1687 law, any person could lawfully apprehend a bondsman without a ticket and cause the slave to "be sent home."[60]

As with the antibarter laws, South Carolina colonists re-created the Barbadian militia structure to enforce these laws against their slaves. Shortly after arriving in the Carolinas, Barbadian immigrants established their own militia in 1671.[61] Its all-encompassing enrollment—every man between sixteen and sixty had to serve—reflected the apprehension colonists felt in their new environment. At first, they feared the Native Americans. The governor and council claimed in 1671 that "the evil of their intentions ha[d] hitherto been prevented by diligent watchings" alone.[62] As time passed, South Carolinians had more reason to worry about the Spaniards, located in nearby St. Augustine, Florida.[63] In 1685 Carolina residents established a watch and built watchhouses to provide "against any hostile invasions and attempts by sea or land, which the neighbouring spaniard or other enemy may make."[64]

The militia's response to external threats also revealed a sense of internal vulnerability. After signaling an alarm, the militia's first act of defense was to gather at central locations, near Charleston or at other designated places, and only then dispatch companies to meet the enemy attack wherever it came.[65] From the whites' perspective, the women and children left behind were easy, undefended targets for slave violence. Alternatively, the slaves could join an invader's forces or take flight.[66] In any case, the absence of white men from large areas of the colony during a threatened invasion posed a problem the Barbadians had not encountered before, and South Carolina's expanding range of settlement (when compared with that of the island of Barbados) meant that the problem would only grow worse with time.[67]

While outlying regions might go undefended during alarms, whites and blacks in the port of Charleston were under surveillance from the town's inception. Although the town's security forces initially responded to many kinds of perceived threats, they formed the beginning of urban slave patrols on the mainland. In 1671, the colony's Grand Council created a night watch using regular constables and a rotation of six citizens as watchmen to aid them every night.[68] From ten in the evening until nearly sunrise, groups of householders were required to keep the peace and detain lawbreakers until the following morning, when justice would be meted out by town officials. Women who headed households had to find a male to serve in their place. Men who did not wish to serve could also provide a substitute, or pay a fine of fifteen pence for each night they did not watch.[69] Occasional reminders were necessary when danger threatened the town; the Grand Council, with a hostile ship offshore in 1692, directed townspeople to be more diligent in their watch duty.[70] These Charlestonians watched for any sign of trouble: fire, Indians, or secretive slave gatherings.

Both in and around Charleston, the growing numbers of slaves meant more runaways, which created problems for South Carolinians that Barbadian planters had not experienced in precisely the same way. Islands—like Barbados—limited the area to which bondsmen could usually flee, but that limitation did not apply to mainland slaves who fled to the woods or Spanish Florida. Ad hoc remedies provided little help. Indians still occasionally hunted runaways, but as relations with the colonists deteriorated, Native American assistance became less reliable. Some individuals chased fugitives, as in 1672, when two men went after a fleeing servant, rumored to be headed for St. Augustine. And militia groups periodically pursued bands of fleeing servants, as one militia unit did in 1673.[71] But from the owners' perspective, a more systematic method of capture and prevention of flight in the first place was absolutely essential if the rapidly increasing slave population was to be controlled. The precedents, as well as the problems inherent in colonists' trading, militia, and town control laws, also prompted Carolina lawmakers to attempt to restrain the growing slave population with the 1690 "Act for the Better Ordering of Slaves."[72]

The 1690 law served as South Carolina's first systematic attempt to control slave behavior, although it was eventually replaced in 1696.[73] The optional right in the 1687 antibartering law for "any person" to capture and send home a slave without a ticket had been transformed into a required duty.[74] As in Barbados, the shift from voluntary effort to mandated duty effectively turned the entire white population into a community police force. All persons had to apprehend runaways and would receive a reward in return; even other slaves could receive the rewards.[75]

Landowners who discovered wandering bondsmen on their property had a duty to apprehend and punish offending slaves, or forfeit a hefty forty-shilling fine.[76] In addition, the militia now had new slave control duties, modeled upon the Barbados experience. Every company captain, upon notice of a runaway's hiding place, had to "raise a convenient party of men" to pursue and capture the fugitive, dead or alive.[77] These groups could be considered the first mainland patrols, although there is little evidence to suggest they were used, and their duties were very limited when contrasted with those of later patrols. Runaways, whether captured by militia or private individuals, were turned over to their owners or to the local sheriff.[78] After the disallowance of the law in 1691, the 1693 assembly immediately moved to replace it.[79] In 1696 the assembly passed a new slave code that took a more comprehensive approach to slave regulation.

With the 1696 law, South Carolina's assembly moved to a more coercive system of private enforcement and directed the Charleston town watch to take an active role in policing slaves. The connections to Barbados were obvious: three-fourths of the Barbadian slave code of 1688, and all of its preamble, were made law by the South Carolina assembly in 1696.[80] The law retained both the pass system, mandating that a slave carry a ticket when away from his master's plantation, and the provisions for returning a slave to his owner or to the local jail. And all whites were required to apprehend bondsmen and give them a moderate whipping if they had no pass.[81] The law protected any white person inspecting a ticket by declaring that if a slave resisted, he could be beaten, maimed, assaulted, or even killed if he resisted or took flight. Even Indians and slaves were rewarded twenty shillings if they delivered runaways back into the hands of the authorities.[82] Militia captains still had to summon groups of men to hunt runaways whenever they were notified of a fugitive's whereabouts, as in the 1690 law. And like Barbadian masters, owners were required to inspect their slave quarters every two weeks and confiscate any weapons or stolen goods.

Recognizing the growing attraction of Charleston for slaves from outlying farms, the 1696 law enjoined town constables to organize white men into groups which would capture, whip, and jail slaves from the countryside found in town on Sundays.[83] Although a planter living away from Charleston could theoretically send a slave there on business, members of the assembly believed it should not be done on Sunday.[84]

The disparity between what masters would allow slaves (typically, a Sunday free from work and a pass to visit town) and what the town might tolerate had already generated security concerns. Assembly members rationalized the restriction by saying that not only did "country" slaves profane the Sabbath there, but that such gatherings "may give them an opportunity of executing any wicked designs and purposes," hinting at insurrection.[85] Finally, any planter who maintained more than one plantation, if separated by more than six miles, had to employ a white overseer for groups of six or more slaves enslaved persons on each farm.[86] Volunteer white police mechanisms, used in 1690, were replaced in 1696 by directives to absentee owners, Charleston constables, and all whites, who now shared the duty to control slave behavior throughout the colony.

Yet the shortage of white South Carolinians forced their continued reliance upon bondsmen for firepower in their seventeenth- and eighteenth-century militia bands. In 1699 the Lords Commissioners for Trade and Plantations must have been appalled to learn of the South Carolina militia's weakness when compared with the slave population it was legally bound to supervise. The militia was "not about 1500 . . . White men," a correspondent wrote, while noting with concern that there were "through the province generally 4 Negroes to one white man."[87] Although this population ratio wildly exaggerated the number of slaves, it offers a telling insight into how some whites feared the growing slave population. But their anxiety about external enemies, like Spain, was still greater. According to laws passed in 1704 and 1708, "one able slave armed with gunn or lance" must be trained for every white man in the militia.[88] The South Carolinians' desperation to fend off the Spanish forced them to put guns in the hands of their own bondsmen, even as they tightened existing laws that limited slave movement and behavior.

Increased alarm about a Spanish invasion, coupled with rumors of a slave insurrection, finally drove South Carolinians to create their first regular, official slave patrols in 1704. The law's preamble noted white residents' immediate worries: "on the sight or advice of an enemy it will be necessary for the safety and defence of the inhabitants . . . to draw together to the sea coast," and this external threat could leave them vulnerable internally to "insurrections and mischiefs." The colony needed two military forces: a militia to repel foreign enemies, and a patrol to leave behind as a deterrent against slave revolts. Every militia captain was to select ten men under his command to serve as patrollers, and that group would henceforth be exempt from militia duty. The patrol became a separate military group that would muster at irregular intervals and "ride from plantation to plantation, and into any plantation," taking up slaves who had no ticket from their master.[89] Fines penalized unwilling slave owners who shirked their patrol duties, and special provisions existed for Charleston and Colleton County. Charleston's night watch would continue to serve its community as the nocturnal patrol. Because of its small population, Colleton County received a partial exemption from the law. Only during an alarm, when Colleton's militia force might be summoned away, would a group of patrollers become exempt from militia service and remain behind, protecting the colonists.[90]

These new mainland patrol groups differed sharply from their Barbadian predecessors in several respects. In Barbados, the militia and patrol were never truly separate, and likely would never have been separated, given the island's relatively small white population. In South Carolina, the need to meet two simultaneous threats made division imperative. Although initially drawn from South Carolina's militia ranks, patrol men would not go with the regular militia to a central location during an invasion; instead, the patrol was to stay behind during the alarm period and remain active during the absence of the other militiamen.[91] Mainland patrols had much more territory to cover, a second key difference. Patrollers not only had authority over slaves they encountered in country lanes but were also required to ride onto plantations and search for slaves lurking there without permission. Up to this time, within plantation boundaries, the overseer or owner had had exclusive authority. Another distinctive characteristic was the deliberate merger of patrol duties with the other responsibilities of Charleston's night watch. And finally, patrols were supplemented by coastal lookouts beginning in 1710. Coastal lookouts, whose primary function was to look for Spanish invasion fleets, would receive two pounds per capture for each slave they caught using boats or canoes near the sea without passes from their masters.[92]

During the first quarter of the eighteenth century, white South Carolinians felt repeatedly besieged by threats from Indians and rebellious slaves, putting the new patrol system under considerable stress. In 1711 a bondsman named Sebastian and several of his followers robbed and plundered numerous houses and plantations.[93] After their deaths at the hands of Indian slave hunters, the 1712 assembly reenacted the 1696 law governing slave behavior almost verbatim.[94] A few months later, in September, the Tuscaroras massacred more than two hundred inhabitants in North Carolina. South Carolina sent men and money to North Carolina, leaving their own colony exposed to other threats. Initially, South Carolina responded to these simultaneous internal and external threats by allowing "meritorious" slaves to be part of the militia during times of alarm. They fought against the Yamassee Indians in 1715, and the most courageous bondsmen were granted their freedom. But another slave insurrection in 1720 brought an end to slaves in the militia and stimulated a major reorganization of patrols.[95]

Historians have often described patrollers as men of very low social rank, but slave patrols between 1704 and 1721 frequently included men of superior social status, not just poor slaveless whites.[96] Wealthy South Carolina men angled for appointments as slave patrollers to avoid having to serve in the militia when it was called away from home. This did not always make them the most vigilant of patrollers, because there was no pay and rewards were very low.[97] Dodging militia service by entering a slave patrol was an evasion that could not last long, and the 1721 legislature promptly closed that loophole. In redrafting the patrol law, the assembly noted that "the several patrols in this Province generally consist of the choicest and best men, who screen themselves from doing such services in alarms as are required and ought to be done by men of their ability."[98] With this failed experiment behind them, the assembly determined that patrols and militia would be formally merged—as in Barbados—with no distinction remaining between them. Henceforth, militia commanders would appoint men to ride patrol within their districts, such that "every person belonging to each foot company and troops of dragoons [would] go a patrolling."[99] Patrollers could also now be fined for failure to carry out their responsibilities.[100] With patrols and militia integrated once more, the law requiring all whites to apprehend slaves (or pay a fine) was altered. The words of the 1696/1712 law were amended to require only overseers to stop and take up wandering slaves.[101] Of course, any person could still capture a runaway and receive the fairly substantial reward of twenty shillings.[102]

Subsequent South Carolina laws increased patrol duties, and briefly implemented a paid system of patrolling in the 1730s. Patrollers were not only to interrogate slaves but to examine "all white servants," too.[103] Patrols could take servants or slaves, whites or blacks, before a magistrate for punishment. This made the duties of rural patrollers much more like the work of the Charleston night watch, which required watchmen to investigate all suspicious activities, not just those of bondsmen. Extra inducements were built into patrolling duties to make the work more attractive. For instance, patrollers who discovered slaves with guns could confiscate the weapons and keep them as their personal property.

In a short-lived experiment with more tangible incentives, the 1734 South Carolina assembly authorized payment for slave patrols, while inadvertently creating a few patrol regulations that would remain in force until the Civil War. Residents of the colony had been vocal in complaining about lax patrolling in the 1720s and 1730s; grand juries protested inadequate patrols every time they decried improper slave behavior.[104] In response, the assembly created paid patrols, citing as its reason that "former acts . . . for regulating patrols have not answered the intention."[105] Patrol captains would now receive £50 per year, and patrollers £25 each.[106] Other incentives were established to make sure that patrols went into action. The militia still formed the pool from which patrols would be drawn, but once chosen to serve, patrollers were exempt from military service for the duration of their appointment; they could avoid attending musters or being called away from their homes during alarms. Patrollers rode together as a "beat company" of five men, visiting each plantation at least once a month to search slave quarters, and without search warrants, they could enter any house, white or black, where slaves were suspected of hiding or loitering without authorization. Members of the beat company lived in the same region that they were required to patrol.[107] Charleston merited its own separate set of two rotating patrols for riding alternate Saturday nights, Sundays, Sunday nights, and holidays.[108] When the assembly reenacted the law in 1737, the most significant modifications ended payment to patrollers, and limited patrol membership to fifty-acre freeholders or forty-shilling taxpayers, and commanders were ordered not to "enlist any person as a voluntary patrolman."[109] The historian H. M. Henry notes that we are left "to conjecture whether irresponsible persons had been attracted to the pay which must have been considerable for that time" or whether there were men who patrolled "for the purpose of wreaking vengeance" on the slaves of others.[110] Certainly the three-year experiment of paying patrollers may have placed an economic strain on the colony.

Inexplicably, the colony ceased paying patrollers at the same time that its slave population had grown enough to sustain a serious insurrection. South Carolina colonists in the late 1730s found the rapidly rising number of slaves formed a greater and greater threat.[111] Moreover, the bondsmen lived as concentrated groups in Charleston or on plantations, not scattered among a farflung white population as slaves did in Virginia. Given slaves' sheer numbers, their participation in acts of everyday rebellion, and the legislature's decision not to continue paying patrollers after 1737, it was perhaps only a matter of time before a slave revolt like the Stono rebellion of 1739 occurred.[112] Some twenty bondsmen gathered near the Stono River and then began attacking white colonists on a bloody march south toward St. Augustine and freedom among the Spanish.[113] Gathering strength, the group eventually numbered between fifty and one hundred members. The colony's militia relentlessly pursued them, killing dozens in skirmishes, while offering rewards for the uncaptured runaways.[114]

The full-fledged slave revolt prompted the 1740 assembly to refine existing slave control laws in dramatic fashion. In response to Stono, a comprehensive slave code was enacted, and the statute's preamble leaves little doubt of the assembly's intention: "[M]any late horrible and barbarous massacres have been actually committed, and many more designed . . . by negro slaves . . . which makes it highly necessary that constant patrols should be established and kept . . . for the better preventing any future insurrections or cabals of the said slaves."[115] Twenty new clauses in the statute tightened the noose on slave movement, slave behavior, and slave importation, restricting many freedoms bondsmen had come to enjoy.[116] Surprisingly, restrictions placed on slaves were not paralleled by increased duties for all whites to ensure their own safety. It would be another three years before the assembly required white men to bring their weapons to church services, when whites were traditionally most vulnerable to surprise attacks.[117] Instead, the assembly placed much of the burden of enforcing slave conduct upon the patrol, reshaping it into the patrol as it would be thought of for more than one hundred years to come.

Beginning in 1740, the contours of patrolling in South Carolina were plainly defined and no longer experimental. Precise directions from the assembly specified that militia officers must meet within three months after the law's passage and mark off their districts into patrol beats, so that each patrol would not have to ride more than fifteen miles. Maps or descriptions of patrol districts were to be posted on every parish church door and entered into the militia company's record books. All slave owners, male or female, absentee or resident, were to have their names written down on a militia list from which patrollers would be drawn.[118] In addition, the law specified provisions for substitute service in great detail, setting out the manner in which substitutes could be hired, and who would pay for defaults of service. Militia officers who failed to choose a patrol group leader at the time of mustering could receive a £100 fine.[119] Patrols found drunk or misbehaving while on duty might also be fined, but those fines were relatively small; presumably, intoxicated patrollers were better than none at all.[120] Some provisions were drawn directly from earlier legislation. For example, in areas where whites outnumbered black slaves, patrols were still not required. Once again, in the city where more slaves resided, Charleston's night watch was singled out for patrol duties. With only minor alterations during the Revolutionary War, the structure of slave patrols in South Carolina would remain relatively unchanged until the Civil War.[121]

South Carolina's patrol system eventually attracted several imitators, especially as settlers moved both south and west.[122] It provided a model for at least one neighboring colony in the eighteenth century: Georgia followed South Carolina's example in the patrol laws it enacted in the 1750s.[123] But to the north, South Carolina's laws were not duplicated. Virginia and North Carolina created strikingly different patrols, different not only from South Carolina, but eventually quite distinct from each other.

Virginia

Although founded and settled earlier than South Carolina, Virginia took longer to develop its own slave patrol system. Virginia's House of Burgesses most likely deferred the introduction of formal patrols because of the colony's small slave population early on and the slaves' great dispersion across the countryside. In similar fashion, the slow introduction of bondsmen into North Carolina delayed even longer that colony's creation of slave control laws. While patrols came into being much later in

Virginia and North Carolina, their structure was affected by forces that seem to have been less intense in South Carolina. For example, the influence of other types of laws on patrols is easier to recognize in Virginia and North Carolina than in South Carolina. The need to regulate suspicious groups like indentured servants, fleeing debtors, and Indians shaped the thinking of Virginia and North Carolina lawmakers when it came to restricting slave movement. In addition, geography, foreign threats, and relatively low populations (both white and black) all played a part in the gradual creation of Virginia's and North Carolina's law enforcement systems for slaves in the seventeenth and eighteenth centuries.[124]

Like the South Carolinians, colonial Virginia settlers feared attack from both Native American and European adversaries. One of their earliest recorded laws required that "dew watch be kept by night."[125] In their lightly settled frontier of roughly 1,300 inhabitants, white Virginians heavily outnumbered Africans in 1625; Indians were the original menace the Virginia militia was designed to repulse.[126] "[A]ll persons except negros" were required by law to have guns because of the threat from Indians, and all white men served in the militia.[127] Virginia and South Carolina's militia shared many similarities during this time, but recapturing runaway slaves was not the primary duty of Virginia's militia at the outset.

Historians dispute why Virginians gradually switched from indentured servant labor to slave labor in the 1660s and 1670s.[128] What they have not disputed is that the switch did take place, probably beginning sometime around 1660. Up to that time, indentured servants constituted a larger group than slaves, and therefore runaway servants posed greater problems for their masters. But fugitive servants or slaves in Virginia found it hard to prevail against both unfriendly Indians and the cold climate, although one maroon community sustained itself for decades in the Great Dismal Swamp on the Virginia–North Carolina border.[129] The first reference to fugitives in legislative records occurred in 1642, when a new law required runaways to serve double their time; the law referred only to servants, since a slave, whose punishment was already a lifetime of bondage, could not serve two lifetime sentences.[130] Whether chasing servants or slaves, the old English procedure of "hue and cry" was initially considered enough to recover them.[131] Although runaway servants and slaves became common enough in Virginia, no regular procedure was implemented to prevent them from escaping—in the seventeenth century colonists worried more about retrieval after the fact than prevention in the first place. Some individuals seem to have stepped into the breach. A 1659 law indicates that Dutch runaway catchers had their means of payment guaranteed: if the owner failed to pay them a reward, the colony's secretary would reimburse them.[132]

Lawmakers initially relied upon independent slave catchers and constables to capture fugitives, but their efforts were not always enough. Low pay and uncertain rewards made pursuit seem unattractive. In 1660 Virginia's House of Burgesses noted that the chief obstacle to capturing runaways was the "neglect of constables in making search according to their warrants." Waving both carrot and stick at constables, the legislature ordered that for every slave or servant a constable apprehended, the master must pay two hundred pounds of tobacco, but if the constable neglected to search diligently he would be fined three hundred and fifty pounds of tobacco.[133] Individual counties with large numbers of runaways were granted the right to "make such lawes" considered necessary to prevent, pursue, or recover runaways.[134] Charles City County took advantage of this option and created a sheriff-led, paid posse of men to search for two runaway slaves who belonged to Theodorick Bland in 1662.[135] The legislature admitted the failure of the "hue and cry" system in 1663, decreeing that in future "pursuite after runaways be made at the charge of the country." They realized that significant financial incentives had to be offered, or no one would make the effort to recapture a fugitive. The charge would be passed along from the county to the master, who was to repay the costs expended in recapturing his slave or servant.[136]

By 1670 lawmakers acknowledged that unreliable slave catchers and constables alone could not keep every Virginia slave on the plantations, so the burgesses began enticing others to lend a hand. Virginia's first experiment to engage all citizens in the capture of runaways came in 1669. Noting that average citizens did not take action unless a runaway's master offered a sizable reward, the legislature mandated a remarkable compensation system. "[W]hosoever apprehends any runaways whither servant by indenture, custome, or covenant, not haveing a legall passe, . . . shall have a thousand pounds of tobacco."[137] After taking a captured servant to a justice of the peace, the captor would receive a note giving him an allowance of one thousand pounds of tobacco, payable after deducting the taxes he owed the following year; the master was then required to repay the county officials the thousand pounds of tobacco. In the following year, the 1670 legislature's first act was to repeal this far too effective law, noting that it was "burdensome on the public."[138] Abuses occurred under the thousand-pound reward system, because it had been loosely worded. No master wanted to pay so much for a slave found close to home, and some frauds had been detected.[139] Now, instead of a thousand pounds of tobacco for capture, the reward was reduced to two hundred pounds "if the runaway be found above tenn miles from his masters' house."[140]

Yet even with such great rewards at stake, Virginia burgesses did not require slaves to carry passes until 1680, and this may have been a side effect of the origins of Virginia's pass system. While South Carolina lawmakers had copied their colony's pass system from the Barbados slave code, Virginia's evolved from a greater mixture of influences. The first persons required to carry passes were colonists leaving Virginia and Indians. Certainly missing slaves were of great concern to the white Virginians who lost their labor, but absconding debtors and Indians were perceived as a greater threat, initially, to the social order. The first passes went to colonists departing from Virginia; after 1642, travelers had to obtain a pass from the governor before they could depart, in order to prevent indentured servants or debtors from fleeing their obligations on the fastest outbound ship.[141] Every few years, laws were reenacted prohibiting ship captains from setting sail with passengers who had no pass.[142]

Like debtors, the members of another marginalized group, Native Americans, were required to carry passes in the seventeenth century. Some colonists perceived all Indians as dangerous and readily resorted to violence upon encountering any Native American; many peaceful Indians died from such unchecked aggression. To control the comings and goings of Native Americans, the colony began issuing them badges or tickets (also called passes) in 1656 so that they could enter colonist villages and trade peacefully.[143] As long as Indians remained close to Virginia settlements, colonists insisted that Native Americans have passes or badges before they entered the villages.[144] Gradually colonists' concerns about identifying trustworthy Indians and capturing debtors diminished, but their fears about slaves remained. Of these three groups, only slaves still needed to be identified and controlled through passes after 1680. In the 1660s and 1670s slaves occasionally carried passes, although they were not required by law to do so.[145] It was not until 1680 that Virginia's legislature decided that bondsmen traveling away from their masters must carry a pass.

The 1680 pass law resulted from Virginia's first recorded wave of slave insurrection panic, which led to additional restrictions such as prohibiting slaves from carrying weapons.[146] It seems to have been an ineffective law, enacted but not enforced, for two years later the Virginia legislature noted that it had not "had its intended effect for want of due notice thereof being taken." As a result, ministers in each parish were required to read the law twice a year to their congregations, or pay a fine of six hundred pounds of tobacco. In addition, all slave masters were enjoined to supervise their own plantations more closely, to prevent truant bondsmen from hiding there.[147] Regardless of whether white Virginians actually knew or heeded these injunctions, the new laws did not prevent rebellious slave activity; in 1687 an actual slave conspiracy was discovered in the Northern Neck counties.[148] The bondsmen had laid their plans during large-scale slave funerals, and as a result, Virginia's colonial council banned all public slave funerals.[149] A few years later, the legislature decided to adopt another experimental approach to recapture runaways. It effectively admitted that private slave catchers and constables alone could not catch enough fleeing bondsmen, and now ordered sheriffs to raise whatever force appeared necessary to apprehend fugitive slaves.[150] The ambiguity that the word "runaway" had in the 1660s is missing in this 1691 statute, which was directed solely at "negroes, mulattoes, and other slaves." Two purported insurrections had scared the Virginians enough to prod them to greater activity, but would it last?

During the following decade, the answer seemed to be yes. In 1705 Virginians created a complex, comprehensive slave code, the first laws comparable to the Barbados statute of 1661 and the South Carolina code of 1696.[151] The 1705 legal structure would serve Virginians throughout most of the colonial era, with only minor alterations.[152] The law incorporated many previously extant laws relating to servants and slaves, including the complete 1691 law allowing sheriffs to apprehend outlying slaves and the 1670 reward system giving two hundred pounds of tobacco to anyone capturing a runaway.[153] Individuals would continue to avail themselves of rewards for capturing runaways throughout the eigh-

teenth and nineteenth centuries, although inflation would slowly de-
value the payments.[154] Unlike South Carolina, Virginia's militia still did
not play a role in recapturing fugitive bondsmen at this time.

But in the decades after 1705, white Virginians seemed to grow increasingly lax about enforcing slave laws, and the possibility of insurrections, real or imagined, rose accordingly. Edmund Jenings, president of
the colony's council in 1709, issued a proclamation to reinforce the law
against allowing slaves to meet without whites in attendance. Jenings
noted disdainfully that "the Tolleration & permission of the Masters,
Mistresses or Overseers of the said Slaves of going abroad and remaining
absent longer time than the Law Allows has been the Occassion of such
Dangerous & Unlawfull Concourses."[155] Royal governors expected the
militia to take a more active part in slave control, but militia members
refused. In 1712 Lieutenant Governor Spotswood wrote that "[t]he Militia of this Colony is perfectly useless," and "the People are so stupidly
averse" to improving the militia that slave rebellions seemed inevitable.[156] After a small insurrection was quashed in 1721, the new lieutenant governor, Hugh Drysdale, predicted that the failed rebellion would
stir up "the next Assembly to make more severe laws for keeping their
slaves in greater subjection."[157]

Drysdale was wrong. Even after the 1721 slave rebellion, the Virginia
legislature postponed taking action or passed prescriptive slave laws that
had no enforcement mechanism. Drysdale resorted to blunt words in his
1723 address to the House of Burgesses, noting that the preceding assembly had refused to pass new laws governing slave conduct, a subject
he viewed as critical. Drysdale said "[y]our Laws seem very deficient"
for preventing insurrections, and he believed the "surest method to prevent any fatal Consequences" was to strengthen the militia.[158] The burgesses ignored his advice about the militia, and instead concentrated on
laws to regulate slave behavior. To prevent insurrections, they increased
the punishment to death for slaves entering into a conspiracy (even for
bondsmen who only discussed it). All meetings of slaves were deemed
illegal, and anyone discovered harboring fugitives had to pay a steep
fine.[159] Baptists may have been a secondary target of the lawmakers,
since they drew large crowds of slaves to their gatherings for prayer and
conversion.[160] All ship captains were required to swear oaths before cus-
toms officers that they would not remove any person from the colony

without a pass, as required by law—neither debtors fleeing their creditors nor slaves escaping from their masters.[161] Drysdale's suggestions about the militia were ignored for more than five years.

Ultimately, in 1727, the burgesses created a law to use the militia against slaves, instituting Virginia's first formal slave patrols. Patrols were designed to operate during times of greatest threat to the colony. Unlike colonial South Carolina's bondsmen, Virginia's scattered slaves usually congregated together in great numbers only at holidays, when freed from their labors. The lawmakers feared what might transpire among the slaves at these times, noting that "great danger may happen to the inhabitants of this dominion, from the unlawful concourse of negros, during the Christmas, Easter, and Whitsuntide holidays."[162] As a result, militia commanders could call out as many white men as they believed were needed to patrol "from time to time." They were particularly directed to disperse "all unusual concourse of negroes" and meetings of slaves; any bondsmen they found gathered could be taken to a constable for punishment, for Virginia patrollers were not yet given the right to discipline slaves. Patrollers called for duty would not be paid unless they stayed on patrol more than two days. Theoretically, these patrol groups could only be called out on the holidays enumerated in the preamble and not at other times during the year.

Attempts by slaves in 1729 and 1730 to create maroon communities or incite rebellions caused Virginians to reenact their patrol law in 1731, 1732, 1735, and 1738.[163] In 1729, Lieutenant Governor Gooch reported that "a number of Negroes, about fifteen" decided to "fix themselves in the fastnesses of the neighbouring Mountains." He correctly assessed the danger permanent fugitives would pose: maroons "would very soon be encreas'd by the accession of other Runaways and prove dangerous Neighbours to our frontier Inhabitants."[164] In the following year, 1730, a series of threatened insurrections placed colonists in a more fearful state. Rumors spread among the slaves that King George had granted them their freedom, but that their masters were keeping it secret; in numerous (illegal) meetings, bondsmen discussed what they should do. Gooch ordered that militia parties be "sent out to Patrole, with Orders to Secure all the Negroes found off their Masters plantations."[165] The chief conspirators were punished and released. Six weeks later, two hundred slaves in Norfolk and Princess Anne counties assembled during the church services of their masters, but again patrols apprehended the ring leaders and the insurrection was suppressed.[166] Gooch later reported that he ordered "the Militia to Patrole twice or thrice in a Week to prevent all Night meetings" in the wake of the second attempt.[167] The legislature must have viewed patrols with greater appreciation after the suppression of several would-be insurrection attempts, which helps explain the renewal of the 1727 patrol law during the 1730s.

In 1736, for reasons unknown, though possibly related to another insurrection scare, the lieutenant governor issued a proclamation to the entire colony regarding slave patrols. Intended to "Oppose and suppress . . . Foreign Invasions of Indians, as [well as] intestine Insurrections of Slaves," the lieutenant governor ordered all county militia commanders to appoint patrols, especially during holiday periods.[168] This may have been a move to publicize the patrol law throughout the colony, or to remind commanders that they had the ability to use patrols. Up to that time, the appointment of patrols proceeded at the discretion of local militia leaders.

The 1727 law creating patrols was expanded in 1738 by broadening the powers conferred on militia commanders. They could order all men to go to church armed with weapons, and appoint patrols to visit "all negro quarters, and other places suspected of entertaining unlawful assemblies of slaves, servants, or other disorderly persons."[169] Moreover, patrollers could take up slaves "strolling about" between plantations without passes and take them to a justice of the peace, who could order them to be whipped. On its face, these changes in Virginia's patrol laws were reminiscent of provisions in South Carolina's 1704 patrol law, but Virginia's law contained a crucial difference: those men on patrol would be exempt from private musters of the militia, and exempt from public, county, and parish levies during their term of service.[170] Through these exemptions, Virginia indirectly compensated its patrollers, offering incentives that South Carolina had experimented with but abandoned. Finally, in 1754, Virginia authorized county courts to pay patrollers ten pounds of tobacco for each twenty-four-hour period that they were on duty, and each patrol captain was obligated to submit written reports of the patrol's activities to the court.[171] With the passage of the 1754 law, the contours of Virginia's patrol system were now complete, remaining largely unchanged until the Civil War.[172]

Although superficial similarities existed, key differences set apart Virginia and South Carolina's slave patrol systems. The language of Virginia's 1738 law contains several phrases and even paragraphs imitative of the wording of South Carolina's 1704 patrol law, and the practices of the two colonies eventually converged along the lines of Virginia's statute. However, the creation of Virginia's patrols ten years earlier to work exclusively during holidays shows that Virginia legislators developed their own ideas about patrols independently of South Carolina.[173] Although their slave patrols were both militia-based, the colonies treated white participation in differing ways. South Carolina's statutes created zones where white residents participated in a night watch rather than the militia (Charleston) or could avoid patrol duty altogether due to limited settlement (Colleton). Virginia made no such distinctions; if enough men resided in an area for a militia to muster, the law required that patrols be established as well. The greatest difference, however, were the financial incentives the Old Dominion provided its patrollers. Virginia gave tax breaks to patrollers, offered exemptions from other onerous duties, and even allowed counties the option of paying patrollers, rewards that went well beyond the militia exemptions offered in South Carolina.

North Carolina

In designing its patrol system, North Carolina most closely followed the example of Virginia at the outset, but eventually developed procedures completely different from those of either Virginia or South Carolina. The original imitation of Virginia seems predictable, since Virginians seeking new tobacco lands first settled North Carolina after 1650, moving from the Chesapeake toward the Albemarle region of North Carolina. Later, South Carolinians made repeated attempts to settle the colony's southeast corner along the Cape Fear River in the 1660s, finally establishing permanent settlements in the 1720s. Free and enslaved populations grew slowly; even as late as 1720, estimates place the black population at only two thousand, while the white population hovered somewhere between four thousand and five thousand.[174] The sparse population of white and black alike, combined with internal leadership disputes and the menacing Tuscarora tribe—which almost wiped out the colony several times—meant that North Carolina existed in "unrest, confusion, slow growth, and armed rebellion" for its first thirty years.[175]

As a result of these circumstances, North Carolina slaves of the seventeenth and eighteenth centuries lived in a more lightly populated world than bondsmen of neighboring colonies—fewer slaves and fewer masters lived in scattered settlements. The meager total population ensured that bondsmen were more likely to live with small white family groups, not set apart from their owners by either space or social distance. Geography continued to limit the numbers of slaves who could enter directly or work in the colony. Lacking deep ocean ports, or rich soil suited to high-grade tobacco, North Carolina never matched or even came close to the large enslaved populations found in neighboring colonies of the eighteenth century.[176] The lack of crowded population centers, such as Charleston, or of high numbers of slaves kept North Carolinians from needing to develop intricate slave control laws until well into the eighteenth century. Indeed, North Carolina's comprehensive slave code, enacted in 1715, was the last to be passed in the three colonies.

Slave-related laws, however, began to appear as early as 1669 in North Carolina, when bondsmen entered the colony with their Virginia and South Carolina émigré owners.[177] One law prohibited taking a slave from his master without a pass or written permission. The passive structure of the law suggests that it was prompted by slave stealing, rather than runaways. As in Virginia, patrolling relied on slave passes, and the pass laws of the colonial period targeted members of several marginal groups, not just slaves. Early in its history, North Carolina acquired the reputation as a haven for those trying to flee obligations elsewhere. Its patchwork pattern of settlement made it an ideal place for runaways to hide. The Virginia attorney general noted in the 1690s that "servants and slaves are daily" fleeing to North Carolina, some with the clear purpose of making for Spanish Florida and freedom.[178] In 1711 Virginia's governor remarked with disgust that North Carolina "has long been the common Sanctuary of all our Runaway Servants and of all that fly from the due execution of the Laws in this and her Majesty's other plantations."[179] Other suspicious characters needed watching, too. Thus, as in Virginia, Indians and debtors in North Carolina had to carry passes or badges. Even those persons wishing to leave North Carolina had to have a written pass from the colony's secretary to certify that they were debt-free and leaving behind no obligations.[180]

But by the mid-eighteenth century, conditions had changed. As native tribes were conquered or retreated into the hinterlands and escaping indentured servants became a rarity, only the restrictions on slaves remained. When county courts finally appointed patrols in the 1750s, the only persons still carrying passes were slaves. The inspection of passes by slave patrollers in North Carolina grew out of an earlier comprehensive attempt to restrict the movement of "questionable" elements of society, just as it had in Virginia.

North Carolina emulated other colonies not only in its pass laws but also in its initial reliance upon private enforcement for controlling slave behavior. Community policing would follow only after the efforts of individuals proved unreliable. As the number of slave runaways increased during the 1690s, the assembly granted rewards to slave catchers and made it illegal to harbor runaways.[181] This law appeared decades after similar ones were passed in Virginia and South Carolina. Even in the eighteenth century, if a slave ran away, white North Carolinians turned to other African Americans or Indians for assistance in recapturing them.[182]

Other similarities existed between North Carolina's slave laws and those of neighboring colonies. North Carolina eclectically borrowed legal provisions for its slave laws from both Virginia and South Carolina. In its first slave control law, the 1699 North Carolina assembly encouraged all white men to capture runaways and convey them to either the provost marshal or the slave's owner and claim a reward. Although comparable to the Virginia law of 1682, this statute did not inflict a harsh penalty on whites who failed to comply. In the 1715 slave code, the North Carolina assembly required all enslaved persons to carry tickets when leaving their master's plantation; the pass had to name their owner and the trip's origin and destination.[183] This pass law mimicked the South Carolina pass laws of 1696 and 1712. North Carolina's laws even imitated the specific language used by other colonies: the 1740 slave law, and virtually every subsequent slave law in North Carolina, spoke of "taking up," or capturing, a runaway, a phrase used routinely in the laws of Virginia and South Carolina.[184] In the same manner that they mentioned taking up stray horses or wandering sailors, white colonists spoke of taking up runaway slaves who tested the limits of their masters' authority.

With minor modifications, the laws passed in 1715 were retained until 1741, when the North Carolina assembly thoroughly rewrote all its laws regarding slavery in the wake of South Carolina's Stono rebellion.[185] Among the intervening modifications were indicators that private enforcement continued to be necessary, and more strongly encouraged. For example, a 1729 law required slaves to keep to the main thoroughfares when traveling, and if the slave was found off the road, it was "lawful for the owner of the land whereon any such slave be found, to give him a severe whipping, not exceeding forty lashes."[186] Likewise, any "loose, disorderly, or suspected person," black or white, found in company with a slave at night could be apprehended, taken before a justice of the peace, and also given a lashing. Married slaves or those who had a pass from their owner would be exempt from this form of punishment.[187] After the Stono revolt, the legislature took even sterner measures. It offered compensation to encourage individuals to take up runaways. A structured reward system was created: 7 shillings, 6 pence, for capturing a fugitive within ten miles of his master's home, and 3 pence more per mile if farther away.[188] Even after formal patrols were established, private individuals could (and did) take advantage of this reward system to apprehend runaways.

North Carolina's slave population began to rise in the mid-eighteenth century, as Cape Fear planters turned more of their energies to cultivating naval stores, lumber, and rice. The British navy needed tar, pitch, and lumber for its ships, materials supplied in abundance along the marshy, tree-choked Cape Fear.[189] Plantations in the region grew so much that their products could support two small commercial centers, Brunswick and Wilmington. The latter steadily expanded, and the entire region soon became the most densely populated slave area of the colony. By 1755 bondsmen in the Cape Fear region outnumbered whites by an almost two-to-one margin, a ratio unmatched in any other part of North Carolina.[190] Swamps near Wilmington provided ideal hiding places that could harbor runaways and thwart all attempts at recapturing them.[191] The salt marshes and high slave population density of this region probably tipped the balance in favor of creating slave patrols in North Carolina, despite the relatively low numbers of slaves colonywide.

The first formal groups resembling patrols appeared in North Carolina in 1753.[192] Although the creation of patrols came somewhat later than in South Carolina (1704) and Virginia (1727), similar fears of slave rebellion appeared to motivate their establishment; Governor Matthew Rowan noted that the slaves had recently attempted to raise an insurrection against their owners.[193] The General Assembly created patrols in a manner quite distinct from either the Virginia or South Carolina models:

county courts, not the militia, were authorized to appoint "searchers" who could enter slave quarters and look for weapons.[194] Searchers, who came to be called patrollers as time passed, shared many of the same privileges as Virginia patrollers.[195] They were exempt from militia duty as well as jury duty and provincial, county, and parish taxes. The justices were to divide their counties into districts, and appoint three freeholders per district as searchers for guns, swords, and other weapons among slaves. Why the legislature decided to place the responsibility for establishing patrols with the county court is a matter of speculation: they may have observed the manner of patrolling in both Virginia and South Carolina and judged those efforts to be inadequate.[196] More likely, they considered the population density of North Carolina and realized that while militia companies might not regularly muster (and not appoint patrols), the county court would almost always convene, and thus the court would be a more responsible agent for this delegated duty.

The first counties to appoint searchers, or patrols, in North Carolina were Chowan and New Hanover. Although not every county appointed patrollers in the 1750s, those with large concentrations of bondsmen quickly took advantage of the new law. Located in the northeast corner of the colony, Chowan had the third-highest number of slaves of any North Carolina county in the 1750s. Chowan's first patrols appeared in 1753, when the legislature initially authorized them. The county court appointed three men in each of four districts to "range in the said district and apprehend such Negroe slaves as they find transgressing."[197] New Hanover, in the colony's southeast corner, had the largest number of slaves of any county in the 1750s, and was the only county in which slaves outnumbered whites.[198] New Hanover named its first patrols in 1759, although the loss of the 1742–1758 court records probably masks the earlier appointment of patrols by that county's court.[199]

Although court records initially named each patroller appointed, eventually the process became so routinized that their appointment barely deserved mention in the court clerk's minute books. In the years after 1769, the clerk of New Hanover county court, John London, simply began recording without elaboration that "Constables, Searchers, and Overseers [were] appointed."[200] Thereafter patrols continued to be named, but their members' identities are often discoverable only through inspection of tax lists. Their jobs entitled them to an exemption from paying taxes, and all patrollers' legally "missing" taxes had to be explained specifically by the sheriff in his yearly financial accounting with the court.[201] This process also held true in Virginia, where annual county tax reports, recorded in the court minute books, reveal the appointment of patrols whose members, year after year, received their tax exemption from the county in exchange for controlling slave movement and illicit behavior.[202]

North Carolina patrols also received other forms of compensation. A patrol's detection of items hidden in slave cabins could prove rewarding, but might also be costly. In New Hanover County, patrols received one shilling for finding a barrel, and greater or lesser amounts for other items they located.[203] If searchers found a hidden gun, they were usually allowed to retain it; James Dotey was allowed to retain a gun he found "as a recompense for his trouble."[204] However, these first patrollers must have had to exercise caution in looking for weapons kept by slaves, for some slaves in the colonial period had a lawful right to possess guns. Any North Carolinian could petition the court for exemptions so that his slaves could carry guns, and early courts were inclined to give these exemptions freely when the owner was a man of great status. When the "Hon. Edward Moseley, Esq.," asked for four gun exemptions for his slaves, the court granted them all on the same day.[205] And a gentleman's complaint might cause the patroller to lose his appointment, and his tax exemption. When William Dry, Esq., complained about patroller David Smeeth, the judges disagreed about whether the searcher deserved a hearing. Apparently the word of a gentleman was enough; Smeeth lost his patrol position without any formal inquiry.[206]

Between 1753 and 1779 North Carolina searchers still constituted a limited form of patrol at most, without several duties required of Virginia and South Carolina patrollers. They had no powers to detain slaves who were traveling between plantations, and they could not enter the homes of whites, searching for slaves absent from their owners. North Carolina patrollers finally acquired these additional responsibilities during the Revolutionary War, most likely as the result of increased concerns about white security.[207] A more important change in 1779, however, was the introduction of direct payment. Already patrollers were exempt from jury duty, road work duty, and militia musters, and received a forty-shilling tax exemption. But the legislature mandated an even greater incentive. County tax money would be paid to the patrollers following their submission of records and proof that they had performed their duties. The decision to pay patrollers constituted the single greatest difference between North Carolina and the other two colonies, for in Virginia, payment remained optional, and in South Carolina there was no payment at all. North Carolina patrollers continued to receive both exemptions and payment for their services until the end of the Civil War.

The methods by which patrol groups developed in the three colonies before the American Revolution shared several common characteristics. At the outset, each colony's legislative assembly attempted to regulate the behavior of its slaves by mandating what a slave should and should not do—a regulation of behavior in the abstract, without much consideration of whether the bondsman would voluntarily obey, or who would be responsible for enforcing the legal provisions if he did not.[208] In short order, each colony turned to requests, and then requirements, that private individuals monitor the behavior of their own slaves and any other bondsmen with whom they came in contact. The reliance on private enforcement seemed natural, since theoretically all white citizens had a stake in preserving their safety and maintaining an orderly society. And given the paucity of settlement in each colony at the outset, reliance on the individual and not a community group was essential if any enforcement action was to take place.

Eventually, white colonial lawmakers determined that they could not rely completely on private efforts to control the slave population. Combining rewards with penalties, each colony groped its way toward a more regulated situation, eventually accepting that some individuals would have to be appointed by the militia or county court in order to enforce the laws pertaining to slaves. By the end of the seventeenth century in South Carolina, and in the mid-eighteenth century in Virginia and North Carolina, legislatures replaced voluntarism (which worked erratically) with colony-sanctioned authority figures who would monitor slave movement and behavior. This shift seems tentative, halting: the early legislation implied a strong preference to have white individuals take action separately, almost a reluctance on the part of colonial officials to create slave patrols. The greatest innovation occurred as a result of this shift from private, voluntary enforcement of slave laws to a public slave patrol system, one in which the community stepped in to supplement actions taken by the individual slave master.[209]

The length of time between first efforts to control slave behavior and the formal institution of patrols in each colony depended upon several variables: first date of settlement, size of slave population, overall population, threatened insurrections, and geographic area and density of settlement. South Carolina adopted its patrol system in 1704, whereas Virginia, which had adopted pass laws before South Carolina, did not create a patrol law until 1727. The fact that Virginia was settled and had slaves prior to South Carolina's initial founding meant that Virginia would be the first to create general slave laws.[210] The density and large number of bondsmen flooding into South Carolina at the end of the seventeenth century, however, prompted lawmakers there to institute their patrols sooner. Likewise, the geography of South Carolina, which encouraged the growth of large, isolated plantations with sizable numbers of slaves, and the development of the first settlement that could be considered "urban" influenced that colony to proceed with slave control laws at an even faster pace than colonies to its north. North Carolina lagged far behind the other two colonies in creating a patrol-like group because it was settled later, had fewer residents until 1700, and even after that date, was so sparsely settled that highly regulated groups like slave patrols would not be necessary for slave control for almost fifty years. Only a threatened slave revolt in the 1750s prompted North Carolina to enact patrol laws.

Even as colonies shifted to using patrols, the private reward system remained in place. Individuals would continue to claim rewards for capturing slaves until the end of the Civil War, and thus the patrols never completely squeezed out private enforcers from pursuing fugitive slaves. Perhaps this should not be surprising, since patrols had multiple duties and were created in at least one colony with something other than runaways in mind. North Carolina's creation of "searchers," who only looked for weapons at their inception, reveals that even at the beginning, some lawmakers expected that patrollers' primary duty was to reveal and destroy the roots of slave rebellions. Tracking down runaways was an early priority in South Carolina, but was only required much later from patrollers in North Carolina.

These differing priorities in the colonial period explain some of the variations found in each patrolling system initially, but not all of them. Certainly, patrols and the laws they enforced developed from experimentation, failures, and evolving perceptions and apprehensions. The process of trial and error becomes clearest when considering the issue of payment. South Carolina lawmakers began by not paying patrollers, then briefly offered pay, and ultimately dropped it altogether. For its patrollers, North Carolina moved from tax exemptions, to including exemption from other duties, to implementing direct payment.

The importance of early failures deserves mention, too. If the hue and cry system had effectively controlled slaves, constables and sheriffs would never have been supplemented with a new institution targeted specifically at slaves. Similarly, if the militia had been capable of handling two different tasks at the same time, that is, rebuffing both the internal and the external dangers, patrols might never have appeared. Evolving apprehensions explain other aspects of colonial patrol development. For example, pass laws that patrollers spent hours enforcing developed out of concerns about numerous seemingly untrustworthy groups, not just slaves. And at first, legislators thought that allowing North Carolina patrols to search slave quarters seemed a large enough grant of power, but with greater threats, patrols gained the expanded authority to control slaves by stopping them on the road.

And yet understanding priorities, experimentation, failures, and changing concerns still leaves some aspects of colonial patrolling unclear. Two of the most intriguing features may always remain a mystery. We will probably never know for certain why North Carolinians decided to continue paying patrollers long after the American Revolution ended, when both South Carolina and Virginia disdained the practice. Why the legislature entrusted slave patrols to the supervision of county courts likewise seems puzzling, although the reliable convening of courts is the most probable reason they, and not the militia, received that responsibility.

The revolutionary era marked the end of extensive experimentation and change for patrolling. The main contours of patrols became evident by that time: except in urban areas, patrols served as separate groups, apart from militia, constables, and sheriffs. They hunted runaways, looked for weapons and stolen goods in slave cabins, questioned slaves they met on the road, and broke up slave meetings. Patrollers could detain and question whites while performing these duties, and enter their homes without warrants. And in Virginia and North Carolina, patrollers received compensation. Even with the main features of patrolling in place, however, institutional development did continue, and would be most apparent in the burgeoning towns and cities that began to dot the three states in the coming decades. After the Revolution, patrollers would have an even more important role in the expanding South.

2

Supervising Patrollers in Town and Country

> I could see at once he was not a militia man, for there was nothing of
> the holiday-look about him. Equally could I see that he was not a
> soldier, for you did not find that smartness and neatness which
> become inseparable from continuous discipline. I was subsequently
> enlightened, and learned that there was a strong force constantly in
> readiness to act. Patrols pass through the city at all hours.
>
> *William Kingsford, a visitor to Charleston in the 1850s*

For a foreign traveler exploring the nineteenth-century South, seeing patrols at work must have been puzzling indeed.[1] Clearly, slave patrols observed some discipline and order that seemed vaguely military, but they did not neatly fit conventional categories of military groups of the day. If patrols were frequently on duty, and had a serious demeanor, they could not be militia men; yet they were not professional enough to be soldiers. And why would cities like Charleston need so many patrols? Despite being told that Charleston had criminals and desperate men who needed watching, William Kingsford finally concluded that "the principal cause of anxiety might be, after all, the slave population."[2]

Kingsford's confusion is understandable. Patrols of the eighteenth- and nineteenth-century South often had military connections, with close ties to the militia. In Virginia and South Carolina, rural patrols drew their membership directly from the militia, so the militia's impact on patrolling merits close attention. By contrast, some patrols had little military oversight—in North Carolina and in towns across the three states, like Charleston, patrol groups answered to county courts, patrol committees, and city councils. And sometimes the boundaries between patrols and other authority groups seemed faint and indistinct. In cities, the line dividing patrols from the night watch and the police blurred. In particular, city councils used patrols not just to control slave behavior but for a variety of other purposes as well. In city patrolling, one can see most prominently the distinctive Southern pattern linking race and slavery with public authority and control.

Patrols and the Militia

The relationship between slave patrols and the militia was an intimate one in all three colonies. In Virginia and South Carolina, the patrol came directly from the militia, chosen by its members. In North Carolina, county courts sometimes used militia rosters to appoint patrollers. For all three colonies, and later states, slave patrols formed the first line of defense against a slave rebellion, with the militia expected to take action should a revolt become large-scale. As "Argus," a letter writer to the *Winyaw Intelligencer,* expressed it, "the patrole is made to depend upon the military commanders, and goes hand in hand with the improvement or deterioration of the militia—surely in this country at least, no arguments will be required to prove the necessity of such a police."[3] Some historians have theorized that because the militia was in decline during the late eighteenth and early nineteenth centuries, it must therefore follow that slave patrols likewise experienced a similar lessening in efficacy. Thus a better understanding of the patrol must proceed from an overview of militia behavior and functioning in the colonial and early federal period. It will then be possible to describe and differentiate the organization and administration of patrols in Virginia and the Carolinas.[4]

In the seventeenth and eighteenth centuries, the English sustained a strong tradition of militia service and brought this background to their American colonies. Englishmen had served in local militia groups for centuries, a visible reminder that reliance upon a standing army alone might encroach upon their liberties. In the seventeenth century, English militiamen routinely put down insurrections and placed limits upon the behavior of dissidents, though by the eighteenth century musters were sometimes not held for years at a time.[5] English colonists in early Caribbean settlements mustered more frequently in response to the various "perils" (Indians, Spanish colonies, slaves) surrounding them.[6] Both

English tradition and Caribbean practice migrated with settlers to Virginia and the Carolinas.

Militia groups formed in mainland colonies almost as soon as the first settlers' ships touched land. The original reason was obvious: self-protection. Colonists had to consider the threat posed not only by Native Americans, who (immediately or eventually) opposed their trespass on Indian lands, but also by foreign powers, who wanted them out of the way to allow conquest and future gains. After the Indians, the Spanish constituted the greatest menace, for their settlement in St. Augustine and claims to large tracts of land in the New World were in direct competition with the earliest English communities. Once slavery became established, free white colonists faced a new enemy, the one least likely to recede with time—the enemy they perceived within their own communities. The variegated protections that the colonial militia provided were obvious to Lieutenant Governor Drysdale of Virginia, who said that a strong militia could simultaneously appear terrifying to "Slaves, [and] formidable to the Indians."[7] In South Carolina, Lieutenant Governor William Bull echoed this sentiment nearly fifty years later, when he wrote that "[t]he defense of the province as far as our own power can avail, is provided for by our militia against foreign and Patrols against domestic enemies."[8] During the seventeenth and eighteenth centuries, regular militia drilling was a sound defensive strategy against a variety of people they considered their adversaries.

When militia companies met, each company captain was responsible for taking a census of white men in his area eligible for service, including those who could serve on patrols.[9] In South Carolina, the "beat" company formed the basic unit of men, comparable to the militia company found in each Virginia and North Carolina county. Originally, militia company lines followed natural geographic divisions that allowed men to muster together without having to cross rivers or mountains, while saving road commissioners money and effort that would have been expended building bridges or roads.[10] Once established, these militia boundaries proved remarkably durable in subsequent decades: a reconstruction of boundaries for sixteen antebellum beat companies in Pickens District, South Carolina, reveals that the companies continued to be bounded by bodies of water and existing roads.[11] Militia company lines also served as boundary lines for individual patrol groups, and their exact perimeters were sometimes recorded in local property record books or company militia roster books.[12] (See Figure 2.) Each militia company might contain anywhere from three to eight patrol groups. Patrols used local landmarks and existing militia divisions to distinguish the limits of their authority and the exact region for which they were responsible.

Militia musters were the site for selecting patrols in Virginia and South Carolina, and in the colonial period, these gatherings began to show signs of rowdiness and excess. At company, or "petty," musters, local men gathered four to six times a year to practice military formations and engage in target practice.[13] Regimental musters and battalion mus-

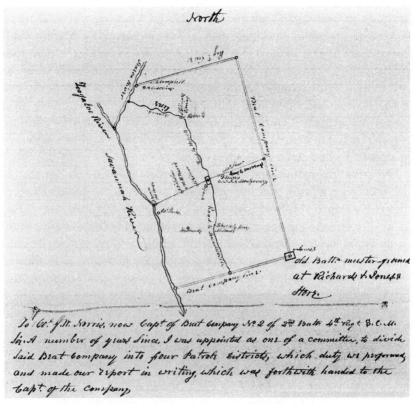

2. Beat lines map, South Carolina

ters were also held once a year, at which the governor and other high-ranking dignitaries would watch the troops go through their maneuvers. The militia was the pride of a community, blending "formality and intimacy" according to the historian Rhys Isaac, who saw in it a male-dominated microcosm of society.[14] Musters displayed both order and discipline in a white society armed against its enemies, but these qualities frequently contrasted with the drunken displays, music, fighting, and political speech making that colonial musters encompassed. Local and regimental musters became a major focus of social life in the colonial and antebellum South, although the revelry was not without its critics. Before and after the American Revolution, citizens in virtually every decade lodged protests against the dissipations of musters.[15] From the earliest militia gatherings, slaves and free African Americans were present, though the law legally limited their participation beginning in the eighteenth century, officially relegating them to the ranks of musicians.[16] Gatherings at militia musters provoked some concern that the martial music and warlike troop movements would incite the slaves attending to take up arms themselves—against white Southerners.[17] Protests like this did not stop nonwhites from attending militia musterings, however.

No observer of musters seems to have been overawed by the military prowess of those involved. Their inability to follow orders, shoot well, or turn out with the required equipment provoked repeated appeals for better discipline. Even in the eighteenth century, the ragged state of the militia led to a series of jeremiads on its dilapidated condition.[18] After 1800, militia groups in many areas met for little more than required musters. Despite their members' sometimes unkempt appearance, however, regular musterings and selections for patrol duty formed a regular pattern of civic duty for eighteenth- and early nineteenth-century males. Interspersed with planting, tending, and harvesting, intermittent calls to militia duty were normal for most Southern white men.[19]

At musters, the beat captain or company captain routinely assigned men to or requested volunteers for patrol duty.[20] If the captain failed to appoint men as patrollers, he incurred a fine. In some cases, the names of all eligible men were placed in a hat and drawn at random.[21] The number of men chosen to serve was determined by law, and varied from four to six, with room for discretionary appointments by the captain if he thought additional men would be useful. New patrol members received a certificate or warrant of appointment which they retained while on duty, in case they were challenged about their authority to enter a person's land.[22] At militia musters, former patrollers gave accounts of their patrol activities, which nights they served, and which houses they visited. Men who failed to serve after being appointed to patrol duty in Virginia or South Carolina could be fined, if the captain decided to hold a court martial.

In addition to selecting patrollers, militia units in the antebellum period continued to meet and drill, which meant that men could be elected to posts with honorific titles like captain, colonel, and major. Routinely, many officers above the noncommissioned ranks were elected by their own soldiers.[23] Once elected, a man ordinarily addressed his troops. John Tompkins, a merchant who later served in the Confederate Army, asked his men to forgive his faults, remember his gratitude at being elected, and faithfully carry out their duties, including patrol duty. By being active patrollers, he asserted, "you will keep afar off those unsatisfied tamperers with our slaves who now throng our Southern country. By it you prevent that most direful of contingencies—a servile war."[24] Service as an officer in the militia for a set number of years could eventually bring exemption from militia (and patrol) duty altogether, and moving up through the officer ranks was commonplace. For example, Virginia resident James Faulkner became an ensign in 1797, a lieutenant in 1806, and captain in 1807.[25] Abuses in the militia election process had their effect on the regularity of patrol duty. Sometimes less qualified but more jovial or easygoing commanders would be chosen, including men known for their leniency in imposing fines for default of patrol duty.[26] Even men who achieved high rank complained about militia elections— as General Wade Hampton III said, "The best officers are sometimes left out because they are strict"—but elections continued even during the Civil War.[27] Joseph Glover, a South Carolina commander, complained that patrolling had waned in 1775 because officers "must be subservant to their mens humours."[28]

Although militia companies experienced a decline of efficacy and enthusiasm in the late eighteenth and early nineteenth centuries, their gradual weakening did not signal the demise of slave patrols.[29] On the contrary, foreign observers, slaves, and those who served on patrols themselves provide ample testimony that patrols continued to be active even as militias appeared to atrophy. This divergence is not easily explained, unless one considers the reasons why the militia formed initially. As other threatening groups receded in the distance, the only remaining menace to the white community was slaves, which a subgroup of the militia—patrols—was specifically designed to control. As long as patrols continued to be vigilant, the Southern militia could diminish its activities and yet be confident that someone was watching its most dreaded adversary. And of course all Southern white men could be called upon in an emergency to join patrols and suppress black insurrections. The formation of volunteer militia groups provided some comfort as well; men who disdained the ragtag public militia could join private military clubs with smart uniforms and a certain social prestige. Although some of these private militia groups attracted men who joined them as a way to avoid patrol duty, other volunteer militias actually wanted greater slave supervision, supervision they believed the regular militia sometimes neglected.[30] Chapter 5 examines the deterioration of the militia after the American Revolution, but episodes of fear and rumored insurrections caused the white community to rediscover periodically its declining militia and the useful though sometimes neglected patrols.[31]

Other Groups That Supervised Slave Patrols

Militia captains were not the only ones to control appointments and movements of patrollers. In North Carolina, the county court had the authority to appoint slave patrollers from the very beginning, and continued to wield that power until the Civil War.[32] Court justices used militia muster lists or local tax rolls to determine who would serve as patrollers. The original delegation of patrol authority to county courts indicates that North Carolinians probably viewed patrolling primarily as a civil, not military, task that should be controlled and regulated by courts, not the militia.[33]

County courts routinely appointed patrollers across North Carolina, and their repeated selection and payment attest to the important role courts believed patrollers played.[34] Even in the mountains, where fewer slaves lived than in other parts of North Carolina, patrols performed their duties in customary fashion.[35] In 1830 the legislature provided for even closer supervision of patrols by creating the local patrol committee. Their decision was prompted by a threatening new pamphlet. In late 1829, an explosive abolitionist tract began circulating throughout the South. David Walker's pamphlet, *Walker's Appeal*, sharply criticized

Southern whites who supported slavery and argued that slaves had the right (as American revolutionaries had in the eighteenth century) to resist oppression with armed force.[36] By 1830 Walker's essay had arrived in Wilmington and other North Carolina cities,[37] and Governor John Owen responded with alacrity, writing to state senators in virtually every county. Owen entreated, "I beg you will lay this matter before the police of your town and invite their prompt attention to the necessity of arresting the circulation of the book alluded to; I would suggest the necessity of the most vigilant execution of your police laws and the laws of the State."[38] Owen followed up his letters by urging the state legislature to reform laws that governed both slaves and free blacks. The assembly responded, nearly a year *before* the Nat Turner rebellion, and revised the administration of slave patrolling within the state.

The North Carolina patrol committee came into being: a group of three men in each county district, designated by the court to appoint, supervise, and dismiss patrols as well as hear complaints brought against patrollers.[39] Courts divided their county into several districts, usually along militia company lines, so multiple patrol committees served in a single county each year.[40] Anxiety caused by the Walker pamphlet, and the limited number of justices sitting on each county court, serve to explain why the legislature wanted courts to delegate patrol supervision to others. Relying on patrol committees allowed a court to focus on pressing business and still provide for the smooth functioning of slave patrols. The patrol committee could be composed of men who lived closer to patrollers, and who would be more likely to see if they were making their rounds. The committee also had the duty of suing those men who refused to serve, in order to collect their fines for nonperformance.

North Carolina court justices chose patrol committee members from among the prominent men of each district. In Panther Branch District, Wake County, the patrol committee of 1857–58 comprised Thomas and Willis Whitaker and Simon Smith, men of means who lived in the same district as the patrollers whom they appointed. The taxes paid by Willis Whitaker indicate that he was the largest landowner and slave owner in the district, with twenty-seven slaves, while Thomas Whitaker and Simon Smith, the other committeemen, were moderately successful men with seven and nine slaves, respectively, and good-sized farms.[41] The Whitaker brothers, Willis and Thomas, inherited most of their wealth from their father, Colonel John Whitaker, one of the wealthy founders of

Wake County.[42] His sons inherited large and thriving farms in Wake and Halifax counties and became active leaders in the community. Willis served with distinction in the War of 1812, owned land in the state capital of Raleigh, and took part in county politics. By 1857, when they were appointed to the patrol committee, the Whitakers were in their late fifties and sixties, men too old to be active patrollers themselves, but who had enough respect among white residents for their choices to carry authority. The fact that the Wake County court chose the Whitakers for the patrol committee suggests that their work was viewed not as a throwaway task, but as a job requiring able men possessing status and prestige within the community. Moreover, as the largest slave owner in the district, Willis Whitaker might well have requested to be appointed to the committee, to prevent patroller abuses and to be sure that the slaves of other owners were properly regulated.

The selection of Simon Smith, the other patrol committeeman, was not solely due to social status, however. Smith lived in a different part of the district from the Whitakers—they lived in the northwest and Smith in the southeast. The court may have been striving to balance the committee by providing geographic distribution of the committee members. But why was Simon Smith, in particular, selected to serve on the patrol committee? After all, other men in the southern part of the district owned more land and slaves than Smith. A map of Wake County from the period offers one likely answer.[43] (See Figure 3.) Most roads in the district ran from north to south. Smith's house stood where three of these roughly parallel north-south roads terminated (within a few hundred yards of each other) at a junction with the main east-west route, the Smithfield Road.[44] In a district riddled with unfordable creeks and rivers, like Terrible Creek and Swift Creek, these roads would prove indispensable for patrollers at work. Any supervision from a committee member would most likely come from a house situated near a main crossroads, such as Simon Smith's. And Willis Whitaker also lived directly on the main north-south highway as it neared Raleigh, the old Fayetteville Stage Road. Thus it seems that North Carolina county courts, by choosing patrol committee members whose houses were located on roads that the patrol itself would use, envisioned some direct supervision of the patrollers ultimately appointed.[45]

Other individuals besides militia captains, county court justices, and patrol committeemen could supervise the movement or appointment of slave patrollers. For example, individual justices of the peace in all three states had the authority to order patrols to search particular areas or hunt for specific slaves. They most frequently invoked this power when they believed fugitive slaves were in the local area, or when someone reported a slave revolt. Additionally, as small urban areas began to expand,

3. Panther Branch District, Wake County, North Carolina, 1871

city councils and town commissions also gained the power to appoint town-based patrols.

Urban Patrols: From Night Watch to City Police

The relative dearth of small towns and their slow growth in the South has been a mainstay of Southern history. In the earliest period, there were few places with enough people that deserved the name of "town." The seventeenth century found Virginia with virtually no cities, a development attributed to the numerous navigable rivers that promoted a scattered patchwork of farms.[46] In spite of deliberate efforts to foster municipal development, Virginia only slowly saw towns emerge and flourish in the eighteenth century.[47] North Carolina's low population in this period also precluded it from having many cities. In the seventeenth and early eighteenth centuries, the urban areas most likely to grow could be found near the ocean at the base of long navigable rivers. Wilmington, at the mouth of the Cape Fear River, and Charleston, at the confluence of the Ashley and Cooper Rivers, both shared these characteristics. Towns like Wilmington and Charleston created their own night watch groups to control slave behavior; these night watch groups constituted the forerunners of urban slave patrols and later the police.[48]

Despite their slow start, towns flourished in Virginia and the Carolinas during the eighteenth and nineteenth centuries. Some historians have theorized that the antebellum South was anti-urban, but urbanization did take place in a very dispersed fashion.[49] The pattern of rivers, settlement, economics, and soil exhaustion combined to dictate that urban places should be populated by fewer than four thousand persons—"urbanization without cities."[50] Within this diffused pattern of settlement, the Old South had "roughly its proportional share of the major and secondary cities" in the United States, but its cities were widely scattered.[51]

As towns expanded across all three states, the urban slave population resident in cities increased correspondingly. Runaway bondsmen eluded pursuing masters by hiding in towns, seeking refuge in their sprawling anonymity. In the eighteenth century, masters in Wilmington, North Carolina, began permitting their slaves to live in lodgings far removed from their owners, a practice adopted in other Southern cities.[52] This pattern of segregated living promoted urban slave communities, gave fugitives better hideaways, and undoubtedly heightened white anxieties during insurrections. White town residents constantly complained that slaves congregated in unruly groups, bought liquor, and hired their own labor to employers, all of which violated laws regulating slave behavior that watchmen should have enforced.[53] Urban growth gave rise to new fears for Southern whites. Clustered together in houses and stores, people and goods concentrated in a town presented a tempting target for a slave bent on arson, vandalism, or theft. Whites worried that urban areas acted like magnets, attracting people who might trade goods or liquor with slaves regardless of what the law permitted. If the local night watch had been completely effective, these illicit slave activities would have gone unremarked.[54] However, the "neglect and supineness of the watch company" in Charleston, for example, was regularly complained of, and in one instance the officer of the watch, William Graves, was accused of selling slaves liquor when he was supposed to be on duty.[55] Nighttime grog shops and petty theft seemed endemic in urban areas, revealing the limits of white control over slaves that some whites felt needed to be strengthened.[56]

Dissatisfied with inadequate night watchmen, town officials wanted authority over their own municipal patrols, which could mimic the routines of county-based patrols without relying on the county. Often county efforts to protect growing cities were insufficient. Patrols appointed by county authorities could exclude townspeople, and hence the town might not be regularly patrolled. If county officials completely neglected to appoint patrols, city authorities had no choice but to create and manage their own patrol. This happened in Columbia, South Carolina, whose civic leaders petitioned the legislature to make them an annual appropriation for the "raising, organization, pay and support of a guard" to protect the city. Columbia's intendant and wardens wrote that "the negligence and inefficiency of the Patrol" in the county, combined with the increasing population and lack of adequate funds for a competent guard, led them to ask for money from the state.[57] In 1832 city officials in Virginia succeeded in gaining control over their own civic patrols with legislation that empowered courts of incorporated towns to appoint and pay patrollers.[58] No doubt some cities petitioned for incorporation specifically to regulate their slaves and have a "proper police," as the citizens of Pearisburg, Virginia, claimed only two years later.[59]

Establishing a city patrol gave the impression of greater safety to whites, while exempting town residents from service in the surrounding area. A townsperson appointed to a county patrol might be ordered to leave the city to visit farms five or ten miles away, while his own family had little or no protection at all. Why should county residents have more security than town dwellers? Citizens of Yorkville, South Carolina, made just this argument in their petition to form their own patrols in 1824, asserting that in the surrounding county "the discharge of patrol duty . . . [was] too seldom for the good order of the slaves in the village." By organizing a municipal patrol, Yorkville residents would also be exempt from serving on county slave patrols.[60] City dwellers and magistrates wanted town patrols, made up of their own citizens, that would patrol their streets. They could look to each other for protection, not to county-provided patrols that might or might not answer their needs.

The pattern of establishing patrols in newly urbanized areas was remarkably similar for places that had relatively little contact with one another. Residents recognized that they needed some patrol force, and at first they relied upon their own efforts to remedy the situation, as the citizens of Raleigh, North Carolina, did prior to 1838. The initial stage might simply be to pass ordinances that banned slaves from city streets after a certain hour, with enforcement left in the hands of private individuals and the existing night watch.[61] Plymouth and Edenton, North Carolina, and Danville, Virginia, residents formed these kinds of citizens' patrol groups in 1808 and 1833.[62] In Georgetown, South Carolina, the need for greater patrol organization was becoming urgent. Pilfering in the surrounding county, and disposing of the goods in town, was common slave practice by 1799, and the ineffective county patrol was blamed for the continuing thefts. In their petition, Georgetown inhabitants claimed that they feared the prospect of slave thefts in town, which led them to form a citizens' town guard. For several months, they worked at guarding Georgetown by regular, nightly duty, but "the hardship of this duty became so great" that they voluntarily raised money to allow the town council to hire a permanent town guard. Some people paid as much as 50 percent of their annual tax assessment for this project, but it became too onerous to continue without state assistance.[63] After relying on its own efforts, a city could request increased powers from the legislature that would authorize it to control and regulate the patrol within town boundaries. The Beaufort town council, which already held a municipal charter, petitioned South Carolina's legislature for an enlargement of the charter to let it administer its own patrols.[64] Like the residents of Yorkville, town authorities would then routinely petition for their citizens to be exempt from patrol duty in the surrounding county.[65]

The next step in creating an urban patrol would be for a town to ask the legislature to allocate funds for a permanent patrol force. Georgetown residents did this as early as 1810, after their own fund-raising attempts did not provide enough money. Relying on precedent, they reasoned that since South Carolina's legislature had already allocated money for a town guard in Charleston, surely it would grant money to Georgetown for the same purpose.[66] The legislature dallied in helping Georgetown, for in 1829 the town petitioned again for the power and money to establish a town guard.[67] Claiming that the Georgetown area was a "very rich and important section of the country" that gave "a very considerable revenue" to the state, inhabitants dwelt on the recent discovery of another slave conspiracy, which forced town residents to serve on patrols for months on end. These petitioners felt "dreadfully harassed by the performance of military duties & [were] wholly unequal to the burden," especially because one-third of the five hundred white men eligible for patrol duty were absentee owners in the summer and early fall. Town residents anxiously pressed for further relief in Georgetown and the state responded with a sizable appropriation.[68]

As urban areas sprang up across each of the three states, some cities stumbled upon ingenious methods to create and organize town patrols. Hiring semiprofessional patrollers and emulating the patrol methods of larger cities became more common. Peter Cuttins, who went from Charleston to Georgetown, South Carolina, as the new captain of the "George Town Guards," borrowed a copy of the rules for the city guards in Charleston and asked the Georgetown city council to duplicate large portions of those guidelines as its own.[69] In the early nineteenth century, work by men like Cuttins went by a variety of names, including town guard, city patrol, or night police, although their duties were the same: to prevent slave gatherings and cut down on urban crime. Cuttins instituted a two-shift guard duty in the town, with the first shift working from 9 P.M. to 1 A.M., and the second shift working until daylight. Cuttins sent laborious notes on his efforts to Governor Stephen Miller, along with his budget for expenses incurred by the new patrols.[70] Georgetown's city council fully supported Cuttins, and informed the legislature that the greatest benefit of the guard was that it protected white inhabitants "against the insurrection spirit that unfortunately pervades a certain class of our population." They noted that Georgetown was in a densely slave-populated area. The guard could "prevent those meetings & conferences" where bondsmen would plot rebellion, and interdict "that dangerous intercourse between the blacks and designing white men" who might profit by inciting unrest.[71] In addition, the guard tended "to remove some of the cause which produce this disaffection" and benefited the entire slaveholding vicinity, not just the town. Slaves taken up by town patrols appeared the following day before a "mayor's court" to answer for their crimes.[72] Governor Miller responded with praise for Cuttins's efforts, and recommended that the legislature continue to support the Georgetown guard, because "reliance has been placed on its vigilance & strength as a security" to that town.[73] Cuttins's work provoked a catastrophic response: shortly after he arrived and implemented new patrol methods, his Georgetown home burned to the ground, which hints at slave retaliation.[74]

Town citizens, like their rural cousins, did not necessarily enjoy patrol work, and only stiff fines managed to keep them at their posts. In many cities one sees a perpetual upward spiral in nonperformance fines, often far outpacing the rate of inflation. Abingdon, Virginia, began with fines of two dollars for every offense in 1811, and in 1812 the fine increased to two dollars for the first offense, five dollars for the second, and ten for every failure to serve as patroller thereafter.[75] Town councils devised elaborate systems to determine who must serve as patrollers, and what would constitute an acceptable reason for failing to make the appointed rounds.[76] In Aiken, South Carolina, the council divided all white men into ten squads of three to seven men each and rotated them on duty throughout the year. Aiken's records reveal that more men appeared for service than paid fines for defaulting.[77] Citizens of Aiken served continuously on urban patrol duty from at least 1839 to 1860, when the "Council Patrol Book" abruptly ends.[78] Patrol service became so routinized in a few urban areas that town councils used preprinted forms to notify individuals when they had been appointed and to indicate when patrol court would be held to fine defaulters.

Some city merchants worried more about the fatigue patrolling inflicted on their workers than whether patrols did their jobs effectively. These storeowners focused on the sluggish behavior of their employees who patrolled by night and labored by day. Employers in urban areas, concerned that the law required overtaxed patrollers in effect to work two jobs, claimed that their laborers were "rendered incompetent to the performance of their daily employments" by virtue of having to work both day and night.[79] Businessmen like these were the most likely to support the creation of paid city patrollers, rather than continue to rely upon private citizens in the local patrol.

The final stage of urban patrol development occurred when a city became so large that hiring a permanent group of men to serve as patrols every night became preferable to relying upon its own citizens for safety. The date of a town's settlement, its rate of population growth, and the number of slaves resident—all these factors would influence how soon town officials wanted a well-regulated, paid city patrol. Alexandria, Virginia, a populous city near the nation's capital, had a night watch by 1800 and hired patrollers a few years later.[80] A much smaller town, Abingdon, Virginia, paid its first patrol in 1857, only a few years before the Civil War.[81] One slave owner who lived in a Virginia town with 25,000 residents recalled two men, Billy Finn and Billy Williams, "whose principal duties consisted in checking the wandering tendencies of the negroes, who were not allowed to be out during the later hours of the night without written permits from their masters." Although he did not think his city was heavily patrolled, forty years after slavery's demise he distinctly remembered the two men responsible for both day and night police work.[82] Some citizens never felt secure with amateur patrollers in their town: a Raleigh citizen criticized town commissioners in 1802 because they did not "appoint a sufficient number of patrollers so as to patrole the streets every night."[83] But average citizens were cheaper than full-time law enforcers like Peter Cuttins, who required more compensation than just a few fines from the mayor's court in Georgetown. Although towns might begin by depending upon state legislatures to pay patrollers, as Georgetown did, eventually too many urban areas petitioned for this kind of appropriation, exceeding the resources available.

Cities then faced the daunting task of raising enough money to pay their patrollers, and town fathers had to determine if their city charter granted sufficient authority to carry out their plans. Some towns asked that their charters be changed, petitioning for the power to raise money to pay patrollers. The resulting widespread municipal legislation can be seen in all three states from the 1810s until the Civil War. The methods used by cities to pay for their patrols, who were now sometimes called police, varied enormously. Under South Carolina law, the informant about a crime received a portion of the fine paid by the convicted wrong-doer. Charleston's town council wanted to pay its guards by using the fines that the guards themselves were entitled to by virtue of doing their jobs, an economy few patrollers must have appreciated.[84] Fayetteville, North Carolina, used private subscriptions instead of taxes, although this practice did not last long.[85] A few urban areas resorted to special patrol taxes, occasionally using fees paid by free blacks, while others allowed their citizens to commute their nonperformance fines (for failing to serve on patrol), and used that money to hire full-time patrols.[86] Cities that had long used townspeople as patrollers, with exemption from county patrol service, typically had to petition the state legislature again for authority to commute citizen fines so that they could hire full-time patrollers. Aiken, South Carolina, set its commutation fee at five dollars a year, or three dollars for any period less than a year.[87] The town of Chester, South Carolina, asked that it be given the power to "compound with all persons liable to patrol duty" for money that "they may deem a fair equivalent for such duty."[88] Citizens like those in Chester would then have the choice of paying a tax to hire patrollers or serving personally when called upon through the year, a practice that mixed ordinary citizens with full-time law enforcers.[89]

Of course, some towns skipped intermediate stages in establishing their own paid patrol forces. Unusual events could spur such developments. For instance, following the discovery and suppression of Gabriel's slave conspiracy in 1800, Virginia's governor James Monroe created the Public Guard of Richmond. While protecting public buildings from potential slave insurrections, the Guard would also round up and punish any slaves found on the streets after curfew.[90] Cities like Wilmington and Charleston had patrols so early in their history that paid patrolling appeared there before practically anywhere else: their size and obvious importance made those cities move quickly from ordinary citizen-patrollers to paid lawmen. Charleston's night watch originally functioned as town patrols until they were replaced by paramilitary city guards that remained on duty until the close of the Civil War.[91] In the nineteenth century, Charleston's routines were so well established that foreign visitors like Fanny Kemble commented upon them. Traveling through the South in the 1850s, a British lieutenant colonel noted that

Charleston's "city guards were actively patrolling the streets day and night, for the purpose, as one of them told [him], of 'keeping down the niggers.' "[92] William Kingsford, passing through a few years later, commented that "[w]hat struck [him] peculiarly in Charleston was the police organization. It is a perfect *gens d'armerie*."[93] Once created, urban patrols could be extremely effective, as in Charleston; one historian has even claimed that Southern city patrols "were much more sophisticated than northern city guards and watches."[94]

Patrols in urban areas, where vigilant guards made nightly rounds, had an important impact on the surrounding countryside. Town and country were never cut off from one another, but were interdependent. Urban patrols encountered novel difficulties when town residents moved just beyond the city limits. Disputes could arise over who should provide and pay for patrol services in outlying, unincorporated regions. A clear example of this development occurred on the outskirts of Charleston.

The area called Charleston Neck or the Cross Roads grew quickly in the early nineteenth century, yet remained beyond Charleston's original boundaries and its patrollers.[95] Afraid for their safety, white Cross Roads residents petitioned more than once for the establishment of "well-regulated Police" to keep order.[96] The thin Neck formed the only land approach to Charleston, and residents believed better patrolling would "add much to the safety of Travellers in general & particularly of the waggoners from the upper country, who are often molested and robbed in the vicinity of Charleston."[97] "[D]isorderly houses, unruly negroes, and wicked and depraved persons of every class" congregated there, and "at least 600 persons" in the vicinity were liable to perform patrol duty. The petitioners wanted a board of commissioners to oversee the "proper arrangement and classification" of the patrol. After all, the petitioners claimed, "[i]n most places in the State, embracing so dense and numerous a population, the powers to regulate the Patrol are given to the municipal authorities," so why not give that power to their commission? Unfortunately, these petitioners were not the Charleston city council, which had earlier been given the authority to organize a guard in the Charleston Neck area, but delayed when it could not raise enough money to pay for patrols. Eventually, Charleston's council collected some taxes to provide patrols in the Charleston Neck area, but it never spent the money. The legislature finally annexed the Neck to Charleston

in 1849 and justified its decision by claiming that the growing population needed an efficient patrol force.[98]

When municipalities complained that their patrols could not enforce
the law beyond town boundaries, they discovered a powerful weapon in
the fight for annexation. The trustees of Charlottesville, Virginia, asked
to have their city limits expanded in 1818 for the same reasons Charleston's town council had given: tippling houses had sprung up on the outskirts of town, leaving patrols with no authority to prevent slaves from
gathering there on Sundays.[99] The town continued to grow as the University of Virginia expanded, and every few years, city trustees would
petition anew to extend Charlottesville's limits, repeating their claims
about the restrictions placed on town patrols.[100] In 1844 citizens living
in the unincorporated area submitted their own counterpetition. They
saw little benefit in being annexed by the city and feared higher taxes to
pay for patrols they did not want (and which might disrupt their profits
from trading liquor to slaves).[101]

Whether a town used hired patrollers or relied upon citizen-patrollers, slaves in cities experienced similar rules designed to constrain their
behavior.[102] Large towns like Wilmington and Charleston required
bondsmen to wear badges. A slave's failure to wear the badge could result in punishment, incarceration, and fines for the slave owner.[103] Although the practice of wearing badges might lapse, it could be reinstated
abruptly when a city needed the revenue badge sales generated or during
times of turmoil like insurrection scares. Urban bondsmen also became
accustomed to the toll of the bell, signaling the end of their free movement for the day. Most towns of any size purchased a bell and set the
time it would be rung to signal the daily curfew. In Abingdon, Virginia,
curfew began at ten o'clock; a patroller on duty who found slaves on the
streets after that time could give them up to fifteen lashes.[104] Towns
varied curfew times to match seasonal variations of the sun's rising
and setting; most established their curfews at 9 or 10 P.M.[105] (See Figure
4.) Occasionally the establishment of a curfew law predated the existence of a local patrol, and violations of curfew would prompt efforts to
create a city slave patrol. For example, the Abingdon council reenacted
its curfew law several times trying to prevent nighttime slave meetings, and eventually established a regular patrol made up of citizens
from each of the six town divisions to prevent more nocturnal gatherings.[106] Although curfew laws and patrols officially restricted the move-

ments of urban bondsmen, they continued to roam at will in practically every town.[107]

Shortly after appointing watchmen or a city patrol, town councils typically built a guardhouse or slave jail to incarcerate wandering and runaway slaves. In Richmond, any slave taken up by the town patrol after 9 P.M. would be carried to "the cage" (a local name for the slave jail) and held until morning.[108] Urban patrols knew these jails quite well, since they frequently brought truants and runaways there for detention.[109] If needed, cities built immense slave jails. While traveling to her

PATROL

REGULATIONS

FOR

The Town of Tarborough.

RULE 1st. Slaves residing in the country whose owners, masters or mistresses for the time being do not live in town, other than such as have wives in town, shall not come to town on the Sabbath day, unless to attend church, or in the night time without written permission from their owners. masters or mistresses for the time being. such permission stating the place or places such slaves shall visit —Provided that they may at all times, come to town, on the business of their owners, masters or mistresses for the time being, without written permissions.

RULE 2nd.   No slave after the hour of nine, P. M (a reasonable time being allowed for him or her to go home or to the place designated in his or her written permission after the ringing of the bell,) shall be on the streets, or absent from the prem-

ises of his or her owner, master or mistress for the time being—or the premises of the owner, master or mistress for the time being of his wife—or the premises of the person, where he may be authorized by his written permission to go—unless he or she be on the business of his or her owner, master or mistress for the time being.

RULE 3rd. If any slave shall violate the foregoing Rules, the Patrol shall have power and it shall be their duty (any two of their number being present) to whip the said slave, either at the time of the offence being committed or at any time within three months thereafter, the number of stripes not to exceed fifteen, unless the said slave shall be guilty of insolent behaviour, or make his escape from the Patrol, in either of which cases the number of stripes shall not exceed thirty-nine.

4. *Patrol Regulations for the Town of Tarborough* (North Carolina)

husband's Georgia plantation, Fanny Kemble visited Charleston and noticed a large, unfinished structure, bigger than any other building in town. When she learned it was to be the new town jail, she asked a laborer working on the structure why Charleston needed one so immense. He informed her that "it was by no means larger than the necessities of the city required; for that they not unfrequently had between fifty and sixty persons (colored and white) brought in by the patrol in one night." When Miss Kemble wondered aloud why the curfew did not keep slaves indoors at night, the man replied that they persisted in going abroad "and every night numbers are brought in who have been caught endeavoring to evade the patrol."[110] Charles Ball, a fugitive slave, knew that his best chance for passing through Richmond was in the daytime, when a single black man could mingle with the city's thronging black residents and not arouse suspicions. Nearing Richmond at night, Ball waited outside the city limits until daylight, when the patrol ceased, and then went through town at midday.[111]

Local and regional variations existed among patrols, although bondsmen may have thought urban and rural patrols were all the same. Cities with paid patrollers could seem more restrictive to town slaves: one ex-slave described how closely patrollers watched the streets of Raleigh, North Carolina.[112] Conversely, a town's or region's lapse in the routine enforcement of slave control laws could inspire a revolt, like Gabriel's rebellion in Virginia at the end of the eighteenth century.[113] A few bondsmen, though, could tell the difference between town and country patrols. The former slave Charley Mitchell thought Lynchburg, Virginia, was filled with patrols "jus' like the country" and equally hazardous for a slave with no valid pass. But Mitchell also remembered that Lynchburg patrols could whip slaves, unlike patrols in the countryside, who had to take the truant country slave to a justice of the peace before the whipping could be administered.[114] Whether immediate or delayed, a beating was still a beating—bondsmen, therefore, had plenty of reason to fear both rural and urban patrollers.

Impetus for Reform: The "Shameful Neglect of Patrol Duty"

From the revolutionary era to the Civil War, changes in slave patrols primarily arose from grievances about patrollers, prompting state legislatures and town councils to take action.[115] In South Carolina, complaints about patrols recurred with the greatest frequency in newspapers, grand jury presentments, and petitions to the legislature. Evidence of protests and petitions to change the patrol laws does not exist to the same extent in North Carolina or Virginia, raising an interesting, yet unanswerable, question: was patrolling worse in South Carolina, or were South Carolinians simply more afraid of their slaves? Although existing records are not sufficiently detailed to permit a comparison of patrols' effectiveness in one state versus another, South Carolinians had at least two extra reasons to be afraid of their slaves: the high density of bondsmen in the Low Country and the practice of absentee ownership, common among planters in that region. A closer look at how South Carolinians criticized patrols provides revealing insight into the fears, real and imagined, of the white community.[116]

Whether patrollers served in urban or rural areas, the most common complaint leveled against them was that they did not do their jobs. Grand juries frequently cited patrollers for their "shameful neglect of patrol duty."[117] "Shameful neglect" could mean many things: patrolling in a haphazard fashion, being drunk while on duty, or not patrolling at all. Although grand juries almost never censured specific men for inadequate patrolling, citizens grew dissatisfied when patrols did not do their job because it was widely believed that vigilant patrollers sustained the "peace & security of the citizens."[118] Newspaper letters and editorials criticized patrols for their laxity, calling for patrols and city guards to increase their vigilance when the extent of crime created "serious apprehensions."[119] Records for several towns indicate that regularly employed patrollers were discharged for sleeping at their posts; the Charleston *Strength of the People* wryly jested that the members of the City Guard probably slept "no more than is necessary" when they were on duty.[120]

Probably the most humorous description of chaotic patrolling came from "A Citizen" who used a Charleston newspaper to vent his anger. "Is it not surprising," he wrote, that

> we hear of so many robberies when we have a guard, whose duty it is to patroll the streets, and instead of that they are skulking or playing whoop and hide, trying to catch negroes . . . I would wish to know if the law is repealed, authorising the city guard to appear in uniform, for it appeared to me those men . . . had none; or if they had it was not visible, they were so much disguised, some of them with clubs and others

with bayonnets—so that I think it is dangerous for a person to send out his servant *even with a pass;* for one does not know who those fellows are, whether they be a set of banditti, or those who ought to guard our property."[121]

Despite the fact that newspapers and grand jurors complained about patrols as ineffective, slaves did not necessarily share the same attitudes. One has only to glance at the index to *The American Slave: A Composite Autobiography* to see the hundreds of references to patrols and slave surveillance in the WPA interviews with former slaves.[122] Almost all former bondsmen recalled patrols working in their neighborhood, and even seventy years later, elderly ex-slaves like Lucy Gallman still remembered exactly who made up the patrol near their home plantation: "The paterollers down there where we lived was Geo. Harris, Lamb Crew, Jim Jones, and Theo. Merchant."[123] If patrols seemed ineffective to Southern whites, former slaves remembered taking shortcuts and altering their behavior to cope with patrollers who manned the main roads.[124] The opinions of Southerners both black and white about slave patrols will be explored more deeply in Chapter 4.

If patrols did not do their jobs, as the complaints suggested, then a complicating factor must be explained: a great many patrollers were paid for their services, either directly or indirectly. In urban areas of South Carolina, and throughout North Carolina and Virginia, courts and cities compensated these men for their work by direct payment or by combinations of tax exemptions and service exemptions.[125] Unlike militiamen, who went unpaid for mustering, slave patrollers were paid by many means. Virginia and North Carolina county courts began regularly paying patrollers in the second half of the eighteenth century.[126] Given the high amount of pay dispersed to these men, over lengthy periods of service, one must wonder that so much money would be squandered for inadequate services rendered. A closer examination of one town reveals the lengths white city residents would go to for security.

Consider the town guard of Georgetown, South Carolina, in 1830, the year before Nat Turner's rebellion in Virginia. In one month, the town spent over $300 on the salaries of town guards alone. During an eight-month span, city patrols received $3,000—this despite fines levied for poor service and men dismissed because they were considered unfit for duty.[127] One possible reason men were compensated for patrol work was that they were indigent: incapable of paying their taxes, they were given community work that could be paid, with the pay being confiscated in lieu of taxes.[128] This interpretation fits with the idea of patrollers as "poor whites" and may have been true in select instances. The majority of patrollers, however, were middling-status taxpayers, a subject explored at greater length in the next chapter. Although citizens complained of inefficient patrols, it is hardly believable that county after county and city after city would have continued to pay patrollers' salaries had they been completely inactive or ineffective.

If payments suggest that patrols did their jobs, then fines for not patrolling could imply precisely the opposite. Supervisory bodies like the militia and county courts could wield both the carrot (payment) and the stick (fines) where patrollers were concerned. In South Carolina and Virginia, militia records show that men regularly paid fines for failing to perform patrol duty.[129] Legislatures and town councils repeatedly increased fines to keep pace with inflation, to make the fines real penalties that men would seek to avoid.[130] As wealth became more concentrated among social elites after 1820, however, even increasing fines did not seem enough. Antebellum reformers wanted change, suggesting that a man's fine for failing to patrol should match the amount of taxes he paid on his property.[131] This must have seemed fairer to ordinary men living in the professedly democratic age of Jackson. To "compel the more punctual attendance of those who from their abilities to pay the fines are seldom or never seen," Charleston petitioners suggested that an extra fine equal to 2 percent of the sum paid in taxes be added to the regular nonperformance penalty—the wealthiest would then pay the most money for neglecting their duties.[132] Indexing fines to the amount of taxes one paid struck some wealthy men as inherently unfair. Affluent gentlemen claimed that such fines would be excessive and "unequal in their operation."[133] Given that legislatures served as second homes to elite men, wealth-based fines stood little chance of enactment. Lawmakers never instituted them, and penalties usually trailed the inflation rate, meaning that some well-to-do white men must have willingly paid fines rather than serve as patrollers.[134]

The links joining patrols to the militia in Virginia and South Carolina made collection of patrol fines that much more difficult in those states.[135] Courts martial had to be held to fine a recalcitrant patroller, and few officers wanted to charge a man with neglecting his duty. After all, each man fined was a lost vote for officers prosecuting the offense. Isaac

Walter, a regimental commander, noted that company captains were reluctant to fine men for just that reason, and he asked his commanding officer whether he could fine men who did not patrol at a regimental court martial, bypassing the officers in the middle who did not want to offend their men.[136]

Walter's complaint about patrol fines, like other patrol-related grievances, should remind us that the efforts of patrols had value in a slave-based society. The cries for reform and complaints suggest that patrol work was valued and desired by members of the white community. Citizens would have neither paid nor complained if they considered patrolling trivial and insignificant.

After their failure to do their job, the next most frequent complaint voiced in the antebellum period about patrols was that they were composed primarily of poor men, and not drawn from all social classes. At least one law in South Carolina, however, suggests that precisely the opposite state of affairs existed at that time.[137] The "poor white" patrol complaint was most common in South Carolina, especially in the later antebellum period. This allegation bore a strong relationship to the absentee ownership customary in that state's Low Country region. Petitioners in Charleston attempted to persuade the General Assembly that the burden of patrol duty fell too often on the poor and that collecting fines was difficult from others who constantly changed their residence— criticisms clearly directed at the peripatetic planter class.[138] Planters who maintained two different homes were required to notify the captain of the patrol company of both the area they were leaving and the one they were going to, since patrols were chosen from white men resident in each district. But by moving their residence seasonally, wealthy men sometimes failed to inform militia officers in either district, hoping to rely on their ignorance and avoid doing patrol duty altogether.[139] The political power wielded by these affluent men, who served year after year in the South Carolina legislature, precluded any reforms to the state's patrol system in terms of either fines or personnel laws.

Complaints about patrollers spurred repeated efforts to change the nature of patrol duty. For some reformers, improving the slave law enforcement system meant trying to disentangle patrols from the militia, and abolish or strengthen one or the other.[140] But the complicated nature of slave patrols, part civil, part military, made this separation impossible, particularly in antebellum South Carolina. Any change in the militia law to make patrolling more rigorous would mean more work and effort for those involved in the militia. So reforms in the laws governing patrols and the militia were slow to come, when they did come. This behavior on the part of legislators (who often had the most wealth and slaves at risk) is succinctly explained by Rawlins Lowndes, a Revolutionary War commander. He foresaw that despite the need for change in the militia law, none would occur because "it is the Militia who form our Legislature, and they have ever been tenacious of the Priviledges they enjoy under this Law & will not submit to any other: indeed, I apprehend, should such an attempt be made, it would give universal disgust."[141] Complaints about the South Carolina system continued from the Revolution to the Civil War: citizens of Beaufort District believed that the patrol law of 1819 was "impracticable, oppressive, and nugatory" in its operation, and they wanted it revised.[142] Governor Thomas Bennett had a constructive suggestion for reform: he urged that the militia and patrol system be abolished in favor of compensated service, a "contagious example" spreading through cities that allowed "commuting such services for an annual contribution," but the legislature refused to adopt his proposal.[143]

Indeed, virtually every proposal to reform the patrol and militia was dismissed by the legislature, as Rawlins Lowndes predicted. In the 1850s, South Carolina's legislative Committee on the Military responded with high indignation to each suggestion about patrol reform. The committeemen saw in slave patrols not just security but virtue. They regretted that some men wished to change or abolish the patrols, because that signaled merely another "instance of the growing desire upon the part of our people to avoid the performance of public duty, and to be allowed to sink down into luxurious habits and slothful and inglorious indolence," a circumstance they regarded as the "first symptom of the decline of a great people."[144] After another governor, James H. Adams, proposed altering slave patrols, the committee fired off a defensive salvo, revealing the thoughts of powerful men on the necessity of patrolling in South Carolina and their unwillingness to change.[145] Their chairman, Samuel McGowan, penned the reply:

> Our state has no other reliance against foreign invasion or internal commotion, than her own citizens organized under the malitia system into an army of about forty thousand citizen soldiers liable to do ordi-

nary malitia duty . . . The militia is a safe national guard, essentially anti-monarchical and republican in its character. The institution of slavery requires that we should keep up the patrol, and it is intimately connected with and based upon the militia system. This is an armed police, and derives its efficiency, as such, from its connection with the militia. If the militia system were abolished, the patrol would fall with it or at least become much less efficient than it is at present.[146]

McGowan rejected the destruction of patrols and the militia system not only because they were essential but also because the critics had nothing to replace them with—it was easier to tear down than to build up, and a proposal to destroy the militia system without replacing both it and the patrol system with some substitute was unacceptable. Indeed, the determination of McGowan and others to fend off critics of patrols supports the notion that their real concern was not wanting to weaken the militia any further, rather than considering all of their options. After all, an alternative system for appointing slave patrols existed in North Carolina under the county courts. Major reform to overhaul the patrolling system in South Carolina, either with or without the militia, never took place.

The stymied impulse for reform in South Carolina compelled some men to supplement local patrolling and establish their own enforcement groups to control slave behavior. In places like Branchville and St. Matthew's Parish, South Carolina, extralegal groups began to take over area patrol duties. The Branchville Vigilant Society had more than twenty members, most of them farmers like J. W. R. Berry, a founder of the group and member of a local well-to-do family. Confronted with a booming slave trade in stolen goods, members pledged "to give no unrestricted passes to negroes" but always to specify where and when the pass would be valid. To enforce their rules, club members granted one another the right to "chastise a negro found with a general pass" even if the slave did not belong to one of the society members. They intended to stop the illegal trade of goods the slaves engaged in, particularly at the railroad station.[147] Slaves who worked for railroads could meet local slaves and pay for stolen property, then dispose of the goods in a different town with little risk of discovery.[148]

The citizens of St. Matthew's Parish also banded together to form "an effective Patrole organization for the suppression of illegal trading with negroes." More elaborate in their planning than the Branchville group, each member subscribed fifty cents for use in rewarding persons who detected bondsmen with stolen goods, with compensation scaled to match the item recovered.[149] Payment would only occur if the slave was whipped; although the rules did not explain why they required whipping, theoretically this could prevent collusion between slave and trader, who might complete a transaction, then ask for the reward without the slave's being punished. Slave owners carefully specified, however, that their private patrol rules gave no one the power to injure, gash, or maim a slave so as to impair his property value. As in Branchville, St. Matthew's patrollers had the right to punish only the slaves of other members found selling goods without an authorized pass. In one unusual provision, the St. Matthew's patrol members provided that the group would pay the legal fees of any member sued by another member for excessively punishing his slave.[150] Anticipating trouble between members for actually carrying out the group's intentions, the organization wisely provided that no man would end up paying for a lawyer to protect himself against a civil suit just for complying with club rules.

On Edisto Island, South Carolina, another extralegal group called the Edisto Island Auxiliary Association established itself not because of excessive slave trading, but to assist the patrol in preventing insurrectionary activities. "[N]otwithstanding the activity and vigilance of our Police officers, the mid-night incendiary has escaped with impunity, and the assassin perfected his schemes of horror." It was time, they thought, for "the zealous aid of every patriotic citizen" to be offered freely. On Edisto, the owners worried about the high ratio of slaves to white residents, which approached fifteen to one. Concerned that they were greatly outnumbered, and "what might be effected, if our police regulations are permitted to be infringed," these Edisto islanders asked to be incorporated as a state-sanctioned body to complement local patrols.[151] Groups like those in Branchville, St. Matthew's Parish, and Edisto sought to control and intimidate slaves, filling a niche between the authority of masters and the power given to patrols by the state.[152]

The close linkages between patrols and militia, county courts, town governments, and extralegal groups demonstrate the pervasive nature of slave control in Virginia and the Carolinas. Even if local patrollers became inactive or ineffective, another method of slave supervision usually evolved to supplement or replace a waning patrol group. The fluid nature of rural and urban patrol groups—constantly renewed through new members—makes it impossible to characterize all patrols, every-where, as either habitually ineffective or habitually conscientious. Even within the same town or region, a slave patrol's competence varied tre-mendously with the turnover of its roster or the immediacy of a rumored slave revolt. If a district or town ceased to be patrolled effectively, a new form of patrol (voluntary or state-backed) emerged to continue super-vising slaves. Only a very few counties never had any type of functional patrol prior to the Civil War.[153] Patrolling had the same appeal of jury duty in the modern era: it might seem onerous, time-consuming, and people might try to avoid serving, but it was indubitably important. Every white Southerner knew that his community could not safely dis-pense with patrolling altogether.

The unwillingness of some men to patrol doubtless inspired the in-creased supervision patrollers experienced in the early nineteenth cen-tury. Abolitionist activities and insurrection scares, the subject of Chap-ter 5, only fueled the concerns local officials had about slave patrols. County courts and patrol committees in North Carolina closely man-aged their patrols by selecting supervisors who lived on or near main roads used by patrollers. Town councils in all three states obviously had even greater opportunities for observing whether the men they ap-pointed were on duty night after night: the concentration of persons in a single place created both the need for regular patrollers and more occa-sions for seeing that they did their jobs. The desire for greater control of city slaves, coupled with more revenue sources (state allocations, com-mutation fees, direct taxation), allowed city officials to develop a more routinized system for slave supervision than existed in rural areas. Cities' reliance upon patrol groups suggests that the standard story of police development in America—from colonial night watch to antebel-lum police officer—needs refinement to include the Southern experi-ence of slave patrols.

Even with heightened supervision, the unpredictable quality of patrol work and repeated efforts by Southern whites to dodge their patrol du-ties prompted multiple efforts to strengthen patrolling, particularly in North and South Carolina. In North Carolina, patrol committees were the byproduct of David Walker's abolitionist pamphlet. In South Caro-lina, the decline of the militia and rising anxieties about slaveholding made nineteenth-century reform efforts urgent, yet political leaders re-fused to instigate any changes. The inability to reform patrolling in

South Carolina by imposing greater order and regularity most likely reflects the sense of individual autonomy that slave owners both experienced and wanted more of in Southern society. The lack of restraint upon their personal freedom caused some white Southerners to disdain the imposition of rules by courts or legislatures upon their way of life. This dominant perspective has led more than one historian to suggest that "[t]he majority of slaveowners, for reasons of either laxity or economic necessity, refused to cooperate in the enforcement of slave controls."[154] If a slave master chose not to give his slave a pass, permit the slave to live on the other side of town from his master's home, or violate curfew without punishment, then this same laxity was bound to creep into patrol efforts as well. No wonder some patrols were delinquent in performing their duty—only the state (through the agency of courts, councils, and militia) could force whites to act in concerted fashion to protect their own self-interest. And some legislatures, like South Carolina's, simply refused to reform patrol practices in order to coerce more public service from their constituents.

Reform required increasing the amount of time each man devoted to protecting the safety and property of others, which was repugnant to Southern white ideas of individual freedom and, indirectly, their sense of personal honor. No white man should have to cower before slaves, it was thought, and patrols were an unequivocal manifestation of white fear. Southern honor required the individual to protect his name and family without the assistance of courts or the community; patrols, by their very nature, were communal, intrusive in the master-slave relationship, and implied that the individual alone could not adequately control his bondsmen.[155] No wonder, then, that some plantation owners refused patrollers admission to their lands, and spurned serving on patrols if their wealth permitted it. Efforts to change and strengthen slave patrols ran directly counter to Southern white notions of honor and self-sufficiency, which, if anything, grew stronger as the nineteenth century progressed.

3

Patrol Personnel: "They Jes' Like Policemen, Only Worser"

"Then the paddyrollers they keep close watch on the pore niggers so they have no chance to do anything or go anywhere. They jes' like policemen, only worser. 'Cause they never let the niggers go anywhere without a pass from his masters. If you wasn't in your proper place when the paddyrollers come they lash you til' you was black and blue. The women got 15 lashes and the men 30. That was for jes bein' out without a pass. If the nigger done anything worse he was taken to the jail and put in the whippin' post."

W. L. Bost, a former slave from western North Carolina,
interviewed by WPA workers in 1937

W. L. Bost and other ex-slaves left extensive information about who served on patrols and what patrollers did, but their impressions of slave patrols as a kind of police have been ignored or forgotten.[1] With the passage of time, our popular understanding of men who hunted runaways has largely become confined to imagery drawn from well-known fiction. For instance, consider the flight of the slave Eliza and her child over the frozen Ohio River in Harriet Beecher Stowe's masterpiece *Uncle Tom's Cabin*. Eliza fled her Kentucky master by crossing the ice to a Quaker settlement in Ohio, but even there she was not safe from the slave catchers Marks and Loker; they continued pursuing her even after her own master had given up all thought of recapturing her. In a book filled with knaves, Stowe describes Marks and Loker as the lowest form of humanity, men who made their living by hunting humans who sought only freedom, men who thought nothing of lying or setting dogs loose on runaways when it served their purposes. These relentless pursuers had no other vocation, no farm or business to tend; Marks and Loker had no official appointment to catch slaves, but worked strictly for their own profit.[2] Although their activities might seem comparable, full-time slave catchers were not patrollers, and the contrasts between them were very pronounced.

The tendency to conflate patrols with expert slave catchers has created misconceptions about who served in patrols, whether they were slave owners, and whether they were rich or poor. And the confusion extends beyond patrollers and professional slave catchers. Scholars have indiscriminately merged the work of patrols with that of other private and public authority figures like overseers and constables. Sorting out their respective duties and rights is essential to understanding slave patrollers and the role they played in preserving the white community's mastery over slaves. Despite historians' generic knowledge that patrols existed, surprisingly little is known about exactly who patrollers were (and this is especially true for the eighteenth century). This gap in our historical understanding about who constituted the slave patrols extends from the earliest histories of slavery to the most recent scholarship.[3] In virtually all books on slavery, patrols appear and disappear so quickly that the reader scarcely knows of their presence in, much less effect upon, Southern society.

Exploring the appointment, authority, and status of slave patrol members will help us understand the ways in which patrols constituted an important presence in the lives of black and white Southerners. Patrollers' night-to-night enforcement of slave control laws undergirded the entire structure of slavery. Serving in patrols gave white men more than the chance to brutalize bondsmen in their community—service also meant camaraderie and social interaction with other whites. Diligent work could be rewarded with authority over one's neighbors in the patrol group and appointment to a leadership position as patrol captain. Understanding who worked as patrollers, and who did not, in the eighteenth and nineteenth centuries will also allow us to evaluate historians' claims that patrollers were white men drawn only from the poorest classes of Southern society.

Who Might Be Chosen to Serve

Property ownership was a prerequisite to patrolling, at least in North Carolina. There, a county court could appoint a man as a slave patroller simply because he was a freeholder of property within the county. County courts selected men from either militia muster rolls or local tax rolls to serve on local slave patrols. Although they paid taxes, free black property owners appear to have been excluded from the selection process. The fact that a man chosen as a slave patroller was then entitled to exemption from road work duty, jury duty, and local militia musters suggests that the slave patrollers chosen were between the ages of sixteen and sixty—the years when all white North Carolina men would have to serve in their local militia or perform other civic duties.[4]

In the eighteenth century South Carolina briefly experimented with a similar plan for enrolling slave patrollers, but then abandoned it. Until 1739 South Carolina's patrollers came from the militia. But after the Stono rebellion, the General Assembly mandated that all owners of plantations, both men and women, should be enrolled by militia officers and selected for patrol duty in their districts.[5] When called upon to serve, women could and routinely did provide substitutes for patrol service. The legislature's rationale for calling upon all property owners was that "all persons, as well women as men, who are . . . owners of settled plantations in any district, ought to contribute to the service and security of that district where their interest lyes."[6] In 1819 the South Carolina legislature changed the requirements for slave patrol duty to exclude women and more closely mirror militia membership. This probably simplified the process for selecting patrollers. All "free white males" between the ages of eighteen and forty-five years of age were liable to be chosen by the local militia captain for patrol duty. After 1819, the rules for selecting patrol members reverted to the method used before 1739—if a man performed militia duty, he could be chosen as a patroller.[7]

As in South Carolina, if a Virginia man served in the militia he was qualified to perform patrol duties.[8] In both Virginia and South Carolina, the first statutes creating slave patrols relied upon laws defining who must serve in the county militia; patrols came from men serving in militia units.[9] Therefore the age guidelines and exemptions from service applied to the militia also applied to patrols in those two colonies and, later, states.[10] The militia laws in place at the time slave patrols were created varied slightly in each colony; all "free male persons" between the ages of sixteen (South Carolina) or twenty-one (Virginia) and sixty years of age must serve in the county militia.[11] These provisions continued in force until the Federal Convention established Congress's power (under the United States Constitution) to regulate state militias.[12] In May 1792, Congress passed a uniform national militia law, limiting enrollment to free white men between the ages of eighteen and forty-five.[13] Thereafter, the majority of men on slave patrol duty in Virginia and South Carolina (after 1819) were also between the ages of eighteen and forty-five.

Although eligibility for the militia seemed all-encompassing, not every middle-aged white male Virginian or Carolinian became a slave patroller. Because of exemptions, many eighteen- to forty-five-year-old men did not serve in the militia or on slave patrol duty. Exemptions existed in every colony or state, so that men in critical professions would not be called away from their work. Judges, members of legislatures, schoolmasters, students, coroners, millers, pilots, and foreigners visiting for a brief time were ordinarily excused from serving as patrol men.[14] Burgeoning nineteenth-century industries, like railroads and canals, might receive exemptions for their workers, too.[15] Curiously, some important professions, like the ministry, did not become exempt from militia or slave patrol work.[16] Even physicians were not always exempt— South Carolina's board of medical examiners, which licensed other physicians to practice, received no exemptions.[17] Doctor Samuel Wells Leland found himself in the ironic position of riding patrol one night and, shortly thereafter, nursing a slave who had been beaten for forging a pass.[18] His humanitarian instincts sometimes allowed him to intervene and prevent a bondsman from receiving a whipping, which may have placed him at odds with other members of his patrol group.[19]

Military exemptions for longtime service affected slave patrol personnel in several ways. South Carolina allowed any man who had served at the rank of captain (or higher) for seven years to be exempt from further militia and patrol work.[20] Although some Carolinians initially interpreted this law as applying only to men who fought during the Revolutionary War, eventually these laws were construed to mean any service, including peacetime militia duty.[21] As a result, many older men between thirty-five and forty-five were not tapped for patrol service because they had already served seven years as commissioned officers. This gradually lowered the age of men who served on patrols, and the young men in Oxford, North Carolina, protested this generational divide; older men tended to have more wealth, and thus had more at stake—why should younger men do the most patrolling?[22] Citizens protested these patrol and militia exemptions, especially when war came again, calling young white men to the battlefront. During the War of 1812, South Carolina citizens urged that no man under forty be exempt from patrolling except those whose "professions or office absolutely forbid their being called out," since the war meant that more men were gone from the state than usual. They wanted all white men to be liable for patrol duty during such difficult times.[23] Another form of military exemption occurred if a man joined a volunteer militia group, and left the state-run militia.[24] Theoretically, a volunteer militia man was subject to the same regulations as in a regular militia unit, including periodic patrol work. Some volunteer companies required only token patrolling efforts from their members, however, and a few volunteer militia groups disdained patrolling altogether.[25]

In the nineteenth century, urbanization and the militia's declining efficacy forced changes upon local slave patrols. In 1839 the power to organize, detail, enforce, and perform patrol duty in incorporated South Carolina towns passed from local militia company captains to the "municipal police of the said towns and villages, who [were] vested with full powers to make all such ordinances relative to the times and manner of performing patrol duty" as they might deem necessary.[26] At the same time, North Carolina and Virginia cities also gained the authority to organize slave patrols through new town charters.[27] (See Figure 5.) In theory, local communities could have limited their slave patrols at that point to slaveholders only if they chose to do so.[28] In practice, however, few communities could afford to use only slaveholders in their patrol forces; there simply were not enough male slave owners of the right age to staff slave patrols throughout an entire year, so town councils rarely limited slave patrols to slave owners alone. Many cities adopted substitution policies, too, which permitted individuals with money to provide replacement patrollers.

Men sometimes escaped patrol work when town residents discovered other pressing city needs. For example, fire companies regularly petitioned for exemption from patrol duty, arguing that firemen must always be at their posts.[29] Fire company organizers feared that if their members were not exempt from patrolling, men would abandon fire companies because of their doubled community obligations.[30] In petitions, a few civic groups even volunteered to limit the number of men who could join their fire companies, in order to keep enough men on active patrol duty.[31] Not everyone was happy when firemen were relieved from slave patrolling; one man's fireman was another man's freeloader. When legislatures granted patrol exemptions to firemen, other citizens resented that they would have to do more patrolling as a result. After the legislature granted the Hamburg Fire Engine Company's exemption, the Hamburg town council petitioned the South Carolina assembly to reverse

5. Virginia, North Carolina, and South Carolina, c. 1840

itself. "[T]he population of the Town is at this time so small as to make the duty verry *onerous*" on the citizens still required to serve as town patrollers, they claimed. Only forty-eight citizens were liable for patrol duty, and they required "thirty five of that number to protect the town" as patrollers each week. To excuse men for an engine company strained town relations to the breaking point; exemptions for fire fighters meant increased patrol duty for every other man in town who was not a fireman.[32]

Occasionally, citizens might ask to be exempted from normal militia and patrol laws altogether due to unusual circumstances. Inhabitants of Moultrieville, on Sullivan's Island, South Carolina, asked for permission to create their own patrol companies "without reference to [an individual's] enrollment in any company beat."[33] Residents on Sullivan's Island changed frequently, as men came and went between the island and the mainland. Some transients claimed they belonged to militia companies on the mainland and should not be called for service during their Sullivan's Island sojourn. Both the legislature and local Moultrieville residents recognized that the short-term visitors simply wanted to evade patrol work. The assembly gave Moultrieville the power to enlist "Inhabitants during their residence into patrol companies without reference to inrollments in any company beat."[34] As a result, patrol duty in Moultrieville was performed by whichever men happened to be temporarily resident in town.

The Appointment Process: Oaths and Warrants

Once summoned for duty, the would-be slave patroller had to be commissioned as an official agent of the county or city. Specific rituals transformed the private individual into a sanctioned officer of the state, like a judge or a sheriff. Receiving legal authority to act as patrollers helped define their status in the white community, and official status provided patrollers indemnity against civil or criminal lawsuits brought by slaveholders who disapproved of their brutal methods.

Joining a slave patrol involved paperwork and meeting with local authorities to be officially licensed as an agent of the white community. After being selected for service, the individual received either a visit from his patrol captain or a written notice summoning him to patrol duty.[35] Notice in hand, the next task of a patroller would be to confirm his new status with a local official. In North Carolina, men chosen as slave patrollers had to appear before a justice of the peace and be sworn in or "qualified," a term used in the nineteenth century. The justice of the peace recited the oath for patrollers, and the patroller either swore or affirmed that he would uphold the law. The oath remained unchanged for one hundred years, even when patrollers no longer went by the name "searchers."

> I, [patroller's name], do swear, that I will as searcher for guns, swords, and other weapons among the slaves in my district, faithfully, and as privately as I can, discharge the trust reposed in me as the law directs, to the best of my power. So help me, God.[36]

Many patrollers had the justice of the peace endorse their appointment slips with the date their oath was administered. Some counties also expected patrollers to consult with court clerks, who provided copies of state or county laws regarding patrols.[37]

After being sworn in, the patroller usually retained his appointment slip, since it indicated that he was an official patroller for a designated period. Alternatively, a justice of the peace could issue the patroller a special warrant to carry while on duty.[38] With his endorsed appointment slip or newly minted warrant, a patroller had official papers to prove he was indeed appointed to his post if someone chose to challenge his authority.[39] One such challenge came from South Carolina lawyer James L. Petigru, who notified M. M. Johnson in 1854 that he should stay off the plantation where he had once been an overseer, unless he was part of a duly appointed patrol. And if he came to the plantation with a patrol, Petigru warned Johnson to be ready to show "your patrol warrant."[40] Other whites physically confronted patrollers in their duties, sometimes ending up in court on charges that they had "resisted a patrol."[41]

Patrol appointment notices and warrants almost completely shielded patrollers from litigious masters, who became angry if patrollers viciously punished local bondsmen.[42] Masters had little recourse against an abusive patroller who chose to ignore community censure, but owners had much greater rights against men who voluntarily "joined" slave patrols without first being appointed and sworn in. "Volunteer patrollers" had no official protection, as an 1817 North Carolina lawsuit proved. In *Richardson v. Saltar,* the defendant, a patroller, took three of his friends (Allen, Bryan, and Singletary, none of them official patrollers) out one night on patrol. At Major Owen's farm, they found a slave be-

longing to a Mr. Richardson, Owen's neighbor. When the bondman produced an invalid pass, Saltar and his friends beat Richardson's slave so
severely that he could not work for days. Richardson then sued the four
men for whipping his bondsman without authority; Richardson claimed
they were not an authorized slave patrol. The trial court acquitted the
four men, but on appeal, the North Carolina Supreme Court remanded
the case for retrial. Their reason: a 1794 North Carolina patrol law stated
that a patrol must have at least two members to be active, and at least
two patrol members must be present when a slave received punishment.[43] The justices deduced that three of the men were not patrollers,
and Saltar could not act as a patrol by himself.[44] Rowan County officials
responded to *Saltar* by allowing a slave thought to be behaving oddly to
be detained by a single patroller, until he could "bring together a requi-
site number of Patrolles to act in the business."[45]

Slave Patrollers and Other Authority Figures

The case of *Richardson v. Saltar* indicates one rough boundary between
officially appointed patrollers and private Southern citizens who controlled slaves. Clear distinctions between patrollers and other authority
figures will be hard to establish, since many Southern whites, not just
slaveholders, actively disciplined slaves and prevented them from obtaining their freedom. Slave patrols were both similar to and different
from expert slave catchers, private citizens who claimed slave-recapture
rewards, overseers, and constables who controlled the slave population
in cities. The titles, obligations, and methods of operation among these
authority figures varied widely, but they were all part of the collective
community effort to control slaves and prevent them from acting like
free men. We need to understand what set apart the slave patroller from
these men with alternative authority over slaves, and what similarities
existed between them such that their overlapping activities could be
confused by others.

Slave patrols were perhaps most renowned for tracking down and capturing runaway slaves before they left the local area. This aspect of their
work is strongly reminiscent of another set of men within Southern society who also tracked and caught runaways, expert slave catchers (also
called slave takers). Slaves sometimes left a plantation temporarily, either for a break from work or to avoid punishment, but other bondsmen

fled with the intent of escaping altogether. Slave patrols responded to all of these possibilities, but a master might decide to employ special slave catchers if he suspected that a bondsman intended to flee the local community permanently. Unlike patrollers who functioned as officials of the county or state, slave catchers were not appointed by their local communities; they merely advertised their ability to capture runaway slaves, and masters hired them for short-term jobs, typically paying ten, fifteen, or twenty-five dollars for capturing a runaway. Marks and Loker, the fictional slave takers of *Uncle Tom's Cabin,* worked up and down the Ohio and Mississippi rivers, just like slave catchers in real life, who frequented the border states and the Deep South.[46] Slave catchers often used trained dogs to reclaim fugitive slaves, but owners usually required that the slaves retaken not be "bruised and torn by the dogs."[47]

Despite their common interest in capturing runaway slaves, the contrasts between slave patrollers and expert slave catchers were marked. Whole communities appointed (and sometimes paid) patrollers to be on duty many nights per year; individuals hired slave hunters and usually paid them more than patrollers to complete a given job, namely, recapturing a specific bondsman in a short period of time. Patrollers handled a variety of tasks, such as searching slave cabins for weapons and dispersing slave meetings. Slave catchers were only concerned with capturing fugitive slaves. Slave patrollers worked in a single community, and almost always remained within their home county, whereas slave catchers might even leave the state to retrieve a fleeing bondsman. A few slave takers, like F. H. Pettis, even resided in Northern cities; Pettis advertised in Southern newspapers that he could find and return fugitive slaves who came to New York.[48] Finally, some slave catchers were able to make their entire living from capturing fugitive slaves.[49] This constitutes a strong contrast to slave patrollers, who were primarily farmers or businessmen, and only occasionally worked as slave patrollers, a task that did not remunerate them enough to replace completely their income from selling crops or goods.

Slave patrols shared common characteristics not only with expert slave catchers but also with ordinary citizens who apprehended fugitive slaves to obtain colony- or state-mandated rewards. From the colonies' founding, a reward system provided incentives for citizens voluntarily to recapture runaways. Even after each colony created slave patrols, individuals could, and did, continue to claim their rewards for finding runaways.[50] The standard procedure required the capturing person and fugitive slave to appear before a justice of the peace, who would issue a certificate stating where the bondsman had been apprehended and how far the apprehender would have to travel to return the runaway to his master.[51] An itemized receipt in this fashion stated explicitly where the slave was taken, so that the owner could not dispute the mileage and refuse to pay.[52] In addition, the colony or state paid a flat fee—typically five dollars in the antebellum period—for the capture of a fugitive slave.[53] Individual owners might also advertise and offer additional rewards for recapturing runaway bondsmen.[54]

The men who served on slave patrols had much in common with private citizens who took advantage of the reward systems that each colony or state had. Ordinary citizens and patrollers both looked for fugitive slaves, but citizens were not appointed to watch for slaves, and after lawmakers created slave patrols, private individuals had even fewer obligations to prevent slaves from leaving bondage. While citizens received a five-dollar reward for each bondsman they captured, patrollers might earn much more than that just for patrolling the roads; depending on the county or town they lived in, they might be paid two or three times that amount for working three months.[55] In fact, patrollers would be paid even if they did not capture any runaways, because they had other duties than just stopping slaves from escaping. Therefore, while slave patrols bore similarities to private citizens who collected rewards for capturing runaway slaves, patrols ultimately had more extensive duties, for which they were often better paid.

Slave plantation overseers served on many slave patrols, and patrollers (as a group) shared some characteristics with overseers. Both patrollers and overseers had responsibility for maintaining order and discipline within the slave quarters, particularly in the absence of a slave owner. James Henry Hammond, a South Carolina plantation owner, had extensive rules for overseers to follow: "The overseer must never be absent a single night, nor an entire day, without permission previously obtained. Whenever absent at church or elsewhere he must be on the plantation by sundown without fail" to see that the slaves were in their houses after curfew, and to discipline slaves who refused to obey.[56] Overseers had to search for weapons in slave cabins, prevent illicit meetings between bondsmen that might lead to revolt, and recapture runaways who left their plantations and might be lurking in the immediate vicinity, stealing from other nearby farms; with slave patrols, overseers formed the first line of defense protecting whites from their unruly laborers.[57] Indeed, the man most likely to capture runaway bondsmen could be the plantation overseer, who was present all the time and had a strong economic incentive to be on the lookout for unfamiliar slaves hanging about the plantation.[58] Not surprisingly, slaves tended to associate patrols with overseers, for both dispensed the worst punishment, a whipping—and after all, slaves knew that only owners could systematically reward them with presents and lenience. The association slaves made linking patrols with overseers would only grow stronger during the Civil War, a topic discussed at greater length in Chapter 6.

Yet however much overseers and slave patrollers protected white interests and controlled slaves in Southern society, an overseer was not required to supervise slaves beyond his own plantation boundaries. He never disciplined every slave in the community; his very presence on a single plantation prevented him from doing so. Slave patrols, by comparison, had to know the activities and movement of all local bondsmen. Overseers and slave patrols also had significantly different and challenging tasks. Overseers not only maintained discipline among slaves on their plantations, but were also expected to assign slaves work, provide them with adequate food, shelter, and medical care, and ultimately produce a profitable crop at the end of harvest season.[59] Overseers worked around the clock, attempting to control slaves both day and night, while patrollers routinely functioned only at night. Plantation owners hired overseers to full-year contracts, but communities appointed slave patrollers for limited spans of time, typically three to six months. And of course the extensive nature of an overseer's job required him to be paid much more than a patroller would make for his part-time service to the community.

Finally, the last men in Southern society whose work seemed comparable to slave patrollers were constables. Like patrols, constables worked for local governments, and both jobs had existed since colonial times. Colonial era counties even appointed constables and patrollers to work side by side.[60] Town councils or county courts appointed constables to carry out a variety of tasks during their one-year term. Constables' pay varied dramatically across time and region; in the seventeenth century, some constables even served without pay. By the eighteenth century, some towns paid constables, and during the nineteenth century, constables performed so many tasks that most towns began paying them well. The jobs they did were multifold: constables summoned jurors and witnesses, caught slaves and took them to jail, and attended court sessions, keeping order in the courtroom.

Slave catching was a major part of the constable's job. Some slave owners employed constables privately to catch their runaways; constables' detailed knowledge of the local area probably gave them every advantage in hunting fugitives. Michael Hancock wrote a friend that he had employed a Richmond constable to take up a slave and have him lodged in the local jail.[61] In Richmond, constables were officially required to patrol streets daily and apprehend slaves who were unable to account for their activities; rural bondsmen who crowded into the city made Sunday the constable's busiest day.[62] A constable in Norfolk, Virginia, named John Capheart left a vivid description of his work, which mimics many of the slave patroller's duties:

> It was part of my business to arrest all slaves and free persons of color, who were collected in crowds at night, and lock them up. It was also part of my business to take them before the Mayor. I did this without any warrant, and at my own discretion. Next day they are examined and punished. The punishment is flogging. I am one of the men who flog them. They get not exceeding thirty-nine lashes. I am paid fifty cents for every negro I flog. The price used to be sixty-two and half cents. I am paid fifty cents for every negro I arrest, and fifty cents more if I flog him. I have flogged hundreds. I am often employed by private persons to pursue fugitive slaves. I have been thus employed since 1838. I never refuse a good job of that kind.[63]

Norfolk city directories listed Capheart as either a constable or a police officer in the 1830s, 1840s, and 1850s. The slave George Teamoh described an evening encounter with Capheart: "I was arrested by Capehart—a noted night watch & cunstable in that city. He asked for my 'pass'—[I] told him I lost it; 'then' said he, 'you must go to jail.' " Teamoh escaped arrest by convincing Capheart that he had smallpox.[64]

Of the various individuals given special responsibilities to control slave behavior in Southern society—full-time slave catchers, private citizens, overseers, and constables—constables were most similar to slave patrols. Both constables and patrollers captured runaway slaves and monitored the movement of slaves in towns, and local officials ap-

pointed both to paid positions. Yet important differences existed between slave patrollers and constables. First, constables performed many
duties for local officials, including summoning jurors and witnesses to
court, or taking prisoners (black and white) to town mayoral courts.
Constables always had an element of process-serving in their assigned
tasks. Patrollers, by contrast, were solely concerned with the activities of
slaves, and rarely had reason to go to court. And second, nineteenth-
century constables sometimes made enough money from their civic duties that they did not need other employment. John Capheart was this
kind of constable, earning his bread by processing papers and flogging
slaves every day. Only men who resided in towns needing full-time slave
patrols could afford to make patrolling their vocation.

Patrollers seemed most like constables because both had duties that
were policelike in nature. Slave patrols and constables eventually gave
way to paid police forces; in cities like Richmond, Raleigh, and Charleston, police performed many jobs, but until the Civil War, their primary task was controlling slaves.[65] "No matter how important crime
control appeared, the true mission of the [Richmond police] force re-
volved around suppressing the city's Negro population."[66] Many Southerners explicitly acknowledged the overlapping nature of patrol and
police duties that targeted African Americans. "With a well regulated police in the way of patrols we can proclaim to the world that it [slavery] is
an inestimable blessing," claimed John Tompkins of Edgefield District,
South Carolina.[67] Slaves like S. S. Taylor claimed that "[p]olice were for
white folks. Patteroles were for niggers."[68] Occasionally the two groups
might work together, as in Danville, Virginia, where the police master
had four slave patrols working for him in the 1850s.[69]

Leadership, Community, and Socializing within the Patrol Group

Not only did slave patrols provide security for white residents in Southern communities, but they also furnished opportunities for white males
to socialize with their neighbors and vie for leadership positions. Members in a slave patrol group could form their own social networks where
rituals of deference and bonding occurred during nightly expeditions.

The physical limits of a patrol's area of operation influenced the formation of social ties within a patrol group. Beat lines conformed to the

natural terrain and grouped men into patrol units with their neighbors in familiar territory; this increased the likelihood of effective patrolling. Patrol beats generally were not larger than ten to fifteen square miles.[70] Within a town, patrols usually divided along geographic lines—north, south, east, and west—so that men would be responsible for areas closest to their homes. The folklorist Gladys-Marie Fry has suggested that in cities, "the districts to be covered by the town patrol were too large, the size of the patrol groups too small, and the visibility after nightfall too limited for the system to be really effective against any slave determined to ramble at night."[71] Although it was true that slave patrols could not be everywhere, every night, rural and urban patrols did limit the nighttime freedom that slaves otherwise had to wander at will. The division of patrol men into units where neighbors worked with neighbors increased the probability that patrolling would be carried out. After all, white men from the same local area were more likely to trade information about pillaging from farms and would have a better idea of where stolen goods or missing slaves could hide. Instead of being required to work in unfamiliar areas, with men unknown to one another, slave patrols were routinely composed of men who knew their fellow patrollers well.

Neighbors who worked together on patrols cooperated not only for the pleasure of being part of a community group but also because their very lives might depend upon such collaboration. In part the forced socialization of patrol groups was linked to the existence of a common enemy: slaves who could rebel. The presence of slaves "meant that any lapse in vigilance, any failure of government, appeared to threaten the white community with annihilation," according to the historian Robert Weir.[72] With their property and very survival at stake, patrollers had to work together and work well.

Masking the serious nature of their work, patrol groups could become quite rowdy and boisterous in carrying out their duties. Slaves like Charity Bowery, born in 1782, remembered that the slave patrol near her North Carolina plantation was "frequently intoxicated."[73] South Carolina patrol groups were particularly well known for excessive drinking, according to slave testimonies and references in colonial law. In the wake of the 1739 Stono rebellion, the South Carolina legislature noted that since "many irregularitys have been committed by former patrols, arising chiefly from their drinking too much liquor before or during the time of their riding on duty . . . any person whatsoever who shall be drunk during the time of his service on the patrol, shall be subject to the penalty of forty shillings."[74] Neither Virginia nor North Carolina's lawmakers ever passed legislation to punish or suspend drunken patrollers.

Yet the very nature of slave patrol work increased the likelihood that patrollers would get drunk, no matter where they lived. Before their evening's work, patrollers usually met at the home of one of their group, eating and drinking to fortify themselves against the long night ahead. Likewise, when they searched the homes and shops of men who sold or traded liquor to slaves, patrollers had plenty of opportunities to acquire alcohol for their own consumption. And a slave patrols might actually loiter in or around liquor shops, like a spider lurking in its web, waiting for slaves to make nocturnal visits.[75]

Socializing and drinking with other patrollers helped pass the time during tedious nights of patrol duty. Captains, the leaders of patrol groups, might have believed it was a duty to entertain their patrollers with food and liquor. Some captains showed a little noblesse oblige in this respect: Charles Lide Burn's patrol captain feted the men in his group with "an oyster supper" before they set out on patrol.[76] The pattern of giving one's patrol food or drink could prove costly to the captain incapable of paying for it. John Jeter learned this lesson the hard way when he unsuccessfully petitioned the governor and legislature to repay him for provisions he gave his company, which performed patrol duty after insurrection rumors caused the state to call out every militia unit across the state.[77] Rituals of hospitality underscored the personal, community nature of patrol work among Southern whites. And bondsmen most likely took advantage of patrollers' occasional inebriation to avoid being captured and beaten. Although patrols were founded on a legal, even bureaucratic basis, their members strengthened social networks during nights of duty spent together patrolling and drinking.[78]

In addition to providing sociable companionship and liquor for their men, patrol captains gave direction and leadership to the patrol group. All slave patrollers were not created equal. At the time of appointment, the county court or militia commander named one man "captain" of each patrol unit.[79] Captains called out patrollers for duty on specific nights, determined where slave patrols would be active, and set the routes patrols followed on a given evening. They kept records of the hours men served on patrol, and submitted these accounts for payment, when permitted. (See Figure 6.) On occasion, they also made more elab-

August 18.th 1799. Chesterfield County _____ D.r

To Peter Baugh, Barnett Moore, Bland Blankenship and James Stewart, Patrollers, To patrolling the Negro Quarters of Edward Featherston dec.d Jesse Cogbill dec.d, Edw.d Goodes. Mrs Brumleys, Elizabeth Walthalls, & the Road to Branders Mill, in all 14 hours at 88 Cents each ____ ____ ____ ____ 352,c

August 22, Chesterfield County D.r To Henry Featherston jr. Peter Baugh, John Womack, & Bland Blankenship. To patrolling the Negro Quarters of Marley Walthall, William Archer, Henry Featherston Sen.r Daniel Hatcher, Edw.d Featherston dec.d, & Kitt Abba, in all 8 hours at 50 Cents each ____ ____ ____ 200c

August 24.th Chesterfield County D.r To H. Featherston jr., Peter Baugh, Barnett Moore, & John Womack; To patrolling the Negro Quarters of Elizabeth Baugh, Wm Worsham, Thomas Bolling, John Stratton, Margarett Baugh, James Deveal, & John Baugh, in all 12 hours at 75 Cents each . ____ ____ ____ 300c

Sept.r 1.st Chesterfield County D.r To H. Featherston jr. Peter Baughh. Barnett Moore, John Womack & Bland Blankenship To patrolling the Negro Quarters of John Friend, and the Road to Petersburg also carrying of a Negro before a Magistrate. in all 8 hours at 50 Cents each . ____ ____ ____ ____ 250c

Sept.r 8.th Chesterfield Cty, D.r To Peter Baugh, Barnett Moore & Bland Blankenshipp, To patrolling the Negro Quarters of ____
turn over

orate notes about the dates and hours of their service in a daily diary format; this record keeping could be useful when calculating how much compensation was owed to both the captain and his men.[80] The leadership role given to patrol captains suggests that men of greater importance filled the position, and evidence bears out that theory. Whereas a majority of patrol members were slave owners (in the colonial period), almost all patrol captains in the colonial and antebellum periods owned slaves, usually in significant numbers.[81]

The leadership of patrol captains comforted white citizens in the local community. Most white Southerners wanted slave patrols to have some form of supervision. The ruthless authority that patrollers could wield over slaves—with the possibility that patrols might damage valuable slaves through excessive whipping—required that slave patrols have supervisors who could check their excesses. Status or obligation could place a man in such a supervisory role. In the eighteenth century, prominent community leaders might become lightning rods for complaints about patrol inefficiency. Colonel Landon Carter received just such a complaint from John Tayloe, a Virginian, in 1771. Tayloe told Carter that "your Patroll do not do their duty, my people are rambleing about every night" and since slaves from all over the county had gathered at Tayloe's property, he believed Carter could expect them to meet at his neighboring home in the near future. Tayloe lamented that "these things would not be so I think if the Patrollers did the duty they are paid for."[82] In North Carolina, not only were individuals designated as patrol captains, but the General Assembly established patrol committees in the early nineteenth century. Committee members did not ride on patrol themselves, but made sure that slave patrollers performed their jobs effectively and lawfully.

The number of men a patrol captain called out to conduct expeditions was constantly disputed.[83] In practice, the number of patrollers on duty in any given night seems to have varied between three and ten, with groups more frequently patrolling in clusters of five or six men. Records for the city of Aiken, South Carolina, between 1839 and 1859 indicate that men were appointed in that town in squads of four to six. Groups that small meant that one unit could perform patrol duty nightly.[84] In rural areas, the size of patrols also varied, but usually consisted of four to six men each.[85] North Carolina courts and patrol committees had great latitude in deciding how many men to appoint to patrol groups. Lawsuits arose about the number of men necessary to patrol when one or two men alone undertook patrol work without more members of their group.[86] In *State v. Hailey*, eight men had been appointed as slave patrollers in Anson County, but only three men were present the night they tried to enter Isham and Lucy Hailey's slave quarters to discipline slaves found there. In the *Hailey* case, a North Carolina court determined that a majority of an appointed patrol group must be present to conduct any searches or administer any kind of punishment to a slave.

The *Hailey* opinion went beyond a mere discussion of whether a patrol needed three men or four present before a slave could be beaten. Court justices, in a rare theorizing moment, touched on the very nature of collective patrol activity, and why slave patrols not only socialized together but sat in judgment together:

> [Patrols] partake of a judicial or quasi-judicial and executive character. Judicial, so far as deciding upon each case of a slave taken up by them; whether the law has been violated by him or not, and adjudging the punishment to be inflicted. Is he off his master's plantation without a proper permit or pass? Of this the patrol must judge and decide. If punishment is to be inflicted, they must adjudge, decide, as to the question; five stripes may in some cases be sufficient, while others may demand the full penalty of the law. All these acts upon the part of the patrol, require consultation and agreement, and a less number than a majority of the whole cannot act . . . it does require that number to constitute (if the expression may be allowed) a court or tribunal for the performance of these duties, and when so constituted a plurality of those present must agree, or no punishment can be legally inflicted. We do not mean that the law requires, on the part of the patrol, any formalities in the discharge of their duties, or that any formal judgment must be pronounced, but that a majority of the patrol, properly constituted, must sanction each sentence passed. If a minority can act, then each individual patroller may act by himself, and every man's property would be subject to the uncontrolled judgment or passion of a single individual. This can not have been the scope and meaning of the act [creating patrols].[87]

The court's opinion explained why slave patrols had to act collectively: an individual might give way to passion and beat a slave for no reason, but sheer numbers in a patrol group, it was thought, could restrain a single white man's aggression.

Patrollers exercised their power not only against slaves in the area but also against whites who challenged the social order as it existed in each community.[88] Some planters, like the South Carolinian R. F. W. Allston, believed that patrol duty was necessary to keep vagabond whites in line. Even men of means had to go on patrol, to keep poor whites from selling illicit goods to slaves. In September 1860, Allston wrote his son that "[p]atrol duty should not be neglected, tho' the duty ought not to be done too annoyingly unless vagabond whites render it necessary."[89] In an essay published in the *Atlantic Monthly* of 1877, Belton Townsend alleged that "aristocratic patrolmen" sometimes used their powers in vigilante fashion to exert social control over whites in the community.[90] The historian John Hammond Moore notes that white class conflict could reveal itself through patrol activity: "Any upstart who threatened the plantation aristocracy might find his slaves whipped and mutilated, fences ruined, or crops damaged, all in an effort to hurt the property owner economically, a stern warning to mend his ways."[91] Patrols not only cemented social bonds between whites, but also reminded transgressors—both black and white—of what was considered acceptable behavior by the masters of Southern society.

Patrol Membership

These last few observations by Allston, Townsend, and Moore contradict the traditional interpretation usually put forth about the status of men who made up Southern slave patrols. Eugene Genovese and other historians of slavery have posited that patrollers came primarily from the lower social classes, often called "poor whites" in Southern communities.[92] Genovese writes:

> Ex-slaves later recalled poor white neighbors as "one of our biggest troubles." Those poor whites would encourage slaves to steal and then cheat them in trade; would steal themselves and blame slaves; would seduce impressionable young slave girls; and above all, provided the backbone of the hated slave patrols, which whipped and terrorized slaves caught without passes after curfew. And besides, the slaves regarded the poor whites as the laziest and most dissolute people on earth; it was probably the slaves who dubbed the poor whites "trash."[93]

In this interpretation, elite Southern whites chose the "dregs" of society to work as slave patrollers, an unsavory social obligation. Casting most patrollers as destitute, non-slave-owning men, historians have relied, perhaps too much, on the 1930s WPA interviews conducted with former slaves, who universally considered patrollers beneath their contempt.[94] These twentieth-century pronouncements by ex-slaves have been read backward in time to paint the patrollers of all periods as being from the lowest social classes. Yet no systematic study has been made of eighteenth-century records to investigate whether slave patrols corresponded to opinions formed about them in the 1860s.

The best information about patrollers and their social status in the eighteenth century comes from tithable (tax) lists compiled in Virginia before and during the Revolutionary War. Tithe-collection documents for two Virginia counties, Amelia and Norfolk, span the period 1750 to 1780.[95] In the seventeenth and eighteenth centuries, each county or parish paid its bills by issuing notes of credit, due at the end of the tax year.[96] Near the end of the tax year, county officials would appoint several men—tithe takers—to make lists of all the tithable inhabitants in their neighborhoods. A person counted as tithable, or taxable, if he was a slave (male or female) over the age of sixteen or a white male over the age of sixteen, able to work and not exempted from tithing by virtue of serving in the legislature or in another honorary post such as a minister. Freed slaves who continued to live in the community also counted as tithables, although their numbers remained low in this period. Failure to declare to a tithe taker all the tithable persons in one's household carried a high fine; the penalty encouraged everyone to cooperate with tithe takers when they drew up their annual tax list. Thus tithe lists usually contain the names of every taxable adult white male or slave in a given household: with names listed, no one could later claim that a particular individual had been deliberately omitted to falsify the tax bill. The head of the household then paid the county taxes for each taxable person in his home.[97]

One can easily identify patrollers on these tithe lists: not only are they indicated by the word "pat" or "patroller" after their names, but they paid one fewer tithe than the total number of people listed in their households. A man who owned two adult slaves should have paid three tithes (two tithes for his slaves and one for himself) but if he was a patroller, he would pay for only two tithes. Serving on a slave patrol conferred a direct monetary benefit on these men.

Amelia and Norfolk counties have several things in common with regard to patrollers: long, steady collections of tithable lists and tithe takers who regularly indicated which men served as patrollers.[98] Other tithable lists for eighteenth-century Virginia are available, but in broken runs. Some tithe takers did not note slave patrollers on their lists at all, even though virtually every Virginia county had patrollers; these omissions may have occurred because each local Virginia county court had the power to exempt patrollers from tithes, but colonial law did not require courts to give patrollers tax breaks.[99] That county courts in Amelia and Norfolk counties gave tax relief to their patrollers created another shared feature for the two areas.

Norfolk and Amelia counties are significant for reasons other than their good records and notations about patrollers. As one of the first counties settled in Virginia, by the mid-eighteenth century, Norfolk was thickly populated, with an urban area in its midst. Located near the Atlantic Ocean on the banks of the James River, Norfolk County's thriving seaport, Norfolk, was the most important commercial town in the colony and the shipping center of eighteenth-century Virginia.[100] Norfolk's location made it an entrepôt for shipping goods out of the colony and receiving incoming merchandise. Fugitive slaves found Norfolk County inviting for other reasons: the Great Dismal Swamp, a magnet for runaways, borders Norfolk County along the south and west.[101] Unlike Norfolk, Amelia County only began to attract numerous white residents in the eighteenth century. One of the fast-growing Southside counties, Amelia lured new settlers to make their fortunes in its rich tobacco lands. After its legislative creation in 1735, Amelia County grew quickly, doubling its population every eight years until the 1750s.[102] In terms of population density, by 1800 Norfolk had a population of more than thirty persons per square mile, while Amelia eventually grew to have more than twenty persons per square mile.[103]

During the mid-eighteenth century, Virginia experienced an overall increase in population, but the rise was most dramatic for slaves. From 1755 to 1785, Virginia's slave population almost doubled, from roughly 119,000 to nearly 230,000 slaves. In 1780 the slaves in Virginia accounted for more than one-third of all slaves living in the United States.[104] Amelia and Norfolk counties experienced that population increase in different ways. In Norfolk County, slaves continued to constitute 30 to 40 percent of all Norfolk residents from 1750 to 1780; as their numbers grew, the number of white residents also grew, keeping the proportions relatively constant. Throughout this period, Norfolk bondsmen lived in small groups, usually one to five slaves per household. In 1780 more than 80 percent of the resident households in the town of Norfolk held slaves; three out of four slaveholders owned between one and four slaves.[105] In 1750 Amelia County bondsmen also started out living in small groups of one to five per household. But by 1782, some 40 percent of Amelia County slaves were living in groups of more than twenty slaves to a household. By the end of the eighteenth century, Amelia County was the largest slaveholding county in Virginia; with more than 60 percent of its population in bondage at the beginning of the nineteenth century, Amelia was a Virginia county with a "black majority."[106]

Detailed Findings from Eighteenth-Century Patrol Records

Tithable records allow us to investigate more closely several aspects of colonial slave patrols: how many patrollers the Virginia militia appointed and their tendency to reappoint the same men to slave patrols again and again; the use of family groups or individuals as patrollers; how long-term residents were employed as patrollers; the slave ownership of patrollers; and patrollers' wealth, relative to that of other members in their communities. With this information we can better evaluate claims made by historians that poor whites constituted the bulk of slave patrol membership.

According to tithe lists, in Norfolk County, 185 patrol appointments were made in the period 1750 to 1780; Amelia County had 50 slave patrol appointments in the same period.[107] In Norfolk, the number of patrollers appointed annually shows a regular increase: in 1751 nine men were patrollers, and by 1768 that number had reached a high of twenty-four patrollers. By contrast, Amelia County had no dramatic escalation in the number of patrollers appointed each year. In fact, in one period the number of appointees to patrol duty distinctly declined. In 1755, only two men served as patrollers, whereas in earlier years, five or six men performed patrol duty. The decline is attributable to Amelia's expanding population. When enough settlers had moved to Virginia's southwest frontier, the legislature created a new county by partitioning Amelia County; the old county lost almost one-third of its acreage in the division.[108] With the loss of land (and population), a decline in the number of Amelia patrollers appears logical. One actually sees a slight increase in the total number of patrollers for Amelia when looking at patrol appointments by decade: eighteen men served in the 1750s and twenty-one were appointed in the 1760s.

Among the men chosen for patrol duty in Norfolk County, officials had a marked preference for using the same men over and over. Forty-three Norfolk men served more than one term as a patroller; as a group, they account for 75 percent of all patrol work done in Norfolk County.[109] Most of these "repeat patrollers" served two or three years at the most on slave patrols, but one unusual man, Jacob Sikes, served eight different years.[110]

With nearly three-quarters of all patrollers in Norfolk County serving for their second or third year, they could not have been inexperienced as patrollers. Moreover, an equal number of repeat patrollers worked in the decades of the 1750s, 1760s, and 1770s. As men retired at age forty-five after serving multiple patrol appointments, younger men replaced them and continued the tradition of several years' patrolling service in the county. These repeat patrollers grew accustomed to their task and occasionally trained novices to join them.

Anecdotal evidence from slave narratives supports the data that the same men repeatedly worked on slave patrols in certain regions. Many years after freedom had been attained, ex-slaves remembered specific individuals who served as patrollers in their communities; as we have seen, Lucy Gallman named George Harris, Lamb Crew, Jim Jones, and Theodore Merchant as patrollers in her part of Edgefield District, South Carolina.[111] William Sykes, a North Carolina slave, said that "Mr. Joe Jones was our regular patteroller and he gave us the very devil."[112] On occasion, a former bondsman recalled that his owner had been a patroller; as a member of the group, the master then gave local patrols unfettered access to his plantation.[113] And yet some ex-slaves thought that patrols always changed their membership: Archie Booker claimed, "Dey didn have de same men on de patrols all de time. Diffunt men come ev'y night."[114]

In several important respects, Amelia County did not replicate Norfolk's pattern of patrol appointments. Of the fifty patroller appointments made in Amelia County, fewer than 10 percent of the men served more than one year. Another distinction set Amelia apart from Norfolk County: Amelia County patrollers usually were unrelated to one another. With only a few exceptions, the Amelia County men appointed all

had different surnames, indicating that they were not from the same immediate family group.[115] Certain families appeared to serve as regular patrollers in Norfolk: fathers, sons, and brothers were a fixture of patrol
duty, unlike in Amelia County. For example, in Norfolk County, the
Portlock and Langley families worked for seventeen and thirteen years
respectively on patrol duty, often with two or three family members riding in the same year. Jacob Sikes, the man who did eight stints as a patroller, had the company of his brother Jesse for six years. Why were
family members repeatedly appointed to patrol duty? The very nature of
patrol duty itself might be a reason. Patrollers spent hours in the saddle,
several nights a month, for months at a time, so family members may
have been chosen because they were more likely to discuss and reach
agreement about when, where, and how to patrol than a group of men
not related at all to one another.[116]

Since Norfolk County regularly clustered family members in patrols,
did sons and younger men get chosen for patrol duty, or did patrolling
fall to the heads of households? In Norfolk County, fathers and sons
served together, suggesting that the fathers chosen for patrol duty could
be in their late thirties or early forties.[117] But if fathers and sons rode together, the sons only rarely still lived under their father's roof; there were
only three or four instances in which a father and son living together
both went on patrol.[118] Men in charge of their own households, who
paid their own tithes separately from their fathers, made up the vast majority of patrollers in both Norfolk and Amelia counties.

In both counties, militia commanders chose men as patrollers only after they had lived in the community several years. Only five of the men
appointed to patrol duty in Norfolk County failed to appear on earlier
tithe lists. Practically every patroller was a regular tithe payer and resident of the county for at least two to five years (or more) before his stint
of patrolling. Likewise, more than 85 percent of these men remained in
Norfolk County for many years after their appointment as patrollers,
bucking the trend among Virginia residents to move to other counties
for richer lands and better prospects.

A similar long-term residence phenomenon can be observed among
Amelia County patrollers. More than 70 percent of the men who became
slave patrollers appear on tithable lists two to five years preceding their
appointment. The length of time their families appeared on the tax lists,
however, might go back only one generation—unlike Norfolk patrollers,

whose families can be traced back for two or three generations. Men appointed to patrol duty in Amelia County were relatively recent arrivals: their families had only been locally taxed for ten years or less. Maps of Amelia County's settlement, showing the location and acreage given in original land patents from the colony, provide clues to this apparent puzzle. Many of the patrollers or their fathers appeared on these maps as first-time land grantees—in other words, these men were farming lands that had never belonged to anyone else except Native Americans.[119]

If Amelia County settlers who became slave patrollers were relatively new arrivals, they did not come alone: of the fifty patrollers, 50 percent owned bondsmen at the time of their appointment.[120] In dividing patrol appointments by decade, the percentage of slaveholding patrollers and nonslaveholding patrollers remained relatively constant for the 1750s, 1760s, and 1770s. This seemed surprising because the percentage of slave-owning patrollers should logically have also increased with time, since Amelia County actually experienced a rise in the percentage of slaveholders during the 1760s and 1770s.[121] In terms of slave ownership, of the 185 patrol appointments made in Norfolk County, 62 percent were slave owners at the time of their appointment. If one removes all men who served more than one term as a patroller from the sample (which could induce a skew in the data), one still finds that nearly 60 percent of the remaining 48 patrollers owned slaves. (See Table 3.1.)

Amelia County patrollers differed strongly from their Norfolk counterparts in another respect: of the Amelia patrollers who owned slaves, a majority owned more than one slave. Most Norfolk County patrollers owned only one slave. If Amelia patrollers owned slaves at the time of their appointment, they usually owned two to five slaves. The largest Amelia County slave owner appointed to patrol duty was Daniel Hardaway, who owned twenty-one slaves and over 1,200 acres when he was appointed in 1770.[122] Likewise, Matthew Wells and Charles Anderson became slave patrollers while owning seven and ten slaves, respectively, in the 1750s.

If half or more than half of all Amelia and Norfolk patrollers owned slaves, how did patrollers' slave ownership compare with that of other white residents, the people living around them not appointed to patrol duty? In Norfolk County, 55 percent of the residents owned no slaves in 1750. Of the remaining 45 percent who did, the vast majority owned one to five slaves. (See Table 3.2.) More than half of white citizens still did

Table 3.1 Norfolk County, Virginia: Slave ownership among slave patrollers, 1750–1780

Slave ownership among	Number (%)
Norfolk County patrollers	
No slaves	70 (37.8)
1 slave	60 (32.4)
2–5 slaves	47 (25.4)
6 or more slaves	8 (4.3)
Norfolk County nonrepeating patrollers	
No slaves	20 (41.6)
1 slave	13 (27.1)
2–5 slaves	12 (25.0)
6 or more slaves	3 (6.3)

Source: Data compiled from Wingo and Wingo, comps., *Norfolk County, Virginia, Tithables, 1730–1750; Norfolk County, Virginia, Tithables, 1751–1765;* and *Norfolk County, Viginia, Tithables, 1766–1780.*

not own slaves, and most slave owners held two to five bondsmen in the 1760s and 1770s.[123] Because 60 percent of Amelia County patrollers owned slaves, they could not have been in the lower economic half of their community: patrollers were more likely to be slave owners than their neighbors.[124]

Similarly, Amelia County patrollers' slave ownership fit in with that of the majority of their white neighbors.[125] In 1768, about 30 percent of all Amelia residents owned no slaves, and half owned one to five slaves. In 1788, 36 percent of all Amelia residents owned no slaves (an increase), while 42 percent now owned one to five bondsmen. The Amelia patrollers, who were evenly divided throughout the period between those who did and those who did not own slaves, fell generally into the middle of these two groups, perhaps being a little overrepresentative of the non–slave owners.[126]

In summary, "poor white" does not describe the status of eighteenth-century slave patrollers from Norfolk and Amelia counties.[127] Typically, these men headed their own households. In both counties, half (or more) of all patrollers owned slaves, usually one to five slaves.[128] The men appointed in both counties conform to the middle-status groups of their respective communities, and some of the biggest land owners and slave owners in the county served on slave patrols. Men of status became

Table 3.2   Slave ownership in Norfolk County, Virginia, 1750

Type of household	Number (%)
No slaves	300 (55.0)
1 slave	90 (16.5)
2–5 slaves	123 (22.6)
6–9 slaves	22 (4.0)
10 or more slaves	10 (1.8)

Source: Data compiled from Wingo and Wingo, comps., *Norfolk County, Virginia, Tithables, 1730–1750*, and *Norfolk County, Virginia, Tithables, 1751–1765*.

patrollers, like tobacco inspectors Thomas Burton and Mark Thomas, or William Craddock, who became a justice of the peace shortly after his patrol service.[129] As a group, slave patrollers were neither wealthy nor at the bottom among the landless and propertyless of their community. White community members knew slave patrollers well, for they had been residents of long-standing, before and after their patrolling work. Some striking differences exist, however, between the two counties' patrollers. Norfolk relied on family groups, and regularly appointed the same men as patrollers again and again. Amelia County spread the duty of patrolling among a much larger group of men, and men chosen in Amelia County usually owned more bondsmen than did their Norfolk counterparts.

The data also suggests two further conclusions. First, despite the fact that a majority of Virginia slaves gradually migrated with their owners out of the Tidewater region into Piedmont counties like Amelia during this period, Norfolk County continued to use a large and growing number of patrollers.[130] Even though Norfolk whites outnumbered their slaves two to one throughout this period, the total rising population of bondsmen in Norfolk was thought to constitute enough of a security threat to warrant using more and more patrollers each year. Norfolk County whites did not feel safe, and so they employed increasing numbers of slave patrols. Second, as Amelia County's total population gained a greater number of slave owners, the continued fifty-fifty division of patrollers between slave owners and non–slave owners indicates that, in fact, the status of patrollers in Amelia may have actually begun to decline toward the end of the eighteenth century.

Changing Nineteenth-Century Patrol Membership

Although slave patrols reflected a "middling sort" status in eighteenth-century communities, after the 1820s the status of patrol members began to change, particularly in South Carolina. In some regions, patrol duty came to be seen as work that was beneath men of high status.[131] A major exception to this trend was North Carolina, where patrolling continued to be the work of men from all classes well into the nineteenth century, and nonslaveholders remained in the minority of patrol groups.[132] Four circumstances affected the changing composition of men who served on patrols in the nineteenth century: growing absentee ownership of plantations, especially in South Carolina, and a concomitant rise in the use of overseers; the creation of a fine system for patrols, and the regular commutation of fines into locally collected taxes for hiring full-time urban patrollers; the development of the patrol committee structure in North Carolina; and a growing belief that patrol work, like police work, should be conducted not by citizens selected at random but by the most capable, diligent residents.

In mid-nineteenth-century letters and journals, the wealthiest land and slave owners sometimes complained that slave patrol work was better left to one's overseer. When called upon to patrol several times at the end of 1855, the rice plantation magnate Louis Manigault became distressed; in a letter to his father, he fumed against his neighbor C. W. Jones (who summoned him to patrol) for being so insensitive to his status and situation. With his overseer gone and unable to hire a new man for at least a month, Manigault simply did not wish to patrol, and he asked his father whether he should sue Jones to avoid the inconvenience. His father, Charles, replied that the patrol captain had "shewd great want of consideration in fixing on the interval between two overseers" in calling upon Louis to patrol, but a lawsuit should be his last resort. Father and son finally hit upon the excuse that Manigault should not have to patrol since he had served as a commissioned officer long enough to be exempt from all militia and patrol duties.[133] The widespread nature of these sentiments in South Carolina, that wealthy men should be left alone and patrol work should be conducted by overseers or poorer men in society, was a tendency noted by South Carolina governor Paul Hamilton as early as 1806. Wealthy slave owners who are most interested in the preservation of peace and order, have, from a mistaken notion of things, thrown the whole of this burthen [patrol duty] on others less fortunately circumstanced, on whom alone the present penalty is coercise.

In his message to the state assembly, Governor Hamilton recommended that fines for failure to patrol be linked to one's tax return, thus making wealthier men liable for heavier fines.[134]

In lowcountry South Carolina, where absentee ownership became quite common prior to the Civil War, overseers regularly served as patrollers, yet even overseers could not always be counted on by other white residents. In Georgetown, where almost half the rice-growing owners departed during the summer months, the grand jury asked the legislature to appropriate money for a police force. The absentee owners should theoretically have been replaced on patrol duty by their overseers, but for health reasons, some owners permitted their overseers to spend up to six months each year away from the plantation. This absence left area slaves with no white supervision and the community without a white man—owner or overseer—who could be tapped for patrol work.[135] Captain William Hayne wrote Governor John Drayton in 1800 to say that "altho' my Company District takes in seventy eight Plantations, yet there are not more than twenty Overseers liable to do duty in my Company."[136] And even if overseers could be called upon to patrol, some white residents considered that leaving patrol duty to overseers was like loosing a fox in a hen house, for overseers would "frequently maltreat the slaves, and commit other excesses in colour of such authority."[137]

If a man did not patrol when summoned to do so, he paid the "nonperformance" fine imposed by the militia or county court. Some wealthy men, like the Manigaults, preferred paying fines to riding on patrol.[138] Charles Manigault wrote his son Louis that "[t]he Leader of Patrol certainly has strong powers as far as his miserable little jurisdiction extends *I presume*—and if it comes to the worst why it won't be very killing to pay."[139] The fine for failure to patrol in South Carolina in 1782 was two dollars for every offense. In accordance with Governor Hamilton's recommendation that one's taxes (and wealth) be incorporated into the fine structure, in 1809 the fine for failure to patrol in South Carolina rose to five dollars plus 50 percent of one's last tax assessment.[140] Virginia also had a system of fines for failing to serve on slave patrols, although the fines imposed were relatively mild and did not increase to match inflation during the nineteenth century.[141] The South Carolina fines could become quite costly: Daniel W. Jordan, master of the Laurel Hill plantation in South Carolina, was fined $12 plus $1 in court costs in September 1860 for defaulting on patrol duty.[142] And yet, despite the cost, men paid nonperformance fines in great numbers: the municipal court in Aiken, South Carolina, repeatedly fined men for defaulting on patrol duty and collected money at every court session in large amounts.[143] Several city councils used the fines to hire men who patrolled on a regular basis, like policemen, rather than rely upon ordinary citizens for patrol work.

By the mid-nineteenth century, the class divide between men of substantial property, who occasionally avoided patrol work, and poorer men who could not afford to hire a substitute or pay nonperformance fines came to be expressed in calls for legislation to protect slave property from abusive, impoverished patrollers. Slave owners stood to lose valuable property when a slave suffered or died from harsh patroller whippings, particularly if the abusers had no assets to pay for the bondsmen they injured. In the South, these differences were apparent enough that men with slave property petitioned the legislature for greater restrictions and penalties on men who cruelly whipped slaves, but who were, in effect, so poor that they could not be sued for the damage they caused.[144] Wealthy owners occasionally sued slave patrollers for whipping bondsmen, but patrollers' status as officials of the state usually protected them.[145]

In some North Carolina counties, the imposition of patrol committees after 1830 to supervise local patrols reinforced the divide between richer and poorer men. As discussed in Chapter 2, wealthier men in each county typically composed slave patrol committees, especially by midcentury. In the 1850s, the Whitaker brothers, members of the most prestigious family in southern Wake County, composed the majority of the district's patrol committee, but they were not expected to go out and perform patrol duty themselves.[146] The Whitakers owned the most slaves in the district.[147] By contrast, the men chosen for patrol duty in Wake County were men like Hugh Blalock, among the lower half of all landowners in the community.[148] Others chosen for patrol work might own one or two slaves and as much as two hundred acres, but they were not in the same social sphere as the Whitakers, who supervised their work.

In a few North Carolina counties like Wake, this trend repeated sporadically—affluent residents supervising patrollers by serving on the local
patrol committee. As a result, some wealthier North Carolina whites
rarely served as patrollers in the mid-nineteenth century, yet could claim
to be performing a civic duty that protected whites from their slaves.

A fourth factor also affected the kind of men chosen for nineteenth-
century patrol work, aside from a belief that it could be left to one's
overseers, paid for through fines, or avoided by serving on a patrol committee. The consequences of slipshod slave patrolling (which might lead
to revolt and bloodshed) led some cautious whites to assert that patrolling should not be assigned randomly or performed haphazardly. Grand
jurors of Abbeville, South Carolina, complained that the district police
imposed onerous duties without regard for the sacrifice of their time
and lost money-making opportunities. Residents of Abbeville contended
that "[u]nder such circumstances it is but reasonable to expect the duties" to be "entirely neglected or discharged in a careless and negligent
manner." They claimed that "whatever is worth doing at all is worth doing well" and that people should be selected to work as patrols in the
district "without a sacrifice of personal interest."[149] The only possible
way this might come about would be to hire men to work full-time as
patrollers. The increasing belief that patrol duty should be competently
performed led, in some instances, to the replacement of volunteer patrols with well-paid officials who could patrol, or police, local slaves
on a daily basis. This impulse toward greater professionalization was
most obvious in urban areas, where nonprofessional slave patrols were
steadily replaced by paid full-time patrolmen who made it their vocation
to ensure the safety of the community.

From the Colonial Era to the Antebellum Period

In the eighteenth century, whether relying upon men of militia age or
slave and property owners, the patrollers who accomplished their mis-
sions were a representative cross-section of citizens—rich, poor, and in-
between—drawn from their communities. The data from the Virginia
counties presents a strong contrast to the traditional view that slave patrols comprised only impoverished whites. However, the wide range of
men who patrolled in the eighteenth century did not persist in every
nineteenth-century locality, for several reasons. The desire of some

wealthy individuals—particularly absentee owners in South Carolina—
to avoid patrol duty led to greater substitution by other persons (overseers) or payment of fines, increasing the likelihood that more lower-status men would be tapped for service. Even the inclusion of lower-status
individuals in patrol groups did not lead to the appointment of free
blacks as patrollers, however. Unlike New Orleans, which relied upon
free blacks in its city guard and patrol forces from 1805 to 1830, no evidence has been found to suggest that free blacks ever served in slave patrols in Virginia or in the Carolinas.[150] Yet not every state experienced a
decline in patroller status: North Carolina counties appear to have retained more mixed-status patrol groups before the Civil War than those
in either South Carolina or Virginia.[151] Perhaps the greatest structural
and social change in patrolling occurred in towns, particularly as urban
areas expanded, with the shift toward commuting patrol fines to hire
full-time patrollers.

Regardless of locality, slave patrollers performed work that, while ap-
pearing similar to the activities of other slave-controlling Southerners,
had unique distinguishing qualities. In terms of status, pay, and community expectations, slave patrols were not overseers, constables, slave
catchers, or purely private citizens hunting rewards. In particular, the official appointment that authorized slave patrollers to act on the community's behalf set them apart. Their indemnification and protection
by courts of law allowed them to discipline, even brutalize, bondsmen
with the legal imprimatur of Southern society. Their duties as patrollers
ranged more widely than constables, their urban cousins in law enforcement. And yet the existence of slave patrols in cities (and citizens' reliance upon them) eventually led to the creation of full-time, paid police
forces in the South—if not before the Civil War, then shortly after its
conclusion. Former slaves could see the resemblance: "They jes' like policemen, only worser."

Knowing who slave patrols were (and were not) provides valuable information, for in a status-conscious society like the South, position frequently determined the range of permissible activities one engaged in.
When considering what slave patrollers actually did in the course of
their nocturnal activities, it is essential to remember that many communities selected their patrols from the full spectrum of the white social
hierarchy. Fiscal prudence demanded no less: a propertyless white patroller could not compensate an owner for a dead or maimed slave.

Financially cautious or paternalistic masters would not expose their bondsmen to such a threat.

A full exploration of what slave patrols did will reveal other reasons why wealthy Southerners remained involved in slave patrolling; patrol activities simply could not be left in the hands of poor whites alone.[152] The responsibilities demanded involvement by men with discretion, prestige, and good character—for slave patrols monitored not only slaves, but the shadowy underworld inhabited by poor whites who traded forbidden liquor and stolen farm goods with them. Indigent whites, who sometimes ran illicit meeting houses where insurrections were discussed, posed too great a threat to the white social order for patrols to ignore. As a result, white men from virtually all social classes learned the habits and routines of slave patrol work.

4

In Times of Tranquility:
Everyday Slave Patrols

> The patrol shall visit the negro houses in their respective districts as often as may be necessary, and may inflict a punishment, not exceeding fifteen lashes, on all slaves they may find off their owner's plantations, without a proper permit or pass, designating the place or places, to which the slaves have leave to go. The patrol shall also visit all suspected places, and suppress all unlawful collections of slaves; shall be diligent in apprehending all runaway negroes in their respective districts; shall be vigilant and endeavor to detect all thefts, and bring the perpetrators to justice, and also all persons guilty of trading with slaves; and if, upon taking up a slave and chastising him, as herein directed, he shall behave insolently, they may inflict further punishment for his misconduct, not exceeding thirty-nine lashes.
>
> *from Edward Cantwell's 1860 judicial hornbook*
> The Practice at Law in North Carolina

Edward Cantwell's description of what slave patrols should do is both encyclopedic and ideal: patrollers were to be perfect disciplinarians who could stop any runaway, prevent any slave crime.[1] Slave patrols this effective, of course, probably never existed anywhere in the American South. Yet laws like this, enacted year after year by state lawmakers and city councils in Virginia and the Carolinas, reveal a shared normative perspective about how Southern leaders wished patrollers would behave. Knowing that men who served as patrols fell short of this ideal has had a curious effect in the modern day. Historians have routinely assumed that since patrollers did not stop every runaway, it matters little what patrols did; their uneven enforcement of the law must have diminished their impact on Southern history and slavery. As a result, the number of prominent slave histories that fail to mention even the existence of patrollers is startling. And when histories do include them, patrols

105

generally appear as little more than straw men, paraded for their inadequacies and little else.[2]

Granted that patrollers were never omniscient or invincible, their presence and activities still affected the behavior of masters and slaves in the South on a day-to-day basis. To determine precisely how patrols affected masters, slaves, and antebellum Southern communities, we need to know what most patrols did, even as we acknowledge that every patrol, every month, did not live up to the high standards set out by lawmakers. Once chosen by militia captains, court judges, or city leaders, how did patrollers carry out their duties during times of relative tranquility? Slave patrols functioned in groups with leaders called captains; knowing how captains directed their patrollers would likewise tell us much about what patrols did once they went on duty. By definition, patrollers' activities took them into repeated (often contentious) contact with bondsmen and their masters—how did slaves describe and react to the "interference" or "benevolent policing" of their patrols? Masters and slaves would of course express different opinions, but further refinements must be possible. Urban and rural slaves, for example, may have held disparate views on patrollers.

Knowing how slave patrols interacted with both masters and slaves will also improve our understanding of their role in the Southern culture of violence. Modern historians readily admit that force and threats underpinned the slave system: slavery studies typically focus on the dominant role of masters, mistresses, or overseers and, to a lesser extent, the domination of blacks by whites throughout the South. Into this equation, we must add another factor—the routine use of violence against slaves by community-sponsored groups such as white slave patrols.

Patrol Duties and Interaction with Slaves

From the time of their first creation, patrols searched slave quarters as one of their three principal duties. Patrols rummaged through slave dwellings looking for weapons of revolt—guns, scythes, knives, but also writing paper, books, and other indications of education.[3] Implements of destruction could come in many forms. Patrols also scrutinized slave quarter inhabitants in search of extra occupants, looking for persons who did not belong on the plantation. Anyone present without permission from his owner would be whipped and then returned to his master or taken to the local jail as a runaway. Patrols sometimes complained that slaves should be compelled to "make lights" when their cabins were searched, and enslaved blacks should be punished for using "impudent language" to patrollers.[4] Failing to have light to see by undoubtedly made patrol duty much more difficult, particularly if one was trying to see under bedding or examine faces closely. Patrols also watched for people missing from a slave cabin as well as those who should have been present but were truant. An absence could signal that a bondsman had turned runaway or was away without a proper pass.

Patrol entries into the homes of slaves provided regular, unwelcome intrusions, which bondsmen occasionally tried to thwart. With no obvious weapons at hand, a slave would be wise not to offend patrollers, for fear of retribution at some later date. Yet some slaves refused to submit to patrol searches. A common slave folktale of resistance and ingenuity tells of patrollers knocking at a slave quarter door, demanding entry. One quick-thinking slave scooped up ashes from the fireplace, opened the door, threw the ashes into the patrollers' faces, and then everyone inside ran past the blinded authorities.[5]

A slave cabin that had lights and music issuing from it might seem a likely target for a patroller visit. Former slaves like Joseph Brooks of Spotsylvania County, Virginia, believed that if a patroller heard too much noise in a cabin "he would walk in and take you out" to receive punishment.[6] And the homes of whites could also be visited by patrollers, if they suspected bondsmen might gather there: the patrollers Peter Ryan and James McBride heard music and noise coming from the home of a former justice of the peace, and with help from the town guard broke up a "negro dance."[7] But even obedient, passive slaves within darkened cabins might fall prey to patrol inspections. Elige Davison, another former Virginia slave, remembered that as bondsmen lay asleep in their own quarters, patrollers would enter and lightly hit them with a whip to see if they were truly tired and asleep at the end of the work day.[8] Although slaves could deliberately remain on their plantations to avoid meeting patrol groups, they might still have regular contact with patrollers.[9]

Patrols more frequently visited slave quarters on plantations where there were few, if any, whites. The greatest concern to slave owners was the idea that slaves might be unsupervised at any time. Even the thought of a slave's being alone on a plantation unnerved Southern whites, despite the fact that the slave might be faithfully working. For that reason, laws in all three states required plantations to have at least one white man present at all times. This created the greatest hardship in South Carolina, where absentee ownership in the Low Country gradually became the norm. Despite this law's obvious importance for security, owners routinely violated it, particularly in the nineteenth century. Even the most respectable men were questioned for not keeping an overseer on the plantation—with errands, emergencies, and frequent changes in overseers, virtually every plantation experienced a time when only slaves were present. For greater security, slave patrols made a point of visiting plantations where owners and overseers were known to be absent. A former slave from Wake County, North Carolina, remembered that after his master died, patrollers came to the plantation every night.[10] Although this may represent an extreme or an exaggeration on his part, slave patrols did scrutinize some plantations with more visits and greater surveillance than others.

A second patroller duty associated with slave quarter searches was the dispersion of slave gatherings of any kind. Independent religious meetings run by slaves alone were a special target. James Smith, an escaped slave, claimed that when patrollers heard hymns and religious music sung by bondsmen, they would follow the music to the slave gatherings, then break up the meetings.[11] As a result, religious worshippers often met in places like swamps, considered inaccessible to patrols. To indicate the meeting place in such a remote location and yet not reveal it to patrollers, the first slave to arrive would break boughs from trees and bend them in the direction of the meeting point.[12] If patrollers did not scatter the worshippers immediately, some who were more sympathetic might allow the meeting to continue and simply object to religious songs they found offensive. James Farley, a former slave in Virginia and Kentucky, reported that "[o]ne time when they were singing, 'Ride on King Jesus, No man can hinder Thee,' the padderollers told them to stop or they would show him whether they could be hindered or not."[13]

But any bondsman caught at a slave meeting (religious or not) was likely to be beaten by patrollers who intruded, especially if the gathering happened at night.[14] A South Carolina ex-slave, Fannie Moore, recalled that the patrol beat one slave they found at a dance until the man died.[15] Night meetings meant more slaves leaving plantations, with or without permission, without supervision from their owners or like-minded men who sought to keep them subservient, so patrols had to restrict these gatherings as much as possible. If meetings could not be held in inaccessible locations, slaves took the precaution of setting out watchers to be on the alert and give warning, should the patrol approach their meeting site.[16] Archie Booker, a former slave from Virginia, remembered that religious meetings often posted lookouts "[c]ose dey hada watch fe de paddyrolluhs."[17] Writing of his experiences in 1857, Austin Steward recalled seeing a slave dance in Virginia interrupted by "the slave who was kept on the 'lookout,' [who] shouted to the listeners the single word *'patrol!'* "[18] Some bondsmen believed patrollers were pressured to administer whippings at slave meetings, or risk losing their positions.[19] Even if a few owners sanctioned slave gatherings, others might prefer patrols to disperse slave meetings with a vigorous show of force.

Although unsupervised church services were the most common focal point for bondsmen, whites worried about any slave meeting that lacked white supervision. For this reason, laws required slave patrols to investigate and break up "any gathering" of bondsmen, without specifying the size or nature of the assembly. Laws of this sort had existed since the eighteenth century, even if they ignored the realities of communal living: a slave family might include six, eight, even ten people, but that kind of group did not demand regular dispersal. So precisely which groups should be separated? If slaves met with poor whites to drink or trade goods, their meetings could draw the attention of patrollers, pitting slave patrols against poor whites in their efforts to control slave movements and behavior. Some patrollers remained uncertain how large a slave gathering had to be before it must be dispersed. H. Milton Blake wrote to the South Carolina governor, asking for clarification about which kinds of meetings and how big a slave group had to be, because "great diversity of opinion as to what constitutes an unlawful assemblage" existed among the members of his patrol group.[20] Merely by congregating in town bondsmen attracted the attention of patrols; many town councils passed laws requiring patrols to disperse any slave gathering in the streets on Sundays.[21]

The third principal activity of patrols was to safeguard areas around plantations and within towns by riding or walking along the roads. Patrols questioned and detained slaves who were away from their plantations without permission, and punished those who offered resistance.

(See Figure 7.) When patrols encountered slaves who could not explain their possession of unusual objects, like guns or horses, patrols confiscated them. The *State Gazette of South Carolina* reported that patrols in 1793 had apprehended a black man, Titus, whose profitable trading had gleaned him two horses, "one poultry cart, and several articles of merchandise . . . [including] linens, and handkerchiefs."[22] Patrols from St. John's Parish carried away guns, linen, and china they found in slave cabins, in addition to five horses.[23] Newspapers used the same words to describe missing horses or runaway slaves apprehended by patrollers: both were objects that had been "taken up," to be reclaimed by their rightful owners.

Slave patrols frequently looked at slave passes while making their rounds. Laws required the slave to carry a pass, or ticket, from her master, which permitted the slave to leave the plantation. A specific pass stated the slave's name, where she had permission to go, on what date, how long the pass was good for ("to North Hampton Plantation until Sunday night"), and bore the owner's signature.[24] Owners had different

7. "The Plantation Police" (1863) by Francis H. Schell

policies about giving passes. Some viewed passes as a reward for work well done during the week, and thus they could be withheld if the owner desired. Other owners thought that regularly giving passes kept slaves content and made them less likely to run away.[25] Directions printed in *DeBow's Review* in 1857 show how the second, more paternalist approach to passes came to be adopted across the South: "No one is to be absent from the place without a ticket, which is always to be given to such as ask for it, and have behaved well. All persons coming from the Proprietor's other places should shew their tickets to the Overseer, who should sign his name on the back; those going off the plantation should bring back their tickets signed."[26] In writing out passes, some owners might fail to name the slave, date, or destination, saying no more than "permit the bearer to pass and repass to ——, this evening, unmolested."[27] Although many masters failed to give specific passes, or occasionally allowed a slave to leave without any written orders, virtually every owner agreed that a slave away from the plantation must have a pass. The irony of expecting all other owners to give passes to their slaves, yet failing to conform personally, was lost on most slave owners, who indulged their belief that they (or their slaves) were above such limitations. When patrollers encountered a slave, they would begin their inquiry by examining the slave's pass.

Patrollers complained about owners who wrote "general passes," or passes good for a whole month, giving slaves great latitude in where and how long they might travel away from their home plantation. Larkin Hundley, a Virginian, wrote this kind of pass for his slave Ben, giving him "permission to pass & repass to his wife . . . for the present month."[28] Owners living near urban areas who allowed skilled slaves to hire their own time—an arrangement under which their owner rented them to a third party and sometimes permitted them to keep a portion of the salary paid—regularly gave this type of pass. Some tickets might not even specify a parish or district within which a slave must remain, granting him tremendous mobility with which patrollers could not legally interfere.[29]

General passes created an obvious hazard for a slave owning society that patrols could not restrain. With a general pass, a slave had immunity from patrols and greater freedom to travel great distances (or commit crimes) without being impeded.[30] When slaves had general passes, "the Patrol has no jurisdiction whatever, except when [slaves] are found under suspicious circumstances, or discovered in some criminal act; and tho' these slaves be met by the latter fifty times in one night, and in fifty different places, yet have they no power to interfere with them in the least degree."[31] Southern whites complained that theft became easier for the slave with a general pass because "no vigilance on the part of [the] Patrol, even tho' it should be prolonged throughout the entire night, can effectually restrain the robberies of evil-disposed slaves; for, under the protection of their general tickets, they can parade our highways from dark till daylight, with the most perfect impunity."[32]

Some owners wanted increased punishment for slaves caught with general passes, and one group of South Carolinians went so far as to request that patrollers be permitted to punish any slave found with an unspecific pass.[33] Such efforts to outlaw general passes were frequent, but met with no success. Patrollers gave general passes more scrutiny, particularly if they did not know the slave they had stopped (or his owner) personally. In response, runaway slaves adopted subterfuges to fool patrols into not looking at their papers. These elaborate bluffs took courage. Isaac Williams, a fugitive slave, believed that traveling directly through a city showed confidence, and that a runaway was less likely to be stopped and questioned there. After passing through Virginia, he and his runaway companions went so far as to light cigars, tilt their hats jauntily to one side, and stroll through the streets when they entered Washington. They looked at everyone directly, not cowering, and although the runaways passed several white officials, no one asked to see their papers.[34]

Occasionally, a master with a sense of humor, or a score to settle with a slave, would give an unusual pass that made patrollers take notice. Fanny Berry, an ex-slave, recalled that John Brice, also a slave in Virginia, received a pass to visit his wife every Saturday. When his master wrote out the pass, the master would laugh, and when patrollers read it, they would laugh, too. John finally got a free black man to read the pass to him:

> To my man John I give this pass
> Pass an' repass to Sally's black ——
> Ef don't nobody like dis pass
> Dey can kiss ——[35]

A few slave owners crafted elaborate slave passes, not as a joke, but to remind patrollers to be considerate in the holiday season. Hugh Lide, planter, slave owner, and state senator from Darlington County, South Carolina, wrote these passes in the 1820s:

> Permit my friends poor sable Dick
> Who scarce can walk without a stick
> To pass to Mr. B—'s plantation
> To see the people of his nation.
> This poor old man has lost his wife
> It touches hard upon his life.
> Then pray permit him to depart
> And seek a wife to mend his heart.
> Christmas comes but once a year
> To give poor nigger happy cheer
> Then let him take his swing in full
> His sop, his tater, and his bull.
>
> Hail gentle patroles as you ride
> See! Here goes York and there his bride
> If you should think they have no vision
> But just to go to Capt. Pugh's
> Pray don't disturb them on the way
> And should they spend the live long day
> In social chat with Dady May
> They have permission so to do
> From Mr. Pierce and Master Hugh[36]

As long as the slave did not overstay the time allowed by his master, patrollers might not molest a slave with a valid ticket.[37] But passes did not always confer safety: Moses Grandy, a former slave of North Carolina, wrote that "[i]f a negro has given offence to the patrol, even by so innocent a matter as dressing tidily to go to a place of worship, he will be seized by one of them, and another will tear up his pass; while one is flogging him, the others will look another way; so when he or his master makes complaint of his having been beaten without cause, and he points out the person who did it, the others will swear they saw no one beat him."[38] Personal animosity between patrollers and slaves could end with the bondsman's getting beaten—but masters might retaliate. In areas where masters regularly gave their slaves passes, one of the most grievous offenses patrols could be accused of was that they beat bondsmen who had valid passes.[39] Patrollers who whipped slaves indiscriminately angered their owners by potentially lowering the property value of their slaves. Conversely, bondsmen who had no passes, but who had enough money to bribe an urban patrol, might be allowed free passage, again incurring the wrath of owners, who complained that patrols either ignored their duties or abused their position of authority.[40]

In addition to searching slave dwellings, breaking up slave meetings, and regulating slave movement, urban patrollers had additional responsibilities. Their work overlapped with what we would today consider tasks of the fire department. Since city fires gathered residents in a central location to fight the fire, they could be used effectively as a ruse at the start of insurrections—and slaves repeatedly started fires for this purpose. In 1826 Charleston city patrols discovered a suspicious "package of combustibles" and prevented a fire from starting.[41] Urban patrols also watched for "strolling" slaves out after the curfew bell had rung, and they checked the tippling houses where blacks and whites might mingle. By checking for fires, vagrants, and any unusual gatherings, city patrollers attempted to control several dangerous threats simultaneously.[42]

Controlling slave movement in cities created special problems for patrols. Urban bondsmen traveled so frequently without passes that alternate methods developed for slave patrols to control their movements. In cities, writing a pass for each job a slave performed could become a tiresome burden for any owner. Some town slaves asked for passes only occasionally, like Governor Dudley's Jack, who asked one evening, "will massa give me a pass, they are whippin 'em out there."[43] Many city slaves went without passes until patrols became active. Rather than force owners to write passes routinely, larger cities like Charleston devised badge systems: a slave's owner purchased a badge from the city, good for one year, that the slave had to wear at all times. Although slaves did not always wear their badges, and some owners flouted the law, badges gave patrollers a means to avoid inspecting passes in the largest Southern cities. Even seventy years after freedom came, one former bondsman declared that he still had his badge and pass to show the patrol, so that no one could molest him.[44]

In urban areas, free blacks or fugitive slaves who had no papers ran the risk of being picked up by city patrollers. Runaways captured by patrollers were usually sent to the guardhouse until reclaimed by their masters. Even free blacks whom the patrollers had no business imprisoning could be placed in the guardhouse by those who were overzeal-

ous. The Savannah, Georgia, patrol incarcerated Olaudah Equiano, eighteenth-century freedman and memoirist, merely for being in a house
that had its lights on after nine o'clock. Only the intervention of a white
doctor, who testified that Equiano was a free man, prevented him from
receiving a whipping the following morning.[45]

Statutes and ordinances (as well as prudence) required free blacks to
carry their freedom papers, and slave patrols—who could not always
distinguish between free and enslaved African Americans—often found
themselves reading freedom papers instead of slave passes. Vulnerable to
being stopped by patrollers as they worked and traveled, free blacks may
have adopted conservative practices in their daily lives, such as staying
away from slave gatherings and tippling houses that might attract patrollers' attentions. Little evidence survives to indicate exactly how patrollers interacted with free blacks, although a few incidents are suggestive.
In the aftermath of Gabriel's rebellion, the "rigid treatment of the Patrols" in Norfolk and the surrounding county drove almost one hundred
Virginia free blacks to state their intention to emigrate to Liberia, a public declaration that some must have hoped would forestall worse treatment at the hands of patrols.[46] Other free black–patroller encounters
ended up in court. One North Carolina freedman, an African American
named William Kees, was charged in Craven County court for attacking
a patrol group in 1856. The patrollers outnumbered him, but Kees tried
to even the odds by wielding "a very large Hickory stick" in his own behalf. It seems unlikely that a single man would initiate an attack on an
armed group of slave patrollers. The indictment noted that patrollers
found Kees "with negro slaves" on the "pathway leading from David R.
Whitford's to George Reel's Quarter," meaning that Kees had probably
not initiated the confrontation, but was defending himself after being
discovered with several bondsmen. The willingness of some free blacks
to help runaway slaves could put the freedmen at risk with local patrollers, who visited their homes too.[47] The scrutiny of slave patrols in
Southern communities probably encouraged less venturesome free
blacks to limit nighttime contact with bondsmen, to avoid patroller brutality and Kees's fate of being taken to court.[48]

Slave patrols had most frequent contact with slaves who left their
plantations repeatedly. This included bondsmen who had family members living nearby and slaves who were courting, trying to woo the part-
ner of their choice. Stories abound of patrollers who encountered male

and female slaves courting outside the bounds of a plantation; in many accounts, the male slave accepted the whipping for both slaves and was embarrassed at being caught. John Thompson, a runaway who success-fully escaped to the North, wrote that one master grew weary of having Thompson court his female slaves, and asked the local patrollers to watch for him and whip him, but they never seemed able to capture Thompson. One evening, patrollers appeared in the slave quarters he was visiting and chased him for more than a mile without capturing him. About two weeks later, however, county officials took the bonds-man into custody to obtain information about some stolen wheat. Al-though he knew nothing of the theft, they whipped him anyhow be-cause the owner of the female slaves complained that Thompson made them unfit for working. Thompson's owner, outraged at this interference and whipping, beat the constable and had the magistrate turned out of office for wrongly abusing his slave.[49]

Fathers and mothers, who moved between plantations to see children and spouses scattered in the region, also encountered patrollers on a reg-ular basis.[50] Many former slaves interviewed by the WPA remembered their father or mother escaping from or outwitting the patrol.[51] Patrol-lers could exploit family relationships: the owner Christopher Dawson thought patrols could easily find his runaway slave Rose because she must be near the plantation where her mother lived.[52] Slave patrols chal-lenged family members about their movements, even when slaves had valid passes, if they suspected slaves were moving about "excessively." One ex-slave recalled that patrollers stopped his father because they thought he was visiting his wife too much.[53] Slave parents talked to their sons and daughters about patrollers, even if the children were too young, like the former slave W. Solomon Debnam, to understand what patrollers did.[54] In some cases, the information they imparted helped their children use more caution around whites, or just scared them into more prudent behavior.

Evading patrollers took speed and ingenuity or faith in the supernatu-ral. Both urban and rural slaves perfected the art of "skinning" over backyard fences—vaulting them while on the run—to escape an ap-proaching patroller. Conjurers and folk doctors prescribed various rem-edies when slaves wanted "to escape the 'patrolers,' " although almost nothing is known about which roots or plants bondsmen deemed most effective against patrols.[55] One Savannah, Georgia, ex-slave remembered that his uncle used magic invisibility to outwit patrollers. The uncle regularly disappeared off the plantation and left no trail, although one time patrollers caught up with him. As his nephew told the story, "One time he git cawnuhed by duh putrolmun an he jis walk up to a tree an he say, 'I tink I go intuh dis tree.' Den he disappeah right in duh tree."[56] Other evasive maneuvers called for more conventional means: slaves rubbed turpentine or manure on their feet, masking their scent from dogs and thus throwing patrollers off their trail.[57]

Evasion, however, was not an inevitable outcome: without a valid pass, slaves caught by a patrol group would be beaten, and the most vivid memories of former bondsmen were beatings they received at the hands of patrollers. Of the ex-slaves interviewed by the WPA in the 1930s who were children or adolescents in slavery times, few had been actually caught or whipped by patrollers. They remembered that patrollers could whip a slave without a pass, however, even though they had not been beaten themselves.[58] In fiction, runaway mothers like Margaret Walker's Vyry might try to escape slavery with their children, but slow-moving toddlers made it easy for patrollers to recapture the entire runaway group. Although the children avoided a patroller's whipping, the parents would not.[59] Other young slaves remembered seeing the patrol riding, although they never met patrols or were threatened by them directly.[60] More often, they knew stories of family members—fathers, mothers, uncles, siblings—who had been caught, or threatened with a beating, by the patrol.[61]

For a female slave a patroller's beating might be the least of her worries. All women held in bondage remained threatened by the possibility of sexual abuse; not only could slave patrols take advantage of a woman's smaller stature, but their searches of slave cabins took them into intimate confines whose beds and privacy could be sexually exploited. A slave woman told her mistress that while a patroller searched her cabin, he appeared "to be very fond of her, tho' she had her Husband hid under Bed."[62] Another slave claimed that patrollers engaged in sexual relations with female slaves, after whipping their enslaved husbands.[63] Recent scholarship suggests that patrollers may not have beaten slave women as severely as slave men due to the feminine style of brief truancy, rather than the prolonged absences of male slaves.[64]

Slaves could also plead with their masters to intercede and stop patroller violence, although most masters usually learned about the brutality that occurred after the fact. One enterprising bondsman, Peter, wrote his absent master to complain about patrollers harassing him and other slaves on the plantation. The patrollers "told a good many miserable lies on me which has given me a great deal of trouble" and the intervention of his master might be the only thing that would stop another beating in the future. Of course, Peter's version of events may not have been the absolute truth: his ingenuity may have extended to distracting his owner with false claims against the area's patrol group.[65]

Slaves might beg to be let out of a whipping from the patrol, hoping that mercy or caprice might avert a beating.[66] Patrollers sometimes toyed with a slave, threatening a whipping, then letting the slave go free. The inherent arbitrariness of punishment added to the fear most slaves felt when they encountered slave patrols. One former bondsman, Alex Woods, recalled how a patrol reacted to a begging slave. He said that patrollers "wouldn't allow [slaves] to call on de Lord when dey were whippin' 'em, but dey let 'em say 'Oh! pray, Oh! pray, marster.' "[67] The harsh punishment a patrol could administer caused one former slave to liken meeting the patrol with being sold to a new master—a slave would seek to avoid both fates at any cost.[68] Few things compared to the agony a slave endured from a patroller beating. One ex-slave from South Carolina recalled what people heard when she was born: her mother screamed as if she were being beaten by patrollers.[69]

On occasion, slaves made deals with patrols, although the reality of white coercion sometimes made the arrangements very one-sided. Patroller Jimmy Stevens started to whip a group of slaves he discovered at a dance, then offered to "let 'em off dat time if dey'd sing and dance some mo'," according to former slave Berle Barnes.[70] In a white folktale about patrols, a Virginian thought that "[t]he men appointed as patrolmen were often in sympathy with the slaves, who would sometimes tell them what they were planning to do."[71] Sympathetic or not, patrollers could be bribed, if slaves had the right goods and patrolmen had weak principles. Enslaved blacks who provided food, liquor, or other goods (stolen or not) could receive safe passage from a patroller, despite not having a valid ticket. However, patrols might make deals with slaves and then renege: in an unlikely alliance, one master aided his slave in getting a patroller to satisfy his part of the bargain, still unfulfilled.[72]

Whether bondsmen bargained with patrollers or tried to outwit them to avoid a beating, slaves made patrolling part of their culture through song. Bondsmen had warning songs that slave children sang to indicate that patrollers were nearby. The most well-known song sung about patrollers, "Run, Nigger, Run," had several variants (see Figure 8).[73] Its lyrics describe the angry owner, the fleeing slave, and the patroller in hot pursuit:

> As I was goin cross de field
> A black snake bit me on my heel
> CHORUS:
> Run nigger run, de Patrol catch you
> Run nigger run, tis almost day
>
> When I run, I run my best
> Run my head in a hornets nest
> CHORUS
>
> Some folks say dat a nigger won't steal
> But I caught nigger in my corn field
> CHORUS

89

110. **RUN, NIGGER, RUN!**

8. "Run, Nigger, Run" sheet music, c. 1867

One had de shovel and de other had de hoe
And if that aint stealin I don't know
CHORUS[74]

Goldie and J. B. Hamilton recorded their versions of this song for Virginia WPA Folklore workers. They remembered alternate verses and a slightly different chorus:

Run Nigger, run, Patty Roller will catch you,
Run, nigger run
I'll shoot you with my flintlock gun.
CHORUS:
Run, nigger run, Patty Roller will catch you,
Run, nigger run, you'd better get away.

I run and jumped across a fence,
Black snake bit for the want of sense,
CHORUS

Run, run, I ran my best
I ran my head in a hornet's nest,
CHORUS

Hornets they went boo, woo, woo,
You'd better bet this nigger flew,
CHORUS

Nigger run and nigger flew,
Nigger tore his shirt tail in two,
CHORUS

Run, nigger, run, run your best
My gal's got jaws like a hornet's nest
CHORUS

I'll load my gun with flint and steel,
I'm gonn' split a nigger's heel
CHORUS[75]

Flight or evasion remained a primary concern for slaves, but avoiding patrollers was easier in song than in reality. In 1844 Moses Grandy, a fugitive slave from North Carolina, wrote that "[a]ll through the slave states there are patrols; they are so numerous that they cannot be easily escaped."[76]

Patroller Equipment and Patterns of Movement

Slave patrols in rural areas regularly used the most common form of transportation available in the eighteenth and nineteenth centuries: they traveled on horseback.[77] Since most slaves they encountered (and most who tried to run away) were on foot, a group of men on horseback had advantages in both speed and range. Patrollers sacrificed silence by using horses, since horses and men made more noise than men alone, but the advantages outweighed any loss of stealth. Charles Ball, fleeing slavery at the beginning of the nineteenth century, evaded patrollers when he heard their horses and remained hidden from his pursuers.[78] Horses were essential in rural areas because slave patrols met in a central location, traveling from their individual residences, and then moved from plantation to plantation, attempting to discover slaves away from their cabins without permission. Although the patrol's work could be done on foot, scouring a countryside with farms scattered a few miles apart could be a daunting task. Patrollers also relied upon horses for purposes of intimidation. A mounted man presents an awesome figure, and the power and majesty of a group of men on horseback, at night, could terrify slaves into submission.[79] And since patrollers carried no distinguishing equipment, in the dark, any cluster of mounted men might be mistaken by a slave for patrollers.

By contrast, in urban areas patrollers regularly worked on foot. With less ground to cover, the noise of horses would draw too much attention to slave patrols who moved through town streets, peering into alleys, checking taverns, and entering slave houses. Whether mounted or on foot, a large part of all patrolling involved movement from place to place, inspecting many locations on a given night. On occasion, rural patrollers also worked without horses, particularly when they had a specific house under surveillance, such as one where they suspected slaves of selling illegally obtained goods.

An excellent example of this stationary patrolling (akin to modern police stakeouts) is found in the diary kept by a young Virginia doctor-turned-planter, Richard Eppes. Eppes made his home at City Point, and like many slave owners on the James River, he owned land on both sides of the river.[80] Eppes recorded an elaborate description of patrolling near his home in Prince George County. One Saturday night in November 1851, three neighbors arrived at Eppes's home and ate dinner. Afterward, the four men went into town on a "patrolling expedition" at one o'clock in the morning. They first stopped at a local City Point tavern, owned by the Dutchman Mark Blitz, and watched a neighboring wharf and store, run by Mrs. Charlotte Penny. When they observed lights inside the store, and a skiff with men near her wharf, the patrollers left the tavern and "took positions to watch—Mr. Meade near the stable, [Eppes] at the corner of Mrs. Penny[']s warehouse on [the] wharfs [and] Mr. Crane at her door to watch & peep." After a short time they heard Mrs. Penny open her door to three slaves; following a short conversation, the bondsmen left the house and went back to the river. Fearing that they would lose their prey, Eppes "jumped off the wharf and made a dash at one but he escaped" and jumped in his boat. Although mistaken identities in the dark created havoc, the slave owners captured their quarry in the end. Eppes tried to overtake one fleeing man, but another patroller, Meade, mistook Eppes for the culprit and gave him several severe blows to the head. The slaves could have gotten away, since they got their boat safely to the middle of the river, "but fearing we had arms & they would be shot" the bondsmen came back to land and surrendered. Two of them turned out to be the cook and carpenter of the prominent slave owner Hill Carter, whose lands lay across the river. Upon examination, the patrollers found two empty bags that had held corn and meal, plus a pistol and cutlass, and three flasks of apple brandy. Mr. Crane, who had been stationed close to the house, claimed he had heard a woman bargaining with the slaves. Later that evening they caught another slave with three bags and a basket of goods to be traded at Mrs. Penny's, but no pass authorizing his visit; Eppes and the others retained the goods and sent the slave back to his owner for a pass. Closer to daybreak, they searched three houses, including Mrs. Penny's and the tavern run by Blitz, looking for the goods missing from the empty bags taken with the captured slaves. Eppes did not record what the search revealed.

On Monday morning, Hill Carter, a friend of Eppes and scion of the powerful Carter clan, came to discuss what should be done about the illicit slave trading. Eppes, Carter, and Meade "agreed to present and prosecute [Mrs. Penny], employing Tim Rives to assist the commonwealth's attorney." Richard Eppes and the other men probably considered their patrolling expedition a success, for it captured the slaves and a suspected liquor trader, and hoped that their discoveries would curtail future thefts in the area. Unfortunately no further information exists about Mrs. Penny's fate once court proceedings began.[81]

Patrollers watched the homes and businesses of free blacks or whites, like Mrs. Penny, when they guessed that these residents had formed ties to slaves through illicit trading or grog sales. The local community might prompt this watchfulness by circulating petitions or rumors that encouraged patrols to target specific individuals. In North Carolina, individuals in Mecklenburg, Iredell, and Cabarrus counties complained about "the cupidity of evil disposed persons located in our midst—who carry on an unlawful traffic with slaves": they expected local patrols to put an end to this kind of underhanded business activity.[82] Patrollers found it easier to keep the suspicious free person under surveillance, through stationary patrolling, instead of attempting to monitor every slave in the neighborhood who might be contemplating a rendezvous with a would-be Mrs. Penny.

Stationary patrolling need not focus only on suspicious whites or free blacks; plantation owners could ask patrols to prevent thefts from their storehouses and fields.[83] J. D. Green, a slave who escaped to the North, described the patroller hired by a neighboring plantation owner to guard his property from repeated thefts by slaves like Green. The patroller "fixed himself under a fence about seven feet high, surrounded with bushes," and when Green went over the fence on his regular raid of the planter's chicken coop, he fell on top of the patroller, scaring both men so much that they ran in opposite directions.[84]

Whether they rode horses, walked a city beat, or hid themselves on a stakeout, patrollers carried weapons. They relied on the instruments of intimidation commonly associated with slavery—guns, whips, and binding ropes. Men could use the guns to threaten or shoot a fleeing slave or to convey information and warnings between patrol groups. Warning shots were rare; they could frighten every household within earshot and were used sparingly, as when a patrol had to break up into smaller parties to search an area. Shots taken at slaves were more common; Sabe Rutledge, a South Carolina ex-slave, recalled that his Uncle Andrew had an eye shot out by patrollers.[85] If a patroller killed a slave in the line of duty (a rare occurrence), the local government usually paid the owner for the dead bondsman.[86] Patrols used whips to beat slaves who were caught away from their home plantations without passes, or who obstructed patrollers in carrying out their duties.[87] City patrols could also use whipping posts to restrain bondsmen while they were beaten.[88] A few slaves reported that patrollers carried paddles instead of whips, but this appears to have been unusual. Ropes could bind slaves to trees or fence rails while they were whipped, or confine them until they could be handed over to town authorities or a slave owner. Patrols used dogs only occasionally, because their barks might give a bondsman too much warning.[89]

Some localities restricted a patroller's use of his whip. In Virginia, patrols had to bring slaves they captured before a justice of the peace before they administered a beating. North and South Carolina seem to have had no formal requirement that patrollers only whip bondsmen with official supervision.[90] Slaves, however, sometimes believed that they had informal rights—one former slave noted critically that some patrols did not wait for dark to administer whippings, implying that patrols which encountered a bondsman at twilight (or before) typically gave warnings, not beatings.[91] Since whites most feared slaves' night gatherings, when they were unsupervised and could plot conspiracies, greater punishments might be expected from a patrol when it encountered a slave at midnight as opposed to twilight.

With his equipment readied, a patroller could go out and challenge slaves on country roads or city streets. The number of nights a patroller spent on duty varied from place to place, and also depended on whether any rumors of unrest or insurrection had recently been heard. Obviously, if any hints of danger were detected, more patrols would be active more nights of the week. During times of relative quiet, however, patrol captains could assemble their patrollers less frequently.

In the Panther Branch District of Wake County, North Carolina, the patrollers of 1857–58 recorded their movements in great detail, providing an excellent overview of how patrollers operated night by night.[92] The district's patrol committee supervised two groups of patrols, and gave them explicit instructions at the outset: "We advise, that you ride at least twice every week for the first two or three weeks, so as to scour the entire district so that you may be able to determine what may be necessary in the future."[93] Orrin Williams, Hugh Black, and Addison King, the three men making up the southernmost patrol group, followed their instructions closely, turning out for twice-weekly rides for the first two months of their service in April and May. The three men were extremely active, catching and whipping three different slaves, and riding to five and seven houses a night in those first few weeks.[94]

Their initial burst of energy did not last. For the rest of the year, the three men regularly rode to only two or three houses in a given night.

Never again would they ride to as many as seven in a single night; for the rest of the year, two-thirds of their rides involved visits to one, two, or three homes in a night.[95] The patrol settled into a pattern of almost-weekly rides: twenty-three of their thirty-four night rides occurred on Saturdays and Sundays, the times when slaves were more likely to be moving from place to place, visiting family and friends, evenings when it would also be easier for the patrollers to spend time patrolling. But it would be wrong to assume that the timing of the Panther Branch patrols became overly predictable: a full third of the rides took place on the other nights of the week.[96] A slave could never be sure that the patrol would not be out on, say, a Tuesday night. It seems likely that these weeknight rides were intended largely for psychological effect, to prevent slaves from assuming that patrols never rode during the week, rather than for regular enforcement purposes. After all, the patrol only caught three slaves during weeknight rides, compared with the fifteen slaves picked up and whipped on Saturdays and Sundays.[97] Hard-worked slaves did not have as much opportunity to wander during the week—masters or overseers would be quicker to spot an absent hand during the week than on a Saturday, with its traditionally easier work-load, or on a Sunday, when most masters expected no work at all, and a bondsman might steal away to visit other places. Fewer roaming slaves in the week meant potentially fewer slaves to be caught by the patrol and consequently less reason to go out riding. But patrollers could never be certain what the slaves were plotting, so weeknight rides had to go on intermittently.

Weekends, particularly Sundays, were times of greater movement for most bondsmen. Slaves went to local religious meetings, visited family members, or hunted wild game to supplement their diets. Freed from their normal tasks, slaves might also use the subterfuge of pretending to go to a religious meeting to camouflage illicit activity.[98] Some services were sanctioned by owners, however, and slaves had sanctuary, so long as the patrol agreed to heed the master's wishes.[99] This was more likely to be the case when slaves held regular religious meetings on the owner's property.[100] Patrols knew these meetings attracted bondsmen, and they often lurked near such gatherings. One North Carolina slave remembered that patrollers waiting outside the church he attended each gave him five lashes because they knew that his master did not give passes to leave the plantation.[101] Many slaves recalled that they needed to have passes to go to church in areas where patrols were vigilant and that in some cases, even having a pass did not prevent them from getting whipped before or after their worship services.[102] Only the wily slave might escape when patrollers broke into his religious gatherings: Anthony Burns recalled that fleeing bondsmen went "through door, window, and even chimney."[103]

Strong evidence exists showing that patrols engaged in abusive behavior to harass congregations (and ministers) of faiths they did not respect. Slave patrollers closely scrutinized Baptists and Methodists, whose ministers encouraged African American attendance and participation in worship. A Baptist minister, James Ireland, recalled that the Anglican rector in Culpeper County, Virginia, made a habit of going to Baptist meetings and publicly disputing with their ministers. On one Sunday, Ireland thought the Baptists would be undisturbed, since the parson would be attending to his duties in his own church. He was wrong. Patrollers descended upon the Baptist meeting and "were let loose upon them, being urged thereto by the enemies and opposers of religion." Ireland was "struck with astonishment and surprise, to see the poor negroes flying in every direction, the patrolers seizing and whipping them, whilst others were carrying them off prisoners, in order, perhaps, to subject them to a more severe punishment."[104]

Like their Baptist brethren, Methodists also suffered from slave patroller attentiveness. On occasion, believers tried to strike back: when King William County authorities warned Baptists and Methodists that slaves attending their meetings would be apprehended, religious leaders from both groups swung into action. The county's sheriff reported that the devout had threatened to use physical violence against county slave patrols. When patrollers invaded a religious meetinghouse, Mr. Charles Neale "through one of them out of the doore" while black and white worshippers overpowered the other patrollers and ejected them from the gathering.[105] Baptists and Methodists threatened the existing social order when they encouraged slaves to attend night meetings and forcibly resist patrollers.[106]

Although patrol members typically ignored the religious beliefs of slaves when they wished, that did not mean patrollers neglected their own observances when they became public officials. Patrol leaders or group members could object to the day chosen for patrolling when it conflicted with their devotions. Samuel Wells Leland appeared to enjoy patrol work: as a country doctor, Leland was accustomed to being called from his bed for medical emergencies, and he considered patrol duty a "very refreshing exercise" after lonely rides by himself. Yet Leland was a devoutly religious man, and he told his patrol captain that he "refused utterly" to go patrolling on Sunday; the captain changed their patrol schedule so that Leland could join their rounds on Saturday nights.[107] Leland apparently saw no conflict between his beliefs and the whippings his patrol administered.

The harvest season and holidays also regulated the patrollers' rides: while Williams, Blalock, and King, the Panther Branch patrollers, rode three and four times a month in June, July, and August, harvest time consumed their energies (and those of the slaves) in September, so they only rode once during the whole month. Their reasons must have been pragmatic: slave field workers were less likely to travel in harvest season, since hard work would be required and supervision on farms would be more acute.[108] In the Panther Branch District of Wake County, the main crops of corn, wheat, oats, tobacco, and cotton would all require heavy work schedules in early fall, before the onset of colder weather. In other regions, patrollers may have modified their activities to match the harvest seasons of different crops. Conversely, at times in the year when whites knew slaves moved around an unusual amount, patrollers became more active. For instance, slaves who hired their time by the year went to county and city gatherings on January 1; they would be scattered about the countryside, changing masters or returning home in greater numbers at the beginning of January, so patrols became more energetic in late December and early January.[109] Likewise, at holidays like Easter and Christmas, more bondsmen were freed from work and likely to travel, so patrols became more active. Williams, Blalock, and King patrolled on Easter Sunday, and on days close to Christmas.[110]

Patrollers did not visit every household in a district where slaves worked, nor did they visit every house the same number of times during the year.[111] Rather, they went to certain homes more often than others, five, six, seven times a year. In Panther Branch District, patrollers went to John Jones's farm an astonishing fourteen times. Clearly some farms received closer attention than others. These well-visited farms have common denominators: a large number of slaves (typically more than five) or closeness of the household to main crossroads.[112] But patrollers attempted to make at least one call during the year at houses where only one or two slaves worked. Interestingly, the patrollers visited the home of Simon Smith, a patrol committee member, three times, and the home of Simon Williams, patroller Orrin Williams's father, once. Slaves of patrollers and committeemen were scrutinized along with other bondsmen in the county, although the prospect of a warm fire and shelter may have drawn patrollers to the Smith and Williams farms as well.

The lists left by Orrin Williams contain names that recur in the same, or similar, order several times during the year.[113] Geographical placement of the homes in Wake County explains this pattern. On May 2, 1857, when the patrollers went to the homes of Nathan Myatt, Dr. Banks, and then Susan Banks, they traveled north on Fayetteville Road. Patrollers rode on Smithfield Road when they inspected the slave cabins of Simon and William Turner, whose farms sat next to each other. Naturally enough, if the patrol used a given road, they would visit certain farms in the same order, time after time.

Patrollers did not have to visit farms in order to carry out their duties, however. As Richard Eppes described in his diary, stationary patrolling around suspected places could take place. On two evenings, the Panther Branch patrollers visited no farms.[114] The first evening, they sat in an "old field"—one not currently in use growing crops—and caught a slave. This suggests that they knew the routes bondsmen used away from the roads and set a trap for the slave they caught.[115] On the other night when they did not visit a farm, they recorded simply "caught runaway." The rest of that evening may have been consumed taking the runaway to local authorities and receiving receipts for his safe delivery to jail or laying claim to the owner's reward. Although patrols preferred to travel on roads and open farmland, where they could easily see their prey, they would travel off beaten paths to get results. They knew slaves used wooded areas to avoid detection.[116] When patrols shifted their areas of surveillance to wooded paths, slaves were sometimes startled by their unexpected intrusions.[117] Charles Ball, who escaped from bondage by traveling through the Carolinas and Virginia, described the pattern of patrolling: "These people [patrollers] sometimes moved directly along the roads, but more frequently lay in wait near the side of the road, ready to pounce upon any runaway slave that might chance to pass."[118] Ball also claimed he knew when South Carolina patrollers were most active: "From dark until ten or eleven o'clock at night, the patrol are watchful, and always traversing the country in quest of negros, but towards midnight these gentlemen grow cold, or sleepy, or weary, and generally be-take themselves to some house, where they can procure a comfortable fire."[119] Sometime after three or four o'clock in the morning, they became active once more. Ball said that "[p]arties of patrolers were heard by me, almost every morning, before day." Ball evaded patrollers by limiting his movement to the hours between midnight and three o'clock.

Once patrollers learned of a runaway slave, they became even more active, if only to thwart the remaining bondsmen who might be tempted by the fugitive's example.[120] The presence of a runaway who stayed in the local area could cause unrest among other slaves, who might shelter, feed, and even run off with him. When slaves fled, they often absconded to remote areas, like the Santee swamps, the Great Dismal Swamp, and the Appalachians, where they found natural hideouts. Patrols loathed searching swamps and mountains, for fear that traps and hidden ambushes could be arranged, hostile Native Americans might appear, or the fugitives would simply melt into the unmapped tracts of wilderness. Patrollers took greater interest in runaways known to have lingered in populated areas, and more men participated in patrols when a fugitive was reported in the vicinity. After Isaac Williams escaped from jail, he went to see his wife who told him there "was a patrol of sixteen or twenty men scouring the country" looking for him.[121] Given patrollers' extra activity when runaways roamed nearby, small wonder that a few slaves thought patrols existed for no other purpose than to track down runaways.[122]

When slaves overtaxed the abilities of one patrol group, or their thefts extended beyond the boundaries of one county or parish, the governor might call out patrol groups in adjoining areas and order them to work in concert. In 1822 South Carolina's governor, Thomas Bennett, took this action after a number of armed slaves moved back and forth between John's Island and St. Andrew's Parish.[123] Because such service would be extensive, lasting longer than a single night, and might involve combat, the men called to arms were compensated for the expenses they incurred.

Interaction with Masters

The relations of patrollers with other citizens ranged from helpful to obstructive. Overseers relied heavily upon patrols, and routinely rode as members of patrol groups.[124] Owners supported this cooperation. Rules for plantation management that appeared in *The Southern Agriculturist* and *DeBow's Review* encouraged overseers to organize their own neighborhood patrol groups and to join any slave patrol that entered their plantations to prevent the abuse of slaves.[125] Overseers' familiarity with patrol methods may explain why they appear to have never barred a patrol from entering property or whipping a slave. By contrast, some masters, generous paternalists or investors sensitive to possible damage to their property, blocked slave patrols from their plantations. Quite a few masters encouraged slave patrols to be more active: they not only permitted patrols to enter their plantations but aided them in patrolling work, and called upon them to capture missing slaves. One former South Carolina bondsman recalled a master holding a slave so that the patrol could administer a whipping.[126] Other owners neither helped nor hindered patrols, but merely wanted to do their own enforcement, without interference from outsiders. As one ex-slave put it, his master did "his own sneaking around" instead of the patrols.[127]

When patrollers encountered direct opposition from whites, at the root of the opposition was the commonly held belief that every man's home was his castle, and no official had the right to enter without permission.[128] Ideas about Southern honor also prompted owners to block patrollers on their rounds: slave patrols were a living reproof to the slave owner, suggesting that he was remiss in controlling his slaves and that the community needed to help him. Little wonder, then, that patrols, acting on instinct, hearsay, or just guesswork, were sometimes obstructed when they tried to enter homes without warrants. After all, patrols needed no warrant to go in a dwelling, unlike other county officials. When the patrollers Ryan and McBride and the town guard tried to enter a house in Charleston, South Carolina, where they suspected slaves were having a party, Justice of the Peace Cunnington appeared at the entrance and angrily demanded, "How dare any man force open the door?" Everyone in the house had a right to be there, he claimed, and Cunnington "gave Mr. McBride some abusive language" when he insisted that slaves were present. Numerous black and mulatto persons were taken into custody after the town guards entered with patroller McBride.[129] According to McBride, when Cunnington asked him what business of his it was whether or not there was a party, McBride responded that he was one of the patrol and he "conceived [it to be] his duty to prevent such doings."[130]

Several former slaves averred that their owners did not allow patrols to enter their plantations at any time.[131] Whether their reasons might be that their slaves were too valuable to be whipped, or that they did not trust their bondsmen with a stranger, or that the entrance of a patrol denigrated the plantation (and thereby harmed the reputation of the owner) is difficult to tell. The former slave Lydia Starks, who lived in South Carolina, said that "Massa Taggart jes' dared anybody ter look lak dey wanted ter whip any o' us. De 'paddle rollers' came on our place one day . . . He run out of de house an' cussed 'em and tole 'em if he needed any whippin' don' on his place, he'd dawn sho do it hisself. Dey didn't come back dere neither."[132] Other slave owners abused patrollers openly, and a few audacious slaves thought that they could then "talk back" to patrollers with impunity, because their masters would protect them.[133] Slaves who lived on plantations where owners denied patrollers access were sometimes called "free niggers," denoting their preferred status.[134] Bondsmen who lived on these havens, however, knew about other nearby plantations where slaves had no immunity from patroller visits.[135] Occasionally, patrols entered a plantation they had been forbidden to enter—after all, the law sanctioned their activities, and they could choose to honor the wishes of an owner or not, as they saw fit.[136] When patrols crept onto a farm in Warren County, North Carolina, and beat up a slave, the master demanded restitution. He received none.[137]

Infrequently, slave patrols encountered masters who confronted them directly. Masters resident on plantations could frustrate patrollers' attempts to "correct" their bondsmen. After a slave's wedding ended, patrollers broke up the party following it and the slave's owner tried to stop them. The owner's wife described the scene: "There were about thirty negroes here and they behaved in a very orderly manner. About ten o'clock just as they were quietly dispersing the patrol came on them and took off seven or eight who had no passes and whipped them. Papa tried very much to get them off but did not succeed in doing it and I find there has been a good deal of talk about it."[138]

Slaves relied upon the sanctity that white masters attached to their lands; numerous former bondsmen remembered being confronted by patrols and running to reach the boundaries of their owners' property, believing, wrongly, that if they could reach the gate or fence barrier at the plantation's edge, the patrol could not whip them.[139] Some owners even gave shelter to the slaves of neighboring owners when the patrol searched their homes, creating an ironic conspiracy of masters and slaves hoodwinking patrollers.[140] These collusions were more likely when the master had specifically invited neighboring slaves to visit a plantation for festive occasions like corn shuckings, quilting bees, or dances.

Slave Evasion and Retaliation

Slaves found the activities of patrollers invasive, occasionally violent, and a general impediment to what they wanted to do. Naturally many worked hard to evade patrollers, while others tricked or taunted them. Bondsmen who could hide in ditches or trees, outrun horses, and disappear into the night had an advantage over their pursuers.[141] One former slave recalled that her father hid in a ditch and made noises like a hog to fool the patrol into leaving him alone. Exploits against patrollers became the stuff of conversation among bondsmen, and a way to gain prestige in the slave community. Slaves who tricked patrollers "[laughed] about it when they got amongst themselves the next day," according to former slaves like Fannie Dorum.[142] To trick patrollers, slaves strung vines across frequently traveled roads or paths in order to knock the patrolman off his horse and, as we have seen, threw ashes in the face of patrollers who tried to search slave homes.[143]

On rare occasions, slaves physically threatened patrollers. In a few instances, a former bondsman mentioned that he had struck a patroller, or knew someone who had.[144] Bertie County slaves Duke, Cuff, and Arthur attacked three North Carolina patrollers, killing the horse of one of them, in 1798; county judges acquitted the men of raising an insurrection but convicted them for killing the horse.[145] In 1857 the Wake County court tried several slaves for "the late riot and resistance . . . to the patrol."[146] Danger to patrollers' property even prompted Cape Fear residents to petition North Carolina's state legislature to change the administration of patrolling, allying it with the militia instead of with county courts. Citizens claimed that patrollers had become afraid of slave retaliation, and were not completing their rounds: pairing patrols with the militia might change this, some white residents reasoned. The damage done by bondsmen in retaliation was hardly trivial. The petitioners reported two patrolmen had had their homes burned down, "while another had his barn and cattle destroyed" by vengeful slaves. The legislature ignored the request.[147]

The former slave Austin Steward recounted in his memoirs a violent confrontation between patrollers and male slaves on the plantation of his Virginia owner. The slave patrols arrived near midnight, interrupting a dance that had been sanctioned by Steward's owner, Colonel Alexander. Telling their womenfolk to hide in a darkened cabin, the male slaves attacked the patrollers as they broke up their party. Led by a newly arrived African slave, called Robert, "[h]and to hand they fought and struggled with each other, amid the terrific explosion of firearms,— oaths and curses, mingled with the prayers of the wounded, and the groans of the dying!" Two patrollers died in the conflict and another had his arm broken, while six slaves perished and two of their fellow bondsmen lay wounded as well. In an unlikely outcome, Colonel Alexander defied local authorities, refusing to hand over the remaining slaves who had taken part in the fighting.[148]

The most renowned patrol attack occurred near Alexandria, Virginia, on a Saturday evening in February 1840. The patrol group, appointed in neighboring Fairfax County, traveled to the edge of Alexandria, where the men encountered several slaves in the late evening. The patrollers determined that two of the slaves had no passes, and they detained the two bondsmen by tying their hands and making them run after the patrols' horses. The patrollers then proceeded through the town of Alexandria and back out onto the country roads in Fairfax County. After a few miles, the patrollers stopped; when one of the men dismounted, slaves hidden in the darkness sprang from the underbrush and started beating him with clubs. One of the patrollers recognized the attackers as the slaves they had stopped earlier at the edge of Alexandria, and demanded to know what they were doing there. The bondsmen responded by beating all of the patrollers, freeing their captives, and fleeing. A doctor, Richard Mason, arrived on the scene and discovered several of the patrollers (whom he had appointed earlier that year in his capacity as justice of the peace) injured and lying on the road. They gave him the identities of the attacking slaves: Alfred, Spencer, and three other bondsmen belonging to Dennis Johnston. At trial, the judges found only Alfred and Spencer guilty of attacking the patrol. Positive identification of the other slaves had not be made, resulting in their acquittal.

When Alfred and Spencer were sentenced to be hanged, confusion broke out. Petitions circulated through the county, requesting clemency from the governor, Thomas Gilmer. The petitioners urged that the condemned slaves be transported out of the state and banished, rather than hanged. These petitions asserted that hanging was too severe a punishment because the other bondsmen were found innocent, and the crime had been rash, but not deliberately malicious. Moreover, the sentences should be reduced because the patrollers had recovered their health, the slaves had good characters, and they had not intended to kill the patrollers or cause a wide-scale slave revolt. Many other prominent citizens rushed to support the court's decision, and demanded that the governor not interfere in the case. Dr. Richard Mason and his cousin George Mason circulated a counterpetition that garnered nearly four hundred signatures.[149] The Masons insisted that the court's verdict be upheld to protect the patrol and set an example, lest other slaves become more rebellious. Moreover, the slaves who attacked the patrol traveled more than three miles to reach the ambush point—not the act of slaves behaving rashly, but a well-planned deliberate assault. George Mason drew a map to show the governor where the night's events had taken place, and to emphasize the distances involved (see Figure 9). Richard Mason

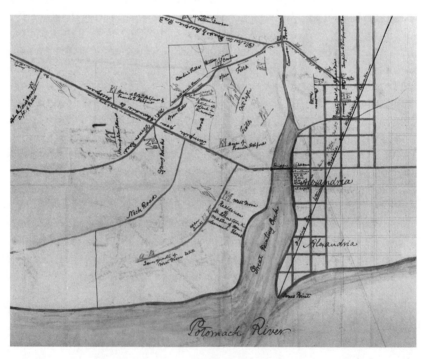

9. *Map of . . . Contiguous Parts of Alexandria & Fairfax,* possibly by George Mason of Hollin Hall, 1840

wrote about his examination of the clubs used in the beatings, some of which measured seven inches in diameter. The slaves had not used saplings, or random branches found on the ground, but oak staves, big enough to injure a grown man.

Nearly fifty letters arrived at Governor Gilmer's office asking him to intervene, or not to intervene, in Alfred and Spencer's case. Some suggested that the slaves' owner, Johnston, wanted their sentences commuted so that he could benefit financially. Others claimed Johnston was uninvolved, and that the patrollers were men of poor character. Richard Mason testified that he had appointed the same men as patrols for years, and knew them to be men of high integrity, well suited for the task, with discretion and good judgment. A few citizens wrote about the confusion surrounding the petitions—facts had been misrepresented to them, and they had signed in ignorance. Now they wanted to have their names removed from the petitions. In the end, Gilmer decided to exercise some clemency, although how he reached his decision remains unknown. The court executed Spencer in May, but Gilmer commuted Alfred's sentence to banishment. He was taken to the state penitentiary and sold to a slave trader who took him out of Virginia. Alfred and Spencer's owner, Dennis Johnston, received compensation for the fair market value of the slaves he lost.[150]

Retaliation against patrollers constituted a form of slave resistance, but did not provoke the same fears or retribution brought on by rebellions or large-scale revolts. Alfred and Spencer plus their accomplices had a limited goal: to free their fellow slaves taken captive earlier that evening, not to escape to permanent freedom or to annihilate the entire slave-owning population. Retaliation by slaves against patrollers, or their homes, must have given at least a few patrolmen second thoughts about whether they wanted to perform their duties with vigor. Patrollers did not expect slave ambushes. When subjected to a bondsman's sudden assault, patrollers had little time to prepare their defenses, and anonymous attacks on their property provided no warning at all. Although attacks and damaged or lost property were unwelcome, their random, infrequent character made patrollers less fearful than hints about slave insurrections, which threatened the entire social structure of white Southern communities.

The episodic quality of revenge taken by slaves like Alfred and Spencer seemed minor when compared with events that could turn Southern race relations upside down. Slave revolts and actual or threatened wars against foreign enemies had that powerful potential, and Southern whites reacted much more forcefully against their slaves during periods of greater peril than during times of relative tranquility. If a slave revolt was ongoing or considered imminent, patrollers had a higher level of preparedness, and their forces were augmented by other white citizen groups. Wars and foreign conflicts provoked the same kinds of white response: the destructive or flight capabilities of all slaves were assumed, and slave patrollers stayed on full alert. Yet even in those dangerous times, the actions and responsibilities of slave patrols continued to be modeled on patroller activities in seasons of calm.

5

In Times of Crisis: Patrols during Rebellions and Wars

I found my short prophecy in regard to the Negroes was already fulfilled and that an insurrection was hourly expected. There had been a great number of them discovered in the adjoining woods the night before, most of them with arms, and a fellow belonging to Doctor Cobham was actually killed. All parties are now united against the common enemies. Every man is in arms and the patroles going thro' all the town, and searching every Negro's house, to see they are all at home by nine at night. But what is most provoking, every mouth male and female is opened against Britain, her King and their abettors—here called the tories.

> *Comment of Janet Schaw, an Englishwoman visiting*
> *Wilmington, North Carolina (1775)*

Slavery always has, and always will produce insurrections wherever it exists, because it is a violation of the natural order of things, and no human power can much longer perpetuate it.

> *Angelina Grimké, "Appeal to the Christian Women*
> *of the South" (1836)*

Keen observers like Janet Schaw in the eighteenth century or Angelina Grimké in the nineteenth recognized the volcanic power that rumbled just beneath the surface of Southern communities.[1] Although large-scale outbreaks of rebellious behavior by slaves remained relatively rare in North America, Schaw and Grimké both realized that human nature rejects enslavement and will fight against it, given the opportunity. At the onset of the American Revolution, Schaw predicted that rumors of freedom would reach the North Carolina bondsmen and turn them against their masters, whether Tory or patriot—and she was right. Grimké understood that even without a war, slavery bred insurrection. Most white Southerners, however, would have ignored or denied Schaw's and Grimké's observations. To admit that danger existed was to concede the possibility of fear; to admit that slaves posed a threat could undermine confidence in an entire way of life.

Slave patrols allowed Southern whites to overlook any day-to-day qualms they might have about slave restlessness. Their errant faith in the docile nature of bondsmen, plus their reliance on the coercion of overseers and patrollers, gave whites reassurance that all was well. And for the most part, that faith went untested: only sporadically did slaves collectively and openly challenge the racial authority system within which they lived and worked. As a result, slave patrols performed most of their duties in quiescent periods, between wars and slave rebellions. But patrols were originally designed to prevent or respond to the worst scenarios slave owners could imagine: slaves free to murder their masters or to run away without impediment. And the insurrections need not even be real for the danger to appear ominous—Southern whites, although they avoided reflecting on slave owning's perils, dreamed vivid racial nightmares. Both owners and nonowners could well imagine slave-created bloodbaths. Their terrors had a grain of truth, for wars and slave insurrections enhanced a bondsman's ability to fight or flee.[2] Indeed, the original impetus for the creation of slave patrols came when colonial legislatures recognized the very real slave-related hazards posed by wars or revolts.

For patrollers, wars and insurrections did not create exactly the same problems. During wartime slave owners would lose runaway slaves, and masters might have to overcome an enemy-inspired insurrection among their laborers. Foreign aggressors sought allies among Southern bondsmen, urging them to revolt, but the more likely outcome was that slaves would escape to enemy lines during wartime tumult. By contrast, during most revolts, riotous slaves plotted first to murder Southern whites and only later to run away, although few bondsmen actually escaped once the shooting started.[3] Not surprisingly, the alarm Southern whites experienced during insurrections usually far surpassed the concern they felt about their slaves during wars with foreign enemies. Patrols could expect full cooperation from Southern whites during both kinds of events, but they would have additional manpower at their disposal and receive greater attention for their actions during slave revolts.

Although slave revolts and wars rarely occurred in the American South, they did happen, albeit much less frequently than in the Caribbean or South America.⁴ Three of the largest revolts took place in South Carolina and Virginia: the Stono rebellion (1739) and the Denmark Vesey revolt (1822) in South Carolina, and the Nat Turner insurrection (1831) in Virginia. Even though actual rebellions happened infrequently, their effects loomed large in the sanguinary imaginations of Southern whites. Wars, by contrast, occurred regularly in the colonial period. The Spanish, French, and Native Americans all attempted to control the South before 1775. Its most numerous invaders were the British, who occupied parts of Virginia and the Carolinas during both the American Revolution and the War of 1812. As citizens of weak colonies and, later, as residents in a fledgling nation, white Virginians and Carolinians had good reason to fear the assistance foreign aggressors might offer their slaves. This chapter considers how slave patrols responded to these two British invasions as well as the changes wrought by slave revolts in Virginia and the Carolinas.

When an insurrection took place, or the rumor of an intended rebellion reached the notice of white slave owners, almost every aspect of regular slave patrols was altered. Their membership, pay, duties, and procedures changed to counter the increased threat that bondsmen presented. Similar adjustments took place when settlements were threatened by war or invasion by an external enemy; during these times, slave patrols became more active, and owners expected greater efforts by patrollers to preserve the white community's safety. Unlike the tranquil times described in the previous chapter, during wars or insurrections, patrols became more vigilant to hamper the movement of would-be runaway slaves. And yet, although the two have much in common, wars and rebellions did have different effects upon slave patrols. The departure of numerous white men from the local community during wartime, for example, created special problems that patrols would have to surmount in order to remain effective. Patrols were not the only ones to notice these changes; slaves understood the greater hazards of these times as well. Charles Ball stated that he knew patrollers "never lay out all night, except in times of danger."⁵

White Unpreparedness and the Likelihood of Slave Revolts

Slave patrols operated within Southern communities even when most white residents refused to acknowledge any vulnerability to their numerous slaves.[6] This unwillingness to practice caution became entrenched as the colonial period wore on, while concerned governors and local officials tried to reverse the trend. The mere presence of slave patrollers, reinforcing notions of white invincibility with midnight rides, may have contributed to this complacency. The more dangerous habits of Southern whites continued unabated, until rumored or real slave rebellions prompted greater support for patrollers. Then apathy gave way to terror and retribution.[7]

In the colonial era, British officials frequently complained about the ill-prepared state of white colonists to defend themselves against their own slaves. In 1712 Colonel Spotswood, lieutenant governor of Virginia, wrote that "the fear of the enemys by Sea (except Pirates) are now happily removed by the Peace . . . but the Insurrections of our own Negros, and the Invasions of the Indians, are no less to be dreaded, while the People are so stupidly averse to the only means they have left to protect themselves against either of these Events."[8] And five years before the American Revolution, South Carolina's lieutenant governor William Bull complained that patrol work was "through human frailty . . . neglected in these times of general tranquility."[9] Grand juries throughout the colonial period condemned men for carrying their guns to church and then handing them over to bondsmen during worship services, but the juries' presentments did not force widespread changes in slave owners' behavior.[10] Despite their apprehension that slaves would rebel, some slave owners persisted in risky practices that all but encouraged bondsmen to revolt, and it often took such a crisis to jolt white Southerners out of their complacency.

Throughout the colonial and antebellum eras, the most vulnerable time of the week for white residents was Sunday, when the majority of the population gathered for church services. In many insurrectionary plans, slaves plotted to attack whites while they were at church by burning the house of worship or killing whites as they left the blazing building.[11] One prime witness in the 1822 Vesey rebellion trials described how the slaves planned to kill white Charlestonians: "We will set the town on fire in different places, and as the whites come out we will slay them."[12] Patrols could not always deter slaves committed to violence. Indeed, the haphazard conduct of Charleston's patrols encouraged the Vesey conspirators to make even more daring plans. One of Vesey's accomplices reportedly told his compatriots that they could get weapons out of an arsenal "as soon as the patrol was slack."[13]

Cities commonly experienced insurrection scares during holidays like Christmas.[14] Towns employed extra patrols in holiday seasons, when there were large numbers of slaves moving from place to place, visiting relatives or enjoying a well-deserved respite from their labors. One of the first holiday-related revolts was quashed in 1766 before it ever began: Lieutenant Governor Bull told his British superiors that "[t]he vigorous execution of our Militia & Patrol Laws for 14 Days before and after Christmas Day . . . disconcerted their Schemes."[15] In 1797 Charleston had another insurrection scare during Christmas week. Newspapers described a clever plot: the powder stores would be blown up while people were in church, and slaves stationed at the church doors would "massacre the citizens as they came out." The bondsmen chose Christmas for their "liberation day" because "they supposed that almost every person would be in some one of the churches; and thus unarmed, or unprepared, fall an easy sacrifice."[16] In a letter to his wife, Robert Scott, a Virginia resident, described a nerve-wracking holiday in 1856. The night before Christmas, rumors of rebellion put the white men of his town on edge. Scott reported that white residents had their "guns loaded & every thing prepared to make a vigorous defence, guards were mounted and recruits called in, in fine the appearance presented must have been truly warlike." Scott was convinced that although the slaves might complain about constraints and the extra patrols, they could not carry out a revolt.[17] Fears about Christmas rebellions persisted even after the Civil War; rumors spread across the South that ex-slaves planned a December 1865 insurrection, a topic explored at greater length in Chapter 6.

Whether slave revolts ended with a massacre or mass flight mattered little to white Southerners: any bloodless getaway could eventually weaken slavery by providing fugitives with a successful example. All rebellions had to be crushed at their inception, every troublemaker recaptured and executed. Colonial and antebellum American slaves dreamed about running away and escaping from white society altogether. In 1729 several bondsmen on a James River plantation in Virginia planned an escape to the mountains and managed to flee with clothes, tools, and provisions. A group of men recaptured the runaways, but Lieutenant Governor William Gooch realized that if their plan had succeeded, the colony would have been placed in great danger. He knew long-term maroons lived in Jamaica's hills, and among other Caribbean islands, threatening the stability of slavery there by providing refuge and models to those still enslaved. And so Gooch wrote that if a small group established itself in the Blue Ridge Mountains, it "would very soon be encreas'd by the accesion of other Runaways and prove dangerous Neighbours to our frontier Inhabitants."[18] This possibility had to be rooted out at its very beginning, to prevent future slave rebelliousness.

As mountainous areas became more thickly settled, creating maroon slave communities remained an option only for slaves who could reach places that were still difficult to search. One such hiding place was the Great Dismal Swamp, along the Virginia–North Carolina border. After they entrenched themselves in the marshes, slaves could resist patrollers for years: the Englishman J. F. D. Smyth considered the Dismal Swamp inhabitants "perfectly safe . . . [and able to] elude the most diligent search of their pursuers."[19] In the colonial period, South Carolina lieutenant governor Bull preferred to use Catawba Indians rather than patrols to root out runaways who reached the swamps.[20] If they grew too bold, however, patrols would try to neutralize them. When large numbers of runaways living in the Dismal Swamp began plundering neighboring settlements, militia and patrol groups received orders to disperse the fugitives.[21] In 1795 Wilmington, North Carolina, was attacked by runaway slaves who hid in local swamps and looted outlying plantations. Hunting parties went into the marshes and killed five maroons in early July, then captured four more a few weeks later. The local editor wrote that "this town has nothing to apprehend as the citizens keep a strong and vigilant night guard."[22] Some twenty years later, one local newspaper advised the "patrol to keep a strict look out" when a large group of maroons gathered in central North Carolina.[23] But even swampy hinterlands could not keep out determined patrollers, particularly when a slave revolt occurred. Following the Turner rebellion, Gates County patrollers scoured the Juniper and Dismal swamps, catching twelve long-term runaways but not Turner's conspirators.[24]

With the growing slave population in the colonial era, it was, perhaps, only a matter of time before insurrections took place. Some African slaves arrived in North America with military training and experience, which doubtless contributed to colonial unrest.[25] In the 1720s the new lieutenant governor of Virginia, Hugh Drysdale, learned about the suppression of an intended revolt in several counties; he speculated that the defeated insurrection would have the effect of "stirring upp" the next legislative assembly to make stiffer laws to keep the "slaves in greater subjection."[26] When Drysdale appeared before the House of Burgesses in

1723, he told the legislators that "[y]our Laws seem very deficient." Given their "late Experience of the lameness" of those laws, Drysdale pushed for stiffer penalties. At the very least, the burgesses should "enquire whether any thing is wanting to enforce those Laws now in being," most notably by improving the militia of the colony.[27] The new laws, however, did not prevent slaves from repeatedly trying to rebel.[28] Like a lit match set next to a powder keg, the idea of freedom continued to place masters in the gravest danger from their own servants.

For patrollers in both the colonial and the antebellum periods, rumors of revolt and actual rebellions provoked similar responses, for white Southerners found it nearly impossible to distinguish between mere rumor and real revolts in their initial stages. Anyone, white or black, who tried to shield slaves from patrollers during those panicked times could receive abuse and physical torment.[29] Innocent slaves found themselves named as insurrectionary accomplices, particularly in areas where bondsmen outnumbered whites. After the Turner rebellion in 1831, slaves in Virginia and North Carolina were apprehended who clearly had no intention of rebelling, merely because someone wanted charges of insurrection brought against them.[30] Joseph Skinner, a North Carolinian, believed that patrols abused harmless bondsmen excessively during insurrection scares. "Not the least outrage has been here committed except by a few patrol . . . much more [is] to be apprehended from the rash unparalleled conduct of the whites than from an insurrection of the negroes."[31] Although Southern whites spent most of their time living in complacent vulnerability, when roused from their torpor, the mortal fear of slave rebellions frequently prompted overreactions.[32]

Patrol Reactions to Slave Revolts

Following the discovery of a slave rebellion, the responses by local patrols before and after the American Revolution form a consistent pattern. When slave patrollers found weapons or other evidence of a conspiracy among slaves, they moved swiftly. They seized all weapons and the suspected slaves were taken into custody. During the 1802 Virginia "Easter rebellion" (a plot formulated by quasi-free slaves who worked as boatmen on the extensive state waterways), patrollers found not guns but a letter naming fourteen men involved in the conspiracy. Patrollers confiscated the letter and detained each of the suspects.[33] Next patrollers handed over all evidence of the revolt and the accused slaves to local authorities—a justice of the peace or a slaveholders' court for trying slave crimes. Although patrols functioned as policelike agents, gathering evidence and suspects for these tribunals, they were not expected to mete out summary justice as they would normally do on regular patrol duty. Instead they investigated the revolt and brought additional evidence or implicated slaves to the court. The court or individual justices of the peace would then be responsible for questioning the bondsmen and reviewing the evidence before passing sentence. During their inquiries, the local jail could overflow with suspects brought in by active patrollers.[34] Thus, during suspected revolts, though slave patrols became much more active, they deliberately restrained themselves from acting as the final arbiters of a slave's fate. The kind of summary justice that patrols ordinarily dispensed—whipping or maltreating a slave—was of secondary importance to discovering the extent of any slave rebellion. Only officers of the court were entrusted with interrogating, torturing, and, if need be, executing a suspicious slave.[35] Little difference existed between colonial and antebellum patrollers when they were investigating a rumored rebellion; in a crisis, local authorities became much more involved in supervising patrol work because the safety of the white community demanded it.

The next level of patrol responses depended upon on how far city or county officials thought the revolt had spread. If required, extra patrols could be dispatched and maintained for a brief period of time.[36] When an insurrection was feared in Chesterfield County, Virginia, in 1810, officials dispatched twice the usual number of patrollers to quell the uprising; nearby Sussex County and Goochland County had done precisely the same thing in the 1760s and 1770s.[37] A few random acts of violence by slaves within a single, contained community could probably be suppressed by more slave patrols. But even with additional men and greater vigilance, patrols alone were thought to be an inadequate response to a large-scale insurrection. Typically, if the rebellion was (or was believed to be) a large one, senior militia officers would be alerted and whole militia units could be called up for service. When Nottoway County patrollers uncovered the 1802 Virginia slave revolt, Petersburg and Richmond militia went on duty, supplementing local patrols.[38] While the militia armed, patrols continued to operate, and eventually the patrols could be subsumed within larger militia units.[39]

Extra patrols might be created through regular appointments by militia captains and county courts, or by local residents in ad hoc fashion. News from Virginia about the 1831 Turner insurrection led Caswell County officials in North Carolina to appoint an extremely large number of men as patrols for the next three months.[40] Back in Virginia, when residents there discovered "hostile designs among the negroes," Joseph Cabell declared that "[w]e shall have a meeting of the neighbours on Friday next, to organize a regular system of patrols."[41] At their meeting, the men grouped themselves into virtually an armed cavalry corps, far better equipped than average patrol groups.[42] Informal patrol groups in North Carolina did not even demand payment for their services when rebellion rumors surfaced.[43] Even though slave owners might say that insurrection rumors they heard were groundless and exaggerated, no one was willing to sit idly by and wait. After patrollers of Bertie County, North Carolina, found evidence indicating an incipient revolt in 1802, patrollers and militia all across eastern North Carolina were out in force, interrogating bondsmen they encountered on the road and searching every slave quarter.[44] In Raleigh, North Carolina, news of the Turner revolt put the patrol of that city "on guard around the clock for several weeks."[45] In Wilmington, a mother wrote her son that he should not worry for her safety: "nearly all the citizens have been under arms, almost constantly, for the last 11 days," and she believed the crisis had passed.[46]

After an insurrection scare, with the white community's weaknesses exposed, Southern men normally exempt from patrol duty served as extra patrollers. In the wake of a slave revolt in 1816, the South Carolinian Rachel Blanding wrote her Philadelphia cousin that even "the Doctor was out on Guard" and a strong guard had been placed on the jail where the slave conspirators were incarcerated.[47] When the bloody outcome of the Turner revolt became known, few scrupled to work as patrols: V. J. Trist wrote her husband that "[a]ll the gentlemen about here are belonging to the band of patrolers."[48] Even North Carolina men who ordinarily refused to carry arms, claiming "freedom of conscience," formed patrol groups when insurrection rumors began to fly. Moravian brethren set up extra night watches in the wake of the Turner revolt.[49] Multiple patrol groups swept through suspected areas, stopping the same slaves again and again. After the 1822 Vesey revolt, Jesse Blackwood, a bondsman, told others that he had been "allowed to pass by two parties of the patrol on the road, but that a third party had brought him back."[50] Whether rumored or real, insurrection scares had their most brutal effect upon slaves, who could hardly withstand the fury of well-armed yet apprehensive whites. White terror led to black terror as militia and patrol groups roamed the countryside looking for victims.

White residents remained uneasy until extra patrols and militia went on duty and the conspirators were caught and punished. After the Vesey rebellion, E. M. Starr, a hatter in Charleston, wrote to a business colleague in Connecticut that "[t]he alarm has subsided and the guard increased so that I think there is no danger to be apprehended from the slaves"—nearly sixty men had been jailed and seven slaves hanged in the previous few weeks.[51] In the wake of the Turner revolt, James Allen wrote his son that he thought nothing would happen, because the slaves were overawed and subdued; at the hint of any new threat, large groups of patrols went out, often several groups each night.[52] Mary McPhail wrote that in Norfolk "we have stricter order observed in the town than i ever saw there is a regular guard provided and a garrison is about to be established."[53]

Whether the revolt was large or small, genuine or imagined, extra patrols conducted interrogations and searched for slave weapons. The young slave Harriet Jacobs vividly described how patrols behaved at the height of the Turner insurrection scare: every home in the town was to be searched, and she knew it would be done by patrols augmented with country ruffians and poor whites. She thought the impoverished whites who joined the patrollers exulted in the task because it gave them the opportunity to "exercise a little brief authority, and show their subserviency to the slaveholders." During the day, they searched houses, and in the night "they formed themselves into patrol bands, and went wherever they chose among the colored people, acting out their brutal will." White men ransacked her house and then proceeded to search the home of every slave and free black who lived outside the city. For two weeks, the patrols abused the bondsmen and free blacks by whipping them, throwing them in jail, and stealing their belongings. "The day patrol continued for some weeks, and at sundown a night guard was substituted." Regular meetings that attracted slaves and free blacks received extra attention from patrols during periods of tension. North Carolina patrollers stopped blacks and questioned them as they emerged from Moravian worship services in September 1831. Finally, with Nat

Turner caught and the rebellion suppressed, affairs returned to their previous state.[54]

The searches and interrogations spared no one, not even white Southerners. While Wilmington residents struggled to put out the latest in a string of suspicious fires thought to be set by an insurrectionary arsonist in the 1840s, patrols stopped a white woman in the street because she was seen carrying bundles away from a shop. Her crime: helping a man evacuate his business records, which happened to be too close to the flames. From a distance they thought she was a person of color, so they demanded her pass.[55] In the aftermath of the Turner rebellion, patrols also searched homes of both rich and poor whites, and did not always stop to ask permission of their inhabitants. V. J. Trist wrote her husband that the cellar of their home had been searched twice in the preceding week, and she learned of the intrusions only after the patrollers had gone.[56]

Vigilance by additional patrols certainly seemed to promote white community safety. When news reached officials concerning an intended revolt in Virginia, Norfolk's mayor, John Cowper, formed a "strong patrole of the citizens" to cordon off his city and take up any suspicious-looking slaves. The men Cowper's patrols captured soon exposed the extent to which the 1802 Easter rebellion had spread, allowing Virginia authorities to crush the insurrection utterly.[57] In another case, auxiliary patrols staved off the beginning of a well-planned uprising. When rumors about the impending Vesey plot reached Charleston's mayor in 1822, he had city patrols pick up two slaves known to have discussed the intended revolt. When their information led nowhere, the mayor "strengthened his patrols, armed his men for extensive action, and waited."[58] With the city guard in readiness for an insurrection, "patrols were ordered on duty with loaded arms." This last detail is noteworthy because "the guard had previously gone on duty without muskets, with sheathed bayonets and bludgeons."[59] Armed and alerted, the extra patrols discouraged bondsmen from taking action on Sunday the 16th, the day originally intended for the uprising.[60]

After the discovery of a slave revolt, patrols were often given specific directions about when and where they were expected to be active.[61] Patrols during periods of unrest typically received precise instructions about their work, unlike normal times, in which they had almost complete freedom to decide how often and where they patrolled. One of the first steps taken by Virginia lieutenant governor Gooch after the 1730 slave rebellion was the "speedy appointment of Partys of the Militia" who were sent out to patrol. He mandated that all patrols be active two or three times a week to prevent all-night meetings, and he gave special orders that all men should carry their arms to church. The extra patrollers took up many slaves found "rambling abroad," and Gooch hoped that these events would inspire the regular militia and patrols to become even more active.[62] After the Turner rebellion, many of the escaped bondsmen fled to the swamps to elude their pursuers. Following explicit orders, the patrols and militia companies searched the swamps and surrounded houses where those slaves were thought to be hiding.[63]

Special signals accompanied these specific directions. During insurrections, officials created distinctive signals to alert patrollers about any new threat, so that they could gather at strategic points and defend their homes from attack if necessary. After discovery of the Vesey plot, Lieutenant Colonel William Yeadon ordered every man with "Patriotism and Honour" in town to assemble upon the signal of drums beating "the Long Roll or To Arms" and the firing of a cannon three times in succession. Bells alone would indicate fire, not an attempted insurrection.[64] Informal groups of patrols, ignorant of these particular signals, created even more confusion when they fired their rifles simply to intimidate slaves.[65] Unusual community signals could be misused or misunderstood, causing even more hysteria. William Byrd Harrison, a Virginia resident, wrote that "a ridiculous scene occured" when a false alarm was given. "[T]he bells began to toll furiously about 10 or 11 oclock, which was to be the signal in case the negroes actually rose" and so the community's white women ran to the town center, where they were to stay for protection—many women arrived wearing only their nightdresses. A white man inadvertently started the commotion by striking his new drum a few times before going to bed; others heard the noise and raised the alarm.[66]

Rebellion (and rumors of revolt) respected no boundaries, and responses to them also knew no state limits. In the immediate aftermath of Virginia's Nat Turner rebellion, the first state militia to arrive came from Murfreesboro, North Carolina, since they were so close to the border county of Southampton—only sixteen miles away.[67] After the 1793 rebellion on the island of St. Domingue, the mayors of Petersburg and Richmond coordinated a simultaneous search of all slaves in their large, adjacent towns. Volunteer guards and patrols busily watched slaves in all other parts of the state as well, scrutinizing every move for anything vaguely rebellious.[68] The influx of refugees to the South from St. Domingue worried officials in Virginia and the Carolinas: how could they prevent their slaves from learning of the successful Caribbean revolt? After banning the importation of slaves from that island, Virginia's legislature increased the punishment for inciting a slave revolt to the death penalty. Near Georgetown, South Carolina, rumors spread that French blacks had landed on their shores in 1802. Governor John Drayton organized a coastal patrol with lookouts, and militia general Peter Horry commanded that Georgetown residents use their militia reserves (alarm men) as a slave patrol. Ironically, these unfounded rumors originated from a commander of the local slave patrol, Peter Nicholson, who lived on the coast.[69] Even with extra protection provided by patrollers, the news from St. Domingue made one Carolinian write "we dread the future."[70]

Slave revolts did not even need to occur in a neighboring county to cause consternation among whites and greater vigilance among patrols. The possibility that an insurrection might spread from one place to another hung like a Damoclean sword over the heads of all white community leaders. The least hint of revolt alerted every official, and governors regularly wrote to one another for the details of slave uprisings.[71] This was particularly true in South Carolina, whose large slave population entailed greater vigilance on the part of its patrols. After receiving news of unrest in Virginia and Maryland, South Carolina's governor Charles Pinckney wrote to his militia company commanders, ordering the "strict and regular performance of the duties of patrole" because "the security of this country depends upon their attention to the Militia Laws, and particularly the duties of Patrole."[72] After hearing about Gabriel's rebellion in Virginia, South Carolina governor Drayton swung into action, writing to his Virginia counterpart, James Monroe, for specifics about the event. At the same time Drayton sent out general orders to all parts of his state for the "patrole law of this state, to be enforced strictly, and steadily," and urged the general assembly to strengthen the laws governing slaves and freed slaves.[73]

Once a threatened revolt seemed fully subdued, the increased number of patrols soon returned to their pre-insurrection state. Even uprisings of great magnitude could not spur whites to maintain their heightened vigilance indefinitely. Only a few short months after the Stono rebellion, for example, a Charleston resident commented that the citizens had grown "fatigued" from "keeping Guard in Town" all through Christmas.[74] Several hundred slaves planned to march on Richmond in Gabriel's abortive 1800 rebellion; once the plot was discovered, "[m]ilitia companies were posted at the penitentiary and the capitol, and patrols swept the outskirts of the city and arrested any slave suspected of taking part in the conspiracy."[75] For days, Richmond resembled an armed camp with a small standing army in its midst.[76] Yet even the direst threat, a massacre like Nat Turner's rebellion, could not provoke whites to continue their extreme vigilance in perpetuity. One short month after the Turner revolt, a North Carolina militia commander wrote that even though he ordered out strong patrols every night, when it came to getting men to patrol "there are many in this County who are quite refractory & scarcely can be brought to do their turn of service." The Carolinians complained that they did not own slaves, were uncertain whether they would be paid for patrolling, and therefore were unwilling to be patrollers.[77] With the decreased postrevolt activity of most patrols, it is not surprising that some former bondsmen, like Irene Robertson of South Carolina, believed slave patrols existed only during times of slave rebellion.[78] Since colonial and antebellum patrols became much more active and visible when insurrections occurred, her inaccurate impression is understandable.

Postinsurrectionary Efforts to Strengthen Patrols

The recurrent problem of insurrections and the intermittent quality of patrols prompted authorities before and after the American Revolution to consider various means of strengthening patrol and militia laws.[79] Merely knowing the law would improve security; quite a few localities had patrol laws reprinted following an insurrection.[80] One proposal, made in the wake of a slave revolt, would have altered South Carolina's patrol laws so that patrollers could enter plantations, note any slave absences, and then whip the missing slaves whenever they were next encountered. Beatings would not be inflicted if the slaves could produce adequate excuses for the earlier absences. This procedure would close a loophole in the existing patrol law, which required the patrol to catch a slave at the time he or she was off the plantation illegally. The proposed law was unsupported in the legislature, and it died in committee.[81] The proposal failed for several reasons. First, no owner would willingly give up the right to whip missing slaves to a stranger, even to a patroller performing his legal duty; this could weaken paternalistic bonds and even encourage slaves who had run away never to return. Further, the law would have been too stringent for a slave who had legitimate reasons to leave a plantation (for example, to visit a spouse or sick child on a neighboring plantation) but who failed to obtain a pass. In addition, the lawmakers might have thought that the proposed law would make it too easy for patrollers to visit plantations and neglect other slave gathering places; patrollers were expected to watch local roads and search less visible places in the woods where bondsmen might meet to trade stolen goods or plan their next revolt.

Sometimes efforts to improve local security focused on changing slave owners' behavior to make patrollers' work easier. Following the Stono insurrection, South Carolina legislators considered passing an unusual law: slave owners would be required to give patrols lists specifying every male slave so that "every Slave might be called by Name, when the Patrols should visit the Plantations." Patrollers needed this information, yet they could not trust slaves to provide it fully and accurately. A roll call of bondsmen would certainly simplify the patrollers' job, since they would no longer have to rely solely upon their memories of which slave belonged where. Surprisingly, the Commons House rejected this simple requirement with no debate.[82]

Following the 1822 Vesey revolt, slave patrollers again requested an accurate local slave census, compiled by whites, to aid them in controlling slave movement. Charleston Neck patrollers asked that absentee owners furnish patrollers with a list of slaves expected to be present on their farms, along with the name of the head slave in charge (this despite state laws that prohibited absentee owners from leaving slaves completely unattended, with no white supervision). Whether patrollers succeeded in making masters comply remains unknown, but seems unlikely.[83] This tool for their work could have been a tremendous help to slave patrols. One possible reason owners would not provide it was the constantly changing numbers of their slave property and, particularly for the plantations near Charleston, the practice of regularly sending bondsmen to town for goods, mail, or errands. If the slaves present and absent constantly fluctuated, no census could ever be accurate. A more subtle explanation may also exist. Slave owners could have resented the notion of having to account for their slaves to any authority but themselves; the very process of making and submitting a list to another white man might suggest submission and a denial of white independence, an inability to manage one's slaves without another man's interference.[84]

Although slave uprisings resulted in strengthened patrol regulations, and a few cities like Richmond created new guard units as a preventative measure to stave off future revolts, little could be done permanently to prevent slaves from rebelling.[85] Every rumor about possible freedom seemed to reach the remotest slave cabin. Reports of the successful 1790s slave revolt in Haiti, solicitations from northern abolitionists after the 1820s, or news about the West Indian slaves' emancipation in 1833 arrived in far-flung slave quarters, although Southern whites did everything possible to interdict such knowledge.[86] Even in the colonial period, when bondsmen were more widely dispersed, false rumors spread like wildfire about their impending emancipation. For example, the Virginia slave revolt in 1730 sprang in part from reports that the English king had ordered colonial authorities to free all Christian slaves, but the order had been suppressed by Virginia owners.[87] Whether they lived in the colonial or the antebellum period, when slaves believed they could expect outside help in their freedom quests, they took even greater chances to reach those (usually foreign) allies whose support might set them free. Rumors of liberation took more concrete form whenever white Southerners went to war with a foreign power. Only extra patrols and additional enforcement efforts restrained slaves from becoming more agitated when they believed that their freedom was at hand.

Wartime and the Fear of Slave Revolt

Although war might initially cause excitement among Southern military men, their enthusiasm for battle was tempered by the prospect of facing internal security threats as well as external dangers. Residents of Virginia and the Carolinas regularly confronted this difficulty, simultaneously controlling their own slave residents and fighting foreign enemies. The dual dilemma existed almost from the first settlement's founding, and was renewed with every foreign conflict. For South Carolinians, conflict with the Spanish remained ever present during the colonial era, but securing whites from their own slaves took top priority: when

Governor Thomas Broughton fretted about possible Spanish invasion in 1737, he doubled the number and strength of local slave patrols and used Cherokee warriors to prevent a slave uprising.[88] During the war against the Dutch in the late seventeenth century, Virginia's officials grew concerned that slaves and indentured servants posed a security threat to their colony.[89] These fears returned during the French and Indian War (1754–1763); South Carolina's governor James Glen mentioned his fears about the possibility of slave rebellion in his message to the legislature and the London Board of Trade.[90] Virginia's lieutenant governor Robert Dinwiddie likewise feared the prospect that Virginia slaves would aid the French, taking advantage of the conflict to gain their freedom. He told Charles Carter in 1755 that he should condemn any slaves caught conspiring during the war, and in the meantime Carter should "act consist[en]t with Y[ou]r good Sense in keeping Patrollers out for the Peace of Y[ou]r Co[un]ty."[91]

Shows of strength and firepower, in addition to extra patrols, provided psychic relief to those white citizens who feared their slaves during wartime. Even before the Revolution, when harassed by the Spanish from the south, citizens of Charleston feared what simultaneous attacks from within and without might produce. After Spanish incursions into Georgia in the 1740s, one Charleston merchant expressed relief that a British man of war would be stationed off the coast, not only to keep the Spanish in line, but also to "keep our Domesticks in awe."[92] Rumors and plots kept surfacing in the French and Indian War, and again when the Indians spared the lives of slaves during Pontiac's uprising (1763–64): "As the Indians are saving & Carressing all the Negroes they take, should it be productive of an Insurrection it may be attended with the most serious Consequences."[93] During the Stamp Act crisis of 1765, "some Negroes had mimick'd their betters in crying 'Liberty,' " which caused great consternation among Charleston's white residents. Henry Laurens reported that, in response, "[p]atrols were riding day & Night for 10 or 14 days in the most bitter weather," which calmed some residents' anxieties, though Laurens thought "there was little or no cause" for real alarm.[94]

The greatest wartime perils confronted white Southerners when their territory was invaded, as in the American Revolution and the War of 1812. Prior to the Civil War, these two conflicts presented slaves in particular areas with their best opportunities for fight or flight. The internal stresses generated by the Revolution gave bondsmen new hope that they might claim their freedom before the war ended. Any time a British army group or ship from the British navy came near a Southern plantation, slaves were quick to take advantage of the opportunity to gain their freedom.

Southern slave owners were not the only ones who seemed cognizant of the likelihood of wartime slave rebellion or flight. Before the Revolutionary War began, British observers and colonial loyalists certainly expected that rebel planters would be less likely to defy the Crown because of the large number of bondsmen they owned. This was particularly true in South Carolina, with its black majority. As Christopher Gadsden explained, South Carolina was a "very weak Province, . . . and [the] great part of our weakness (though at the same time 'tis part of our riches) consists in having such a number of slaves amongst us . . . slavery begets slavery."[95] South Carolina's situation mirrored the anxieties of its slaveholding neighbors during the Revolution. White Virginians worried that the chaos of war would only breed opportunities for slave insurrections or, worse, that the British would do everything in their power to encourage a general rebellion among the slaves.[96]

The American Revolution

By the mid-1770s incessant rumors circulated that the British would not merely incite the slaves to revolt, but would go so far as to arm them against their white masters.[97] As early as 1774, the Virginian Arthur Lee read a pamphlet in London which suggested that the patriots might not go to war if their slaves were inspired to revolt against them. Likewise, James Madison thought a bill freeing slaves had been introduced in Parliament, although no such bill has ever been located.[98] This type of volatile gossip spread with lightning speed. In May 1775 the *South-Carolina Gazette* printed a letter from London in which the writer speculated that the English government had sent 78,000 guns to America to "put into the hands of N*****s ."[99] "Perhaps nothing could have corroded the ties of loyalty that still bound South Carolina whites to Britain so quickly as a fear that its ministry might be in secret league with their slaves."[100] While the patriots might be uncertain about how to respond to a British military attack, they knew how best to forestall a threatened slave insurrection: call out more armed patrols. The Charleston General Committee responded quickly, ordering city inhabitants to patrol every night in the summer of 1775; meanwhile, the first Provincial Congress ordered three militia companies to patrol the city day and night.[101] South Carolina's governor, Lord William Campbell, newly arrived in the colony, found himself accused of having transported arms for the slaves in the ship that had borne him from England. Campbell thought Charleston's "ceaseless militia and slave patrols" only incited slaves to think rebellious thoughts, rather than prevent them.[102] Moreover, the belief that one royal governor planned to arm slaves in rebellion led to rumors that other royal governors had similar plans. North Carolina's governor Josiah Martin wrote that "a most infamous report . . . [was] propagated among the people that I had formed a design of arming the Negroes and proclaiming freedom to all such as should resort to the King's standard."[103]

The British were not the only ones who could play upon the fears of slave insurrection to achieve their own ends. In one instance, patriots also used the ostensible threat of slave insurrections during the Revolution to arm slave patrols: the armed men could then be deployed against local British military forces. In Charleston, after the royal lieutenant governor retired to the country for the summer season in 1775, Charles Pinckney, the local militia colonel, ordered inhabitants to "do Patrole Duty and to Mount Guard every night, which duty had till then been done by a Town Guard." A loyalist wryly noted that "the Reason assigned for this Order was Certain information which they pretended to have received that an Insurrection of the negroes was meditated." In fact, the patrolling pretext placed arms and ammunition in the hands of every man associated with the rebel cause.[104]

After the Revolutionary War began, South Carolina and Virginia both required more men to assist regular slave patrols. The demands of the military created a dire shortage of men available to patrol; meanwhile, some plantations had no white supervision at all.[105] Supplementary men, typically overseers who could not legally be inducted into the militia, often worked together as units to control slaves, supporting other patrol groups.[106] Enlisting overseers as additional patrollers vexed some colonial residents, who believed that these supplementary patrollers exploited the slave patrol needs of their state to avoid serving in the militia, at a time when the revolutionary cause was going poorly.[107] Many Virginia residents protested the use of overseers as supplementary patrollers. For example, 259 people in Amelia County, Virginia, petitioned state authorities, saying that there were more than 250 overseers capable of bearing arms and that they should be compelled to do more than just patrol duty. The petitioners showed their mistrust of the overseers left behind when they said that "we apprehend [the duty of patrolling] will be done but slightly if intirely trusted to them"; they wanted the overseers to share the hazards of war with the other men called to arms.[108] Other residents worried that despite the additional patrollers, the overall patrol work done was too lax during such a tense war period. Such laxity, they thought, only encouraged slaves in their rebellious tendencies.[109] In 1779 North Carolina responded by increasing the fines of men who refused to patrol.

Just as some men sought to avoid patrol work, others surprisingly embraced it during wartime struggles. Moravian men who claimed "freedom of conscience" and who would not fight the British took up arms as patrollers when reports of slave revolts circulated. Following the rumors about royal governors Campbell and Martin, New Bern's Committee of Safety warned that "there is much Reason to fear, in these Times of general Tumult and Confusion, that the Slaves may be instigated and encouraged by our inveterate Enemies to an Insurrection, which in our present defenceless State might have the most dreadful Consequences." The committee urged the Moravians and other whites in neighboring counties to scour suspected places and "to patrol and search the Negro Houses."[110] The historian Jon Sensbach ironically describes the contradictory behavior of Moravian brethren who pleaded exemption from actual military service during the Revolution while hoarding "arms and ammunition in case of a slave uprising."[111]

As in peacetime, rumors of slave revolts during the Revolution were more common than actual rebellions. One such rumor launched an extremely active response by patrollers in North Carolina. In July 1775 reports of an intended slave revolt in Beaufort, Pitt, Edgecombe, and Craven counties caused the Pitt County Committee of Safety to place patrollers on alert and order them to shoot any slaves found armed who did not surrender their weapons. Even after ten or more slaves were punished, rumors persisted that more slaves were arming themselves, and the whites posted guards along the roads at night.[112] Alarmed by rumors, Edenton whites formed a guard of eight men to patrol the town nightly in May 1775.[113] Even patrollers, though, had divided allegiances in the Revolution. In 1777 North Carolina loyalist John Llewelyn encouraged patroller David Taylor to incite Chowan County slaves to run away and then capture rebel governor Richard Caswell. The plot unraveled when the patriotic Taylor revealed Llewelyn's schemes to local authorities.[114]

Genuine slave revolts occurred infrequently during the Revolution, but one such instance provides unusual insight into how local patrollers responded. The thriving port town of Wilmington, North Carolina, had a large slave population, and in 1775 experienced a short-lived revolt in which great numbers of bondsmen took to the woods with weapons and were hunted down by whites. In consequence, the Wilmington Committee of Safety disarmed all slaves and ordered "Patrols to search for, and take from Negroes, all kinds of Arms whatsoever."[115] During this same uneasy time, Janet Schaw, a visitor to Wilmington, attended a dinner far from her own lodgings; afraid for her safety, Schaw delayed returning to her residence that night "till the Midnight patrol arrived." It was commanded by an acquaintance, who escorted her home. She wrote that "under his protection therefore I marched off at the head of a party stopping at the different houses in our way to examine if the Negroes were at home . . . While the men went into the houses, I stayed without with the commander."[116] Temporarily, the slave revolt caused Wilmington patriots and Tories to put aside their differences to confront the danger the slaves presented.[117] Patrols searched the homes of all slaves, a curfew was imposed, and the revolt was suppressed.[118]

In Virginia, a few counties like Richmond began to pay their patrollers at a high rate to encourage them to be active on their rounds. Prior to the war, county officials had paid patrollers small amounts for their nightly work. County levies during the Revolution reveal the heightened concern Virginia officials felt about controlling slave movement through more rigorous patrols. For example, total expenditures for all Richmond County jobs and services in 1776 were estimated at 18,272 pounds of tobacco, of which 6,920 pounds, or roughly one-third, was paid to nineteen men for patrolling that year. By the following year, Richmond authorities had reduced their expenditures on patrols to 3,915 pounds of tobacco, nearly a quarter of the annual budget. Even in 1781, close to the war's conclusion, patrols still constituted, by far, the largest single item in the county's budget. Only when the war was over did patrol expenditures drop below 17 percent of Richmond County's annual expenses.[119]

British Intervention and Dunmore's Proclamation

The slaves certainly knew they could obtain their freedom with the help of the British, if they waited for the right moment. The mere arrival of British troops in Norfolk from St. Augustine produced insurrectionary tendencies among slaves in the vicinity.[120] In the South Carolina trial held after the discovery of a suspected 1775 revolt, one slave, Sambo, reported that another slave had suggested that when war with the British began, the slaves should "[j]ump on shore, and join the [British] soldiers," for "the war was come to help the poor negroes."[121]

Colonial authorities recognized the dangers they faced, and both the Committees of Safety and the new independent governors (in their capacities as commanders-in-chief of the militia) used their authority to order patrols to be more vigilant.[122] Shortly after the battles of Lexington and Concord, the clerk of the Virginia Committee of Safety in Williamsburg sent a circular letter to all the commanding officers of county militia. The commander in Westmoreland County received direct orders from the committee to begin training and equipping his men, in apprehension of attacks by both land and sea. In the postscript the committee's clerk, John Pendleton, enjoined him to "Keep up a regular patrol."[123] This injunction was reiterated six weeks later, when the newly chosen governor, Patrick Henry, repeated the order in another circular letter to county militia commanders. (See Figure 10.) Taking note of Dunmore's proclamation, Henry wrote on November 20, 1775, "I take the Liberty to enclose you a Copy of the Proclamation issued by Lord Dunmore; the Design and Tendency of which, you will observe, is fatal to the publick Safety. An early and unremitting Attention to the Government of the SLAVES may, I hope, counteract this dangerous Attempt. Constant, and well directed Patrols, seem indispensably necessary."[124]

In the six months prior to his November proclamation, Dunmore did not openly announce his intention of inviting slaves to rebel, although he had plans to do so as early as March 1775.[125] During that six-month period, Dunmore "initiated a policy of unofficial slave solicitation" by sending small ships to coastal areas and inviting slaves aboard.[126] "For nearly a year, Dunmore led or ordered spoiling operations along Virginia's waterways, causing considerably more fear than havoc."[127] Bondsmen were more likely to run away to the British than to rebel and kill their masters, although insurrection rumors abounded in Chesterfield and Prince Edward counties, Norfolk, and Williamsburg. "Throughout the war, blacks capitalized on the unsettled conditions brought on by civil strife, roving armies, and the weakened mechanisms of control to seek their freedom. Wherever the British army marched, slaves followed."[128] And Virginians knew their vulnerability, even before Dunmore made public his declaration: in June 1775 James Madison wrote to his friend William Bradford that "[i]t has been imagined our Governor has been tampering with the Slaves & that he has it in contemplation to make great Use of them in case of a civil war in this province. To say the truth, that is the only part in which this colony is vulnerable; & if we should be subdued, we shall fall like Achilles by the hand of one that knows that secret."[129] In response to Dunmore's depredations and anticipating armed conflict with the British, Virginians organized themselves into independent companies. This generated some confusion about which Virginia groups should take responsibility for slave patrolling at the outset of the Revolution.[130] Despite the confusion, however, white

SIR,

AS the Committee of Safety is not fitting, I take the Liberty to enclose you a Copy of the Proclamation issued by Lord **Dunmore**; the Design and Tendency of which, you will observe, is fatal to the publick Safety. An early and unremitting Attention to the Government of the S L A V E S may, I hope, counteract this dangerous Attempt. Constant, and well directed Patrols, seem indispensably necessary. I doubt not of every possible Exertion, in your Power, for the publick Good; and have the Honour to be, Sir,

Your most obedient and very humble Servant,

P. H E N R Y.

HEAD QUARTERS, WILLIAMSBURG, *November* 20, 1775.

10. Patrick Henry broadside, 1755

Virginians scoured the coastline, "patrolling the porous coast, securing canoes and small craft" to prevent slave escapes to the enemy.[131]

Dunmore finally declared martial law and issued his famous proclamation on November 7, 1775, granting the freedom of all indentured servants and slaves (belonging to the rebels) "that are able and willing to bear Arms" and who joined the British against the rebels.[132] Dunmore was well aware of the vulnerability that planters faced if their laborers chose to revolt, and wrote that "[m]y declaration that I would arm and set free such slaves as should assist me if I was attacked has stirred up fears in them which cannot easily subside as they know how vulnerable they are in that particular."[133] Slave owners could not countenance the change in British policy: how could the British, who had represented law and order in colonial government, actively encourage lawlessness and disorder by slaves against their masters? Colonists believed that if they published the news of any offer like Dunmore's, "20,000 Negroes would join" the British army from South Carolina and Georgia.[134] Rebel officers stationed militia and patrols along the Virginia coastline to prevent Dunmore's troops from passing across it and to prevent slaves from joining Dunmore's men.[135] Newspapers published the proclamation in full, to inform and warn outlying areas. As a result, patrol groups doubled in towns like Williamsburg, watching local roadways—for a brief time, white Virginians became an exceptionally vigilant community.[136]

Estimates of whether slaves responded to or ignored Dunmore's proclamation varied. News of the unrest among slaves caused by the proclamation was exaggerated, according to Matthew Pope, who wrote to an English friend that wrong and malicious accounts of slave behavior were being circulated—revolt was not contemplated. Pope enclosed a clipping with his letter that said a "strict patrol" was being kept in Yorktown.[137] Pope, however, would not have found agreement among the many Virginia planters who lost slaves during this time. John Banister wrote in 1781 that although general orders existed at British headquarters to destroy tobacco and leave other property unmolested, "they have taken almost all the Negroes on the River, with the Stocks of Cattle & Horses." He expected to lose the rest of his slaves to the British before the war's end.[138] Similarly, Robert Carter Nicholas complained that the British did not wait passively for bondsmen to reach their lines, but sent boats "up the Rivers, plundering Plantations and using every Art to seduce the Negroes."[139]

Many Virginians lost slaves either to the British or to slave patrols who caught them trying to reach the British. Bondsmen recaptured by patrols during the war were usually jailed and sometimes sent to the state-owned lead mines. Many slaves so captured died while in the state's keeping and were effectively lost to their owners.[140] Large slave owners like John Willoughby or Edmund Pendleton regularly petitioned the state legislature for recompense in either case: Willoughby's slaves went to the British, while Pendleton's ended up in the lead mines, but both men's slaves sought the freedom offered by Dunmore's proclamation.[141] As Pendleton observed, when the British plundered the homes of rebels, the slaves departed as "willing captives."[142]

Despite the fact that Virginians increased the number of patrols (and in some cases their pay) to allow almost constant vigilance over their bondsmen, large numbers of slaves fled to the British, although how many successfully reached Dunmore has never been precisely determined. British armies moved up and down Virginia's rivers many times, and the historian Allan Kulikoff concludes that three thousand to five thousand slaves managed to join Dunmore's forces.[143] Of course once Dunmore was forced off the mainland in December 1775, any slaves seeking shelter with him had to come by water.[144] That considerable numbers of slaves could and did join Dunmore suggests that however vigilant patrollers along the Virginia coast were, even their best efforts could barely restrain determined slaves who sought refuge with the British. Of course, slaves (and their owners) became aware that that refuge might disappear for good once the royal governor and the off-coast Royal Navy vessels departed Virginia's shores. In July 1776 Dunmore and the British did just that, leaving the Virginia coast and setting sail to the south with many colonial slaves.[145] Dunmore's withdrawal did not abate the threat that slaves might aid the British: General Henry Clinton renewed Dunmore's offer in June 1779, promising freedom to slaves (of patriots) who agreed to help the British for the rest of the war.[146]

The movement of the war to the Deep South in 1778 raised great concerns for South Carolina's slave owners. "What had been a trickle of runaways in 1775–1776 became a flood after the British inaugurated their southern offensive in late 1778."[147] The offensive merely heightened fears Southerners felt at the war's outset: as early as 1776, Georgia sent slave patrols over the Savannah River into South Carolina to search slave quarters for weapons that could aid the British or be used in rebellion.[148]

In April 1778 Charleston militia leaders ordered patrols out on duty every night at ten o'clock, to continue on guard until dawn. Local officials added new restrictions on slave movement in 1780, after the British captured Charleston.[149] Although the British threat seemed less severe at the very end of the war, observers still worried about bondsmen finding ways to reach the British. Even in 1783 "An Old Suffering Merchant" sent an open letter to the *South-Carolina Weekly Gazette*, warning other Charlestonians to "keep a strict eye over your black walking property." But knowing how many slaves had attained literacy, he described his fears in roundabout fashion, stating that "[i]t would be highly improper to explain in a newspaper" why he thought they might find their way to enemy lines. By war's end, South Carolina runaways numbered upwards of 10,000, and contemporary estimates of slaves who stole themselves ranged as high as 55,000 for the whole South.[150]

At the close of the Revolutionary War, unrest and numerous manumissions led to stricter regulations governing free blacks and to renewed efforts to control runaways. North Carolina's General Assembly in 1785 ordered free blacks in the urban areas of Wilmington, Washington, Edenton, and Fayetteville to register with town commissioners and wear a badge on their left shoulder proclaiming them to be free blacks.[151] These regulations ultimately made the work of city patrollers easier in the years to come. Meanwhile, in 1787 South Carolina's assembly recruited Catawbas to kill or capture runaway slaves living in maroon communities on the state's southern border, reviving a long-standing policy of encouraging Indians to act like patrollers in the pay of whites.[152]

Revolutionary War Patrols Revisited: The War of 1812

The renewal of conflict with the British in the War of 1812 reminded Southern slaveholders of the insurrectionary fears they had experienced in the Revolutionary War. Additional slave patrols were posted, and white residents felt familiar anxieties when the holidays arrived, during which time slaves enjoyed greater freedom of movement to visit their family members.[153] One of James Monroe's correspondents wrote that "[t]he disaffection of the blacks is daily gaining extent & boldness which may produce effects, at the approaching festival of Xmas . . . The same heedless Imbecility that destroys our Efforts against the external

Enemy, paralyses every thing like vigilance & Police, in respect to the more dangerous internal population."[154] It was not enough to raise troops against the British: the *Richmond Enquirer's* editor wanted to know "[a]re all the necessary steps taken to screen us from the efforts of our own population?"[155]

Virginia residents proved reluctant to use their militia against the British, not because they feared their old enemy, but because of the danger posed by their slaves, who would be that much stronger when the militia left to fight the British.[156] Similarly, Vice President Elbridge Gerry's son described increased wartime patrolling in Washington, D.C., as an indispensable replacement for the militia's presence. In his diary he recorded that "[a]s the militia are ordered off, I expect to patrole more frequently, and this is very necessary, for the blacks in some places refuse to work, and say they shall soon be free, and then the white people must look out . . . Should we be attacked, there will be great danger of the blacks rising, and to prevent this, patroles are very necessary, to keep them in awe."[157]

During the War of 1812, the possibility of slaves either being captured by or escaping to freedom among the British worried many slave owners, particularly in Virginia. North Carolina's Outer Banks and treacherous coastal waters made it less vulnerable to British raiding parties, while Virginia's network of riverways from the Atlantic looked positively inviting to English sailors. Joseph Cabell, a wealthy Virginia planter, corresponded with his friend John Hartwell Cocke about the chances that slaves would either escape or be captured as spoils of war: "The British were nearly opposite to us in the Potomac during my stay there [at his home, Corotoman plantation], & were burning vessels, plundering along the Maryland shore, & receiving refugee slaves from both shores in great numbers. About the 7th inst. [of November 1813] they received about 200 negroes that went off from their owners in Westmoreland and Northumberland counties."[158] In no case did slave owners think that either patrols or local militia would stop determined bondsmen from escaping, or the British from taking slaves at will. But that did not stop them from proposing stronger measures to prevent slaves from absconding.

Where possible, Virginians increased their patrols during the war. Coastal areas were particularly vulnerable, and whites there took extra precautions. At Norfolk, "besides the usual patrole guard, a large number of the citizens" formed a volunteer patrol group to watch the river approaches to British ships; the group captured or shot half a dozen runaways and broke up several runaway encampments.[159] Along Virginia's vulnerable Eastern Shore, Accomack County officials increased the total number of men working in patrols by approximately a third, from roughly 100 patrollers per year prior to the war to 164 in 1813 and over 200 in 1814.[160] In Chesterfield County, slave patrols had been submitting their reports to the county court since the Revolution, but in 1813 and 1814, they provided detailed lists of the homes they visited on their rounds.[161] Along the Chesapeake Bay, "armed patrols of whites constantly scoured the coastal areas shooting suspected escapees on sight" in the last two years of the war.[162]

Although courts occasionally appointed additional men as patrollers, as during the Revolution, the size of patrol groups in the War of 1812 appears to have been very steady. James Martin, captain of a Virginia patrol group, recorded the names of the same five or six men who served with him on patrol about once a week during 1813. The men patrolled anywhere from six hours to twelve hours each during the weeks of September, October, and November. In Accomack County, Eastern Shore patrol groups also were made up of five or six men each, although the total number of active patrol groups increased substantially.[163] The battle over exemption from patrol duty that had raged during the Revolution also renewed itself in 1812. Some petitioners in South Carolina asked that none be exempt from patrol duty except those over the age of forty and men in specific, limited professions, since liberally granting exemptions from patrol work in wartime tended to "dampen the spirit of patriotism."[164]

Once again, county courts and military commanders took steps to improve the performance of patrol duty. Judges in Warren County, North Carolina, ordered that patrollers receive fresh copies of their patrol regulations during the war.[165] In 1812 the commander of the 3rd South Carolina regiment noted that great abuses were sustained across the state "from the want of due attention to patrole duty" and he ordered that every captain fully conform to the patrol laws, "except in those places where the establishment of regular night guards render it unnecessary." To ensure that his orders were carried out, Colonel Peter Edwards ordered that at the "end of every two months, each Captain will report to his Lieutenant Colonel" the number of times patrol duty had been performed, the number of men who defaulted from patrol duty, and the fines levied as a result.[166]

Wars and slave revolts caused slave owners to manifest greater vigilance in controlling their slaves than they normally used during times of relative tranquility. Although conflict with foreign enemies could limit patrols' ability to use all available men on patrol duty, they usually became larger and more active in wartime and in periods of insurrection (real or imagined). Whites tended to debate the membership of patrol groups more during wartime, when militia units might be drawn away from protecting the local community. As in times of slave insurrection, no person wished to leave his home without protection from the potential depredations that unsupervised slaves could cause. During wars and revolts, patrols received more direction about where they should be active, and the number of hours that they served was longer than average. In addition, local ad hoc groups sprang up to assist patrols when necessary. Even though patrols could not always prevent a determined bondsmen from reaching the safety of enemy lines and freedom, additional patrols staved off slave revolts and suppressed excessive slave movement.

The expansion of slave patrols during these periods of danger increased not only the number of men serving as patrollers but also the total number of households that had a stake in carrying out patrol work successfully. In normal times, slave patrol duty was merely one of many community functions that all white men, at one time or another, were called upon to perform, like jury duty or road work. Under the threat of rebellion or in the face of war, the patrol was no longer a small group carrying out one of many public tasks—patrollers performed the single most important community job whites could imagine, protecting the lives of white inhabitants by controlling slave behavior. As a result, the patrol's status as preserver of community peace (temporarily) gained in stature. Once the threat subsided, however, slave patrols were once again only one of many community duties that men performed without great fanfare.

The same characteristics that slave patrols developed during wars and rebellions reappeared immediately before the Civil War. Near Camden, South Carolina, regular militiamen continued to drill for battle while an insurrection was quashed by supplementary patrols. As one white Carolinian put it, "[t]he minute men are to do guard duty and negroes prevented from going about after [the] bell ring[s]"; in other words, the older men and younger boys who constituted the minute men, or home guard, would be responsible for patrolling the streets while the able-bodied men prepared to go to war.[167] In some areas, prewar anxieties about the behavior of slaves led to the creation of ad hoc civilian groups to control slaves and punish them if necessary. Citizens of Ninety Six District in South Carolina feared seditious activities among their slaves, so they established the "Military Vigilance Poliece" [sic] to swear in juries of residents and prosecute bondsmen for insurrectionary activities. One slave was hauled in just for saying that "the negroes would be free before long." All the prominent men of the area participated in this policing effort, including the magistrate and the local doctor.[168]

After the beginning of armed conflict between the Union and Confederate armies, slave patrols no longer continued to function as they had before. Although some familiar aspects of nocturnal patrolling would persist, patrols were significantly altered. As we will see in the following chapter, the Civil War radically changed slave patrols in terms of membership, repetitive appointments, efficacy, and stability. And at the war's conclusion, although slave patrols ceased to be active in the American South, their work was all too enthusiastically continued by other community groups like local police and the Ku Klux Klan.

6

Patrollers No More: The Civil War Era

> Will our people be wise for once in their lives, and inaugurate a rigid
> police patrol on their plantations all over the country? It is very
> doubtful. They have been warned so often, of so many things, that a
> deep apathy seems to have settled upon them. It is in the highest
> degree necessary that we should scour the country frequently, at night;
> visit all places where slaves resort, especially suspicious ones; put a
> stop to the stealing of hogs, which threatens to leave us almost
> without meat for the next year; prevent all practices that tend to
> demoralize the negro, and render him worthless, troublesome, or
> insubordinate; in short, carry out the provisions of the patrol laws.—It
> is best that this should be done at all times; but it is especially
> important, now that so many of our neighbors are in the army, and so
> many more are just in the act of departing from their homes to assists
> [sic] in repelling the advance of the invader, leaving so few behind
> them.
>
> *Editorialist for the* Camden (S.C.) Confederate
> *after the introduction of conscription in 1862*

Slave revolts and wars before the 1860s had only fleeting effects upon
the dominance that white Southerners exerted over their bondsmen.[1]
These struggles usually drew away a mere fraction of the adult male population to fight, leaving more than enough white men in each community to maintain order and discipline in the slave system. Neither of the
two wars that had intruded most upon Virginia and the Carolinas—the
American Revolution and the War of 1812—had as its ultimate goal the
destruction of the slave society that existed in the American South. Slave
insurrections and wars against the Indians, Spanish, French, and British
did not permanently end slavery or destroy the need for slave patrols.

But civil war with an American enemy would be different. Fighting
their own countrymen, Southerners would be challenged to sustain
their slave system against great opposition. The Civil War, lasting four

167

and a half bloody years and contested almost completely within the Southern slave states, threatened the very existence of slavery even before slavery's abolition became an official objective of Union leaders. During the conflict, Northern armies moved through and occupied parts of Virginia dozens of times; areas of North and South Carolina were besieged or occupied by Union troops as early as autumn 1861.[2] The continuing proximity of enemy armies created new stresses in slaveholding communities that few local slave patrols had encountered before.

Northern armies were not the only obstacles slave patrols confronted—their own Confederate army repeatedly sapped the manpower needed to maintain strong, effective patrols. As the war dragged on, more and more men were conscripted into the Southern army, men who would have served on slave patrols had they remained in their local communities. By war's end, the Confederate government called upon practically every able-bodied white male to fight, compelling men to leave their homes and go wherever the army took them. The growing absence of adult white men from local communities changed the personnel and procedures of slave patrols in each locale, particularly those closest to the actual fighting. Small wonder, then, that the Camden newspaper editorialist believed that patrols were "especially important, now that so many of our neighbors are in the army": Confederate army personnel demands would create both the greatest need for and the greatest disruptions of slave patrols in Southern history, short of the disappearance of slavery itself at the war's conclusion.

With the war lost, fears that Southern whites had about African Americans did not diminish—if anything, their anxieties about racial control increased in 1865. Ultimately, although slavery and patrols were legally dismantled, vestiges of the patrol system survived. In the immediate aftermath of the war, informal patrols sprang into being; later, with occasional help from Union army officers, city and rural police squads revived patrolling practices among the freedmen. During Reconstruction, old patrol methods would resurface among both the postwar Southern police forces and the Ku Klux Klan.

Growing Tension Immediately before the Civil War

In the late 1850s, as the question of slavery's legitimacy increased sectional divisiveness, Southern slaveholders took additional precautions to safeguard their slave property. These precautions usually included extra patrol rounds by locally appointed slave patrols—and more patrol groups were appointed by many townships—or by privately formed groups that behaved like slave patrols in all but name. In 1859, after news reached North Carolina of John Brown's abortive plans to lead slaves in revolt with arms taken from the Harpers Ferry arsenal, newspapers across the state urged the organization of extra patrols.[3] In South Carolina, Beaufort District residents held a meeting on October 31, 1859, and "five new vigilance committees were created to better enforce the patrol laws, and their ranks were quickly filled."[4] Lynchburg, Virginia, had nine neighborhood vigilante groups actively patrolling in 1860, in addition to its militia.[5] The mandate of these vigilance committees was to keep slaves subordinated as well as to inquire into the activities of suspicious whites. David Gavin, a South Carolinian, wanted "free negroes, persons of Colour and all white persons who have not a visible means of an honest living" investigated by patrols or a police force during the secession crisis.[6]

The tense atmosphere allowed for the creation and expansion of vigilante justice groups and newly created paramilitary corps that moved in tandem with (or in some cases subsumed) the patrol system in the months before the attack on Fort Sumter. These patrol-like vigilance committees sometimes created new problems, because they were not bound to respect the traditional limits that law or custom placed upon regular slave patrols. Their eagerness to discipline whites was a significant alteration to the antebellum slave patrol's customary behavior.[7] The historian Stephen Channing has documented the rising tide of patroller activism in South Carolina immediately prior to the war: "When a vigilance patrol broke up a nest of whites secretly trading with slaves in coastal Georgetown, there was some grumbling about this use of their authority."[8] Elsewhere in South Carolina, the Edgefield Riflemen of Beaufort took turns as nightly patrols in 1860, practicing their maneuvers in military fashion while they policed the nocturnal affairs of their bondsmen.[9]

Southerners worried that their slaves were less subservient because Northern abolitionists had "infiltrated" their states and corrupted those in bondage. Masters wanted a system of isolation, to keep dangerous abolitionist ideas out and slaves in. Giving voice to ideas shared by many Southern masters, one Georgia planter described how he intended to protect his "entire social system": he would hermetically "*seal* by the most rigid police all ingress and egress" to and from his plantation.[10]

Full-scale vigilance would shield and protect a plantation, or a state, from abolitionists. And that vigilance would have to be on a massive scale that left no home unprotected. Declared one prewar editorialist, "let us teach our daughters how to defend themselves . . . to load and shoot the gun and revolver with facility" and make sure that "patrol duty [is] regularly performed," so that no home would be left totally defenseless in the face of black violence.[11] Fear of abolitionist activities did not abate in the year before the November 1860 election. In February "the sea island of St. Helena [was] crisscrossed by extra patrols, as the island was distressed by rumors of the discovery of Sharp's rifles and meddlesome abolitionists," while in August Newberry, South Carolina, residents established a special committee to reinforce performance of the patrol laws "in the wake of evidence of 'tampering' with local blacks."[12] Whether abolitionists actually ventured to St. Helena or Newberry remains unclear, but the reactions of whites there are instructive—they believed that abolitionism could lead to only one thing: slave revolts.

To prevent these revolts in the last twelve months before war came, patrols swung into high gear and white leaders advocated rigorous enforcement of all slave control measures. In Washington County, North Carolina, reports of an 1860 slave insurrection caused "as many as 50 persons" to go on guard, in addition to the local slave patrol's activities.[13] Suspicious fires in Charlotte prompted two hundred additional men to enlist as city patrols until the incendiary could be found.[14] As the prospect of war drew closer, the newspaper editor Arthur Simkins became a vocal advocate for more assertive patrols and vigilance activities to prevent insurrections. He used his Edgefield, South Carolina, *Advertiser* to spread those opinions among upcountry planters.[15] Badge laws that had been selectively enforced in 1850s suddenly became more stringent; James D. Johnson, a free black tailor in Charleston, remembered freedmen who had paid taxes for thirty years or more being forced in 1860 "to go back to bondage and take out their Badges" like slaves.[16]

Efforts to maintain control over slaves and suspicious whites were not limited to formal patrols, ad hoc vigilance committees, or paramilitary groups. Other community associations, like agricultural societies, that had long been accustomed to discussing slavery and plantation work habits focused on the need for increased slave patrolling in the immediate prewar period. These gentlemen's clubs switched from discussing the latest innovations in planting and harvesting to considering how to increase their community's security. Several agricultural societies either debated or actually formed their own patrol groups to supplement the work done by regular patrols. The Beech Island Agricultural Club in South Carolina, of which James Henry Hammond was a member, debated this proposition in December 1859: "There is a class of white men about here that a patrole would do good in Katching those Hunting Fishing & Steeling raskals, the patrole could not chastise them, but they could take them up & prosecute them & this should be done." J. M. Miller recommended that the club establish its own patrols, and another member, J. M. Clarke, agreed with him, saying that "the blame of not having [a] patrole is with the officers of the Beat Company." Hammond disagreed with Clarke and Miller, urging that judicial officials and not the militia take charge of patrolling. Hammond declared that "patroling is a very grave thing & should be done right not by young men going patroling drinke & carowsing[.] there is no mischief done in the early part of the night, patroles should be out from 1 Oclock to day, that is the time & then not over 3 or 4 times a month . . . we must have a majistrate & let the patrols be under his control." Hammond was alone in his views, for other club members sided with Clarke and Miller. J. D. Everett said of patrols that "if we do anything we must do it ourselves," and Dr. Cook concurred, averring that "[w]e want patrols and when they go out they should patrole properly not make a frolick of it as is generally the case & *we should form some plan to have it done.*"[17] But in 1859 the men did nothing. Two years later, after the war had been under way for almost twelve months, Miller suggested that a committee divide the neighborhood into districts and organize patrols. With little discussion this time, the society appointed a patrol committee, consisting of Miller, Clarke, and Cook.[18]

The club members' discussions of whether or not to form their own private patrol group left no firm evidence that the men acted as their own patrols. Yet their deliberations about taking the law into their own hands are reminiscent of another group of South Carolinians who almost a century earlier had tried to control "troublesome" people in the absence of local courts and jails in the restless 1760s. Dubbed the "Regulators," these "ambitious, commercially oriented slaveowners" were comparable to men in the 1850s Beech Island Agricultural Club in attempting to control their local area by suppressing groups that threatened them: unruly slaves and suspicious, rascally whites.[19] Although the

Regulators responded violently to the spread of banditry, their demands were for local jails, local courts, and other measures to prevent crime. In his study of the Regulators, Richard M. Brown has called them men who strove to "stamp out crime and chaos so that ambition and enterprise could gain their rewards."[20] Like the Regulators, well-to-do members of the Beech Island Agricultural Club viewed it as their prerogative to dominate the local area they inhabited. Unlike the Regulators, who abandoned their vigilante ways when their demands were met by the colony's legislature, however, the men of the Beech Island Agricultural Club received no relief from their legislature to help them control assertive slaves.

In the months that followed Abraham Lincoln's November 1860 election, new patrol groups and "Minute Man" volunteer organizations sprang up across the South. These groups served the multiple purposes of augmenting local surveillance of suspicious whites and assisting the slave patrols with their increasingly important duties. The certainty that slaves would revolt rose to an almost feverish pitch after Lincoln's election. The Minute Man groups, in addition to helping patrollers with their work, also distributed propaganda about what the appropriate response to Lincoln's election should be: secession.[21]

The First Year of the War: Patrols Increased

Apprehensions that troubled Southerners immediately before the war, particularly after John Brown's raid, only increased once the Civil War started on April 12, 1861. The onset of hostilities with the North amplified the innate insecurities white Southerners had about their own slaves. Even if the threatened revolts never materialized, the fear white Southerners experienced was real.[22] The English newspaperman William H. Russell described this suppressed (yet pervasive) fear shared by many Southerners as he traveled the country in 1861. Crossing South Carolina only ten days after the war began, Russell recorded that "[t]here is something suspicious in the constant never ending statement that 'we are not afraid of our slaves.' The curfew and the night patrol in the streets, the prisons and watch-houses, and the police regulations prove that strict supervision, at all events, is needed and necessary."[23]

White expectations of impending slave revolts inspired most communities to appoint more patrols in a hurry.[24] In North Carolina, communities like Granville County doubled their slave patrols in 1861, while in

South Carolina, nearly seventy citizens of Kirksey's Cross Roads enrolled as patrollers "in view of the uncertainty of the times."[25] Anticipating that cities, with their larger slave populations, would endure greater unrest, South Carolina's General Assembly gave small municipalities more latitude to organize their own urban patrols by mandating that all towns with between 500 and 2,500 persons form separate patrol beats.[26] Greater watchfulness became the rule and not the exception for all patrols, as well as for the men who appointed them. For example, Governor Francis W. Pickens of South Carolina ordered a closer police watch around Charleston, and he expected Mayor Charles Macbeth to increase the town watch.[27] Men not immediately called upon for military duty were drafted into or volunteered for patrol work. In Danville, Virginia, the town government drew up a list in April 1861 of all white male residents who did not belong to either the volunteer military companies or the home guard in order to require those men to patrol the town "as a police" under the captain of the patrol. All men who did not patrol were fined one dollar for each absence, while those who did serve were paid one dollar for each night's service.[28]

With mobilization and many men volunteering for active military service, the numbers of men available to patrol became uncertain. Governor Pickens complained in late 1861 that the patrol system had lately become "deranged by the breaking up of the Beat Companies" as masters went off to war; he advocated that military provost marshals send their assistants to patrol areas where white men had become scarce.[29] In South Carolina, commanders were ordered to take new censuses of persons in their local area who were eligible for militia and patrol duty, and return the lists to militia headquarters.[30] Ironically, efforts to strengthen patrols "came at precisely the moment army service depleted the number of eligible males, including many who had previously performed patrol duty."[31]

In the first year of the war slave patrols functioned side by side with other groups, like vigilance committees and home guard units, to restrict the movement of slaves. Some young men, turned down by the army for medical reasons, ended up acting as patrols at the war's beginning when they joined the home guard. Initially rejected by the Confederate army because of a disability, twenty-two-year-old Wilbur Davis joined the Holcomb Guards, a home guard unit on patrol duty in Albemarle County, Virginia. Davis knew that "there was much apprehension at the outset [of the war] as to the behavior of the slave—some fearing insurrection after so large a part of the able bodied men were off in the army. It was thought a strong home guard would be needed to protect our homes[,] to patrol the county[,] and keep the negroes in place." Although Davis and his fellow guardsmen diligently made their patrol rounds, they discovered nothing to confirm their suspicions. In his wartime reminiscences, Davis wrote that "[t]he negroes were invariably all right, and always at home—go where we would. We took the darkest nights by preference for our investigations, and after a few weeks becoming satisfied that they had no idea of any insubordination, we gave it up."[32] Prominent citizens in Fayetteville, North Carolina, wrote their mayor in July 1861, telling him to "count us in" when he organized security measures for the town. They offered to help maintain order, property, and secure the public interest by providing men for a home guard "or policial service."[33] Regardless of the name they used while on duty, Southern white men eagerly volunteered for extra patrol duties in the first year of the war.

Given the psychological distress most white Southerners experienced over the possibility of, or the certainty of, slave revolts, it would be a mistake to assume that "[r]egular slave patrols for the most part ceased to function in the summer of 1861, when the men who filled their ranks joined the armies."[34] Although a few communities cut back on their patrols, most neighborhoods continued to rely on patrollers or home guards—like Wilbur Davis—to control their slaves during 1861, although important changes had already begun to occur.[35] In the 2nd Battalion, 4th Regiment, of the South Carolina militia, a unit on reserve duty, officers still assigned patrollers to duty in 1861–62, but the men selected to patrol were older than those of prewar years. Aaron Dobbins was thirty-nine when he was assigned as a patroller, for example, and Samuel Williford was forty-eight at the time of his appointment.[36] Patrolling did continue, and in several communities paid quite well in 1861 and 1862. In Danville, Virginia, patrolling was significantly strengthened at the beginning of the war; some men earned fifteen dollars a month for patrolling during the war's first year.[37] In Davie County, North Carolina, local officials paid each man an additional four dollars over his regular pay for extra patrolling in 1861.[38] North Carolina's adjutant general attempted to compensate for the loss of white men in some communities by increasing county patrols where needed. Twenty mounted men could be raised as special patrols if local justices of the peace deemed their use necessary; these groups later came to be known as county policemen, with multiple duties that included controlling slaves as well as hunting for deserters.[39]

The increased activities of some patrol groups in 1861–62 included attempts to root out maroon communities that in an earlier time might have been left unmolested. A Marion, South Carolina, newspaper reported that a group of men searching for runaways destroyed a maroon camp in a local swamp where corn, squash, and peas were growing—clearly not a recent settlement. Although the adult runaways evaded capture, they left behind two small children, who were taken into custody by patrollers.[40]

After a year of war, the group of men available for patrolling, or any military service, was beginning to be stretched thin, particularly in South Carolina. In 1862 James Chesnut, chief of South Carolina's Department of the Military, reported to the governor that more than 32,000 men had been called to arms by the state and the Confederate government, leaving behind fewer and fewer men to meet the demands of patrolling. Those left by virtue of exemptions from state service were few. Overseers, exempted from state military levies because of the important role they played in the state's agricultural interests, made up a large portion of those who remained behind. In fact, overseers were deemed "so essential to a proper system of police" that the state did not call them for active service.[41]

The initial exemption of overseers from military duty altered the composition of slave patrols even in the first year of the war. Once the Civil War began, the "role of the overseer assumed even greater importance with the departure of hundreds of thousands of able-bodied southern whites for the fighting front."[42] Because overseers received automatic exemptions from military service in 1861 and early 1862, they formed the core group of male residents in any given area. Consequently, overseers were repeatedly tapped for patrol duty during this period.[43] This may have led slaves to associate patrolling even more closely with overseers' work in the WPA interviews of the 1930s.

Conscription in 1862 and the Emancipation Proclamation of 1863

On March 29, 1862, Confederate president Jefferson Davis requested that the Confederacy pass a law conscripting all white men between the ages of eighteen and thirty-five into the Southern army. In the year since the war had begun, many men had volunteered for duty, but Davis was concerned that too many of those men were actually teenagers, or men unfit for military service due to advanced age. Davis wrote that the youngest and more elderly men, who formed the "proper reserve for home defense," should not be sent away from their homes. Conscription of those between eighteen and thirty-five meant that only youths who needed additional military training before joining the army and older men who would maintain "order and good government at home" would stay in their local communities.[44] The Confederate Congress debated Davis's suggestion through much of April 1862, and eventually passed a conscription act that required all men between eighteen and thirty-five to serve for a total of three years in the army. Men could hire substitutes, and a supplementary act was passed a week later that specifically exempted state officials, railroad workers, clergymen, teachers, and hospital personnel.[45] Overseers did not receive an exemption from this first attempt to raise a Confederate army via conscription, despite the efforts of many planters. The comprehensive nature of this first American conscription act has led some historians to assert that the men left in local militias could "at best be little more than a pathetic band of the aged, the decrepit, and the resentful."[46]

The Confederate Congress's failure to exempt overseers from the draft prompted immediate consternation among those most concerned with patrols and the safety of local areas. Even before the draft began, large slave owners feared that their overseers would join the Confederate army. The South Carolina planter James B. Heyward wrote to the Confederate military protesting the enlistment of his overseer, stating that overseers formed "the best civil police system that can be invented."[47] Many planters, like Heyward, complained to the Confederate Congress, urging that overseers be exempted from the new conscription law in order to continue their work as patrollers. In October 1862, Congress responded. "[T]o secure the proper police of the country" it passed a second exemption act, which excluded one white man—the owner or overseer—from conscription on each plantation of twenty or more slaves, and one white man on each plantation where state law required one to be kept.[48] The exemption permitting one man to stay home if he owned or supervised twenty slaves came to be known as the "twenty-nigger law," and was bitterly unpopular among non–slave owners and small farmers. Although the law was revised in May 1863 and eventually repealed in February 1864, reducing the total number of exemptions granted, exemptions under its provisions were obtained in great numbers.[49] Through this and other methods, many avoided direct military service in the South; estimates of all men exempted from the Confederate military run as high as 40 percent of the eligible adult male population.[50]

Planters obtained exemptions for their managers by arguing that they needed overseers not only for harvesting and plantation supervision but also to perform slave patrol duty in local communities. Owners typically provided affidavits to local military officers, cosigned by other local residents, affirming the need for an overseer's continued presence. In one such affidavit, Robert F. W. Allston wrote in 1863 that if his overseer Joseph M. Thompson were allowed to remain on his Georgetown District plantation, "[i]t would contribute materially to the Police of the locality in which he resides."[51] One year later, Allston again petitioned to have his own and his son's overseers exempted from military service, using patrolling and supervision along the PeeDee River as a main reason for his request. He wrote that "[f]or the security and proper police of his negroes together with the direction of their labor in producing, preparing and transporting his produce of grain . . . [the overseers] named herein . . . [are] absolutely necessary."[52] But even when owners fought to keep their overseers, the overseers might patriotically choose to enlist in the army and forgo their exemption. Most planters reported that experienced overseers became harder to find and employ as the war dragged on.

The forcible removal of so many Southern men from their communities due to conscription made the enforcement of patrol laws increasingly difficult at a time when white residents needed even greater reassurances about their own safety. Fewer and fewer counties could continue to appoint patrollers every month, as Richmond County officials did in North Carolina throughout 1862. Then in September 1862 Abraham Lincoln issued the preliminary Emancipation Proclamation, declaring that all slaves in areas where rebellion persisted would become free on January 1, 1863. The wildest fear of many Southern citizens had been realized: the slaves would be free.

The hysteria white Southerners experienced at the start of the war renewed itself in the aftermath of the Emancipation Proclamation.[53] Running for reelection in 1863, the Confederate congressman Archibald

Arrington told North Carolina voters that he had not wanted to support the twenty-slave exemption from conscription, but that the Emancipation Proclamation and the need for greater local patrolling had persuaded him it was necessary, no matter how unpopular.

> At that time I thought it absolutely necessary for our safety, and more especially for the safety of the families of our soldiers, that the most vigilant and efficient police should be kept over our slaves. Lincoln's infamous proclamation was then staring us in the face; proclaiming that all slaves should be free on the first day of January 1863 . . . If we could all have foreseen at that time that the proclamation would have had no deleterious effect, the law would not have been passed . . . And who knows but that it was this precautionary step on the part of Congress that preserved the loyalty of our slaves and averted the horrors of a servile insurrection.[54]

Arrington's statement reminded fellow North Carolinians of the panic that gripped Southern citizens following the Emancipation Proclamation and the widespread slave revolts they had expected that never came. Slave patrols—even as their numbers declined—played a vital role in maintaining discipline on wartime plantations. With fewer whites available for hire as overseers, slave owners were forced (sometimes reluctantly) to rely upon the heightened supervision of their neighbors riding in slave patrols to prevent insurrections, slave crime, and large numbers of runaways. North Carolina's legislature even considered strengthening its patrol laws in the spring of 1863, but decided that existing laws were sufficient for wartime.[55]

Following the Emancipation Proclamation, reports persisted that slaves intended to revolt, and in at least one case, in Camden, South Carolina, an insurrection was actually discovered. The uprising "was very weak and ill-arranged" according to one local resident; the slaves involved were hanged and extra patrols ordered to duty.[56] That Union troops might instigate an insurrection became a widespread rumor when a letter proposing a slave rebellion, signed by a Union officer, was found in a captured federal steamer off the North Carolina coast in May 1863. Copies of the letter were forwarded to Jefferson Davis and Robert E. Lee, although no insurrection seems to have developed from the Union plan. Local North Carolina authorities took steps—assigning men additional patrol duty—to prevent any insurrectionary behavior.[57]

In 1862 and 1863 frightened citizens petitioned state authorities, requesting guns, powder, and protection from their own slaves. Yet even if more guns and gunpowder could be found, where would the extra men to patrol come from? Some governors, as in South Carolina, gave beat captains unprecedented powers to impress men for up to a week's duty on patrol. They realized, however, that this might strip parts of a neighborhood of the only remaining white men on plantations. After the local militia captain was given the power to compel a week's patrol service from men remaining in the county, Theodore Gourdin complained that for miles around "[t]he only effective man is my overseer and four hundred and seventy fore resident negroes in the beat." If the overseer was gone for a whole week, "that beat would be perfectly exposed" to all kinds of slave plotting and meetings. His fears mounted as the number of slaves in his neighborhood increased dramatically with the arrival of refugee slaves, moved there by nervous owners. Gourdin pointed out that more than six hundred slaves in the adjoining beat effectively surrounded his plantation.[58]

If state militia units were mobilized for full active duty, the patrols could be utterly deprived of capable adult men. "Since the ages of persons subject to militia and patrol service were the same, the calling away of the militia to perform active military service deprived the communities of the old men and boys capable of patrolling the beats."[59] Even if patrolling was carried out with a vengeance after the Emancipation Proclamation, the ongoing drain of militia units from most communities in 1862 and 1863 meant that many local slave patrols simply did not have the men to be as active as they had once been. Indeed, the sporadic nature of wartime patrolling caused some slaves to think that the patrols had ceased to function. A few bondsmen believed patrols could not afford to be as ruthless in their dealings with slaves because whites did not have the manpower or desire to give offense to slaves whom they encountered during wartime.[60]

The changes in patrol personnel became marked in the months following full conscription. The ages of the men available to perform patrol duty were clustered among the young and those beyond middle age. In 1863 a militia census in Beat No. 2 of the 2nd Battalion, 4th Regiment, of the South Carolina militia counted fifty-one men of serviceable patrol age—between the years of sixteen and fifty. Many of the men were very young or past middle age: thirteen of the fifty-one were under the age of twenty, while at the other extreme twenty-one of the men, nearly half, were over the age of forty.[61] Responding to the conscription laws, the town of Abingdon, Virginia, expanded its patrol to include men from sixteen to fifty-five, instead of calling upon the men in the customary sixteen to forty-five age group.[62]

In areas not completely bereft of white men, patrols continued to be appointed throughout the war, and local authorities tried to share the work among all those remaining in the community. As in the antebellum period, men served as patrols in family groups. In Henry County, Virginia, the number of appointed patrollers increased from four and five per patrol group in the prewar period to an average of six men per patrol group during the war. The county court appointed patrols every three months from 1861 through August 1864. Of the 195 men who served as patrols from the late 1850s to 1864, most patrollers chosen actually served for only one three-month period. A few men served repeatedly: Drury Bocock, Overton R. Dillard, and James Gregory served five or more three-month appointments as patrollers. All three men served as patrollers both before and during the war. If a man was appointed but could not serve, he might hire a substitute patroller, assuming that he could find someone capable of serving. This prewar practice continued throughout the Civil War.[63]

The changing composition of local patrols, particularly the use of younger and younger men, did not go unnoticed by citizens who were alarmed at the possibility of imminent slave revolts. The editor of the Camden, South Carolina, *Confederate* newspaper printed a letter in November 1862 complaining that children were now working as slave patrollers.[64] Although the letter writer was exaggerating, young men in the community might have leapt at the opportunity to patrol. Serving in a slave patrol or home guard unit was perceived as good training for a young man who might eventually be sent into real combat with the Northern enemy. Some men advised their younger friends and relations to join the home guard, for through drilling and patrolling the youths would acquire the conduct of soldiers while still at home. William Blackford suggested to his brother in Virginia that he should join the home guard in order to "harden your muscles by exercise and then you wont mind exposure."[65]

Even men who were technically exempt from patrol service, due to their status as students or professors at universities, for example, often ended up performing slave patrol duty sometime during the war. Thomas Anderson, a cadet at the Arsenal Academy in Charleston, was ordered to patrol in 1863, despite the fact that in the prewar period he would have been exempt from patrol duty.[66] Charles Phillips reported that when a home guard was formed to patrol near the University of North Carolina, in Chapel Hill, "all the preachers & others of the Faculty" joined it.[67]

Specially formed patrol units found that conscription vitiated their prior exemption from the Confederate army. Groups set up by state officials to combat known runaway threats were subsumed into the army as the number and types of exemptions were limited in 1863 and 1864. Jere Pearsall, leader of a patrol group in Kenansville, North Carolina, wrote to Jefferson Davis, asking that his special patrol unit be spared from absorption into the Confederate army. The North Carolina governor had ordered the militia commander of the county to establish a special patrol, which Pearsall described as "the ounce of preventive in place of the pound of Cure." County residents had funded the purchase of a pack of dogs, which not only helped them recapture slaves but also prevented desertions to the enemy, Pearsall asserted. He also claimed that "since the organization of this Company, there has been *no* attempt of escapes by the Slaves *but one,* (save in the Raid in July) and the whole number of negroes . . . were Captured & returned to their owners through this Company." Pearsall's request that Davis grant a special exemption to his patrol group went unfulfilled. The secretary of war, James Seddon, noted on the petition that he could not "conceive that a better use could be made of the men than by conscription."[68]

As slave owners entered the Confederate army in ever-increasing numbers, some slaves lost the shield that had previously protected them from brutal slave patrols. A former Virginia slave, Mollie Booker, recalled that "[th]e paddyrollers use to bother my father somepin' awful. Dey'd come an' beat him anytime. Once he went an' got his bossman to run dem away. Dey waited years ontil de war come an' de bossman went to war." The patrollers' wartime revenge took a horrible toll. One night the slave patrol came and "got paw right out of bed, took him out in de road an' beat him turrible. Dey tol' him dey's beatin' him fur tellin' his ole bossman dat time. Momma an' we all kids stood in de door an' cried."[69] Of course, conscription took both slave owners and slave patrollers into the army. Henry Baker, a former bondsman, reminisced about the time the slaves heard that a patroller, Jeff Coleman, had been killed in the war and "de 'niggers' jes shouted en shouted, dey wuz so glad he wuz dead cause he wuz so mean tuh dem."[70]

Some planters chose not to rely on sporadically operating slave patrols, and instead hired extra patrollers for their own plantations, whom they paid collectively to perform extra duty. Former slaves like Hannah Crasson and Solomon Northup remembered that owners hired their own private patrollers during the Civil War.[71] Owners were more likely to hire their own slave catchers to watch the roads and routes that led away from their plantations if they had slaves prone to flight. Whether these private patrols were considered legal (since they were composed of men not appointed by a lawful body) was obviated by general laws that allowed all white men to interrogate and capture wandering slaves. Administering whippings, however, which could potentially damage a slave's property value, was theoretically prohibited. Years later, ex-slave George Fleming of South Carolina thought that wartime patrols were composed of anyone who wanted to join, as long as his master was willing to pay.[72]

Not every owner welcomed the presence of slave patrollers, however. In the antebellum period, some slave owners did not allow "strangers" to discipline their slaves or even enter their plantations, and this practice persisted during the Civil War. In places where wartime slave patrols continued to be active, more than one owner insisted upon administering his own whippings, and would not leave that task to patrols.[73] As war came closer to some parts of the South, increasing numbers of slaves and masters took refuge in new homes and new regions, where slaves or their owners were less likely to know or have long-established relationships with local patrollers, perhaps intensifying the anxieties both groups felt about slave patrols.[74]

Although some masters wanted nothing to do with local patrollers, others asked that they do more than any prewar patrol might have done. After Stephen, one of her slaves, ran away, Adele Allston of South Carolina wanted the local patrol to search the homes of Stephen's relatives and then imprison the runaway's older family members to keep good order among her remaining slaves.

If you could get a small military force, or the patrol and have Mary's house surrounded and searched, and James likewise at the same time you might find out something more . . . I think Mary and James should be taken up and sent to some secure jail in the interior and held as hostages . . . And they should understand that this is done by the police of the country, who require that the older negroes should endeavour to influence the younger ones to order and subordination while this war lasts, and that they will be held responsible for the behaviour of their children. For this course to have the best effect it ought to be universal, and ought to be required by the police of the country.[75]

Adele Allston worried that Stephen's example might encourage her other slaves to abscond to the enemy armies marching ever closer to her plantation in 1864, but no evidence suggests that the local slave patrols ever fulfilled her request.

One final change in the Confederate conscription law further undermined the strength of local slave patrols. In February 1864, running low on men, the Confederate Congress amended the conscription law to draft men between the ages of seventeen and fifty into military service for the duration of the war.[76] This resulted in the loss of practically all men who constituted the remaining home guard in most communities. From this point forward, any patrolling done would be carried out by the very old, the very young, and men severely injured in the war who had returned home as invalids.

Approaching Armies, Captured Areas, and Diminishing Patrols

The likelihood that slaves would flee to areas controlled by Union armies increased as a Northern army moved into a local community. Previously docile and obedient slaves disappeared in the night, passed through enemy lines, and gave themselves to Union army commanders, who, at the outset of the war, were somewhat puzzled about what they should do with their new recruits.[77] Owners reduced the number of passes they issued to slaves (or ceased giving them altogether) when a Northern army approached their lands, and Southern commanders warned masters to move their slaves away from enemy lines.[78] Slave owners knew that at the first opportunity, slaves would fly to the lines of the oncoming Union army, and if the men were available locally, extra patrols would be mounted to prevent this predictable increase in slave runaways. Slaves believed that patrollers during the Civil War were posted explicitly to prevent their running away, more than any other of-fense.[79] Whole plantations might grind to a halt, as the entire workforce went over to the enemy side. This happened to Thomas Robins, a Vir-ginia overseer who repeatedly noted escapes from his plantation during 1862 and 1863 as slaves ran off and joined the Union army.[80] Virginia, the location of many of the war's battles, experienced an explosion of runaways, so much so that the Confederate army established three special depots to hold fugitive slaves until their owners could reclaim them.[81]

The approach of Union troops often drew forth Confederate forces, and Southern troops served as erstwhile slave patrols where they had picket lines near the Union army.[82] Southern commanders realized that slaves were not only a commercial commodity, but had vital information about military strength and roads that would be valuable to any would-be Northern invader. Along the vulnerable Atlantic Ocean, Sea Island planters pressed Southern generals to catch and return their fugitive slaves.[83] Confederate army picket lines doubled on the York River in February 1864, to prevent slaves from escaping to nearby Union troops, but one Richmond newspaper editor thought that a determined bonds-man could still successfully "run the blockade" of patrols.[84] Military ne-cessity took precedence over slave owner appeals: only infrequently did the Confederate army hunt down and return runaways, attack slave groups that menaced Southern pickets with Northern weaponry, or lo-cate troops with a primary purpose of preventing slaves from running away.[85] The greatest army patrolling efforts made on behalf of planters appear to have occurred in South Carolina. For example, Dr. Francis Parker of Georgetown convinced Confederate officers to use cavalry for patrol work in 1862.[86]

Bondsmen made their own way to freedom, sometimes with assis-tance from Northern troops, and only occasionally hindered by patrols. The advancing Union army forcibly carried them off a few plantations. Such incidents were a frequent occurrence for planters near the front lines like William Wickham of Virginia, who lost about thirty slaves to the Northern army.[87] Bondsmen who found their way to freedom occa-sionally returned to help other slave groups escape to Union lines.[88] In 1863 Colonel Lawrence Keitt wrote to his superior about the "plunder-ing expeditions" conducted by the Northern navy along South Carolina's coast with the assistance of fugitive slaves, and the immense difficulty of patrolling the entire shoreline where "for long distances a barge or small

boat can land anywhere at high tide." Keitt placed three cavalry companies and two infantry companies on patrol to stop slave escapes.[89] In the
dark, bondsmen may have found it hard to distinguish between Confederate and Union troops. Slaves had to be cautious, if they did run away:
men on horseback all looked the same at night, and the difference between friendly Northern liberators and unfriendly slave patrollers could
be difficult to determine.[90]

In communities garrisoned by Confederate troops or menaced by
Union troops, new procedures effectively restricted slaves and masters
alike. Once Confederate troops entered a local area, it was not uncom-
mon for slave quarters to be searched thoroughly by military units, independent of the local slave patrol group. On Argyle Island, in the Savannah River along the South Carolina–Georgia border, Louis Manigault
reported that part of General Harrison's brigade came to search all the
houses, including the slave quarters.[91] With the approach of Union
troops to Southern towns, town councils began to issue passes to white
inhabitants, ironically turning a system of control that had once been
aimed solely at slaves into a universal requirement for all residents.[92]
Passes specified the complexion, hair and eye color, height, and age of
the person given permission to leave the restricted area. Such passes became commonplace in the largest cities of the South, such as Charleston
and Richmond.[93] The Englishman W. C. Corsan, complaining bitterly
about the system in 1862, noted that "no one can move about any road,
river, or railroad—no, not even from county to county" without a military pass from a provost marshal.[94]

Rapid population growth and the sizable presence of Confederate
troops in Southern cities accelerated changes for urban patrols.[95] The
changes actually amplified two trends that existed in the prewar period:
a shift of patrol functions to urban police groups, and heightened vigilance over urban slaves on a daily basis—much more than rural slaves
received. In Richmond and Charleston, these trends became especially
pronounced. After the Confederate government adopted Richmond, Virginia, as its capital, the population tripled in 1861–62. Joseph Mayo,
mayor of Richmond from 1853 until after the war, increased the number
of police to handle the rising amount of both slave and white crime. In
December 1861, for example, he had eleven men patrolling on day beats
and seventy-two men working at night.[96] High levels of crime and the
disorders of war meant that Richmond police did not have time to give
city slaves and free blacks the close attention they had received in pre-

war years. Louis Cei finds that during the Civil War the Richmond "police arrested whites far more than blacks." The extraordinary growth of the town, coupled with its status as the Confederacy's new capital, meant that police simply could not restrain all crime.[97]

The strain on Richmond's urban policing resources became too much, and President Jefferson Davis finally proclaimed martial law in March 1862, appointing military police to guard Richmond.[98] Thereafter the town's provost marshal would control slave discipline, supplementing the actions of the police.[99] Provost marshals across the South could use their power over slaves ruthlessly. In Georgetown, South Carolina, the provost marshal executed several male slaves for running away, a punishment far greater than most masters (or slave patrols) would have inflicted.[100] As the war dragged on and more towns fell under military jurisdiction, the existing community relations that might previously have tempered slave patrol excesses began to disappear. Bondsmen may have discovered that transgressions easily forgiven by patrollers in the prewar years yielded deadly consequences in the latter part of the Civil War.

In Charleston, the provost marshal and Confederate military troops carefully enforced the laws relating to slave movement. On July 30, 1863, the Confederate provost marshal instructed city guards that "[a]ll slaves coming into the city without tickets or passports, [shall] be arrested and sent to the Provost Marshal's office." While stationed in Charleston, the 4th Brigade of the 19th Regiment of the South Carolina militia was ordered to active patrol duty. Brigadier General DeSaussure mandated that "in each of the Beat Companies of Said Reg[imen]t . . . a rigid military patrol be performed twice in each week." Each captain was to give a report to his colonel about the patrolling, and the colonels, in turn, would report to DeSaussure.[101] While most of the regiment was busy in Charleston proper, an artillery company, augmented by a mounted company of "Farmer's Rangers," was responsible for patrolling nearby Charleston Neck.[102]

The declining number of able-bodied men available for urban patrolling left a mixed impression upon city slaves, but most remembered that municipal patrols were in force until the very end of the Civil War.[103] One slave recalled hearing about patrollers working "near surrender-time."[104] Smaller towns had better luck keeping up their patrols near the end of the war. Patrolling continued in Danville, Virginia, until the town surrendered to the Union army in 1865.[105] Towns like Roxboro, North Carolina, that had abandoned patrolling in 1861 reinstated their patrols in 1865, perhaps fearing the disorder to come.[106] In cities where patrollers were in short supply, as in Wilmington, North Carolina, urban slaves capitalized on the shortage of able-bodied men for patrolling by increasing their activities and becoming more daring about forbidden movement at night.[107]

As Union armies moved nearer their homes, Southern whites pleaded with community leaders to appoint more slave patrollers, while others despaired that nothing could stop the slaves from acting as they pleased. In 1864 a North Carolina resident, James Williams, wrote his local county judge that "I deem it necessary that some one should suggest to you the idea of having some patrols appointed for this district. If there ever was a time it was needed it is now." Williams was quick to point out that he had already served his military duty, however, and had no intention of patrolling himself. He told the judge, "Don't make a mistake and appoint me for I have served my apprenticeship."[108] In Pasquotank County, North Carolina, local authorities ordered out the local slave patrol as the Union army drew near, to ensure that their slaves did not run off to the enemy.[109] Meanwhile, a South Carolina plantation mistress worried that the home guard, the last line of defense standing between her and her slaves, might soon be taken away to fight the Northern invaders. She wrote, "If the men are going, then awful things are coming, and I don't want to stay. My God, the women and children, it will be murder and ruin. There are many among the black people and they only want a chance."[110]

In the last few days before a Southern town was overrun by Northern troops, city officials might call upon every resident able to pull a trigger to keep the peace and defend it. Such groups were variously known as local "police and guard" forces. No distinction was now made between the functions of slave patrols and police or home guard; patrol work functions, at that point, were fully melded with those of civic defense. For Southern whites, enemy soldiers had become as dangerous as slaves roaming with impunity.[111]

Slave Control under the Union Army during and after the War

Union armies occupied parts of the South during the war and after its conclusion, with authority over both free and unfree Southerners. At the war's beginning, Northern policies aimed at eventual reconciliation with the slaveholding South: more than one Union officer locked up runaway slaves so that their masters could reclaim them.[112] Further, General George McClellan ordered Union officers to suppress "all attempts at Negro insurrection" among Southern regions that Northern armies controlled in 1861.[113] The policy of catching and returning slaves to their masters ended following the adoption of the Confiscation Acts of 1861 and 1862 and Lincoln's subsequent issuance of the Emancipation Proclamation. From that point forward, bondsmen who could make their way to the Union lines would be received, put to work, and paid as contrabands, serving as army support personnel or as field hands working on captured plantations. The slaves were "fully aware of the causes of the invasion" and knew that it involved their freedom; thousands flocked to the Union army wherever it traveled.[114] But even with a contraband policy in place, Union commanders needed control mechanisms to stave off the complete chaos that accompanied the massive influx of bondsmen into their encampments.

As the Northern invaders advanced into the South, Union troops could not control all parts of the occupied land with equal vigor. If Northern troops did not come to a town immediately after it was clearly behind Union army lines, local citizens would constitute themselves into armed forces to guard against slaves, raiders, and strangers. One South Carolina man wrote that "[w]e have no military rule here, as I suppose they [the Union army] do not consider the place of sufficient consequence to need troops. A company of civilians have been formed, however, armed with shot guns or whatever arms they can get."[115]

One man who had served in the home guards during the war, John F. Flintoff, recorded that on May 27, 1865, he joined the police of Caswell County, North Carolina, "which is the only authority in our land for a time."[116] Patrols continued to function near Buffalo Forge in the Shenandoah Valley until Union troops arrived in late May 1865.[117] Lowcountry whites in South Carolina organized as "scouts"—guerrilla bands, really—who tried to force slaves to continue in their subordinate roles, although the scouts' alleged purpose was to put an end to the plundering that accompanied the Union army's arrival.[118] Without protection from either the Confederate or the Union army, white Southerners residing behind Union lines relived the terror they had experienced at the war's beginning and after the Emancipation Proclamation: they *knew* "bloodthirsty" freedmen would try to murder them. In 1865 several of South Carolina's most prominent residents petitioned the Federal Military Command for protection from the newly freed slaves; ironically, these former masters pleaded for Union troops to safeguard them from the "insurrectionary" freedmen who surrounded them.[119]

After entering a newly occupied Southern area that they intended to garrison, Union troops began dispensing justice during the initial occupation period. The role of the Union officials in this transition from one era to another in law enforcement was not blameless; they were often as racist as the white Southern men they replaced. But they sometimes succeeded in breaking up disturbances between blacks and whites, as they did in Hilton Head in April 1866.[120] Both Union officers and white Southerners recognized that the old slavery regime had ended wherever occupying forces held sway. But they did not necessarily agree about the limitations freedmen should observe under that Northern occupation.

Surprisingly, rural slave patrols and city police controlling urban freedmen continued to operate for a short time under Union occupation, either with or without direct supervision.[121] A few civic leaders chose to consult Northern commanders of the occupying forces, as the town council of Abingdon, Virginia, did in May 1864. Abingdon residents realized that it would "be useless to put out patrols of citizens" unless the "co-operation of the military authorities of the town" could be effected. They invited the local Union army provost marshal, Captain Martin, to a town council meeting to discuss security. Martin agreed to help the police of the town, and furnished men to work with the town patrol.[122] Northern officers could sometimes be persuaded to aid local patrols, on the principle that they were maintaining order and discipline in the newly conquered territory. The turmoil that coincided with the breakdown of slavery and Union occupation "convinced both native whites and Federal military officials of the necessity for establishing mechanisms to check the black threat to law and order."[123] White Southerners might long for the return of slavery, but Northern officers pragmatically applied any useful techniques they could find to keep their new territory under control.

These makeshift alliances between Union officers and Southern whites could be uneasy. In 1865 a majority of white Southerners, for example, expected that white men would continue to sweep black people from the streets by mid-evening—a continuation of their previous experience. Emma Holmes recorded in her diary that because Union soldiers patrolled the streets at night, she anticipated that Columbia's freedmen also would not be "allowed . . . to be out after a certain hour, just as formerly."[124] If white patrols appeared to interfere with Union activities, however, Northern authorities quickly prohibited their outings. In areas like Norfolk, Southern white patrols were suppressed by Union officers, who viewed them as a threat to Northern domination.[125]

The task of controlling newly freed slaves grew enormously for Union commanders in charge of Virginia and Carolina cities as word spread about slavery's end and freedmen flocked to urban centers. After their liberation, Charleston freedmen went out to the surrounding countryside and told their rural cousins that they were free. To the consternation of white residents, rejoicing country slaves soon thronged the streets of Charleston. Elias Horry Deas wrote his daughter that to his dismay, the freedmen would not stay out of Charleston, where they claimed "they [were] free."[126] One commander ordered that country slaves be given access to Georgetown, South Carolina: Rear Admiral John Dahlgren decreed that "colored people are to be allowed to come into the town freely."[127] Some rural slaves, however, even after being told about their freedom, were afraid to leave their plantations for fear that patrollers would bring them back again.[128] And Southern whites fully expected that country freedmen would be turned out of the city by Union troops or a new civil government, and that order, as they had known it before the war, would be restored.[129]

Slaves flooded into Southern cities, looking for lost relations, seeking food, and testing their newfound freedom, particularly from the patrols and the passes they had known before. The pass system had been one of the most resented aspects of slavery, and slaves frequently traveled to prove to themselves that their freedom was real. Eric Foner succinctly describes the motives impelling many freed slaves to relocate to urban areas: "In the cities, many blacks believed, 'freedom was freer.' Here were black social institutions—schools, churches, and fraternal societies—and here too, in spite of inequities in law enforcement, were the army . . . and Freedmen's Bureau, offering protection from the violence so pervasive in much of the rural South."[130] The growth of the urban freedman populace was spectacular: in Richmond, where there had been 12,000 slaves in 1860, the number had grown to 30,000 freedmen by 1865.[131]

Virginia whites were discomfited to find "[s]qualid villages of freed-men [growing] up at the various towns along the Chesapeake Bay, at Alexandria, at Arlington, and at numerous other points throughout the State."[132] The rapid expansion of the slave population in Charlottesville, Virginia, "caused alarm both to the military and civil authorities as well as to local whites." The local county court considered "the expediency of appointing a special police force to prevent marauding and to preserve the peace generally."[133] City dwellers surrounded by multitudes of strange, unfamiliar freedmen stood in terror, waiting for the insurrection that never came. One Wilmington, North Carolina, newspaper editor described the panic thus: "We are really slumbering on a volcano . . . [and the] general eruption is likely to occur at any time."[134]

The rapid influx of freed slaves to cities created a state of chaos, impeding Union occupation activities and frightening Southern whites. The federal authorities issued "order after order urging the freedmen to remain on the farms."[135] They tried to forbid the freed slaves from leaving their plantations unless work could not be found at all. The freedmen ignored the orders, if they even knew such orders existed, and continued to pour into the cities in overwhelming numbers. Finally, military authorities established a pass system, and "Federal authorities enforced it with a vengeance."[136] All persons, white or black, army or civilian, needed a pass. Northern officials hoped the pass system would prevent the possibility of famine and forestall trouble between freed slaves and local whites—even Union troops got into fights with freed slaves, and separating all whites and blacks was a partial goal of the re-instituted pass system.[137]

Reports taken from Union-occupied areas read so similarly to those covering prewar Southern patrol work that, without knowing the dates of an area's occupation, it is occasionally difficult to determine whether Southerners or Union army troops were enforcing the pass system. This notice, for example, appeared in an 1862 North Carolina newspaper: "Taken up and committeed to the Jail of Onslow County on the 4th day of Oct. 1861, a negro man by the name of Ben Boss, the said negro is of a copper color weighs 165 pounds . . . and says he is a free man." Such a notice could have been printed by Southern papers at any time in the early nineteenth century. However, this notice was printed at the behest of a Union provost marshal in a pro-Union newspaper following New Bern's occupation in January 1862.[138] To former slaves, it may have seemed as if little had changed: white men still attempted to control their mobility.[139]

The reinstitution of a pass system, applicable to free blacks and former slaves alike, posed problems for those entering large cities, and was especially troublesome for laborers with steady jobs. The *Richmond Times* reported that "the streets are now constantly patrolled by cavalry, who have instructions to pick up all colored people," assisted by provost guards who entered workshops and searched house to house for passless freedmen.[140] Procuring a pass and having to show it to every white officer revealed to freedmen that the new pass system confined both free blacks and former slaves to a dependent status that could easily lead to abuses. Even black families that had been free for generations complained that they were "required to get some white person to give us passes to attend to our daily occupation, without which we are marched off to the old Rebel Hospital, now called the negro bull pen."[141]

Objections to the new pass system were even more vociferous because Union army officers often delegated enforcement of the pass laws to local police forces, composed of Southern whites, who were all too eager to reimpose the old restrictions of servitude.[142] Their racist attitudes toward law enforcement were no doubt augmented by the need to prevail over some enemy, any enemy, given their recent defeat at the hands of the Northern troops. Richmond provides an excellent example of how easily earlier patterns of racial control reappeared after the war.[143] Once the Union army captured Richmond in April 1865, it established martial law. By June, federal authorities had allowed Mayor Mayo to create a new police organization, one that was reorganized under provisional mayor David Saunders in December as a unified day and night force. Police officers joined Union army soldiers in sweeping freedmen from the streets.[144] But could Richmond police officers, so accustomed to viewing slaves as presumptive criminals, learn how to treat the freedmen fairly?[145] Faced with a prodigious number of freedmen entering the city and federal troops stationed in the area ready to intercede if the former slaves experienced too much harsh treatment, new policemen had to work within constraints that their prewar predecessors had never encountered.[146]

Albert Brooks, a free Richmond stablekeeper before the war, experienced firsthand how little things had changed under the new regime. He was arrested at his place of business by a Richmond policeman, who told him that "all niggers that did not have a paper from their master, show-ing that they were employees, must be taken to jail and hired out for 5 dollars per month." At that point the policeman, acknowledging the os-tensible authority of the occupying forces, handed Brooks over to a fed-eral cavalry soldier who took him to the city jail where he was locked up by the Richmond jailer, "the same one who has kept the jail for many years." After Brooks was released and given a pass from a Union officer, Brooks discovered that he would be required to show it several times a day; as Brooks put it, "[I would be] obliged to show [the pass] to Mayo's police, who stop me on nearly every corner of the street, and make it nearly impossible for me to carry on my business." By forcing him to carry a pass and present it on demand, Southern police intended Brooks to remain in a dependent, controllable status forever.[147] Brooks and oth-ers like him contacted leaders in the African American churches of Rich-mond to rally support for their cause.

At Brooks's urging, the African American community in Richmond protested this renewal of prewar police measures by taking their griev-ances to Northern newspapers and President Andrew Johnson. In June black Virginians sent a description of their treatment to the *New York Tribune,* castigating the "daily mounted patrol, with their sabers drawn, whose business is the hunting of colored people." For Northerners unfa-miliar with Richmond's police, they spelled out the brutal history of Mayo and his men.

> For a long series of year he [Mayor Joseph Mayo] has been the Mayor of Richmond, and his administration has been marked by cruelty and injustice to us, and the old Rebel police now again in power have been our greatest enemies. It was Mayor Mayo who in former days ordered us to be scourged for trifling offenses against slave laws and usages; and his present police, who are now hunting us through the streets, are the men who relentlessly applied the lash to our quivering flesh.[148]

The African Americans also sent a delegation to the president, who took quick action. Virginia's governor replaced Mayor Mayo, and "[b]y the time the delegates returned and reported back to their constituents the pass and curfew laws had been repealed, the civilian government re-moved, and the offending army officers replaced."[149]

When Union commanders conducted elections and then handed con-trol of a Southern city back to its residents, the changes could have a dramatic impact on the daily lives of urban freedmen. When the coastal city of Portsmouth, Virginia, fell to the Union army in 1861, the residents saw their first African American policemen, chief of police, and justices of the peace. Prior to 1861 no police force had existed in Portsmouth; instead, patrollers had the same duties as "policemen of today," according to Jane Pyatt, a former slave interviewed in the 1930s. In 1866, when civic elections were held again, Pyatt reported that "a mayor was elected head of the city, and the colored policemen, Justice of Peace, and Chief of Police was done away with. In their places, a [civilian] provost-marshal with a white staff was appointed."[150]

Union army officers were not the only Northern outsiders thrust into the midst of conflicted relations between freed slaves and Southern white policemen. Besides providing food, clothing, and guidance to newly liberated slaves, officials of the Freedmen's Bureau also found themselves in the unlooked-for position of siding with former slaves in their grievances against aggressive policemen. Although it did so rarely, the Freedmen's Bureau occasionally charged the police with robbing and beating former slaves. "Colonel Whittlesey wrote that the police of Johnston and Sampson [counties] as well as Duplin counties are not only inefficient, but are often engaged in robbing freed men and others who sympathize with them." Another Freedmen's Bureau officer corroborated his evaluation that the Duplin County, North Carolina, police were "armed enemies . . . against the rights and property of the Freed people."[151] Bureau agents did not always protect freedmen from whites who terrorized them, of course, but blacks could often find shelter from abusive whites at bureau offices.[152]

Accustomed to imposing their will upon slaves and free blacks before the war, Southern police groups in the immediate postwar regime did not realize they could not resume their violent ways so long as the occupying Union army remained to supervise their actions. In the Second Military District (North and South Carolina), after granting Southern citizens the right to choose their own police groups, Union commanders ended up taking that prerogative back and dictated the composition and authority local police squads would have.[153] In 1867, Capt. J. W. Clous removed police officers from duty in Wilmington, North Carolina, claiming that they used "unnecessary and unwarranted violence in making arrests." In future, Clous ordered, "any officers selected would have to be cleared through the Charleston commander's office."[154] He also re-moved from office town guards in Sumter, Lancaster, and other South Carolina townships for using excessive violence.[155] Clous then took di-rect action against still-active slave patrols by removing their authority in several city charters. For example, the Lancaster city charter, passed in 1840, had its entire fifth section, authorizing patrols, suspended on July 29, 1867, by special order of Clous's military command.[156] Finally, to draw the teeth of newly created police groups, Clous stepped in the following year to set forth the exact composition of local police forces. He authorized the courts of Jones, Craven, Lenoir, and Pitt counties to organize and employ an armed police force "to be composed of loyal citi-zens, white and colored in the ratio of registered voters."[157]

With the loss of control over their civic and state governments, South-ern whites faced a changing society in which they were ever more fearful of their former slaves. After emancipation, freedmen acquired weapons in growing numbers, and the prospect of former slaves with loaded fire-arms brought back the rumors of imminent "negro risings." In towns like Pineville, South Carolina, former slaves openly drilled and dis-played their weapons.[158] Any rumor would set white citizens to loading their guns and mounting guards.[159] Southern whites wanted the freed-men disarmed and helpless; only then could they be made to stand in awe of the whites, who sought to continue the psychological and physi-cal domination of their former bondsmen. "The occasional discovery of a cache of arms confirmed the worst fears and intensified the campaign to disarm the black population."[160] In North Carolina, particularly in the Cape Fear region, bands of county police (some with legal authority and some without) searched freedmen's homes looking for weapons and "stolen property," a euphemism routinely adopted for all goods they found in a freedman's possession. Naturally, the stolen goods often ended up in the hands of county police who retrieved them but did not necessarily return them to their white, allegedly rightful, "owners."[161]

As in the prewar years, fears about these supposed threats to white security mounted precipitously at the holiday season, when freedmen were seen more frequently in town, visiting family members and buying yearly supplies. No one knew better than the freedmen that insurrection rumors would ultimately result in white-on-black violence: the former slaves could count upon some scapegoat to be flogged or killed to satisfy the psychological demons that haunted Southern whites. In the immediate aftermath of the Civil War, the most widespread insurrection rumors swirled around Christmas 1865.

Insurrection Scares of 1865

White fears of insurrections by freedmen flared in December 1865, but several anxious months preceded the holiday panic. Tensions mounted in the wake of white-black confrontations, like those in Wilmington, North Carolina, in the late summer of 1865. Following the "daily outrages" that African American Northern troops allegedly committed on white residents, or the insolent behavior witnessed from former slaves, white Wilmington citizens complained of their "well-grounded fears for the safety of our unarmed and defenseless people." Planning to "arm the police and to form a *posse comitatus* of all white residents," they requested rifles from Governor William W. Holden when they informed him of their insurrection fears.[162] Their hysteria provoked Samuel A. Duncan, a Union general stationed in the area, to investigate. He reported that their fears were "utterly groundless, and absurd in the extreme."[163] Months later, the Wilmingtonians claimed that the former slaves were armed and "performing military drills."[164] Governor Holden also received requests from residents of Hyde and Hertford counties asking to be allowed to form militia units in response to the supposed insurrection threats. The white Hertford citizens asked for a patrol band to ward off "domestic violence and disorder."[165] Similar requests to other state governors prompted them to order "militias to patrol the countryside and disarm blacks," while town officials "authorized the employment of additional police."[166]

In fact, North Carolina residents had been given the means to protect themselves by Union general John M. Schofield, commander of the Department of North Carolina in 1865. He authorized the formation of county militia companies, commonly called "county police," to stop roving marauders.[167] Although Schofield intended the police units to repress bandits and not freedmen, militia companies (largely composed of Confederate army veterans) provided security for white residents by overawing former bondsmen with shows of force that bore a strong resemblance to prewar slave patrols. In the Cape Fear region, the head of a county police force violently murdered four freedmen for their refusal to turn over the crop they had planted and harvested on their former master's lands.[168]

The Christmas insurrection panic was not limited to North Carolina alone. Virginia's governor, F. H. Pierpont, received multiple letters from citizens requesting weapons or the right to raise a military company for self-defense, claiming that "a general insurrection of the negro population about Christmas is contemplated."[169] Although some white Virginians calmly acknowledged that the rumors might be false, county courts appointed large police forces to patrol their counties, ready to stave off any revolt.[170] One Virginian placed his sole faith in the local patrol's ability to protect him and other whites, saying that "we have an armed patrol which keeps perfect order and makes them [the freedmen] stand in some fear."[171] In South Carolina, one vigilante committee voted to disarm all local freedmen to prevent any planned insurrection, while another such group formed in Kingstree and took more extreme action, whipping several freedmen.[172] South Carolinian Jane Pringle wrote to General Dan Sickles in 1865, predicting that an insurrection would definitely take place during Christmas week and earnestly entreating that Union troops intervene to protect whites in her neighborhood against their former slaves.[173] Dan T. Carter, who has closely studied the Christmas insurrection scare, finds that "[i]n many respects, the insurrection panic of 1865 was a recapitulation of those which had taken place during the antebellum period. There was the same preoccupation with 'outsiders,' with nonconformist white southerners, and with assertive blacks."[174]

Although the Christmas 1865 uprising never materialized, the fears of many Southerners translated into direct action against former bondsmen. Moreover, their insurrection fears were reinforced by news in November 1865 that British West Indies black residents had revolted, causing some Southerners to wonder whether their former slaves would show them any mercy.[175] White Virginia and Carolina residents formed their own patrol groups or extralegal forces to disarm and terrorize the freedmen, calling upon their prewar experience as patrollers to guide them in the world of Reconstruction.[176] Some observers think the 1865 Christmas insurrection rumors might be attributed to calculated, Machiavellian motives of Southern whites: the threats may have been falsified to allow whites to disarm the freedmen without opposition, in order to control them with greater ease later.[177]

The End of Legal Slave Patrols

The Thirteenth Amendment and the Civil War ended slavery in the United States, but the use of slave patrols and their methods did not terminate so neatly or conclusively. Although some Union army commanders could dictate the end of patrolling, as J. W. Clous did in Lancaster, South Carolina, the occupation forces took no concerted action against slave patrols. Rather, a hodgepodge of state and local government laws ended the official patrolling era. Insurrection fears, like those that surrounded Christmas 1865, however, prompted the continued use of patrol techniques by Southern whites in the postwar era, either legally by means of county and city police or illegally by vigilante groups.

Southern whites' insurrection fears and worries about armed, assertive freedmen only increased after the war's close because, despite the presence of the Union army, official state governments no longer existed. Each community thought that it was on its own until a state government could be created. At the earliest opportunity, Southern state legislatures rewrote their constitutions. In attempting to prevent legal chaos, the state constitutions of 1865 "did not materially change or alter the system of government that had existed in each state previous to that time."[178] In North Carolina, although the new state constitution abolished slavery, laws pertaining to slavery and patrols remained on the books. Only in October 1865 did the legislature repeal laws related to slavery, including those authorizing patrols.[179] When the Virginia General Assembly met in February 1866, its members repealed all "acts and parts of acts relating to slaves and slavery," including chapter 98 of the Code of 1860, authorizing the continued use of slave patrols.[180] South Carolina lawmakers, expressing their disdain for the Northern forces, never formally repealed slavery—they merely acknowledged its failure to continue as an institution: "The slaves in South Carolina having been emancipated by the action of the United States authorities, neither slavery nor involuntary servitude . . . shall ever be re-established in this State."[181]

Having ended slavery and repealed its supporting laws, South Carolina legislators next considered how they would confine the freedmen through new laws. All Southern states enacted "Black Codes" in the two years following the war's end, with South Carolina leading the way.[182] The new codes relied upon laws enforcing labor contracts and prohibiting vagrancy to restrict former slaves to agricultural pursuits and control their movements. The Black Codes put laws into place that could be enforced by county or voluntary militia units, much like the slave patrols of old. Although technically outlawing slavery, South Carolina's legislature reenacted its militia and patrol laws in September 1865 as part of its new code at the urging of its provisional governor.[183] Governor Benjamin F. Perry wanted the militia restored to prevent insurrections, and the legislature passed new laws that virtually reenacted the prewar status quo. The law provided for enforcement of the patrol laws by either militia or patrol groups or by volunteer police forces (in effect, volunteer patrollers).[184] Even before the new laws went into effect, however, some South Carolina planters like E. P. Millikey thought they would never be tough enough. He wrote: "As for making the negroes work under the present state of affairs it seems to me a waste of time and energy . . . No sheriff & Posse or Patrol, under civil rule, will suit our wants. We must have mounted Infantry."[185]

In 1866 Governor Perry proclaimed that South Carolina militia organizations would continue to act as militia and patrols, and that they would be "charged with the police and patrol duty of the country," so long as that did not interfere with the formation of private volunteer companies for police purposes. Indeed, he hoped to stimulate the formation and enforcement of militia and patrol laws by volunteer patrol groups.[186] The governor anticipated that once the Union military commander got wind of his proclamation, he would officially outlaw the state-mandated militia and patrol duties, thus leaving the voluntary groups outside the authority of both the governor and the Union army commander.[187] Governor Perry wrongly assumed that the army commander would invalidate the new patrol law; in fact, his successor, Governor James Orr, vetoed it first. Orr assumed that since slavery had ended, patrol laws would be null and void. The rest of the South Carolina Black Code was set aside by military edict. The quickness with which the laws were nullified after their enactment makes it almost impossible to determine whether they had any practical effect.[188]

The overall harshness of South Carolina's laws, clearly designed as race control laws with discriminatory features, prompted angry reaction in the North and encouraged other Southern states to exercise greater legerdemain when they passed their own Black Codes in 1866. Instead of creating laws that mandated different punishments based upon race, they would have to find another method of enacting the legal restrictions they wanted to place upon freedmen.

As in South Carolina, white constituents in Virginia and North Carolina wanted their own Black Codes to delineate all aspects of freedmen's lives. The impetus behind creating these new codes came, in part, from the continuing flow of freedmen toward each state's cities. Virginia newspapers led the movement for a Black Code and antivagrancy laws. The *Richmond Times* and *Lynchburg Virginian* complained in 1865 of the "idle, vagabond" freedman, whose only apparent source of income must be petty theft; both newspapers expected the state government to enact antivagrancy laws to protect the property and safety of whites.[189] Lynchburg's editor ardently suggested that

> the most stringent police regulations may be necessary to keep [freedmen] from overburdening the towns and depleting the agricultural regions of labor. The military authorities seem to be alive to this fact and are taking measures to correct the evil—But the civil authorities, also, should be fully empowered to protect the community from this new imposition. The magistrates and municipal officers everywhere should be permitted to hold a rod *in terrorem* over these wandering, idle, creatures. Nothing short of the most efficient police system will prevent strolling, vagrancy, theft, and the utter destruction of or serious injury to our industrial system.[190]

In November 1865 the newspaper renewed its appeal for a stronger system of antivagrancy laws to "be revived and rigidly enforced."[191] The reinstitution of measures that resembled the patrols' prewar powers seemed only logical to Southern whites.

The Virginia legislature responded to these suggestions by passing a criminal antivagrancy law that empowered any white person, including the "special county police, or the police of any corporation," to take up and then hire out for three months any people without obvious means of employment.[192] Although the impartial language could theoretically have applied to either whites or former slaves, in practice the law was directed only at African Americans. Southern whites of all classes could not give up their compulsive desire for authority over the lives of freedmen. General Terry, the Union army officer in command of Virginia, annulled this statute, because he believed that "[t]he ultimate effect of the statute would be to reduce the freedmen to a condition of servitude worse than that from which they have been emancipated, a condition which will be slavery in all but its name."[193]

North Carolina, like many Southern states, also passed antivagrancy

laws as part of an attempt to write a comprehensive, new Black Code
that would restrict the freedmen to agricultural labor and keep them on
plantations permanently.[194] However, military officials forbade the enforcement of the antivagrancy laws in North Carolina, and the attempt
to reinstitute widespread slavery through legal chicanery prompted
swift, unilateral action by the United States Congress in 1867.[195]

Dissatisfied with the unrepentant attitude of many Southern lawmakers, Republican legislators at the federal level took over the laws governing military occupation of the South. The Reconstruction Act of 1867
declared that no legal government existed in the ten Southern states, and
then divided the area into military districts with army commanders.
Congress required the military commanders to "suppress insurrection,
disorder, and violence, and to punish, or cause to be punished, all dis-
turbers of the public peace and criminals."[196] Legislators created the
Fourteenth Amendment, guaranteeing equal protection to all citizens
under federal law, passed the Civil Rights Act, and prolonged the existence of the Freedmen's Bureau. Congress also enfranchised former male
slaves and disenfranchised most Southern white men who had served in
the Confederate war effort—the very men accustomed to serving in local, state, or federal government offices in the South.

The requirements that Congress imposed during Reconstruction convinced many Southern whites that local governance had become a sham.
By handing town and state governments over to former slaves and Republican "scalawags," under the eagle eye of Union officers and Freedmen's Bureau agents, Southern whites believed that their traditional
racial arrangements had been turned upside down. Accustomed to legislation that vindicated slavery and controlled slaves, and yet denied those
laws with the invalidation of their Black Codes by Congress and the
army, some Southern whites resorted to extralegal means to continue
their dominance over the race they deemed inferior.

Referring to the effects of the Civil War, Wilbur J. Cash wrote that
"Reconstruction was . . . simply an extension of that war, on lines yet
more terrible and exigent. And so its effect was to hammer home the
war's work, including, specifically, the essential military tone and organization. During these thirty years the South was like nothing so much as
a veteran army."[197] While Cash's observation applied to the cohesion of
Southern classes and the respect ordinary soldiers gave their command-

ers in the years following the Civil War, his comment also aptly describes other aspects of the white postwar South. The "military tone and organization" that helped the South retain its individualistic demeanor also allowed white Southerners to apply military precision to the new police forces that flourished in the postwar years. The patrol techniques that they knew so well before the war would become even more forceful when melded with the military training that virtually all adult white men received in the Confederate army. Postwar police forces would transform patrolling into a highly effective but still legal means of racial oppression, building upon the practices that many prewar police forces had used when acting as urban patrollers. But the merging of patrol work with military experience for Southern whites found other outlets besides police forces.

After the Civil War, the violent methods of slave patrols would also be adopted and renewed by groups dedicated to white supremacy at all costs, even by illegal means. The seemingly unrestricted brutality of patrols would find its mirror image during Reconstruction in the extralegal activities of vigilante groups that operated outside virtually all social restrictions. As slaves, bondsmen had often been protected from patrollers by their masters, who (for paternalistic or materialistic reasons) did not wish to have their "property" damaged by roving slave patrols. With slavery's abolition and the end of property rights in slaves, freedmen found they had no guardians to protect them from the rebirth of patrol-like violence in the postwar period. White Southerners visited retribution upon freedmen who had little means of protecting themselves from the next incarnation of slave patrols: the Ku Klux Klan.

Black Freedom, White Violence:
Patrols, Police, and the Klan

Former slaves envisioned that freedom would mean they could "do like a white man."[1] Freedom for them not only implied an end to forced labor, corporal punishment, and the separation of families, but also held the promise of education, economic advancement, and freedom of movement. They thought that emancipation would end the use of racial controls like the pass system and slave patrols. Their high hopes were dashed in the war's immediate aftermath, when many Union commanders allowed Southern whites to use city or county police forces to harass and threaten freedmen just as they had done in prewar patrols.

Northern whites expected that freed slaves would have the right to earn wages in exchange for their labor. Believing the position of Southern freedmen to be analogous to that of African Americans in the North, Northern whites thought that former slaves would be accorded basic rights. However, Union commanders and Northern congressmen generally did not expect that freedmen would have, or indeed deserved, all the rights of white men. Not every Northerner believed that freedmen should vote or sit on juries. Indeed, Northerners' own state laws prohibited such behavior in many instances.[2] The victors anticipated that Southern whites would extend to freedmen basic privileges, while retaining (and perhaps privately acting upon) their racial prejudices.

Southern whites wanted to reassert the social, economic, and political domination they had enjoyed before the Civil War. Although they knew slavery was technically dead, old habits of racial superiority died hard. They assumed that freedmen would have to be controlled and forced to work; otherwise, whites believed, lazy, larcenous former slaves could only survive by leading lives of crime. In the two years after the Civil War, Southerners tried to force freedmen to share the same restricted legal status that free African Americans had held in the antebellum South, only to have Union army commanders or the United States Congress invalidate their laws and integrate their lily-white legislatures. Stymied in their attempts to regulate freedmen with Black Codes, white Southerners could not easily use legal means immediately after the Civil War's conclusion to reestablish formal racial controls.

These three differing views of how freedmen would live in the postwar South competed with one another for dominance in the late 1860s and 1870s. While the North remained willing to impose its views through the Union army and the Freedmen's Bureau, former slaves began to realize how difficult achieving their ideals of freedom would be. With the enfranchisement of freedmen and their election to integrated Southern state legislatures, ex-slaves could enact laws that recognized their new legal status. But the chasm between enactment and day-to-day reality remained wide. Some Southern whites, seeing their authority stripped away by the army, the Freedmen's Bureau, and laws that required them to treat freedmen like equals, turned from legal to extralegal measures to reassert control over their former bondsmen: they resumed patrolling, this time as vigilantes. Ultimately violence defined the scope of former slaves' freedoms, making Southern whites' vision of postwar race relations the dominant one in the Reconstruction of Virginia and the Carolinas.

Union Leagues, Black Militias, and Vigilante Justice after 1867

Having lost control of their state governing apparatus after March 1867, Southern whites experienced dismay when newly enfranchised freedmen elected their own integrated legislatures. Freed slaves formed Union Leagues to learn civic responsibility and increase their political participation—but from the perspective of Southern whites the leagues promoted an unfortunate awareness of and sympathy for the Republican party. At the ballot box, guarded by the still-present Union army, former slaves voted for Republicans in overwhelming numbers. Once elected to state offices, Republicans lost little time in re-forming local militias to contain all able-bodied males (including freedmen) and providing weapons to the new militia groups.[3] Disdaining to march side by side with former slaves as fellow citizen-soldiers, most white Southerners refused to participate in the restored militias. Other whites were banned from the new militias because of their service in the Confederate army. But failing to muster and drill with the new militias did not mean Southern whites ignored their activities. On the contrary, armed and potentially dangerous freedmen brought images of insurrectionary horror to the minds of former slave owners.[4]

In addition to the state-created militia, freedmen also formed voluntary militia units to practice and drill with weapons. One of the first such volunteer militia groups assembled in Richmond in 1866.[5] Armed with rifles and sabers, former slaves marched around the city with banners flying. Although disbanded by Union army edict, the group later reunited and continued its military exercises. New black volunteer militias were training in every town and county.[6] South Carolina's former governor Milledge Luke Bonham believed that local freedmen were "forming . . . secret military organizations." He described a barbecue and training camp for fifty former slaves, complete with a drillmaster who wore epaulettes—the height of indignity for Bonham, since in his eyes they represented the authority of Southern military organization. Bonham feared that the creation of "[s]uch organizations of one race must of necessity lead to similar organizations of the other for self[-]preservation," and warned that no white man would "quietly submit to unauthorized and armed negro domination."[7]

Indeed, white Southerners did not "quietly submit," but began collectively organizing in three ways. The least militant of the new white groups were restrictive agricultural associations designed to retain economic dominance over the freedmen. In Edgefield, South Carolina, white planters formed an Agricultural and Police Club that drew upon the prewar plans of the Beech Island Agricultural Society.[8] Their objective: to pursue a "united and systematic plan with respect to the regulation of our colored population." The club's rules included selling no land to freedmen or Republicans and enticing no laborer to break his labor contract. In addition, the planters created their own white police force, reminiscent of the slave patrol, "to ensure that all blacks and whites observed these conditions."[9] Whites who did business with black farmers could find themselves threatened by such voluntary patrols, as one Sumter businessman did in 1870, or put out of business altogether.[10]

More ominously, white planters organized their own militia-like groups as voluntary clubs. Whites created a "mutual aid club" to control blacks in Rockbridge County, Virginia, as early as May 1866.[11] Rifle clubs sprang up across all three states in response to the Union Leagues and African American militias. Governor Daniel H. Chamberlain believed that South Carolina had more than 240 gun clubs in 1876.[12] Although club members claimed to be gathering for recreation, drilling and military organization were never far away from any of their meetings.[13] In Charleston, rifle clubs met on alternate nights in every ward, so that several thousand white men could be quickly mobilized against freedmen at a moment's notice.[14]

The third and most frightening form of collective action taken by Southerners was the formation of white vigilante groups. The Ku Klux Klan had many predecessors following the Civil War, and these gangs frequently included Southern veterans.[15] Returning Confederate soldiers pillaged and robbed the homes of freedmen, sometimes in collusion with local authorities.[16] Southern whites looked to veterans to restore the old racial regime: north of Charleston, Harriet Palmer hoped that Southern soldiers returning from the war would once again regulate freedmen by patrolling.[17] The veterans understood military discipline and applied it. Around Greenville, South Carolina, planters organized themselves into beat companies and sent out patrols, as in the old prewar days.[18] They took away weapons that freedmen had acquired and forced those living in rural areas to obtain passes from former masters.[19] African American military forces were to be disarmed or intimidated. Near Pineville, South Carolina, "scouts" from a white guerrilla band attacked a new freedmen's military group.[20] In the war's aftermath, "[a]rmed bands of white men patrolled the country roads to drive back the Negroes wandering about," according to observers like Carl Schurz.[21]

Certain Union army officers made it easier for vigilante groups to wield influence. Officers like General E. R. S. Canby refused to disperse Union troops to protect freedmen and continued to rely upon white Southern law enforcement to keep the peace, well aware that its agents could not always be trusted to safeguard freedmen's rights.[22] Near Lumberton, North Carolina, Confederate veterans preferred joining "police guard" units to the Klan, since Union army officers there would arm and deputize them to keep order in the community. If the veterans sometimes persecuted freedmen or Union sympathizers, Northern authorities often chose to turn a blind eye.[23]

This ad hoc postwar patrolling, through economic associations, rifle clubs, or vigilante groups, was slowly replaced by a more organized method of white intimidation. Following the Reconstruction Act of 1867, accounts of night riders "regularly appeared in Republican newspapers [and] letters written by southern Republicans." In disguise, they traveled to freedmen's lodgings where they took weapons and whipped former slaves.[24] Their avowed purpose was "to take the law into their own hands, in defiance" of law and the Union army.[25] Collectively these night riders came to be known as the Ku Klux Klan.

The Klan Forms and Spreads to Virginia and the Carolinas

The first Klan met in Pulaski, Tennessee, in 1865.[26] Claiming boredom, six young men created the club (they said) to play pranks on local freed men; club members rode around dressed as ghosts to scare former slaves. Even this supposedly innocuous beginning contained indefensible elements of terror. The historian John Hope Franklin has written that the young Ku Kluxers "could hardly have been unaware of what they were doing. Even if they were bored and impatient with life, as has been their defense, [night riding] was nothing new for [them]. Nor were wanton attacks on helpless Negroes new. If the young men were looking for fun, they did not have to go beyond the nearest Negro settlement, and furthermore, they would be performing a service to the white community if they whipped Negroes to keep them in line."[27]

In the first year or two after the war, perhaps the boys did little more than try to scare freedmen by preying on their fear of the supernatural. Shifting from burlesques and jokes, however, these first KKK members began borrowing techniques of the prewar patrollers. Groups of disguised white men on horseback broke up religious and social gatherings, confiscated freedmen's firearms, and increased the psychological terror they inflicted by riding at night. Men in the KKK had made the transition from pranks to systematic brutality by 1867. By then, Klan members routinely resorted to violence—beating, lynching, and shooting—to punish freedmen for their political convictions and to prevent the enforcement of the Fourteenth Amendment.[28]

The rapid increase in Klan membership after 1865 may also account for its quick descent into violence. The Klan attracted many to its ranks, including bushwhackers, desperadoes, and banditti already at large across the South.[29] And of course it became impossible to tell "real" Klan members from others who merely used its white sheets to hide their own actions. When former slave patrollers "disguised themselves and spiced their visitations with the ghostly mumbo jumbo the Klan had made popular, the distinction between them and 'legitimate' Klansmen grew blurred."[30] Whether these groups were sanctioned by the real Klan or not, it seems likely that even informal Klan activities were tacitly approved by elite members of white Southern society. The social hierarchy that existed in the South before the war persisted during Reconstruction, and Klan outrages would not have continued without the support (implicit or explicit) of leading whites. Thus we cannot blame all Klan activity on the South's poor whites any more than one can describe the slave patrollers as being exclusively from the bottom of Southern society.[31]

The loss of white political power, matched with the rise of black militias and Union Leagues, prompted Southern whites of many classes to join the Klan, where they could resume the activities of slave patrollers.[32] Some would have preferred to see a formal, all-white militia system restored. Any place where Southern whites were permitted to reestablish their militia would ultimately lead to the "restoration of the old patrol system," but all-white militias would have to await the departure of Union troops.[33] In the meantime, vigilantes and the Klan would scare freedmen into political and social submission to Southern whites. "Ultimately, as a former Confederate officer put it, the Klan aimed to regulate blacks' 'status in society.' "[34] For whites, these reasons merged into one long political agenda with interrelated goals. As one Klansman said, he joined the group to foster the "promotion of the Conservative-Democratic party, undermining of the Republican party, the desire for a white man's government, and the suppression of Negro equality."[35]

Combined with the new postwar political situation, Southerners had a long-standing tradition of self-help—a willingness to use violence without waiting for official legal sanction—that almost mandated the creation of a vigilante group like the Klan.[36] Self-help had its roots in many interlocking elements of Southern culture: honor, slavery, and the South's residual frontier nature that caused many to doubt the efficacy of centralized justice and law enforcement.[37] Although violent groups changed in membership through the decades, they formed a continuing tradition in the South predating even the Regulators of the 1760s and continuing through the age of slave patrols.[38] And of course the recent Civil War provided a body of men with military training and violent tendencies who made ideal members for Klan enclaves.[39] The recruitment of Confederate war heroes like Nathan Bedford Forrest into the Klan helped the KKK retain its chivalric image long after it lapsed into racial violence.[40]

The Klan also allowed militant whites to reassert psychological dominance over the freedmen who seemed such an ominous threat, just as patrols had done in the prewar period. With the demise of paternalistic relations that had shielded former slaves from some violence, membership in the Klan provided an outlet for white aggression that no longer had to be tempered by the master and slave façades of affection and subservience. That need for dominance had been strengthened by the alleged "threats" that emerged in the new postwar regime (for example, militias and the Freedmen's Bureau). Whites who had once mistrusted their slaves but controlled them through physical intimidation now sought to control the freedmen in order to diminish their fears.[41] Terror was the key. Aggression and insecurities emanating from emancipation were not the only psychological needs driving Southern whites after the war's end. Freedom for slaves elevated the status of African Americans, but in the minds of Southern whites that freedom implicitly lowered the status of all whites in society.[42] The mere fact of black freedom was psychologically damaging to the self-perceptions many whites held about themselves in the postwar era, and violence against freedmen (through the Klan or otherwise) was a means by which to repair, or at least mask, that damage.

While using patroller methods, Klan violence drew upon beliefs and attitudes that had fostered slavery as an institution. Pseudoscientific proof that African Americans were racially inferior, phrenology, biblical injunctions legitimating slavery, the "white man's burden" that Southerners believed obligated them to civilize the slaves they commanded—these doctrines and others had bolstered the continued existence of slavery in the South.[43] After emancipation, these beliefs did not disappear; all the prewar arguments in favor of slavery were reborn as justifications for continued violent episodes of racial control by the Klan.

Having started and spread across Tennessee like wildfire, the Klan slowly worked its way into other states. The KKK gained many followers in South Carolina before expanding to states both north and south. Prince McElhannon, a Georgia freedman, recalled a conversation he had with a white neighbor about the Klan's appearance in his state: "I said to old Mr. Whitehead, 'They tell me that people have got to rising out of the ground.' He said, 'Prince, that is not so; it is just like the old patrollers. It was first in South Carolina and then it came here.' "[44]

In Virginia and the Carolinas, the Klan had its strongest foothold in the Piedmont regions.[45] The mid-state Piedmont farms contained almost equal numbers of whites and African Americans, and medium-sized farms outnumbered both extremely large and extremely small properties.[46] In a few locations the Klan operated with impunity: in North Carolina counties like Caswell, Orange, and Alamance, the sheriff, deputies, and all important local officials were members of the KKK.[47] In South Carolina, the Piedmont region was also where the newly formed African American militia units had been most heavily armed by the governor. Some areas were virtual Klan strongholds, like Spartanburg, Union, and York counties in South Carolina. In places where blacks heavily outnumbered whites, as they did through most of South Carolina's Low Country, whites realized that they were vulnerable to counterattacks from the freedmen, and the Klan was slower to take root in those districts.[48] However, despite being outnumbered by blacks, the Klan briefly appeared even in coastal areas. Describing the Klan's uneven manifestation, Eric Foner explains that "no simple formula can explain the pattern of terror that engulfed parts of the South while leaving others relatively unscathed."[49]

The Klan had a relatively brief though brutal reign of terror in Virginia and the Carolinas. In North Carolina the Klan first appeared in late 1867, and in all three states, it gained additional strength in the spring of 1868, when new Republican state governments began forming.[50] From 1868 to 1871, the Klan accounted for at least "26 murders and 213 floggings" in North Carolina.[51] In response, blacks were willing to use their own self-help methods to thwart the Klan: in 1868 they marched armed with only fence rails near Wilmington, and ended Klan activities there for a time.[52] In Virginia the KKK was first mentioned in 1868 when Klan members began visiting the houses of freedmen at night, threatening them because of their political opinions.[53] Where the KKK seemed most powerful, as in Charleston and Columbia, South Carolina, the Union army sent additional troops in 1870–1872.[54] In other places, like Lynchburg, the Klan appeared only briefly in 1868.[55] After 1871 the Klan became less active because some of its political objectives had been achieved. In North Carolina the Republicans lost power in 1870, and in South Carolina the governor withdrew weapons from local African American militia units in 1871.[56]

The Klan's violent methods attracted renewed federal attention, and Congress responded to the latest wave of terrorism. Congress passed the Ku Klux Klan Act of April 1871, making it illegal to conspire to prevent freedmen from enjoying their full civil rights and allowing federal law enforcement to intervene when state officers failed to act. Congress then conducted a series of hearings in 1871, with special attention given to South Carolina, since Klan outrages seemed most conspicuous there. Calling dozens of witnesses to testify, congressmen tried to understand the KKK's beatings and brutality. The hearings, however, did little to stop the violence Klan members used to intimidate former slaves into forgoing their political rights. Only after Reconstruction ended, with federal troops withdrawn and state politics returned to the hands of white planters, did Klan groups disband or become quiescent across the South.[57]

Slave Patrols versus the KKK

Similar methods shared by slave patrols and the Klan reveal the violent legacy that patrolling left after the Civil War. The KKK worked at the local level, usually acting against regional targets. Patrols also had worked locally and focused on specific plantations or areas, attempting to restrict slave movement. Both patrollers and Klan members operated primarily at night, using horses to move about in rural areas. Like slave patrols, the Klan drew its members from every white social class; after all, theoretically every white Southerner was united in wanting to limit the new civil rights of freedmen. Klansmen, like slave patrols before them, required freedmen to have passes to travel on the roads. They let it be known that all black dances and social meetings should be over by eleven o'clock, and the gatherings had to remain small—they did not want to give former bondsmen the opportunity to plot "insurrections."[58] In particular, they wanted all African Americans disarmed: Klansmen took guns away from both ex-slaves and blacks who had been free before the Civil War so that their militia groups would be helpless.[59] Restraints upon mobility, socialization, and property ownership that slave patrols had legally imposed continued almost without interruption under the extralegal enforcement of the Klan.

The features shared by the KKK and slave patrols also seemed obvious to Belton Townsend, a white Southern reader of the *Atlantic Monthly*, who rebuked Maryland's Democratic senator Reverdy Johnson for his supposed ignorance of the Klan's unique Southern bloodlines. Townsend wrote that:

> Reverdy Johnson was startled and indignant at the atrocities of the Ku-Klux. But a moment's reflection would have convinced him that their deeds were not so unnatural as, at first sight, he evidently regarded them. The Ku-Klux Klan with its night visits and whippings and murders was the legitimate offspring of the patrol. Every Southern gentleman used to serve on the night patrol, the chief duty of which was to whip severely any negro found away from home without a pass from his master. . . . in the good old times they used to hunt down runaway negroes with hounds and guns, brand them, beat them till senseless, and while patrolling at night flog negroes who had passes, "just to hear them beg and hollo."

Townsend went on to explain that respectable white members of Southern communities were shielding Klansmen from discovery, making it almost impossible to prosecute and convict them for their violence against freedmen.[60]

Like Townsend, former slaves noticed the similarities between prewar slave patrollers and the Ku Klux Klan. For whites like Reverdy Johnson, the differences between patrols and the Klan may have seemed obvious, created by the great divide of war: one set operated before the Civil War, the other afterward. But that division was not so clearly drawn for ex-slaves who had seen both groups operate. Maria Leland, a former slave, talked about the Klan and patrollers as if they worked at the same time.[61] Freedmen such as Randall Lee knew of "patrols who were active *after* the war," and more than a few former bondsmen claimed that the Klan functioned before the Civil War.[62] Some confused the two groups, like ex-slave J. T. Tims, who recalled that "[i]t was before the war that I knew 'bout the Ku Klux. There wasn't no difference between the patroles and the Ku Klux that I knows of. If th'd ketch you, they all would whip you. I don't know nothin' about the Ku Klux Klan after the War."[63] When questioned about slave patrols, some elderly ex-slaves talked of the patrol and the Klan as if they were one and the same thing. While one WPA editor in the 1930s noted this down as the delusion of a "crazy" slave, the similarities between patrol and Klan methods were not lost on freedmen.[64]

Even if they distinguished between patrollers and Klansmen, many former slaves recognized that both groups shared a common enemy, directing their energies against African Americans. Charlie Harvey knew that the Klan persecuted freedmen with guns.[65] Laurence Gary, from Newberry County, South Carolina, distinguished between patrols and the Klan, but said that his master, Dr. John Gary, kept the Klan off his plantation and away from his laborers.[66] One Greenville, South Carolina, ex-slave said that after the war, the patrol was called the KKK.[67] Other former slaves merely alluded to the similarities of the two groups and said they feared both.[68]

As the victims of Klan violence, former slaves feared the living men who wanted to subdue them far more than the supernatural terrors that Klansmen tried to invoke with their white sheets. Sometimes borrowing from trickster tales passed down in folklore, freedmen, as noted earlier, triumphantly reported the cunning deceptions they practiced upon slave patrollers—tying vines across roads, throwing ashes into their faces—but no comparable successes can be discerned from their discussions of battling the Klan, no small victories recorded except mere existence.[69] Ex-slaves rarely retold spooky stories of Klansmen in ghostly garb; instead, their memories focused on the systematic use of terror and the men they knew who belonged to the Klan, some of whom they could identify. The freedwoman Frances Andrews described the Klan most simply: "They went to negro houses and killed the people."[70] Former slaves like W. L. Bost recognized the KKK's political agenda—"if they find a Negro that tries to get nervy or have a little bit for himself, they lash him nearly to death"—and understood that the Klan was a more menacing threat for blacks than patrollers had ever been.[71]

Despite their many similarities, slave patrollers and the Klan differed because of the lack of legal immunity available to Klansmen and the psychological terror their white sheets inflicted on victims black and white. State and local authorities appointed patrollers and gave them the power to carry out their duties; if they failed to act patrols could be legally censured. Although many white Southerners certainly condoned the KKK's activities, Klansmen had no official immunity for their actions. Lacking such protection, Klan members could be brought to trial for any illegal activities. Though convictions usually proved impossible, Klan trials were held.[72] The absence of state-provided immunity meant that most KKK members sought to disguise themselves.[73] White sheets and other subterfuges provided protection from being prosecuted in court, and the disguises lent an air of intrigue that enhanced the psychological effects of night riding, emboldening the abuser while scaring the victim. Terror and mystery might, on occasion, even go farther than physical abuse, particularly if Union army troops remained stationed nearby.[74]

While patrollers and the KKK both sought to dominate African Americans, the Klan had a "moral agenda" that went beyond the patrols' old objectives. Klansmen sought to prevent the decline of Southern society into "barbarous" practices, which for them included miscegenation and the appearance of racial equality in day-to-day settings. Whether that meant beating whites and former slaves who lived with each other as man and wife, or terrorizing whites who treated African Americans as peers, the KKK intended to reinstate what it perceived as the antebellum code of correct race relations.[75]

The Klan had political goals that went well beyond what slave patrols tried to accomplish. Klansmen wanted to prevent freedmen from buying land, voting Republican, or presuming to act like their white "superiors."[76] In North Carolina, Klan members burned the homes of freedmen, murdered and ambushed other ex-slaves, then imported guns and began carrying them to even further intimidate the freedmen before the 1870 election.[77] In South Carolina, Klansmen shot rifles into freedmen's cabins and confiscated political literature of the Republican party. Before the November 1868 election, Abbeville Klan leaders announced their intentions to "patrol that whole Co[unty] the night before the election" and they went so far as to assassinate two legislators.[78] Emancipated slaves had to be terrorized into acceding to plans that were not in their best interests, so the Klan resorted to ghastly brutality. While patrollers inflicted forty lashes, at most, to prevent slaves from moving around, the Klan readily shot or killed hundreds. Moreover, the KKK destroyed property and drove off workers who would have made their communities economically stronger. Former slaves and white Republicans found

KKK coffins on their doorsteps, warning them to leave the South.[79] Ku Klux Klan outrages led many freedmen to abandon their cabins and sleep in the woods, or even flee the state.[80]

Booker T. Washington eloquently described this extreme quality in the Klan's brutality when he reviewed the major similarities shared by slave patrols and the KKK.

> The "Ku Klux" were bands of men who had joined themselves together for the purpose of regulating the conduct of the coloured people, especially with the object of preventing the members of the race from exercising any influence in politics. They corresponded somewhat to the "patrollers" of whom I used to hear a great deal during the days of slavery, when I was a small boy. The "patrollers" were bands of white men—usually young men—who were organized largely for the purpose of regulating the conduct of the slaves at night in such matters as preventing the slaves from going from one plantation to another without passes, and for preventing them from holding any kind of meetings without permission and without the presence at these meetings of at least one white man.

But Washington recognized that the similarities concealed crucial differences that distinguished the Klan from its predecessor in racial violence.

> Like the "patrollers" the "Ku Klux" operated almost wholly at night. They were, however, more cruel than the "patrollers." Their objects, in the main, were to crush out the political aspirations of the Negroes, but they did not confine themselves to this, because schoolhouses as well as churches were burned by them, and many innocent persons were made to suffer. During this period not a few coloured people lost their lives.[81]

The Klan's willingness to inflict tremendous property damage and other violence, including murder, upon blacks (and the white Republicans who joined them) marked the beginning of a new era in Southern racial violence. With the loss of property rights in their slaves, white Southerners who became Klansmen no longer had any compunction about maiming or killing freedmen—no pecuniary loss was involved for them or other whites. While some slave patrollers enjoyed violently attacking slaves, ultimately few slaves died at the hands of slave patrollers. A slave's death would have constituted a significant financial loss for his owner. The Klan's record tells a different story: the number of freedmen maimed, killed, or frightened into leaving the South runs into the thousands. Antebellum owners did not tolerate such high levels of violence and property losses from slave patrollers. Moreover, patrols were supposed to keep slaves at their workplace; the Klan often forced freedmen away from their homes, diminishing productivity. The demise of slavery and the absence of all state and local controls over Klan activity permitted such brutality to continue unchecked during Reconstruction.

Klan, Army, and Police Vie for Control

Violence against freedmen ran rampant during Reconstruction because Southern-born law enforcers refused to pursue or prosecute Klan members. Indeed, white Southerners had little or no incentive to restrain the Klan, for they viewed it as their true instrument of "law enforcement" after the Civil War. One unreconstructed Southern historian could scarcely restrain his praise for the role that the Klan played in protecting white society from disorders: "Crime and violence of every sort ran unchecked until a large part of the South became a veritable hell through misrule which approximated to anarchy. Called into existence by this state of affairs, the Ku Klux lifted the South from its slough of despond by the application of illegal force which overthrew Reconstruction and ultimately restored political power to the white race . . . [then] the supremacy of the white race and Anglo-Saxon institutions was secure."[82] From this perspective, the Klan was the true keeper of the peace with its violent methods conveniently overlooked. Necessity justified the use of any means available. Law enforcement (and racial control) rested in the hands of any white man who owned a gun and was willing to use it on the Klan's behalf.[83]

The Klan's widespread appeal and actions made it a force that only the Union army could surmount. In South Carolina, Union and Spartanburg counties were described as being in an insurrectionary state in 1870. Eventually President Ulysses S. Grant declared martial law in nine counties in March 1871, in an attempt to quell activities of the Klan. Even then, the army could not be everywhere, safeguarding every freedman from Klan attacks. General Alfred H. Terry, Union army commander in charge of North and South Carolina, analyzed the situation in 1871. He believed "that the entire United States Army would be insufficient to give protection throughout the South to everyone in possible danger from the Klan."[84] Terry suggested that an example be made of the Klan in South Carolina, since that might make suppression of the Klan easier elsewhere. His recommendations led to congressional inquiries into the Klan, and the continued quartering of troops in South Carolina long after Union forces had left other Southern states. However, a Northern army could not garrison the state indefinitely. Federal troops withdrew from South Carolina in April 1877.

Federal troops and the Klan were not the only ones struggling to control Southern race relations during Reconstruction. In cities, white law enforcement groups frequently failed to protect freedmen. When armed vigilantes attacked freedmen around Wilmington in 1867, "civil authorities [were] unable or unwilling to arrest and punish" the offenders.[85] Often it seemed that white police officers merely wanted to goad African Americans into questionable actions to justify their injury by those in authority. As was the case in Richmond, if police were not using undue force in arresting former slaves, white officers were beating black suspects for no reason. Southern white authorities often assumed that blacks could only be lawbreakers, not law-abiding citizens, much less uphold the law as police officers themselves.[86]

Southern Reconstruction police forces in many towns opened their ranks to African Americans reluctantly. In a few Southern cities, like Montgomery and Vicksburg, they were admitted in great numbers by 1870, but in Virginia and Carolina towns that was rarely the case. Richmond had no black policemen in 1870 or in 1880, and Norfolk had only a few in 1870: they made up only 3 percent of the force, compared with a city population that was nearly half black. Even these gains were short-lived; by 1880 Norfolk once again had no African American policemen.[87] Even if blacks were appointed, white community members would not always accept African Americans as law enforcers. In cities that hired blacks as policemen, the officers were frequently criticized. When Raleigh's town leaders appointed four black policemen, one newspaper announced, "this is the beginning of the end."[88] Charleston's more racially balanced police force in 1876 was actually held accountable for not stopping racial violence—black-on-white attacks, as had occurred during the September rioting in that city—aggressively enough.[89]

In towns that did hire freedmen as policemen (either willingly or at the behest of occupying Union forces), ex-slaves-turned-lawmen even encountered active resistance.[90] Authorities in Graham, North Carolina,

appointed a "night police force consisting of three negroes who were instructed to stop all persons . . . who came on the streets after nine
o'clock, and ascertain their business." Ironically, their duties looked very
much like those of old patrollers controlling the nighttime movements
of slaves. But the irony was lost on local whites, who saw only black men
presuming to act like law enforcers. A group of thirty disguised white
men rode into town "with the purpose of frightening the police." They
exchanged gunfire with the policemen, but apparently no one was
wounded.[91] After African American policemen and white civilians
traded gunshots that resulted in the death of a white man in 1876, some
white Columbia residents decided that local law enforcement had become too lax. They resolved to take matters into their own hands. One
white man recalled that at night he "checked with [his] company of Vigilantes. All that night we rode through the negro quarters. Everything
was quiet, but every now and then a door would open, but when they
saw us on our horses, the door would slam shut. Once or twice we heard
some one call out 'Watch out, here come de patterolls.' "[92] Even under
army occupation and despite an integrated police force, former slaves
recognized the trademark behavior of white Southern men who would
willingly use violence to preserve their racial dominance.

The legacy of slave patrols lasted beyond the straightforward adoption of
their methods by the Ku Klux Klan and other vigilante groups of the
postwar era. Memories of white law enforcers' control over the actions
of slaves and former slaves endured even into the twentieth century.
Through collective social memory, the deeds of patrollers, Klan, and
white policemen often fused in the minds of freedmen when they recounted tales of racially motivated violence.[93] Meanwhile, white Southerners in the late nineteenth and early twentieth centuries retained a
deep-rooted conviction that law enforcement should remain exclusively
in the hands of white society. They assumed that law enforcement officers should rightfully be white and only white.[94] These ideas about
white law enforcement stemmed not only from patrolling but also from
strongly embedded ideas about Southern honor that dictated that white
men must rule while black men remained subservient.[95] For whites, patrols did not carry negative associations in the postbellum era. Nineteenth-century lawyers used patrollers as illustrations of proper police
behavior well after slavery's end. In criminal digests, arrests made by

slave patrollers continued to be used as examples of lawful and unlawful arrests by policemen in the 1880s.[96]

The language used to describe slave patrols also permeated police activities long after patrols were gone. The "beat," originally used as a geographic means of organizing slave patrol groups in South Carolina and other states, became the basic area that policemen supervised.[97] The policeman's beat has become a common phrase in American parlance, much the same way that Americans expect a policeman to "patrol" his rounds. The origins of both words predate the creation of slave patrols, but their use in the context of law enforcement today owes much to their application in the slaveholding South.

Beyond the language and ideas that slave patrols left after their demise, patrollers used techniques that later police forces would find extremely productive. Patrols employed systematic surveillance methods, like the stakeout Richard Eppes participated in, that policemen would later adopt as part of routine law enforcement. Patrollers also acted with greater discretion and lack of supervision, much as policemen did until the 1960s and the advent of more modern due process concerns. Through at least the first half of the twentieth century, policemen had great latitude to confine, question, brutalize, and release suspects without recourse to more formal judicial settings, just as slave patrollers had done on their nightly rounds for the sake of racial control.

In the new regime of Reconstruction, Southern whites were forced to adopt laws and policing methods that appeared racially unbiased, but they relied upon practices derived from slave patrols and their old laws that had traditionally targeted blacks for violence. To resolve this apparent contradiction, the more random and ruthless aspects of slave patrolling passed into the hands of vigilante groups like the Klan. The KKK provided an outlet for the racial aggression that white Southerners could no longer legally inflict through patrolling or slave ownership. Both the methods and the targeted victims of Klan violence—denounced by federal officials—were secretly approved of by many white Southerners who came to see the Klan as the South's true "law enforcers." Meanwhile, policemen in Southern towns continued to carry out those aspects of urban slave patrolling that seemed race-neutral but that in reality were applied selectively. Police saw that nightly curfews and vagrancy laws kept blacks off city streets, just as patrollers had done in the colonial and antebellum eras. Former slaves knew how insignificantly things had changed. Freedmen like W. L. Bost and J. T. Tims recognized that precious little difference existed between the brutality of slave patrols, white Southern policemen, or the Klan.[98] The work of controlling "marginal" members of Southern society had merely shifted from slave patrollers to Klansmen and policemen. Although slavery had died, the white community's need for racial dominance lived on.

Abbreviations

Archives

DU	Rare Book, Manuscript, and Special Collections Library, Duke University, Durham
LC	Library of Congress Manuscript Collections, Washington, D.C.
LV	Library of Virginia, Richmond
NCC	North Carolina Collection, Wilson Library, University of North Carolina at Chapel Hill
NCDAH	North Carolina Division of Archives and History, Raleigh
NYHS	New-York Historical Society, New York
PRO	Public Record Office, London
SCDAH	South Carolina Department of Archives and History, Columbia
SCHS	South Carolina Historical Society, Charleston
SCL	South Caroliniana Library, University of South Carolina, Columbia
SHC	Southern Historical Collection and Southern Folklife Collection, Wilson Library, University of North Carolina at Chapel Hill
UVA	Special Collections Department, University of Virginia Library, Charlottesville
VHS	Virginia Historical Society, Richmond

Journals and Published Series

AHR	*American Historical Review*
AJLH	*American Journal of Law and History*
BPRO	W. N. Sainsbury, comp., *Records in the British Public Record Office Relating to South Carolina, 1663–1710*, 5 vols. (Atlanta: Foote and Davies, 1928–1947)
CRNC	William L. Saunders, ed., *The Colonial Records of North Carolina*, 10 vols. (Raleigh: Hale, 1886–1907)
CWH	*Civil War History*
JAH	*Journal of American History*
JNH	*Journal of Negro History*

JSH	*Journal of Southern History*
KKK Hearings	U.S. Congress, *Report of the Joint Select Committee to Inquire into the Condition of Affairs in the Late Insurrectionary States,* 13 vols. (Washington: Government Printing Office, 1872), House Reports, 42d Cong., 2d sess., no. 22.
NCHR	*North Carolina Historical Review*
OR	*War of the Rebellion: A Compilation of the Official Records of the Union and Confederate Armies,* 128 vols. (Washington: Government Printing Office, 1880–1901)
SCHM	*South Carolina Historical Magazine*
SC Statutes	Thomas Cooper and David J. McCord, eds., *The Statutes at Large of South Carolina,* 10 vols. (Columbia: A. S. Johnston, 1836–1841)
SRNC	Walter Clark, ed., *The State Records of North Carolina,* 15 vols. (Raleigh: Hale, 1886–1907)
VA Statutes	William Waller Hening, ed., *The Statutes at Large; Being a Collection of All the Laws of Virginia from the First Session of the Legislature, in the Year 1619,* 13 vols. (New York: R. & W. & G. Barton, 1809–1823)
VCRP	Virginia Colonial Records Project (microfilm series on deposit at LV, VHS, and UVA)
VMHB	*Virginia Magazine of History and Biography*
WMQ	*William and Mary Quarterly*

Notes

Introduction

1. The few historians who have examined policing in a historical context include Roger Lane, *Policing the City: Boston, 1822–1885* (Cambridge, Mass.: Harvard University Press, 1967), Eric Monkkonen, *Police in Urban America, 1860–1920* (Cambridge: Cambridge University Press, 1981), and Dennis Rousey, *Policing the Southern City: New Orleans, 1805–1889* (Baton Rouge: Louisiana State University Press, 1996).

2. Edward L. Ayers, *Vengeance and Justice: Crime and Punishment in the Nineteenth-Century American South* (New York: Oxford University Press, 1984); Michael S. Hindus, *Prison and Plantation: Crime, Justice, and Authority in Massachusetts and South Carolina, 1767–1878* (Chapel Hill: University of North Carolina Press, 1980).

3. Michel Foucault, *Discipline and Punish: The Birth of the Prison,* trans. Alan Sheridan (1975; reprint, New York: Vintage Books, 1979), *Madness and Civilization: A History of Insanity in the Age of Reason,* trans. Richard Howard (1961; reprint, New York: Pantheon, 1965), *Archaeology of Knowledge,* trans. A. M. Smith (1969; reprint, New York: Pantheon Books, 1972).

4. The influential E. P. Thompson's body of work in this area, including *Whigs and Hunters: The Origin of the Black Act* (New York: Random House, 1975), led to many similar studies, including Douglas Hay et al., eds., *Albion's Fatal Tree: Crime and Society in Eighteenth-Century England* (New York: Random House, 1975), and Peter Linebaugh, *The London Hanged: Crime and Civil Society in the Eighteenth Century* (Cambridge: Cambridge University Press, 1992). Allen Steinberg's book tackles comparable ground in considering the depersonalizing shift from private to public law enforcement. *The Transformation of Criminal Justice: Philadelphia, 1800–1880* (Chapel Hill: University of North Carolina, 1989).

5. See, for example, Peter C. Hoffer and N. E. H. Hull, *Murdering Mothers: Infanticide in England and New England, 1558–1803* (New York: New York University Press, 1984); Douglas Greenberg, *Crime and Law Enforcement in the Colony of New England, 1691–1776* (Ithaca, N.Y.: Cornell University

Press, 1976); Bradley Chapin, *Criminal Justice in Colonial America, 1606–1660* (Athens, Ga.: University of Georgia Press, 1983). For notable exceptions, see Hindus, *Prison and Plantation,* and Rousey, *Policing the Southern City.*

6. Eugene Genovese, *Roll, Jordan, Roll: The World the Slaves Made* (New York: Vintage Books, 1976); Daniel Flanigan, *The Criminal Law of Slavery and Freedom, 1800–1868* (New York: Garland Press, 1987); and most recently, Thomas Morris, *Southern Slavery and the Law, 1619–1860* (Chapel Hill: University of North Carolina, 1996).

7. "Forging the Shackles: The Development of Virginia's Criminal Code for Slaves," in David J. Bodenhamer and James W. Ely, Jr., eds., *Ambivalent Legacy: A Legal History of the South* (Jackson: University Press of Mississippi, 1984), 125; Philip J. Schwarz, *Twice Condemned: Slaves and the Criminal Law of Virginia, 1705–1865* (Baton Rouge: Louisiana State University Press, 1988).

8. Slave patrols also had a naval connotation, as the British navy moved to interdict the slave trade in the early nineteenth century by positioning ships near Africa and among the Caribbean islands. For a brief fictional account of nineteenth-century seafaring patrols, see C. S. Forster, *Admiral Hornblower in the West Indies* (New York: Bantam Books, 1960). For purposes of this study, naval slave patrols have been omitted.

9. Bertram Wyatt-Brown, *Southern Honor: Ethics and Behavior in the Old South* (Oxford: Oxford University Press, 1982).

10. Frances A. Kemble, *Journal of a Residence on a Georgian Plantation in 1838–1839,* ed. John A. Scott (Athens, Ga.: University of Georgia Press, 1984), vii.

11. Despite reviewing numerous patrol records, I have uncovered no evidence that a woman ever served on patrol instead of providing a substitute.

12. H. M. Henry, *The Police Control of the Slave in South Carolina* (Emory, Va.: n.p., 1914). Henry's brief though wide-ranging work, despite being flawed by his racist views, surpasses later work done by Shirley J. Yee, "The Origins of the Southern Slave Patrol System: South Carolina, 1690–1810" (master's thesis, Ohio State University, 1983).

13. Benjamin Franklin Callahan, "The North Carolina Slave Patrol" (master's thesis, University of North Carolina at Chapel Hill, 1973).

1. Colonial Beginnings and Experiments

1. Epigraph: Reprinted in *DeBow's Review,* n.s., 1 (1849): 296.

2. Carol Bleser, ed., *Secret and Sacred: The Diaries of James Henry Hammond, a Southern Slaveholder* (New York: Oxford University Press, 1988), 142, 149.

3. Stephen Channing, *Crisis of Fear: Secession in South Carolina* (New York: W. W. Norton, 1974).

4. Among the many excellent books that emphasize the work of individual masters are Drew Faust, *James Henry Hammond and the Old South: A Design for Mastery* (Baton Rouge: Louisiana State University Press, 1982); James Oakes, *The Ruling Race: A History of American Slaveholders* (New York: Alfred A. Knopf, 1982); Michael P. Johnson and James L. Roark, *Black Masters: A Free Family of Color in the Old South* (New York: W. W. Norton, 1984).

5. In discussing the use of slave labor and law in British North America, I have not included slave-owning explorers who only visited coastal areas.

6. Historians have been hard pressed to determine the exact beginning of settlement in North Carolina: "[It] is difficult to tell exactly when they came." Hugh T. Lefler and Albert R. Newsome, *The History of a Southern State: North Carolina*, 3d ed. (Chapel Hill: University of North Carolina Press, 1973), 17, 128. See also Harry R. Merrens, *Colonial North Carolina in the Eighteenth Century: A Study in Historical Geography* (Chapel Hill: University of North Carolina Press, 1964), 19–20.

7. See Bruce H. Mann, *Neighbors and Strangers: Law and Community in Early Connecticut* (Chapel Hill: University of North Carolina Press, 1987); David T. Konig, *Law and Society in Puritan Massachusetts: Essex County, 1629–1692* (Chapel Hill: University of North Carolina, 1979); and Peter C. Hoffer and N. E. H. Hull, *Murdering Mothers: Infanticide in England and New England, 1558–1803* (New York: New York University Press, 1984).

8. The debate about whether colonists created their own laws *sui generis* or re-created the intricate legal world they left behind has had many combatants. The best collection of these differing viewpoints in one volume is David H. Flaherty, ed., *Essays in the History of Early American Law* (Chapel Hill: University of North Carolina Press, 1969), which includes essays by George L. Haskins, Zechariah Chafee, and Julius Goebel. See also Paul S. Reinsch, *The English Common Law in the Early American Colonies* (New York: Gordon Press, 1977), originally published in the *Bulletin of the University of Wisconsin*, no. 31 (Economics, political science, and history series), vol. 2, no. 4 (1899). Recently, historians working in this area have agreed on the importance of remembered behavior during the settlement period, followed by a gradual accretion of formalistic laws emanating from higher legal authorities, such as legislative assemblies or English government proclamations. See David G. Allen, *In English Ways: The Movement of Societies and the Transferal of English Local Law and Custom to Massachusetts Bay in the Seventeenth Century* (New York: W. W. Norton, 1982), 209.

9. *Somerset v. Stewart* Lofft I, 98, Eng. Rep. 499 [KB. 1772]; Peter Kolchin,

American Slavery, 1619–1877 (New York: Hill and Wang, 1993), 17–18. New scholarship challenges this sharp distinction and suggests that Englishmen were far more familiar with other forms of servitude in England than has previously been thought. See Michael Guasco, " 'Seek not to keep the commons of England in Slavery': English Conceptions of Slavery and Early Colonial Settlement" (paper delivered at the Omohundro Institute for Early American History and Culture Colloquium, June 6, 1998), and his "Encounters, Identities, and Human Bondage: Foundation of Racial Slavery in the Anglo-Atlantic World" (Ph.D. diss., College of William and Mary, 2000).

10. This process has been elaborated by Bradley Nicholson, "Legal Borrowing and the Origins of Slave Law in the British Colonies," *AJLH* 38 (1994): 38–54.

11. Despite suggestions to the contrary by Oscar and Mary F. Handlin, "Origins of the Southern Labor System," *WMQ,* 3d ser., 7 (1950): 206, this position continues to have the approbation of South Carolina scholars. For an analysis of the controversy, see M. Eugene Sirmans, "The Legal Status of the Slave in South Carolina, 1670–1740," *JSH* 28 (1962): 462–473. See also Sirmans, *Colonial South Carolina: A Political History, 1663–1763* (Chapel Hill: University of North Carolina Press, 1966), 64–66; Peter H. Wood, *Black Majority: Negroes in Colonial South Carolina from 1670 through the Stono Rebellion* (New York: W. W. Norton, 1975), 52.

12. Elsa V. Goveia, "The West Indian Slave Laws of the Eighteenth Century," *Revista de Ciencias Sociales* 4 (1960): 84. See also Gwendolyn M. Hall, *Social Control in Slave Plantation Societies: A Comparison of St. Domingue and Cuba* (Baltimore: Johns Hopkins University Press, 1971), 77; Alan Watson, *Slave Law in the Americas* (Athens, Ga.: University of Georgia Press, 1989), 40–124; and Jonathan Bush, "Free to Enslave: The Foundations of Colonial American Slave Law," *Yale Journal of Law and the Humanities* 5 (1993): 417–470. The French laws about slaves were codified in the *Code Noir* (1685), which bore a strong resemblance to English colonial slave laws. Its codification came too late to influence patrol laws in Barbados of the 1650s and 1660s, although the local laws it codified may have included some patrol-like groups. Goveia, "West Indian Slave Laws of the Eighteenth Century," 92–93. The only portion of the *Code Noir* that related even indirectly to patrolling was Article 16, in which the king urged "all our subjects, even if they are not officers and if there is no other conflicting law, to pursue these offenders [runaway slaves], to arrest them and to lead them to prison." Translation courtesy of David Ferris and Charles Donahue of Harvard Law School.

13. Colin Palmer, *Slaves of the White God: Blacks in Mexico, 1570–1650* (Cambridge, Mass.: Harvard University Press, 1976), 122.

14. Herbert S. Klein, *Slavery in the Americas: A Comparative Study of Virginia and Cuba* (Chicago: University of Chicago Press, 1967), 70. The *hermandad* was also employed in 1550s Mexico. *Recopilación de leyes de los reynos de las Indias*, 4 vols. (1681; reprint, Madrid: Ediciones Cultura Hispanica, 1973), libro VII, título V, leyes XXI–XXII. One scholar dates the Mexican *hermandad* closer to 1570; see David Davidson, "Negro Slave Control and Resistance in Colonial Mexico, 1519–1650," *Hispanic American Historical Review* 46 (1966): 244, which includes a discussion of the *Recopilación*.

15. Hall, *Social Control in Slave Plantation Societies*, 75–76. On rewards to slave hunters, see Klein, *Slavery in the Americas*, 156. *Rancheadores* searched the homes of free blacks, looking for runaways, causing Spanish authorities to enact laws preventing *rancheadores* from disturbing free blacks. *Recopilación*, libro VII, título V, ley XIX.

16. Demoticus Philalethes [pseud.], *Yankee Travels through the Island of Cuba* (New York: D. Appleton and Co., 1856), 38–42, reprinted as "Hunting the Maroons with Dogs in Cuba," in Richard Price, ed., *Maroon Societies: Rebel Slave Communities in the Americas*, 3d ed. (Baltimore: Johns Hopkins University Press, 1996), 60–63.

17. Michael Craton, *Testing the Chains: Resistance to Slavery in the British West Indies* (Ithaca, N.Y.: Cornell University Press, 1982), 94. Hiring primarily freed slaves as slave catchers was most common in colonial Brazil, where they worked as *capitães do mato* (bushwhacking captains). C. R. Boxer, *The Golden Age of Brazil, 1695–1750: Growing Pains of a Colonial Society* (Berkeley: University of California Press, 1962), 170. See also Peter Voelz, *Slave and Soldier: The Military Impact of Blacks in the Colonial Americas* (New York: Garland Publishing, 1993), 332–336.

18. Frederick P. Bowser, *The African Slave in Colonial Peru, 1524–1650* (Stanford: Stanford University Press, 1974), 105. Eventually, the use of slaves to hunt runaways was suppressed in the Spanish empire so that slaves "would have no pretenses to take leave from their master." *Recopilación*, libro VII, título V, ley XXII.

19. Rolando Mellafe, *Negro Slavery in Latin America*, trans. J. W. S. Judge (Berkeley: University of California Press, 1975), 101. Fernando Ortiz, *Los negros esclavos, estudio sociológico y de derecho público* (Havana: Revista bimestre cubana, 1916), 351. Eventually the Spaniards collected the ordinances and decrees together and compiled them as the *Recopilación* in 1681.

20. For example, in British-held Antigua, rewards of six hundred pounds of sugar or tobacco were offered to any person, free or slave, who captured and delivered a fugitive slave to authorities. "An Act for bringing in Runaway Negroes and Incouragement of such who shall bring them in," July 9, 1680, PRO C. O. 154/2, p. 349 (fol. 145). One author described the system

of recapturing runaways as a "free-for-all" in which anyone could participate. Luis M. Diaz Soler, *Historia de la esclavitud negra en Puerto Rico* (San
Juan: Editorial Universitaria, 1974), 207.

21. Jerome Handler, *The Unappropriated People: Freedmen in the Slave Society of
Barbados* (Baltimore: Johns Hopkins University Press, [1974]), 13.

22. Hilary Beckles, *Black Rebellion in Barbados: The Struggle against Slavery,
1627–1838* (Barbados: Antilles Publications, 1984), 33.

23. Richard S. Dunn, *Sugar and Slaves: The Rise of the Planter Class in the English West Indies, 1624–1713* (Chapel Hill: University of North Carolina
Press, 1972), 240.

24. Although some professional slave catchers may have been former slaves
themselves, I have found no clear evidence to support this proposition for
Barbados.

25. "An Addition to the Act for Restraining the wandring of servants and Negro's," *Acts and Statutes of the Island of Barbados. Made and Enacted since the
Reducement of the Same, unto the Authority of the Common-wealth of England*
(London: W. Bentley, [1654]), 147. The solution, from the legislature's
point of view, was to allow the slave catcher to keep the slave until retrieved by his master, thus gaining the labor of the slave in the interim.

26. "An Act for the Better ordering and governing of Negroes," Sept. 27, 1661,
PRO C. O. 30/2, fols. 16–26. The act was amended in 1676, 1682, and ex-
tensively revised in 1688. For the text of the 1688 act, see either Richard
Hall, comp., *Acts Passed in the Island of Barbados. From 1643, to 1762, inclusive* (London, 1764), 112, or PRO C. O. 30/2 (Acts of Barbados, 1645–
1682). Barbadian law for 1682–1692 is in PRO C. O. 30/5. The laws regulating slaves from the 1640s and 1650s have been largely lost. Michael
Craton, *Sinews of Empire: A Short History of British Slavery* (New York: An-
chor Books, 1974), 176.

27. The preamble to the earlier 1652 law noted that "it hath been by dayly experience found, that many great mischiefs have risen in this Island, . . . by
the wandring of Servants and Slaves, on Sundayes, Saturdayes in the after-
noon, and other dayes . . . by stealing and filching their Masters goods
and provisions, and bartering and selling them." "An Act to restrain the
wandring of Servants and Negro's," *Acts and Statutes of the Island of Barbados,* 81.

28. This role probably began with retrieving indentured servants. See "An Act
for the good Governing of Servants, and Ordering the Rights between Masters and Servants," clause XXIV (1661), which noted that "all Constables
within this Island are hereby required to apprehend all Run-aways that
they shall know of by credible Information, then in safe Custody convey
from Constable to Constable, until they come to the Common Gaol, or to
their Master or Mistress."

29. "An act for the Governing of Negroes," clauses I, II (1688), *Acts of Assembly, Passed in the Island of Barbadoes, From 1648, to 1718* (London: John Baskett, 1721), 137.

30. Hilary Beckles, *Natural Rebels: A Social History of Enslaved Black Women in Barbados* (New Brunswick, N.J.: Rutgers University Press, 1989), 167. See also Beckles, "Rebels without Heroes: Slave Politics in Seventeenth Century Barbados," *Journal of Caribbean History* 18 (1983): 1–21.

31. Goveia, "The West Indian Slave Laws of the Eighteenth Century," 82; Barbara Bush, *Slave Women in Caribbean Society, 1650–1838* (London: James Currey, 1990), 27–29.

32. Jerome Handler and Frederick Lange, *Plantation Slavery in Barbados: An Archaeological and Historical Investigation* (Cambridge, Mass.: Harvard University Press, 1978), 90–91; Beckles, *Natural Rebels,* 74–75n13, 84–85.

33. "An Act to Prohibit the Inhabitants of This Island from Employing their Negroes and Other Slaves in Selling and Bartering," passed January 6, 1708, in Hall, comp., *Acts Passed in the Island of Barbados,* 185–186, cited in Beckles, *Natural Rebels,* 76.

34. Beckles, *Black Rebellion,* 21.

35. The militia in Barbados was no doubt originally modeled upon the militia of England, but by this time England's militia was in disarray and decaying from internal political struggles. J. R. Western, *The English Militia in the Eighteenth Century: The Story of a Political Issue, 1660–1802* (London: Routledge & Kegan Paul, 1965), 27–28, 52. On the English militia, see Lindsay Boynton, *The Elizabethan Militia, 1558–1638* (London: Routledge & Kegan Paul, 1967), and Douglas Edward Leach, *Arms for Empire: A Military History of the British Colonies in North America, 1607–1763* (New York: Macmillan, 1973).

36. Handler, *Unappropriated People,* 110.

37. Ibid., 33; Jerome Handler, "Freedmen and Slaves in the Barbados Militia," *Journal of Caribbean History* 119 (1984): 2–3.

38. Handler, "Freedmen and Slaves in the Barbados Militia," 2–3.

39. Governor Willoughby to Privy Council, December 16, 1667, W. N. Sainsbury, J. W. Fortescue, and Cecil Headlam, eds., *Calendar of State Papers, Colonial Series, America and West Indies,* 43 vols. (1860; reprint, Nendeln, Liechtenstein: Kraus, 1978), vol. 5 (1661–1668), 526, cited in Beckles, *Black Rebellion,* 31.

40. Note that patrols appear in Barbadian law under the island's militia organization, and not under its theoretically comprehensive slave code; we shall see this again when we examine mainland statutes. It is unclear exactly when slave patrols were first used in Barbados. The first statutory mention of patrols in Barbados occurs as a reaffirmation of prior customary practice in "An Act for the Settlement of the Militia of this Island" (1697 restate-

ment of the militia law), in William Rawlin, comp., *The Laws of Barbados, Collected in One Volume* (London: n.p., 1699), 226, clause XXXVIII ("Provided also, That Horse Petrols do Duty *as formerly* every Saturday Night, Sunday and Sunday Night, and other Holy-Days, in such manner as hath hitherto been usual in this Island; all which being duly observed, will tend to the Liberty, Safeguard and Quiet of the Inhabitants of the Place" [emphasis added]). The original of this law is missing from the PRO, which has copies of no Barbadian laws between 1692 and 1698. Patrols were used by the 1680s, but no earlier reference to patrols exists in the militia legislation of 1676, 1682, or 1688. The particular care taken with the 1697 militia act was based on the Barbadian lawmakers' belief in the continued hostilities between France and Britain in King William's War (1688–1697), which they did not know had concluded at the time this law was enacted.

41. After troops returned home, forged papers began circulating among white Barbadians, designed to prove the alarm had been real. In the papers, a (supposedly) rebellious slave wrote to his fellow conspirators, saying that "our design is discovered but not be [*sic*] disheartened. Let us begin the next Sunday about Midnight, do not let us minde the Patrol or Companyes." Barbadians believed the white author of the papers wanted to prove the insurrection had been real, to justify any fearful expressions he may have voiced during the alarm. Unsigned circular dated November 29, 1683, enclosed in an extract of an unsigned letter from Barbados discussing the false alarm and the scattering of these forged papers among white Barbadians, December 18, 1683, PRO C. O. 1/53, fols. 264–66. Craton is unsure of the authenticity of these documents but believes them to be slave-authored, *Testing the Chains*, 110.

42. Comments by Lieutenant Governor Edwyn Stede following the Monmouth rebellion, Minutes of Governor's Council 1660–1686, March 16, 1685/6, PRO C. O. 31/1, fol. 386. See similar remarks in the Journal of the Assembly 1684–1694, PRO C. O. 31/3, fol. 145, as well as Stede's earlier comments of February 16, 1686 regarding the rebellion, Minutes of the Governor's Council, PRO C. O. 31/1, fol. 676.

43. A full search in the Journal of the Barbados Assembly (PRO C. O. 31/2, 31/3, 31/5) and the Minutes of the Governor's Council (PRO C. O. 31/1, 31/4, 31/5) has produced no information about patrols other than that included in this study.

44. These restrictions included the reintroduction of the ticket system, and the prohibition of slaves' owning any item that could be used for islandwide communication, like drums or horns.

45. "An Act for the Encouragement of all Negroes and slaves that shall discover any Conspiracy," October 27, 1692, PRO C. O. 30/4, fol. 158.

46. Handler, *Unappropriated People,* 30; Beckles, *Black Rebellion,* 35, 52.

47. Dunn, *Sugar and Slaves,* 243.

48. In this earliest period, North and South Carolina had not yet been separated as colonies. I refer to settlement areas as North or South Carolina, however, because of their eventual status as separately administered colonies and states.

49. Sirmans, *Colonial South Carolina,* 27. See two dissimilar evaluations of the connection between Barbados and South Carolina: Jack Greene, "Colonial South Carolina and the Caribbean Connection," *SCHM* 88 (1987): 192–210, and Kinloch Bull, "Barbadian Settlers in Early Carolina: Historigraphical Notes," *SCHM* 96 (1995): 329–339.

50. Population estimates drawn from Wood, *Black Majority,* 143, 152. See also Russell Menard, "Slave Demography in the Lowcountry, 1670–1740: From Frontier Society to Plantation Regime," *SCHM* 96 (1995): 280–303.

51. "An Act for the Encouragement of the Importation of White Servants," in Cooper and McCord, eds., *SC Statutes,* vol. 2, 153 (1698). In fact, few laws from the period before 1685 on any subject remain for the historian. Those that we know about are frequently given only as titles to the laws, without reference to their substantive provisions. See Charles Lesser, *South Carolina Begins: The Records of a Proprietary Colony, 1663–1721* (Columbia: South Carolina Department of Archives and History, 1995), 257–284, for a list of all acts omitted from Cooper and McCord's compilation.

52. Lords Proprietors' instructions for the government, June 5, 1682, *BPRO,* vol. 1, 174.

53. Lords Proprietors to unnamed correspondent, October 18, 1690, *BPRO,* vol. 2, 293.

54. On Native Americans' slave-hunting abilities, see James Merrell, *The Indians' New World: Catawbas and Their Neighbors from European Contact through the Era of Removal* (Chapel Hill: University of North Carolina Press, 1989), 99n16.

55. Marvin L. Michael Kay and Lorin Cary, " 'They are Indeed the Constant Plague of Their Tyrants': Slave Defense of a Moral Economy in Colonial North Carolina, 1748–1772," in Gad Heuman, ed., *Out of the House of Bondage: Runaways, Resistance, and Marronage in Africa and the New World* (London: Frank Cass, 1986), 40.

56. Some historians have erroneously concluded that the first law to refer to slaves and their rights or restraints was the 1690/1 law. Actually, several laws prior to 1690/1 referred to slaves, either in specific provisions, or indirectly, like the 1683 and 1687 laws to inhibit trading by slaves. It is more correct to say that the 1690/1 law was the first law directed primarily at slaves, designed to regulate many aspects of their behavior. I have retained

the Old Style/New Style notation commonly in use prior to 1752 (and the adoption of the Gregorian calendar in England) where original sources indicated both years.

57. This problem was present from the formation of the colony. Alexander S. Salley, Jr., ed., *Journal of the Grand Council August 25, 1671–June 24, 1680* (Columbia: State Co., 1907), 17. The ongoing nature of this problem is noted in H. M. Henry, *The Police Control of the Slave in South Carolina* (Emory, Va.: n.p., 1914), 80–89, and the variety of marketing canvassed in Philip D. Morgan, *Slave Counterpoint: Black Culture in the Eighteenth-Century Chesapeake and Lowcountry* (Chapel Hill: University of North Carolina Press, 1998), 250–252.

58. "An Act Inhibiting the Trading with Servants or Slaves," in Cooper and McCord, eds., *SC Statutes,* vol. 2, 22 (1686/7). White servants would not need passes from their masters until 1744, primarily because their numbers were never very large: in 1708, only 120 white men and women were servants in South Carolina. Wood, *Black Majority,* 144. Even then, the disparity of treatment between white and black servants and slaves would mandate different levels of evidence and punishment for servants wandering away from their masters. See A. Leon Higginbotham, *In the Matter of Color: Race and the American Legal Process—The Colonial Period* (Oxford: Oxford University Press), 157.

59. "An Act Inhibiting the Trading with Servants or Slaves," in Cooper and McCord, eds., *SC Statutes,* vol. 2, 23 (1686/7).

60. Ibid. (emphasis added). This type of town control over slave barter expanded as settlements grew. Town ordinances required slaves to carry tickets in order to trade goods in Wilmington, North Carolina by 1765. See Donald R. Lennon and Ida B. Kellam, eds., *The Wilmington Town Book, 1743–1778* (Raleigh: Division of Archives and History, 1973), 164–165.

61. Salley, ed., *Journal of the Grand Council, 1671–1680,* 10–11. The militia laws were continuously renewed, in 1683, 1685, 1686, 1687, 1690, 1691, 1693, 1696, 1697, and throughout the eighteenth century.

62. Ibid., 8. These early militia were so diligent that the Grand Council eventually ordered them to cease watching in order to maintain the health of their men. Ibid., 38.

63. In part, this was due to the Carolinians' willingness to harbor and trade with pirates, who raided near Spanish Florida and then were freely received on the South Carolina coast. The ties that the Spanish formed with neighboring Indian tribes also provoked conflict, since the South Carolinians regularly sold Indians into slavery who were under the protection of the Spanish.

64. "An Act for the Better Security of that Parte of the Province of Carolina,

that lyeth Southward and Westward of Cape Feare, . . .," in Cooper and McCord, eds., *SC Statutes,* vol. 2, 9 (1685). A 1703 law provided for lookouts aimed at Indians from the West and Spaniards from the South. Osgood notes that there were eight watchhouses on the coast, and one of their duties was to look for slaves. Herbert L. Osgood, *The American Colonies in the Seventeenth Century,* 3 vols. (New York: Macmillan, 1904–1907), vol. 1, 70. Their apprehension appeared well founded: South Carolina was invaded in 1706 by the Spanish and French. Wood, *Black Majority,* 125.

65. "An Account of the Invasion of South Carolina by the French & Spaniards . . .," 1706, and "Account of the Invasion made by the French and Spaniards upon Carolina in which Attempt they were Defeated . . .," August 1706, *BPRO,* vol. 5, 166–167, 174. See also Salley, ed., *Journal of the Grand Council, 1671–1680,* 36–37. This threatening scenario, in which all the men are drawn to one place and thereby make their society vulnerable to slaves, provides a leitmotif for Southern white fears until emancipation. Local fires or distant wars (against the British in 1776 or Northern armies in 1861) provided a strong rationale for tight slave security measures. See Chapter 5.

66. The Spanish promised freedom to those slaves who could reach St. Augustine.

67. In the initial formation of the town watch, persons living in "outward plantations" were still required to come in to town to do their duty on watch. The Grand Council acknowledged that they were essentially doing double duty, watching not only their plantations but also the town, and thus partially excused them from watch duty. The vulnerability of outlying homes was a reality from the first. Salley, ed., *Journal of the Grand Council, 1671–1680,* 12.

68. The watch is referred to as "regular" in council minutes for the 1670s and 1680s. Ibid., 11. The first extant town watch statute is from 1685. "An Act for Clearing the Lotts and Streets of Charles Town, and for the Settlement and Regulation of a Night Watch in the Said Town," in Cooper and McCord, eds., *SC Statutes,* vol. 7, 1–3, clauses III, IV, V (1685). The law was reenacted, unchanged, in 1687 and 1690. "An Act for the Settling and Continuing a Watch in Charles Town," ibid., vol. 7, 4 (1690). Other versions of it were enacted in 1692, 1693, 1696, 1698, 1701, 1703, and many years following. This form of town watch is comparable to that found in many other towns farther north in British North America. See, for example, Roger Lane, *Policing the City: Boston, 1822–1885* (Cambridge, Mass.: Harvard University Press, 1967), 10–29, on Boston's early watch system.

69. "An Act for Clearing the Lotts and Streets of Charles Town, and for the Set-

tlement and Regulation of a Night Watch in the Said Town," in Cooper and McCord, eds., *SC Statutes*, vol. 7, 3, clause V (1685). Shirking one's duty was known, since they planned to cope with the "great neglect" of skipping one's turn at watch by determining if "any person or persons shall *really* be sick," suggesting they could tell the difference between true illness and malingering. Alexander S. Salley, ed., *Journal of the Grand Council of South Carolina, April 11, 1692–September 26, 1692* (Columbia: State Co., 1907), 11 (emphasis added).

70. Salley, ed., *Journal of the Grand Council, 1692,* 5, 43.
71. Salley, ed., *Journal of the Grand Council, 1671–1680,* 45, 63–64. Slaves could also flee by ship, and the council took steps to require all ship passengers to obtain certificates showing that they were on legitimate business or were debt free before they could leave the colony. Ibid., 20, 32–33.
72. Cooper and McCord, eds., *SC Statutes*, vol. 7, 343 (1690/1). The law was actually passed February 7, 1690/1, but it has been described by many historians as the statute of 1690. I have retained the 1690 dating here to avoid confusion.
73. The laws passed in 1690/1 were part of the local assembly's revolt against the proprietary government. The revolt was accomplished by entering into an alliance with Seth Sothel, a proprietor who arrived in South Carolina in 1690/1. He claimed the governorship and worked in tandem with some colonists (passing the 1690/1 slave law, among others) until the other proprietors in England suspended him from office and set aside all laws passed under his administration. See *BPRO*, vol. 3, 31–33, 37–38; Sirmans, *Colonial South Carolina,* 48–50; Higginbotham, *In the Matter of Color,* 430n116.
74. "An Act Inhibiting the Trading with Servants or Slaves," in Cooper and McCord, eds., *SC Statutes*, vol. 2, 22 (1686/7).
75. "Act for the Better Ordering of Slaves," ibid., vol. 7, 344, clause IV (1690/ 1). This parallels the right in the 1686/7 slave trade law. "An Act Inhibiting the Trading with Servants or Slaves," ibid., vol. 2, 23 (1686/7). This requirement also extended to women. On slave rewards, ibid., vol. 7, 345, clause VI.
76. "An Act for the Better Ordering of Slaves," ibid., vol. 7, 343, clause I.
77. Ibid., clause IX.
78. Ibid., clause IV.
79. Alexander S. Salley, Jr., ed., *Journal of the Commons House of Assembly,* 21 vols. (Columbia: State Co., 1907–1946), vol. 1692–93, 8, 15, 17, 24, 27, 34 (passed into law September 1693). The text of this 1693 law is lost, although it is believed that the assembly simply reenacted the 1690/1 law.

Thomas J. Little, "South Carolina Slave Laws Reconsidered, 1670–1700," *SCHM* 94 (1993): 99.

80. Sirmans, "Legal Status of the Slave in South Carolina," 466.
81. The text of the 1696 law, "An Act for the Better Ordering of Slaves," is in Governor Archdale's Laws, fols. 60–66, SCDAH. On the legal requirement to capture runaway slaves, see clause 2, fol. 60. The law was reenacted with minor changes in 1698. Although both of these laws were omitted from the Cooper and McCord *SC Statutes* compilation, the reenactment of the 1696 law in 1712 is reprinted in vol. 7, 352–365. This has caused several historians to date the first comprehensive slave law inaccurately as 1712, instead of 1696. Sirmans, "Legal Status of the Slave in South Carolina," 466n13.
82. "An Act for the Better Ordering of Slaves" (1696), clause 12, fol. 64, Governor Archdale's Laws, SCDAH.
83. Ibid., clause 7.
84. Ibid., clause 8.
85. Attempts to limit slave access to Charleston were part of an effort to restrict the alcohol trade between whites and slaves, which would remain largely unsuccessful in the eighteenth and nineteenth centuries. In 1702 the assembly summoned Charleston constables to appear for questioning, and to reprimand them "for their Past negligence" in restraining slave gatherings. The assembly confronted them with William Harvey, a notorious white man who hosted slave "Caballs" in his "Rat Trap" in Charleston. Salley, ed., *Journal of the Commons House of Assembly* (1702), 99.
86. "An Act for the Better Ordering of Slaves" (1696), clause 29.
87. Randolph to the Board for Trade and Plantations, June 28, 1699, *BPRO*, vol. 4, 88.
88. "An Act for Raising and Enlisting Such Slaves as Shall be Thought Serviceable to this Province in Time of Alarm" and "An Act for Enlisting Such Trusty Slaves as Shall Be Thought Serviceable to This Province in Time of Alarm," in Cooper and McCord, eds., *SC Statutes,* vol. 7, 347, 349 (1704, 1708). The first law did not limit the number of slaves that could be enrolled, but the second did not allow the number of slaves to be greater than the number of white men, an alteration noted by Thomas Nairne in 1708. *BPRO*, vol. 5, 204.
89. "An Act to Settle a Patroll," Cooper and McCord, eds., *SC Statutes,* vol. 2, 254–255 (1704).
90. According to Wood, St. Bartholomew's Parish (which corresponded to Colleton County at that time) had only 47 taxpayers and 144 slaves in 1720. In 1704, the numbers would have been considerably less. Only St. Helena

Parish, closer to Florida, and St. James Santee Parish, on the colony's northern frontier, had a smaller number of taxpayers. Wood, *Black Majority,* 146–149. Although I have discovered no connection, it is possible that Colleton's religious stance also influenced the drafting of the bill. Sirmans, *Colonial South Carolina,* 86–87.

91. Henry suggests that this initial distinction probably accounts for the old alternative patroller name "alarm men." *Police Control of the Slave,* 31.
92. In addition they received 6 pence per mile for returning the slave to his master, or to the guardhouse in Charleston. "An Act for Reduceing the Watches and Look Outs Placed and Appointed on the Sea Coast of This Province to a Lesser Number, and Regulating and Providing Convenient Necessaries and Allowances for the Same, and Also Encouraging the Taking up of Servants and Slaves," in Cooper and McCord, eds., *SC Statutes,* vol. 2, 354 (1710).
93. Herbert Aptheker, *American Negro Slave Revolts* (New York: Columbia University Press, 1943), 171n30.
94. "An Act for the Better Ordering and Governing of Negroes and Slaves," in Cooper and McCord, eds., *SC Statutes,* vol. 7, 352–365 (1712).
95. Aptheker, *Slave Revolts,* 174–175.
96. For example, see Bill Cecil-Fronsman, *Common Whites: Class and Culture in Antebellum North Carolina* (Lexington: University Press of Kentucky, 1992), 5, 78–79, or Shirley J. Yee, "The Origins of the Southern Slave Patrol System: South Carolina, 1690–1810" (master's thesis, Ohio State University, 1983), 45. Yee relies on John Hope Franklin, *The Militant South, 1800–1861* (Cambridge, Mass.: Belknap Press of Harvard University Press, 1956), 190, for part of her evaluation.
97. See the preamble to "An Act for Reduceing the Watches and Look Outs Placed and Appointed on the Sea Coast of This Province to a Lesser Number, and Regulating and Providing Convenient Necessaries and Allowances for the Same, and Also Encouraging the Taking up of Servants and Slaves," in Cooper and McCord, eds., *SC Statutes,* vol. 2, 354 (1710).
98. "An Act for the Better Settling and Regulating the Militia," in Cooper and McCord, eds., *SC Statutes,* vol. 9, 639, clause XXVI (1721).
99. Ibid.
100. Ibid., 640, clause XXVIII. The fine equaled the amount paid by "defaulters at musters of the foot company." The assembly also repealed the 1704 patrol law.
101. "An Act for the Better Ordering and Regulating of Negroes and Slaves," ibid., vol. 7, 352 (1712) and "An Act for the Better Ordering and Governing of Negroes and Other Slaves," ibid., vol. 7, 371 (1722), based on a comparison of the words in clause 2 of each law.

102. "An Act for the Better Ordering and Governing of Negroes and Other Slaves," ibid., vol. 7, 378 (1722).

103. Ibid., 640, clause XXVII. Wood observed that "[t]he tendency to associate 'Servants' and 'Slaves' together in these statutes may derive from the loose structure of the labor system in early Carolina, or it may stem from the fact that 'all negroes and slaves' were accounted as freehold property rather than chattel property." *Black Majority,* 51n63.

104. *South Carolina Gazette,* no. 9, March 23–30, 1733/4, 1–2 ("Charleston Negroes congregating in large unruly groups on the Lord's day"); *South Carolina Gazette,* no. 165, March 19–26, 1737, 1 ("negroes permitted to cabal in the streets on the Sabbath"); *South Carolina Gazette,* no. 197, October 29–November 5, 1737, 1 ("laws concerning Sabbath not enforced, negroes cabaling"). It is difficult to gauge the level of civilian discontent in the period preceding 1733, given the absence of a local newspaper to record such sentiments. I am indebted to Alex Moore (University of South Carolina Press) for allowing me access to his card files on eighteenth-century grand jury presentments in South Carolina sources.

105. "An Act for Regulating Patrols in this Province," in Cooper and McCord, eds., *SC Statutes,* vol. 3, 395 (1734).

106. Fifty pounds in South Carolina currency would be worth roughly $680 in 1991. John J. McCusker, *How Much Is That in Real Money? A Historical Price Index for Use as a Deflator of Money Values in the Economy of the United States* (Worcester, Mass.: American Antiquarian Society, 1992), 333, table A-3.

107. After an extensive comparison of boundary lines for sixteen beat companies and sixteen townships in Pickens District, Jean Flynn concluded that "the beat companies were bounded by geographical features such as bodies of water and then existing roads." Jean M. Flynn, *The Militia in Antebellum South Carolina Society* (Spartanburg: Reprint Company, 1991), 160.

108. "An Act for Regulating Patrols in this Province," in Cooper and McCord, eds., *SC Statutes,* vol. 3, 398, clause VI (1734).

109. "An Act for Establishing and Regulating of Patrols," ibid., 456 (1737). Patrollers were further exempted from parish offices, working on the roads, and jury duty. In 1736, the Commons House of Assembly also considered, then rejected, the possibility of putting patrols under the authority of county magistrates or patrol commissioners, rather than the militia. J. H. Easterby, ed., *The Journal of the Commons House of Assembly, November 10, 1736–June 7, 1739* (Columbia: Historical Commission of South Carolina, 1951), 34, 42–43.

110. Henry, *Police Control of the Slave,* 33.

111. For population statistics, see Wood, *Black Majority,* 152, 218–238; Mor-

gan, *Slave Counterpoint,* 40–41. Several historians have argued that the physical threat confronting white colonists was dwarfed by the variegated psychological threat that the slaves posed. See Winthrop Jordan, *White over Black: American Attitudes toward the Negro, 1550–1812* (Chapel Hill: University of North Carolina Press, 1968), for the colonial period, and Channing, *Crisis of Fear,* 17–57, for the late antebellum period.

112. Wood, *Black Majority,* 211–217, 298–307.

113. Ibid., 308–326.

114. Ibid., 318–319.

115. "An Act for the Better Establishing and Regulating Patrols," in Cooper and McCord, eds., *SC Statutes,* vol. 3, 568, preamble (1740). The assembly considered, but rejected, the possibility of paying patrols again. J. H. Easterby, ed., *The Journal of the Commons House of Assembly, September 12, 1739–March 26, 1741* (Columbia: Historical Commission of South Carolina, 1952), 26, 37. The price tag may have simply been too high; legislators calculated the cost of patrolling throughout the colony at close to £25,000 annually. J. H. Easterby, ed., *The Journal of the Commons House of Assembly, May 18, 1741–July 10, 1742* (Columbia: Historical Commission of South Carolina, 1953), 293.

116. "An Act for the better ordering and governing of Negroes and other Slaves," in Cooper and McCord, eds., *SC Statutes,* vol. 7, 397–419 (1740).

117. Ibid., 417. This provision came several years after similar measures were taken in Virginia.

118. Ibid., 569, clause II. The extensive rules for substitute service were likely drafted with female owners in mind.

119. Ibid., 571, clause VI.

120. Forty shillings per offense. Ibid., 572–573.

121. In 1850, Judge Withers commented on this stability in *State v. Boozer et al.,* when he said "Our fundamental code, now time-honored, is that of 1740. It was enacted soon after a violent, barbarous and somewhat servile bloody attack at Stono. Not a few of its provisions took their hue from the exigency of the occasion, and that it has faded somewhat in the lapse of time is only the usual inevitable consequence of all police systems in the shape of positive terms, which cannot have the quality to keep up with the advancement of a community." 36 S.C.L. (5 Strob.) 21 (1850).

122. Patrolling based upon a militia structure, without pay, was enacted for rural areas in Florida, Alabama, Mississippi, and Tennessee. On Mississippi, see J. Michael Crane, "Controlling the Night: Perceptions of the Slave Patrol System in Mississippi," *Journal of Mississippi History* 61 (1999): 119–136.

123. "An Act for Regulating the Militia of this Province and for the security and

better Defence of the same," January 24, 1755, in George De Renne and Charles C. Jones, Jr., comps., *Acts Passed by the General Assembly of the Colony of Georgia, 1755 to 1774* (Wormsloe, Ga.: n.p., 1881), 21, clause 25, and "An Act for Establishing and Regulating Patrols," July 28, 1757, indexed in Robert and George Watkins, eds., *Digest of the Laws of the State of Georgia . . .* (Philadelphia: R. Aitken, 1800), 50.

124. On the multiple meanings of time in Virginia and South Carolina's slave societies, see Morgan, *Slave Counterpoint,* 18–19.

125. Hening, ed., *VA Statutes,* vol. 1, 125–128 (1623). The law was reenacted in 1631/2, ibid., 173.

126. Edmund Morgan, *American Slavery, American Freedom: The Ordeal of Colonial Virginia* (New York: W. W. Norton, 1975), 404, 420–423.

127. Hening, ed., *VA Statutes,* vol. 1, 226 (1639).

128. For contrasting theories, see Morgan, *American Slavery, American Freedom,* and Winthrop D. Jordan, *The White Man's Burden: Historical Origins of Racism in the United States* (New York: Oxford University Press, 1974); see also Russell Menard, "From Servants to Slaves: The Transformation of the Chesapeake Labor System," *Southern Studies* 16 (1977): 355–390.

129. Klein, *Slavery in the Americas,* 71, 181. Although there were more *cimarróns* in Cuba, slaves escaped to and lived in or around the Great Dismal Swamp until the Civil War. See Hugo Leaming, "Hidden Americans: Maroons of Virginia and the Carolinas," 2 vols. (Ph.D. diss., University of Illinois at Chicago Circle, 1979). For a foreign observer's impressions of Dismal Swamp maroons, see J. F. D. Smyth, *A Tour in the United States of America,* 2 vols. (Dublin: Price, Moncrieffe, 1784), vol. 1, 101–102.

130. Hening, ed., *VA Statutes,* vol. 1, 235–253 (1642). This law was reenacted again in 1654, ibid., vol. 1, 401.

131. Ibid., 483 (1657).

132. Ibid., 539 (1659).

133. "Apprehending of Runawayes," ibid., vol. 2, 21 (1660).

134. Untitled order, "Whereas a proposition relating to the proposition . . .," ibid., 35 (1660/1).

135. Warren Billings, ed., *The Old Dominion in the Seventeenth Century: A Documentary History of Virginia, 1606–1689* (Chapel Hill: University of North Carolina Press, 1975), 158.

136. "An act concerning the pursuite of runawayes," in Hening, ed., *VA Statutes,* vol. 2, 187 (1663). This law was ultimately repealed in 1684, having been found "very inconvenient." "An act repealing an act, concerning the pursuit of runawayes," ibid., vol. 3, 12 (1684).

137. "Against Runawayes," ibid., vol. 2, 273 (1669).

138. "An act concerning runaways," ibid., 277 (1670).

139. Under the new law, certificates for runaways would have to be sworn to in county court, where local knowledge would prevent frauds from proceeding too far. Ibid., 283 (1670).
140. "An act concerning runaways," ibid., 277 (1670). The law was reenacted several times. See "An additionall Act about runawayes," ibid., vol. 3, 28 (1686).
141. Ibid., vol. 1, 243 (1642).
142. For example, "Concerning passes," ibid., vol. 2, 130 (1661); "An act to prevent clandestine transportation or carrying of persons in debt, servants, and slaves, out of this colony," ibid., vol. 3, 270 (1705).
143. Ibid., vol. 1, 415 (1656).
144. "Concerning Indians," ibid., vol. 2, 142 (1661); "An Act prohibiting the entertainment of Indians without badges," ibid., 185 (1663).
145. See the establishment of a reward system in 1669, below, that speaks of "servants by custom" [slaves] not having legal passes, which suggests that some slaves carried passes prior to that time.
146. "An act for preventing Negroes Insurrections," in Hening, ed., *VA Statutes*, vol. 2, 481 (1680). There were small-scale slave plots in 1663 and 1672.
147. "An additionall act for the better preventing Insurrections by Negroes," ibid., 492 (1682).
148. The Northern Neck of Virginia is the peninsula bounded by the Potomac and Rappahannock rivers and the Chesapeake Bay.
149. Aptheker, *Slave Revolts*, 166.
150. "An Act for suppressing outlying Slaves," in Hening, ed., *VA Statutes*, vol. 3, 86 (1691). Justices of the peace had to order the sheriff to apprehend runaways using this method.
151. Dunn, *Sugar and Slaves*, 245.
152. Klein, *Slavery in the Americas*, 52. It also contained references to indentured servants, with provisions applicable only to them, but the bulk of the law related to slaves and their treatment. The 1705 law would be slightly amended in 1723 to incorporate regulations about slaves marketing goods and owning property.
153. "An act concerning servants and slaves," in Hening, ed., *VA Statutes*, vol. 3, 447–462 (1705), esp. 455–456, 460.
154. City Sergeant Register 1841–1846, Richmond, VHS, confirms that runaways were continually brought to the city jail for incarceration by private citizens, who received five dollars plus a small fee for each mile that they had transported the slave.
155. Edmund Jenings, president of the Council of Virginia, 1709 proclamation, PRO C. O. 5/1316, fols. 166–169, *VCRP* reel 40.
156. Spotswood to the Commissioners for Trade and Plantations, October 15, 1712, PRO C. O. 5/1316 fols. 384–385, *VCRP* reel 40.

157. Hugh Drysdale to the Commissioners for Trade and Plantations, December 20, 1722, PRO C. O. 5/1319 fols. 82–84, *VCRP* reel 41.

158. Governor's speech to the General Assembly at the opening of the session, May 10, 1723, PRO C. O. 5/1319 fols. 107–108, *VCRP* reel 41.

159. "An act directing the trial of slaves, . . . ," in Hening, ed., *VA Statutes,* vol. 4, 128–129 (1723). The direct connection between the changed laws and the insurrection is attested to by Drysdale in his letter to the Commissioners for Trade and Plantations, PRO C. O. 5/1319 fols. 111–117, esp. fol. 114, *VCRP* reel 41.

160. Chapter 4 discusses the attack of slave patrols on a Baptist gathering.

161. "An Act for Amending the Act concerning Servants and Slaves . . . ," in Hening, ed., *VA Statutes,* vol. 4, 173 (1726).

162. "An Act for making more effectual provision against Invasions and Insurrections," ibid., 197–204, esp. 202–203 (1726/7). Whitsuntide is the first few days of Pentecost, which occurs seven weeks after Easter.

163. "An Act, for reviving the Act, for making more effectual provision against Invasions and Insurrections," ibid., vol. 5, 24 (1738). This is not the same law as the 1738 act creating greater regulation of the patrols, which it immediately follows.

164. William Gooch to the Commissioners for Trade and Plantations, PRO C. O. 5/1322 fols. 10–13, *VCRP* reel 42. Another maroon community on the Maryland frontier apparently developed in 1728–29, and one of the runaways returned to Prince George's County, Virginia, to encourage other slaves to join them there. Allan Kulikoff, *Tobacco and Slaves: The Development of Southern Cultures in the Chesapeake, 1680–1800* (Chapel Hill: University of North Carolina Press, 1986), 328–329.

165. William Gooch to the Commissioners for Trade and Plantations, September 14, 1730, PRO C. O. 5/1322 fols. 158–159, *VCRP* reel 42. I am grateful to Philip Schwarz for his assistance in locating this material.

166. William Gooch to the Commissioners for Trade and Plantations, May 28, 1731, Lambeth Palace Library, Fulham Palace Papers, *VCRP* reel 591. See also abstract of letter from Gooch to the Commissioners for Trade and Plantations, February 12, 1730/1, PRO C. O. 5/1322 fols. 160, *VCRP* reel 42.

167. William Gooch to the Commissioners for Trade and Plantations, February 12, 1730/1, PRO C. O. 5/1322 fols. 161–163, *VCRP* reel 42. See Gooch's proclamation ordering patrols to be active, October 8, 1730, PRO C. O. 5/1322 fols. 212–213, *VCRP* reel 42.

168. Proclamation of William Gooch, October 29, 1736, PRO C. O. 5/1344 fol. 40, *VCRP* reel 48.

169. "An act, for the better Regulation of the Militia," in Hening, ed., *VA Statutes,* vol. 5, 19 (1738).

170. Ibid.
171. "An Act for amending the act, intituled, An act for the better regulation of the militia," ibid., vol. 6, 421–422 (1754).
172. The state finally settled on fifteen pounds of tobacco per twelve hours in 1777. "An act for regulating and discipline the Militia," ibid., vol. 9, 273. In the 1850s Virginia experimented with, and then discarded, a completely voluntary militia. See Kenneth McCreedy, "Palladium of Liberty: The American Militia System, 1815–1861" (Ph.D. diss., University of California, Berkeley, 1991), 192–193.
173. Compare Yee, "Slave Patrol System: South Carolina, 1690–1810," 8.
174. Marvin L. Michael Kay and Lorin Lee Cary, *Slavery in North Carolina, 1748–1775* (Chapel Hill: University of North Carolina Press, 1995), 19. Their estimates are drawn from Saunders, ed., *CRNC* vol. 1, 720, 722, vol. 2, xvii, 419, vol. 3, 433; Evarts B. Greene and Virginia D. Harrington, *American Population before the Federal Census of 1790* (1932; reprint, Gloucester, Mass.: P. Smith, 1966), 156; Merrens, *Colonial North Carolina,* 20–21. William S. Powell places the white population closer to 30,000 in 1730, *North Carolina through Four Centuries* (Chapel Hill: University of North Carolina Press, 1989), 105.
175. Lefler and Newsome, *History of a Southern State: North Carolina,* 43. On the chronological limits of North Carolina's settlement during the eighteenth century, see Powell, *North Carolina through Four Centuries,* 78.
176. U. S. Bureau of the Census, *Historical Statistics of the United States: Colonial Times to 1970,* 2 vols. (Washington, D.C.: Bureau of the Census, 1975), vol. 2, table Z 1–19, 1168. In 1750, North Carolina had roughly 19,000 slaves, as compared with 100,000 in Virginia and 40,000 in South Carolina. As a percentage of each colony's total population, Virginia's slaves made up more than 40 percent, South Carolina's slaves over 60 percent, while North Carolina slaves were only about 25 percent of its total population in 1750.
177. 1669 marked the first time lawmakers acted upon the latitude granted them by the English constitution under which North and South Carolina was settled (which permitted slavery). "The Fundamental Constitutions of Carolina, Drawn up by John Locke," March 1, 1669/70, clause 110, reprinted in Saunders, ed., *CRNC,* vol. 1, 204 (1670).
178. Barth. Fowler, attorney general of Virginia, to Deputy Governor of North Carolina, August 27, 1699, in Saunders, ed., *CRNC,* vol. 1, 513.
179. Lieutenant Governor Spotswood to the Earl of Rochester, July 30, 1711, in Saunders, ed., *CRNC,* vol. 1, 798.
180. "An act for restraining the Indyans from molesting or injureing the inhabitants of this government, and for securing to the Indyans the right and property of their own lands," in Clark, ed., *SRNC,* vol. 23, 87–88 (1715);

"An act for entering of vessels, and to prevent the exportation of debtors," ibid., 44–45 (1715).

181. Susan H. Brinn, "Blacks in Colonial North Carolina, 1660–1723" (master's thesis, University of North Carolina at Chapel Hill, 1973), 49.

182. *North Carolina Historical and Genealogical Register,* vol. 2, 315, and vol. 3, 286; Cindy Hahamovitch, "Crime, Law, and Authority in Colonial North Carolina, 1700–1750" (master's thesis, University of North Carolina at Chapel Hill, 1987), 43.

183. "An Act Concerning Servants and Slaves," (1715), in Clark, ed., *SRNC,* vol. 23, 63–64. Other parts of the 1715 North Carolina code limited slaves' ability to keep weapons, hold meetings, or steal boats, but the law did not simply copy Virginia or South Carolina slave laws whole-sale. Roger Brooks, "North Carolina, 1715: Reflections in the Statute Law" (master's thesis, University of Virginia, 1987), 40, 50. On the timing of the 1715 law's passage, see Hahamovitch, "Crime, Law, and Authority," 44–45.

184. Hening, ed., *VA Statutes,* vol. 6, 24 (1748) (runaway sailors to be "taken up"); ibid., 563 (1755) (deserters to be "taken up"); [John F. Grimké], *The South Carolina Justice of the Peace . . .,* 2d ed. (Philadelphia: R. Aitken & Son, 1796), 534 (absent servants to be "taken up").

185. Prior to 1739, there were no reports of slave rebellions in North Carolina of any size.

186. "An additional act to an act for appointing Toll-books, and for preventing people from driving horses, cattle, or hogs, to other persons' lands," in Clark, ed., *SRNC,* vol. 23, 114, section VII (1729).

187. Ibid., section IX.

188. "An act concerning servants and slaves," ibid., 191, chap. 24 (1741).

189. For the purposes of this discussion, "Cape Fear" includes New Hanover and Brunswick counties.

190. Kay and Cary, *Slavery in North Carolina,* table 1.2 (Lower Cape Fear), 226. In the next twelve years, the density of slave population in this district would almost double. Ibid., table 1.4, 229.

191. R. H. Taylor, "Slave Conspiracies in North Carolina," *NCHR* 5 (1928): 23; David Cecelski, "The Shores of Freedom: The Maritime Underground Rail-road in North Carolina, 1800–1861," *NCHR* 71 (1994): 177–179.

192. "An additional act to an act concerning servants and slaves," in Clark, ed., *SRNC,* vol. 23, 388 (1753). Compare Yee, "Slave Patrol System: South Carolina, 1690–1810," 8.

193. Matthew Rowan to Captain William Wilkins, February 1, 1752/3, Governor's Papers, NCDAH.

194. "An additional act to an act concerning servants and slaves," in Clark, ed., *SRNC,* vol. 23, 388.

195. See August 8, 1759, fol. 75 verso, New Hanover County court minutes, 1738–1769, NCDAH ("Searchers, or Patrols, appointed for the . . .").

196. The legislative records for this period are unrevealing on the motives behind this law's creation or structure.

197. July 1753, fols. 205–207, Chowan County court minutes, 1749–1754, NCDAH.

198. Statistics drawn from Kay and Cary, *Slavery in North Carolina,* table 1.1, 221.

199. February 1759, fol. 71, New Hanover County court minutes, 1738–1769, NCDAH.

200. Ibid., April 1769, fol. 205. Eventually the court would order that the first day of each term be set aside for appointing patrols, road overseers, and handling other types of routine, repetitive tasks. May 1793, fols. 60–61, New Hanover County court minutes, 1786–1793, NCDAH.

201. See, for example, October 1768, fol. 191 verso, New Hanover County court minutes, 1738–1769, NCDAH; April 1771, fol. 10, New Hanover County court minutes, 1771–1779, NCDAH.

202. See Virginia tax levies for Princess Anne County starting in the late 1730s or Spotsylvania County in 1758, LV; other counties, like Richmond, did not start paying patrollers through their levies until the 1780s. See Chapter 3 for similar data in Norfolk and Amelia county tithable lists for the 1750s–1780s. Alternatively, one can trace the use of patrols through the appointment slips issued to patrollers, which served as their legal permission to enter the homes of others without warrant. The earliest extant slips are found in North Carolina, in Richmond County (1786) and Onslow County (1795). Patrol, Miscellaneous Officials' Bonds and Records, Richmond County, and Patrol, Officials' Bonds and Records, Onslow County, NCDAH.

203. September 1766, fol. 144 verso, New Hanover County court minutes, 1738–1769, NCDAH.

204. January 1783, fol. 92, New Hanover County court minutes, 1780–1785, NCDAH. This must have been contested, because an earlier court record had already granted Dotey the gun. Ibid., October 1783, fol. 105. The right to keep weapons found eventually disappeared with the patrol law changes of 1779.

205. Well-to-do whites wanted gun exemptions to provide protection for their property on farflung plantations. Guns also gave slaves the means to supplement their normal diet. June 1741, fol. 50, New Hanover County court minutes, 1738–1769, NCDAH.

206. Ibid., September 1761, fol. 105.

207. A 1779 law allowed patrollers to check passes, take up slaves, and return

them to their owners. "An Act to amend an Act, entitled, An Additional Act concerning Servants and Slaves . . ." in Clark, ed., *SRNC*, vol. 24, 276–277 (1779).

208. Jonathan Bush has succinctly described this quality in Virginia slave laws: "They are more akin to lengthy police measures, listing crimes and consequences but little more." "Free to Enslave," 433.

209. This conception parallels a similar finding (based on a contrasting analysis of English and Roman slave law) in Watson, *Slave Law in the Americas,* 66.

210. Virginia enacted a pass law in 1680, as opposed to South Carolina's 1687 law.

2. Supervising Patrollers in Town and Country

1. Epigraph: William Kingsford, *Impressions of the West and South during a Six Weeks' Holiday* (Toronto: A. H. Armour & Co., 1858), 77.

2. Ibid. Kingsford may have chanced upon similar newspaper commentary in the 1857 *Charleston Courier,* which stated that city slaves were "peculiarly susceptible to the influence of military display" among the reorganized city guards. January 17, 1857, cited in Clarence Smith, "William Porcher Miles, Progressive Mayor of Charleston, 1855–1857," *Proceedings of the South Carolina Historical Association* [12] (1942): 31.

3. *Winyaw Intelligencer* (Georgetown, S.C.), March 8, 1819.

4. For greater background on the colonial militia, see William L. Shea, *The Virginia Militia in the Seventeenth Century* (Baton Rouge: Louisiana State University Press, 1983); James Titus, *The Old Dominion at War: Society, Politics, and Warfare in Late Colonial Virginia* (Columbia: University of South Carolina Press, 1991); Marvin L. Michael Kay and William S. Price, Jr., " 'To Ride the Wood Mare': Road Building and Militia Service in Colonial North Carolina, 1740–1775," *NCHR* 57 (October 1980): 361–409; David W. Cole, "The Organization and Administration of the South Carolina Militia System, 1670–1783" (Ph.D. diss., University of South Carolina, 1953); Jean M. Flynn, *The Militia in Antebellum South Carolina* (Spartanburg, S.C.: Reprint Company, 1991); John W. Shy, "A New Look at Colonial Militia," *WMQ*, 3d ser., 20 (1963): 175–185; Shy, *A People Numerous and Armed: Reflections on the Military Struggle for American Independence,* rev. ed. (Ann Arbor: University of Michigan Press, 1990); John E. Ferling, *A Wilderness of Miseries: War and Warriors in Early America* (Westport, Conn.: Greenwood, 1980).

5. J. R. Western, *The English Militia in the Eighteenth Century: The Story of a Political Issue, 1660–1802* (London: Routledge & Kegan Paul, 1965), 11–12, 27, 52.

6. P. F. Campbell, "The Barbados Militia, 1627–1815," *Journal of the Barbados Museum and Historical Society* 35 (1976): 103, 110, 113.

7. Hugh Drysdale, Lieutenant Governor, to the Virginia House of Burgesses, May 10, 1723, PRO C. O. 5/1319 fols. 107–108, *VCRP* reel 41.

8. Bull to Earl of Hillsborough, November 30, 1770, Records in the British Public Record Office relating to South Carolina (microfilm), vol. 32, 383.

9. This practice continued in the antebellum period as well. See Colonel John Hill's order about making rosters, December 4, 1840, Edgefield Military Record, 9th Regt., South Carolina Militia, SHC.

10. Frederick C. Holder, *Bailey A. Barton Muster Roll Book of Pickens District, South Carolina* (Oconee, S.C.: Oconee County Historical Society, n.d.), "Introduction," x.

11. Flynn, *Militia in Antebellum South Carolina,* 160. Similar evidence exists for North Carolina companies. See the patrol appointment for December 1849, which gives Broad Creek, Smith's Creek, and the Neuse River as patrol boundaries, Slave Patrols 1845–1849, Craven County Slave and Free Negro Records, NCDAH.

12. In South Carolina, beat lines were sometimes copied into record books of mesne conveyances. See "Order to copy lines of the beat and post them," Brigadier General W. Thompson, Jr., to Col. Wilson Barton, March 8, 1834, Townes Family papers, SCL.

13. Kay and Price, "To Ride the Wood Mare," 361–409; Holder, *Bailey A. Barton Muster Roll Book,* "Introduction," i.

14. Rhys Isaac, *The Transformation of Virginia, 1740–1790* (Chapel Hill: University of North Carolina Press, 1982), 104.

15. See, for example, grand jury presentment, Colleton District, April 6, 1852, S.C. General Assembly papers, Index number 0010 015 1852 00008 00, SCDAH.

16. These early laws were frequently ignored. Free and slave African Americans served in the militia before and in the army during the Revolutionary War, and free blacks served in the North Carolina militia until 1812. Complaints made after the passage of the federal militia act of 1792 suggest that local groups persisted in allowing persons of color to participate in militia musters, and not always just as musicians.

17. Petition of Inhabitants of Kershaw District, undated, S.C. General Assembly papers, Index number 0010 003 ND00 01869 00, SCDAH.

18. See, for example, Lieutenant Governor Francis Nicholson to the Privy Council and the Commissioners for Trade and Plantations, August 20, 1690, PRO C. O. 5/1390 fols. 109–110; Governors' messages to the S.C. General Assembly, no. 701, Governor Charles Pinckney, November 22, 1797, S.C. General Assembly papers, SCDAH.

19. See the diary of Washington Taylor, in which he indicates regular attendance to musters at least four times a year, starting in 1835 (the diary's beginning), and continuing to 1855 (the diary's end), SCL.

20. For example, see August 30, 1837, Edgefield Military Record, 9th Regt., South Carolina Militia, SHC. Militia records in Virginia and South Carolina reveal who served as patrollers in parts of those states. Unfortunately, the widespread destruction in South Carolina during the Civil War has meant the loss of most of its militia records. Private families preserved most surviving militia records in the SCL and SHC.

21. Jean M. Flynn, "South Carolina's Compliance with the Militia Act of 1792," *SCHM* 69 (1968): 26–43, esp. 29.

22. These warrants suffered from frequent handling, folding, and subsequent annotations, which can be seen on patrol appointment slips in all three states. For more on the warrants, see Chapter 4.

23. The higher militia offices ultimately went to men based on seniority, reckoned by the number of years they had served as officers. At the highest level, a governor customarily selected his own adjutant general and staff.

24. Address to "Brother officers" by J. W. Tompkins, undated (c. 1859), Tompkins Family papers, SCL.

25. Military commissions and records, James Faulkner, Box 9, Militia service, Faulkner Family papers, VHS.

26. Petition of Officers and Privates of the First and Second Brigades, undated, S.C. General Assembly papers, Index number 0010 003 ND00 00390 00, SCDAH.

27. Wade Hampton to Mrs. Singleton, September 5, 1861, Hampton Family papers, SCL.

28. Return of the Officers and the whole of the men . . ., September 22, 1775, Glover Papers, SCHS, cited in Philip D. Morgan, *Slave Counterpoint: Black Culture in the Eighteenth-Century Chesapeake and Lowcountry* (Chapel Hill: University of North Carolina Press, 1998), 308.

29. Mark Pitcavage, " 'An Equitable Burden': The Decline of the State Militias, 1783–1858" (Ph.D. diss., Ohio State University, 1995).

30. Kenneth McCreedy, "Palladium of Liberty: The American Militia System, 1815–1861" (Ph.D. diss., University of California Berkeley, 1991), 325–326.

31. Pitcavage, "An Equitable Burden," 429.

32. Virginia briefly experimented with a totally voluntary militia in the 1850s, while requiring that country courts appoint patrollers. McCreedy, "Palladium of Liberty," 192–193.

33. Attempts to shift control of patrols from courts to the militia failed in 1815 and 1819. "A bill to amend the militia laws and also the several acts now in

force within the state relative to patrols," General Assembly Session Records, November-December 1815, Box 1, NCDAH; "A bill to regulate and change the mode of appointing patrols in the several counties of this state," ibid., November-December 1819, Box 1, NCDAH.

34. Hundreds of these appointment slips, creased from being carried during patrol duty, are preserved in the NCDAH, which houses the largest collection of patroller appointment slips in the American South. Fiscal officers of the county courts preserved the slips after patrollers surrendered them in return for compensation. The longest complete runs, some twenty to sixty years of patrol appointment records, exist for Cleveland County, Henderson County, Perquimans County, and Warren County, NCDAH.

35. John C. Inscoe, *Mountain Masters: Slavery, and the Sectional Crisis in Western North Carolina* (Knoxville: University of Tennessee Press, 1989), 99. Appalachian patrols became most active when large numbers of slaves entered the region, in the summer resort season or during gold rushes.

36. David Walker, *David Walker's Appeal,* rev. ed. with an introduction by Sean Wilentz (1829; reprint, New York: Hill and Wang, 1995).

37. John Hope Franklin, *The Free Negro in North Carolina, 1790–1860* (New York: W. W. Norton, 1971), 64–72.

38. Circular letter of John Owen, August 19, 1830, Governor's Letter Book, 1828–1830, NCDAH.

39. "An act for the regulation of the patrol," chapter XVI, section III (1830), *Acts passed by the General Assembly of the State of North Carolina, at the Session of 1830–31* (Raleigh: Lawrence & Lemay, 1831), 17–18.

40. These divisions mimicked tax collection districts and census districts.

41. In 1856, Willis held twenty-seven slaves. The next highest assessed male taxpayers, William Myatt and Simon Turner, had only six slaves on their farms. The second-largest number of slaves were held by widow Susan Banks, who had seventeen. Panther Branch District, Wake County Tax Returns, 1856, NCDAH. In the 1860 federal census, Willis is listed as owning fifty-five slaves, which indicates not only his growing wealth but some slaves who were probably hiring themselves out in the nearby capital, Raleigh, who were also counted among his household in Panther Branch District. Panther Branch District, Wake County, Population of the United States in 1860, Eighth Census, United States Census Office (microfilm).

42. Vance E. Swift, "Colonel John Whitaker: Judge, Revolutionary War Patriot, Squire of Echo Manor, Wake County, North Carolina," (Raleigh: n.p., n.d.), Genealogical Collection, NCDAH. Colonel Whitaker held practically every important county office and served as justice of the peace for ten years, in addition to owning a tannery, brickyard, and lumber mill. Other material in this section on the Whitaker family is from Vance

E. Swift, "Colonel John Whitaker," in Lynne Belvin and Harriette Riggs, *The Heritage of Wake County, North Carolina, 1983,* (Winston-Salem, N.C.: Wake County Genealogical Society, Hunter Publishing Co., 1983), 568–569.

43. Map of Wake County, Drawn from actual Surveys by Fendol Bevers, County Surveyor. Published by Nicholas & Gorman, Raleigh, n.d. [1871], Map Collection, NCC.

44. Where the current state highway 42 and state road 2736 meet, a quarter mile from the Middle Creek Baptist Church. Whether the church was a drawing point for slave preaching is unknown, but this may have been an additional incentive for appointing Smith to the patrol committee.

45. Memoranda generated by the Wake County patrollers of 1857–58 suggest that their nightly routes usually took them along these roads and past the committee members' homes. See Chapter 4.

46. See Hermann Wellenreuther, "Urbanization in the Colonial South: A Critique," *WMQ,* 3d ser., 31 (1974): 653–668.

47. The assembly passed port town bills on multiple occasions. See Hening, ed., *VA Statutes,* vol. 1, 412–414; vol. 2, 172–176, 471–78; vol. 3, 53–69, 404–419. See also John C. Rainbolt, "The Absence of Towns in Seventeenth-Century Virginia," *JSH* 35 (1969): 348.

48. See Chapter 1. On the use of early policing mechanisms targeted at African Americans, see Homer Haskins and Richard Thomas, "White Policing of Black Populations: A History of Race and Social Control in America," in Ellis Cashmore and Eugene McLaughlin, eds., *Out of Order? Policing Black People* (New York: Routledge, 1991), 65–86; Richard C. Wade, *Slavery in the Cities: The South, 1820–1860* (New York: Oxford University Press, 1964), 80–82, 98–106.

49. For a rebuttal, see Lyle W. Dorsett and Arthur H. Shaffer, "Was the Antebellum South Antiurban? A Suggestion," *JSH* 38 (1972): 93–100.

50. David R. Goldfield, *Cotton Fields and Skyscrapers: Southern City and Region, 1607–1980* (Baton Rouge: Louisiana State University Press, 1982), 32, and Goldfield, *Region, Race and Cities: Interpreting the Urban South* (Baton Rouge: Louisiana State University Press, 1997), 43–45.

51. Leonard P. Curry, "Urbanization and Urbanism in the Old South: A Comparative View," *JSH* 40 (1974): 51.

52. James H. Brewer, "Legislation Designed to Control Slavery in Wilmington and Fayetteville," *NCHR* 30 (1953): 156–157. Brewer speculates that masters may have also been willing to let slaves live in separate dwellings due to the greater fees gained from slave hiring.

53. Complaints about slave behavior of this kind began in the colonial period and continued intermittently until the Civil War. Examples can be found

in Brewer, "Legislation Designed to Control Slavery in Wilmington and Fayetteville," 157–158, 160–162, or the grand jury presentments printed in the *South Carolina Gazette*, March 23–30, 1733; March 19–26, 1737; November 5, 1744; May 1, 1756.

54. For a theory about why Charlestonians permitted their night watch to grow lax in the face of such assertive slave behavior, see Philip D. Morgan, "Black Life in Eighteenth-Century Charleston," *Perspectives in American History*, n.s., 1 (1984), 216–222.

55. Grand jury presentment, *South Carolina Gazette*, April 15, 1745, and May 1, 1756.

56. Wade, *Slavery in the Cities*, 152–155.

57. Petition of the Intendant and Municipal Wardens of Columbia, 1820, S.C. General Assembly papers, Index number 0010 003 1820 00039 00, SCDAH.

58. "An act concerning patrols," chapter XXI, March 1832, in *Acts Passed at a General Assembly of the Commonwealth of Virginia, begun and held at the Capitol, in the City of Richmond, on Monday, the fifth day of December, in the Year of our Lord, one thousand eight hundred and thirty-one, and of the commonwealth the fifty-sixth* (Richmond: Ritchie, 1832), 19–20. The legislature explicitly denied this power to unincorporated towns.

59. Citizens and Freeholders of the Town of Pearisburg, December 10, 1834, Giles County legislative petitions, LV.

60. Petition of Citizens of Yorkville, November 1824, S.C. General Assembly papers, Index number 0010 003 1824 00151 00, SCDAH. A similar law existed in Virginia, "An act exempting the night watch from military duty in time of peace," April 1839, chap. 30, *Acts of the General Assembly of Virginia, passed at the Session commencing 7th January, and ending 10th April, 1839, in the sixty-third year of the Commonwealth* (Richmond: Shepherd, 1839), 24.

61. See the classification of all male residents into groups to serve as a watch or patrol at the beginning of each year, W. C. G. Carrington, comp., *Laws for the Government of the City of Raleigh, Containing all legislative enactments relative thereto, and the ordinances of the Board of Commissioners, now in force; from the first act of incorporation to 1838* (Raleigh: Raleigh Register, 1838), 56–57. This private to public shift parallels the development of regulations that were privately enforced during the initial period of patrol establishment in colonywide laws. See Chapter 1.

62. October 5, 1808, *Edenton (N.C.) Gazette*, cited in Guion G. Johnson, *Ante-Bellum North Carolina: A Social History* (Chapel Hill: University of North Carolina Press, 1937), 128–189; Town of Danville, Minutes, 1833–1844, 22, LV.

63. Grand jury presentment, Georgetown District, November 6, 1799, S.C. General Assembly papers, Index number 0010 015 1799 00004 00, SCDAH.

64. Petition of Intendant and Wardens of Beaufort, undated (c. 1818), S.C. General Assembly papers, Index number 0010 003 ND00 00196 00, SCDAH.

65. See, for example, Petition of Citizens of Town of Cheraw, undated, S.C. General Assembly papers, Index number 0010 003 ND00 02424 00, SCDAH.

66. Petition of Georgetown Inhabitants, 1810, S.C. General Assembly papers, Index number 0010 003 1810 00075 00, SCDAH.

67. The state gave them $500, which they claimed was inadequate, because the location of the town made labor that much more expensive to hire. Ibid. See also the Georgetown District grand jury presentment of November 9, 1829, claiming that it needed a strong town guard because of the dangerous "business carried on at night with the color'd population," S.C. General Assembly papers, Index number 0010 015 1829 00004 00, SCDAH.

68. Petition of the Town Council of Georgetown, November 16, 1829, S.C. General Assembly papers, Index number 0010 003 1829 00025 00, SCDAH. On the rebellion, Jane Gwinn, "The Georgetown Slave Insurrection of 1829," in Charles Joyner, ed., *Black Carolinians: Studies in the History of South Carolina Negroes in the Nineteenth Century* (Laurinburg, S.C.: n.p., 1969).

69. Governors' messages to the S.C. General Assembly, no. 1472 (13–21), Governor Stephen Miller, December 3, 1830, S.C. General Assembly papers, SCDAH. Charleston later studied the watch and police systems of New Orleans and Savannah in 1855. Smith, "William Porcher Miles," 30–39.

70. Governers' messages to the S.C. General Assembly, no. 1472, Governor Stephen Miller, appended document, Peter Cuttins to Stephen D. Miller, n.d., S.C. General Assembly papers, SCDAH.

71. Governors' messages to the S.C. General Assembly, no. 1472, Governor Stephen Miller, appended document, Georgetown Town Council to Stephen D. Miller, November 12, 1830, S.C. General Assembly papers, SCDAH.

72. Newspapers that typically listed all the business of the mayor's court later transformed these listings into "police blotter" reports, which continued to describe offenses committed by slaves and free blacks apprehended by town patrols. See, for example, the *Richmond Examiner,* where this change-over occurs in early September 1849.

73. Governors' messages to the S.C. General Assembly, no. 1472, Governor Stephen Miller, December 3, 1830, SCDAH.

74. *Winyaw Intelligencer* (Georgetown, S.C.), November 18, 28, and December 9, 1829.

75. "An act to restrain negroes from wandering about the streets after night," June 26, 1811, and "An act respecting patroles in the Town of Abingdon," September 11, 1812, Town of Abingdon Trustee & Council Minutes, 1778–1803, vol. 1, 75–76, 82, LV. See a similar rise in default rates in Aiken Municipal Court Docket, 1839–1866, SCDAH.

76. See, for example, Town of Abingdon Trustee & Council Minutes, 1778–1803, vol. 1, 64, 75–76, 82, 86, 106–107, 154–155, 197–198; vol. 2, 8–9, 49–50, 93, 128, 147–149, LV.

77. Based upon a comparison of Aiken Town Council Patrol Book, 1839–1859, with Aiken Municipal Court Docket, 1839–1866, SCDAH, which records the fines for defaulters. The Aiken records are among the most complete urban patrol records available in the three states.

78. Aiken Town Council Patrol Book, 1839–1859, SCDAH. Fines for failure to patrol continue to appear in the Aiken Municipal Court Dockets for 1860 to 1865, suggesting that patrols were appointed during the Civil War.

79. Petition from residents of Richland County (Columbia), undated, no. 373, S.C. General Assembly papers, SCDAH.

80. James R. Caton, *Jottings from the Annals of Alexandria: Legislative Chronicles of the City of Alexandria* (Alexandria, Va.: Newell-Cole Co., 1933), 80–82.

81. December 22, 1856, 126, Town of Abingdon Trustee & Council Minutes, 1830–1864, LV.

82. "Negro Slaves as I have Known them," 1904 reminiscence, J. Willcox Brown private papers, LV.

83. *Raleigh Register,* May 4, 1802, cited in Franklin, *Free Negro in North Carolina,* 197.

84. Petition of the Mayor and Aldermen of the City of Charleston, undated, S.C. General Assembly papers, Index number 0010 003 ND00 02332 00, SCDAH. The petition was denied by the assembly's judiciary committee.

85. In December 1845, Fayetteville town residents "recommended the employment of a Town Guard, and authorised the levy of a special tax to defray the expense thereof, [and] the Commissioners, in obedience to these instructions, partially relinquished the Municipal Patrol, and established the present system." In the first year the town paid patrollers with private subscription monies and out of the city's general fund, because it was an inconvenient time of year to collect the tax. Receipts and disbursements for Fayetteville for 1845, City of Fayetteville, Miscellaneous Records 1769–1917, NCDAH.

86. November 1840, Taxes on African-Americans, Gates County, and 1840 Guilford County returns, both in Governor's Papers, NCDAH. Towns that did this typically allowed citizens to pay all their nonperformance fines in one lump sum. For one city that commuted fines, see petition of the Intendant and Wardens of the town of Camden, 1830, S.C. General Assembly papers, Index number 0010 003 1830 00089 00, SCDAH.

87. See, for example, *The Charter of the Town of Aiken, with the By-Laws and Ordinances, Passed by the Town Council in June 1860* (Charleston: A. J. Burke, 1860), 23.

88. Petition of citizens of town of Chester, December 5, 1853, S.C. General Assembly papers, Index number 0010 003 1853 00092 00, SCDAH.

89. *Charter of the Town of Aiken,* 6.

90. *Richmond Enquirer,* January 6, 1807; Douglas Egerton, *Gabriel's Rebellion: The Virginia Slave Conspiracies of 1800 and 1802* (Chapel Hill: University of North Carolina Press, 1993), 164. On Richmond's transition from patrol to police, Louis Cei, "Law Enforcement in Richmond: A History of Police-Community Relations, 1737–1974" (Ph.D. diss., Florida State University, 1975), 7.

91. See Edward P. Cantwell, *A History of the Charleston Police Force from the Incorporation of the City, 1783 to 1908* (Charleston: Furlong, 1908), and William H. and Jane H. Pease, *The Web of Progress: Private Values and Public Styles in Boston and Charleston, 1828–1843* (Athens, Ga.: University of Georgia Press, 1991), 100–101, 165.

92. Arthur Cunynghame, *A Glimpse at the Great Western Republic* (London: Richard Bentley, 1851), 264; Frances A. Kemble, *Journal of a Residence on a Georgian Plantation in 1838–1839,* ed. John A. Scott (Athens, Ga.: University of Georgia Press, 1984), 38–39; William Faux, *Memorable Days in America: Being a Journal of a Tour of the United States* (1823), vol. 12 of *Early Western Travels,* ed. Reuben Thwaites (Cleveland: A. H. Clark, 1904–1907), 103.

93. Kingsford, *Impressions of the West and South,* 77.

94. W. Marvin Dulaney, *Black Police in America* (Bloomington: Indiana University Press, 1996), 6. Dulaney offers no evidence in support of this assertion, however.

95. Petition to the General Assembly, undated, no. 2125, S.C. General Assembly papers, SCDAH. See also grand jury presentment, May 1847, S.C. General Assembly papers, Index number 0010 015 1847 00006 00, SCDAH, suggesting that a more rigid police be established on the Neck.

96. Memorial from Inhabitants & Proprietors of Charleston Neck, undated, S.C. General Assembly papers, Index number 0010 003 ND00 00255 00, and the legislature's response to the petition of inhabitants on Charleston

Neck, December 22, 1822, S.C. General Assembly papers, Index number 0010 004 1822 00076 00, SCDAH.

97. Memorial of the Inhabitants of Charleston Neck, undated, S.C. General Assembly papers, Index number 0010 003 ND00 00255 00, SCDAH.

98. Memorial of the Intendant and Wardens of the City of Charleston, undated, S.C. General Assembly papers, Index number 0010 003 ND00 00227 00, SCDAH. Another group of citizens also got involved, petitioning the legislature not to believe the "commissioners" because they were merely a few people who had not announced the meeting publicly, and should "not be considered a fair representation of the citizens" of Charleston Neck since the meeting had been held at an inconvenient time. They stressed that the "commissioners" portrayed the situation as one of "absolute misrule, and the most imminent danger," which was not true. Petition of Charleston Neck residents asking that powers of the Commissioners of Cross Roads not be enlarged, undated, S.C. General Assembly papers, Index number 0010 003 ND00 00253 00, SCDAH.

99. Albemarle County legislative petition, December 14, 1818, LV, calendered in H. J. Eckenrode, ed., *Fifth Annual Report of the Library Board of the Virginia State Library, 1907–1908,* under the title of *A Calendar of Legislative Petitions Arranged by Counties: Accomac-Bedford* (Richmond: Superintendent of Public Printing, 1908), 35. Revolutionary era petitions have been traced and described for all Virginia counties in Randolph W. Church, comp., *Virginia Legislative Petitions: Bibliography, Calendar, and Abstracts from Original Sources, 6 May 1776—21 June 1782* (Richmond: Virginia State Library, 1984).

100. See, e.g., citizens of Charlottesville, December 12, 1832, Albemarle County legislative petitions, LV, described in Eckenrode, *Calendar,* 41.

101. Citizens of Charlottesville, January 16, 1844, Albemarle County legislative petition, LV, described in Eckenrode, *Calendar,* 49.

102. A list of many nineteenth-century slave control city ordinances can be found in Claudia Goldin, *Urban Slavery in the American South, 1820–1860: A Quantitative History* (Chicago: University of Chicago Press, 1976), 133–138.

103. Charleston began issuing badges in 1800. Ordinance for the Better Ordering and Governing of Negroes and other Slaves, July 16, 1800, in Alexander Edwards, comp., *Ordinances of the City Council of Charleston* (Charleston: W. P. Young, 1802), 193.

104. "An act to restrain negroes and mulattoes from behaving disorderly and for other purposes," undated, 63, Town of Abingdon Trustee & Council Minutes, 1778–1803, LV. In Aiken, S.C., the curfew was 9 P.M. from October to March, and 10 P.M. for the rest of the year. *Charter of the Town of Aiken,* 17;

in Tarborough, N.C., the curfew was 9 P.M. year round. *Patrol Regulations for the Town of Tarborough,* NCC.

105. Nine P.M. all year in Tarborough, N.C., with "a reasonable time being allowed for him or her to go home or to the place designate in his or her written permission after the ringing of the bell . . ." *Patrol Regulations for the Town of Tarborough,* NCC.

106. "An act to restrain negroes from wandering about the streets after night," June 26, 1811, and "An act in addition to the act concerning patroles," October 20, 1831, 75–76, 106, Town of Abingdon Trustee & Council Minutes, 1778–1803, LV.

107. Enforcement efforts were uneven. In Richmond, city authorities simply stopped enforcing the pass law between 1852 and 1854. Goldin, *Urban Slavery,* 48–49.

108. Clippings from Richmond newspapers on slavery in Virginia, 100–105, William Price Palmer scrapbook, VHS.

109. *Wilmington Chronicle,* September 24, 1795.

110. Kemble, *Journal of a Residence on a Georgian Plantation,* 38.

111. Charles Ball, *Slavery in the United States: A Narrative of the Life and Adventures of Charles Ball, A Black Man . . .* (1837; reprint, Detroit: Negro History Press, 1970), 354–355.

112. George P. Rawick, ed., *The American Slave: A Composite Autobiography,* 19 vols. (Westport, Conn.: Greenwood, 1973–1976), vol. 7(1), 31.

113. Gerald W. Mullin, *Flight and Rebellion: Slave Resistance in Eighteenth-Century Virginia* (London: Oxford University Press, 1972), 141; Egerton, *Gabriel's Rebellion,* 18.

114. Rawick, ed., *American Slave,* vol. 5(3), 111.

115. The creation of North Carolina's patrol committees in 1830 stemmed from the perceived threat of abolitionism.

116. I am indebted to Lacy Ford for his discussion of these issues with me. Certainly white fears would have increased during any rumored or actual revolt, but these anxieties seem to have been evenly spread among all three states. On white fears and the growing physical/social distance between masters and slaves in the Low Country, see Morgan, *Slave Counterpoint,* 120, 221, 278.

117. See, for example, grand jury presentments, January 19, 1770, January 21, 1771, January 20, 1772, Charleston Court of General Sessions Journal 1769–1776, SCDAH; grand jury presentment, Marlborough District, 1823, S.C. General Assembly papers, Index number 0010 015 1823 00019 00, SCDAH; grand jury presentment, Abbeville, 1853, S.C. General Assembly papers, Index number 0010 015 1853 00001 00, SCDAH. On eighteenth-century grand juries, see A. G. Roeber, *Faithful Magistrates and Republican*

Lawyers: Creators of Virginia Legal Culture, 1680–1810 (Chapel Hill: University of North Carolina Press, 1981), 86–88, 185–187. One should bear in mind that presentments only contain complaints about failure to perform any civic duty; they never contain positive statements about persons performing their jobs adequately.

118. Grand jury presentment, Orangeburgh District, April 1819, S.C. General Assembly papers, Index number 0010 015 1819 00009 00, SCDAH.

119. *Charleston Evening Courier,* October 26, 1798.

120. *Strength of the People* (Charleston), September 21, 1809; Governors' messages to the South Carolina General Assembly, no. 1472 (13–21), Governor Stephen Miller, 1830, S.C. General Assembly papers, SCDAH (Benj. H. King, Levi Hewit, and James Downey all discharged for sleeping on the job in 1830).

121. *Strength of the People* (Charleston), October 6, 1809.

122. Donald M. Jacobs, ed., *Index to the American Slave,* (Westport, Conn.: Greenwood, 1981), 257–258. See Rawick, ed., *American Slave,* vol. 3(4), 81, for questions asked and 170–171 for a lengthy description of patrols.

123. Rawick, ed., *American Slave,* vol. 2(2), 101. See also ibid., vol. 2(1), 251–252; ibid., vol. 14(1), 29–30, 83, 293; ibid., vol. 15(2), 330, 402; Charles L. Perdue, Thomas E. Barden, and Robert K. Phillips, eds., *Weevils in the Wheat: Interviews with Virginia Ex-Slaves* (Charlottesville: University Press of Virginia, 1976), 56, 253.

124. Rawick, ed., *American Slave,* vol. 2(1), 319–320.

125. In North Carolina and Virginia, county courts had the option to pay patrollers' salaries, as did cities in all three states. Each court and city had different rates of compensation.

126. Many Virginia patrol records are linked to county tithable lists. Among the earliest payments recorded are those from Southampton County Patrol Returns and Lists for 1754–1755, LV.

127. Governors' messages to the South Carolina General Assembly, no. 1472 (13–21), Governor Stephen Miller, December 3, 1830, S.C. General Assembly papers, SCDAH. The state paid for this service, not the town.

128. Timothy Lockley suggests this analysis, based upon evidence from Savannah, Georgia, in 1819, in *Lines in the Sand: Race and Class in Lowcountry Georgia, 1750–1860* (Athens, Ga.: University of Georgia Press, forthcoming).

129. May 18, 1850, January 29, 1853, September 24, 1853, August 20, 1854, June 3, 1855, Edgefield County Sheriff, Militia & Road Duty Fines & Executions, 1836–1837, 1840–1855, SCDAH. Some men apparently sought appointment in North Carolina patrols in order to avoid fines for missing militia musters. Memorial of the Field Officers of the Twenty-fifth Regi-

ment, December 26, 1846, Petitions, Box 7, General Assembly Session Records, November 1846–January 1847, NCDAH.

130. Grand jury presentment, October 21, 1771, published in *South Carolina Gazette,* no. 1879, November 7, 1771; *South Carolina Gazette,* December 10, 1772, for Georgetown, November 26, 1772. See also Governors' messages to the South Carolina General Assembly, no. 768, enclosed letter of Paul Hamilton to John Drayton, October 19, 1800, S.C. General Assembly papers, SCDAH.

131. Governors' messages to the South Carolina General Assembly, no. 768, enclosed letter of Paul Hamilton to John Drayton, October 19, 1800, S.C. General Assembly papers, SCDAH.

132. Petition to the S.C. General Assembly, no. 119, 1798, S.C. General Assembly papers, SCDAH.

133. Grand jury presentment, Colleton District, April 4, 1845, S.C. General Assembly papers, Index number 0010 015 1845 00005 00, SCDAH.

134. Report of the Committee on the Lieutenant Governor's Message No. 5, December 12, 1800, S.C. General Assembly papers, Index number 0010 004 1800 00060 00, SCDAH.

135. The collection of fines in urban areas provides a useful contrast; fines for not patrolling were collected routinely in towns, perhaps because there were fewer opportunities to avoid contact with city officials. The presence of volunteer militia companies, particularly in South Carolina, compounded the difficulties of routine patrolling. Some volunteer companies came into being as a response to lax patrolling; others existed simply to help men escape from regular beat companies where they would be liable to patrol duty. Although all volunteer companies theoretically did patrol service, it is virtually impossible to ascertain whether the volunteer companies were more or less active in carrying out their patrol duties. No records have been discovered that link actual patrol service to the volunteer companies. What is certain is that their existence complicated the regular militia's system of meting out and collecting fines, as well as appointing men to serve on patrol in the first place.

136. Col. Isaac W. Walter to Robert Young Hayne, June 25, 1828, Robert Hayne papers, SCL.

137. On wealthy men serving as patrollers in the colonial period, see Chapter 1.

138. Petition to the S.C. General Assembly, no. 119, 1798, S.C. General Assembly papers, SCDAH.

139. Order to appear for Regimental and brigade drill parade, September 9, 1861, Louis Manigault scrapbooks, SCL.

140. John Washington wanted to do away with foot soldiers in favor of cavalry, which could more easily intimidate or squash slave rebellions. Washington

to Calvin Jones, July 29, 1811, Letters, Orders, and Returns, 1807–1812, Adjutant General's Department, NCDAH. See also Calvin Jones to Governor Montford Stokes, December 28, 1830, Governor's Papers, vol. 61, NCDAH, proposing a citizen's cavalry as a strengthened form of patrol.

141. Rawlins Lowndes to "Dr Sir" [General Lincoln], January 30, 1779, Rawlins Lowndes papers, SCL.

142. Grand jury presentment, Beaufort District, November 19, 1835, S.C. General Assembly papers, Index number 0010 015 1835 00001 00, or 0010 015 1835 00002 00, SCDAH.

143. Governors' messages to the South Carolina General Assembly, no. 1296, Governor Thomas Bennett, November 27, 1821, S.C. General Assembly papers, SCDAH. Even other committees within the S.C. legislature urged that the militia and mustering be eliminated to improve the state's agriculture. See, for example, Report of the Committee of Agriculture, undated, S.C. General Assembly papers, Index number 0010 004 ND00 01146 00, SCDAH. The committee calculated that in ten years, a man would lose seventy days at various battalion, regimental, and company musters. After all those days spent mustering, the committee concluded: "[W]here we ask is the equivalent good to them, or the country? We think it is not to be found."

144. Report of the Committee of the Military, undated [c. 1850s], S.C. General Assembly papers, Index number 0010 004 ND00 01139 00, SCDAH.

145. The governor included a presentment from Sumter District to support his proposal. The Sumter District grand jury complained that "the present military system" was "odious and oppressive in its opperations and a *nuisance*." April 10, 1855, S.C. General Assembly papers, Index number 0010 015 1855 00031 00, SCDAH. The presentment was unclear about whether the district objected to having a militia, or just to its particular structure. The presentment was signed by John Belton O'Neall, the famous South Carolina jurist profiled by A. E. Keir Nash in "Negro Rights, Unionism, and Greatness on the South Carolina Court of Appeals: The Extraordinary Chief Justice John Belton O'Neall," *SCLR* 21 (1969): 141–190.

146. Response of the Committee of the Military, 1855, S.C. General Assembly papers, Index number 0010 004 1855 00087 00, SCDAH.

147. November and December 1860, Branchville Vigilant Society journal, SCL. See also article 3 in the patrol manuscript, Franklin William Fairey papers, SCL, for the establishment of an effective patrol in St. Matthew's Parish, discussed below, relating to "conductors, engineers, or any other person connected with" the railroads who traded in illegal goods.

148. For another example of this type of group, see Germanton volunteer patrols, March 1814, Miscellaneous Records-Patrollers, Stokes County, NCDAH.

149. For example, a slave caught with eggs, fruit, poultry, potatoes, or tur-
nips was worth three dollars to the detecting white man. A slave caught
with corn, peas, rice, cotton or livestock without the appropriate pass was
worth five dollars to the capturing white person. Patrol manuscript,
Franklin William Fairey papers, SCL.

150. Article 5, ibid.

151. Petition of the Edisto Island Auxiliary Association, November 18, 1823,
S.C. General Assembly papers, Index number 0010 003 1823 00151 00,
SCDAH.

152. Other extralegal groups are well described in Stephanie McCurry, *Masters
of Small Worlds: Yeoman Households, Gender Relations, and the Political Culture of the Antebellum South Carolina Low Country* (New York: Oxford University Press, 1995), 117–118, and Alan January, "The South Carolina Association: An Agency for Race Control in Antebellum Charleston," *SCHM*
78 (1977): 191–201.

153. These counties were uniformly in the westernmost edge of the three states,
where slaveholding was not pervasive and the population was much lower.

154. Brewer, "Legislation Designed to Control Slavery in Wilmington and Fayetteville," 162.

155. On Southern honor and manhood, see Bertram Wyatt-Brown, *Southern
Honor: Ethics and Behavior in the Old South* (Oxford: Oxford University
Press, 1982), and Kenneth S. Greenberg, *Honor and Slavery: Lies, Duels,
Noses, Masks, Dressing as a Woman, Gifts, Strangers, Humanitarianism,
Death, Slave Rebellions, the Proslavery Argument, Baseball, Hunting, and
Gambling in the Old South* (Princeton: Princeton University Press, 1996).

3. Patrol Personnel

1. Epigraph: George P. Rawick, ed., *The American Slave: A Composite Autobiography,* 19 vols. (Westport, Conn.: Greenwood, 1973–1976), vol. 14(1),
141. Although Bost acknowledged that both the patrol and the Ku Klux
Klan used violence against blacks, he made a clear temporal distinction between the two groups. Compare ibid., vol. 14(1), 141, 144.

2. Stowe, *Uncle Tom's Cabin, or, Life among the Lowly* (1852; reprint, New
York: Library of America, 1982), 86–88, 231.

3. See, for example, Ulrich B. Phillips, *American Negro Slavery: A Survey of the
Supply, Employment, and Control of Negro Labor as Determined by the Plan-
tation Regime* (1918; reprint, with a foreword by Eugene D. Genovese, Ba-
ton Rouge: Louisiana State University Press, 1966), 476, 485; Kenneth
Stampp, *The Peculiar Institution: Slavery in the Ante-bellum South* (New
York: Knopf, 1956), 214–215; Eugene D. Genovese, *Roll, Jordan, Roll: The
World the Slaves Made* (New York: Vintage Books, 1976), 618–619; Peter

Kolchin, *American Slavery, 1619–1877* (New York: Hill & Wang, 1993), 122.

4. "An additional act to an act concerning servants and slaves," in Clark, ed., *SRNC,* vol. 23, 388–390 (1753).

5. Owners and nonowners alike might evade patrol duty by using the substitute system. By the nineteenth century, each state had provisions that allowed men to send hired substitutes on patrol.

6. "An Act for the better establishing and regulating patrols," in Cooper and McCord, eds., *SC Statutes,* vol. 3, 569, sec. II (1740).

7. Men above the age of forty-five could only be chosen if they owned slaves. "An Act to provide for the more effectual performance of patrol duty," ibid., vol. 8, 538, sec. II (1819).

8. Individual cities that received the right to select their own patrols sometimes used different standards.

9. South Carolina: "An Act to Settle a Patroll," in ibid., vol. 2, 254, sec. I (1704); Virginia: "An Act for making more effectual provision against Invasions and Insurrections," in Hening, ed., *VA Statutes,* vol. 4, 197–204, sec. XVIII (February 1726/7).

10. In South Carolina, the patrol remained separate from the militia until 1721. The laws governing who must serve in either the patrol or the militia, however, were the same. See Chapter 1.

11. South Carolina: "An Act for the Better Settling and Regulating the Militia, and Appointing Look Outs," in Cooper and McCord, eds., *SC Statutes,* vol. 9, 617 (1703); Virginia: "An Act for the settling and better Regulation of the Militia," in Hening, ed., *VA Statutes,* vol. 4, 118–126, sec. II (1723).

12. U.S. Constitution, art. I, sec. 8.

13. "An Act more effectually to provide for the National Defense by establishing an uniform Militia throughout the United States," May 8, 1792, chap. 33, sec. 1, in Richard Peters, ed., *The Public Statutes at Large of the United States of America from the Organization of the Government in 1789, to March 3, 1845,* 17 vols. (1848; reprint, Buffalo: Dennis & Co., 1961), vol. 1, 271–274.

14. See, e.g., "An Act for the better Regulation of the Militia," in Hening, ed., *VA Statutes,* vol. 5, 16, chap. II, sec. 3 (1738); "An Act for the Better Settling and Regulating the Militia, and Appointing Look Out," in Cooper and McCord, eds., *SC Statutes,* vol. 9, 620, sec. X (1703). Other exempted professions also existed. The precise wording of exemptions changed with time. See Cooper and McCord, eds., *SC Statutes,* vol. 9, 634, sec. IX (1721); ibid., vol. 9, 649, sec. XV (1747); ibid., vol. 9, 673–674, sec. XIV (1778).

15. See Sally E. Hadden, "Law Enforcement in a New Nation: Slave Patrols and

Public Authority in the Old South, 1700–1865" (Ph.D. diss., Harvard University, 1993), 141.

16. In North Carolina, this proposition was tested in court; the minister lost. *Elizabeth City v. Kenedy* 44 N.C. (Busbee) 89 (1852). Not every religious group that sought exemption from militia duty avoided patrol work; Moravians in North Carolina routinely refused to fight foreigners but willingly served on slave patrols. Jon Sensbach, *A Separate Canaan: The Making of an Afro-Moravian World in North Carolina, 1763–1840* (Chapel Hill: University of North Carolina Press, 1998), 207–208. Ministers and religious groups who sought exemption from patrol work regularly relied on substitutes. Virginia originally developed its militia and patrol substitution system for Quakers, who objected to serving in either group on religious grounds. See "An act to amend the act for regulating and disciplining the militia, and for other purposes," in Hening, ed., *VA Statutes,* vol. 10, 417 (1781).

17. Report of Military committee, rejecting the petition of the Medical board of South Carolina, December 13, 1820, S.C. General Assembly papers, Index number 0010 004 1820 00115 00, SCDAH.

18. July 9, 1853, and August 3, 1853, Samuel Wells Leland diary, SCL. Given that in 1853, doctors were exempt from patrol service in South Carolina, Leland's presence on the patrol is puzzling. He may have waived the right to his exemption, or he may not have practiced medicine full time.

19. March 30, 1854, Samuel Wells Leland diary, SCL.

20. "An Act to organize the militia throughout the State of South Carolina, in conformity with the act of Congress," in Cooper and McCord, eds., *SC Statutes,* vol. 8, sec. XXIII, 492 (1794). Virginia never developed a comparable exemption.

21. Governors' messages to the South Carolina General Assembly, no. 866, James B. Richardson, November 24, 1803, S.C. General Assembly papers, SCDAH.

22. Records of the Commissioners of the Town of Oxford, Petitions, undated (c. 1840), Granville County, NCDAH. The tendency to appoint youthful patrollers could create religious tensions; in Salem, North Carolina, the patrol appointment of young men to discipline slaves seemed to threaten their "Brotherly character" as Moravians, which church leaders deplored. Sensbach, *A Separate Canaan,* 208.

23. Petition of citizens and inhabitants of Newbury District, 1814, S.C. General Assembly papers, Index number 0010 003 1814 00039 00, SCDAH.

24. A man joined a volunteer militia group by notifying his former militia company that he was enrolled in a volunteer group. Membership in volunteer militia units carried prestige within the community, and volunteer militia units became popular in the early nineteenth century.

25. Memorial of the Inhabitants of Charleston Neck, undated, S.C. General Assembly papers, Index number 0010 003 ND00 00255 00, SCDAH. The disdain for patrolling among volunteer militia may have been class related, since those units attracted the wealthiest men who could afford the fees to join. One or two volunteer militia groups formed specifically to crack down on slave behavior, however, and they increased patrol duties for their troops. See Chapter 2.

26. "An Act to reduce all Acts and Clauses of Acts, in Relation to the Patrol of this State, into one Act, and to alter and amend the same," in *Acts and Resolutions of the General Assembly of the State of South Carolina, Passed in December, 1839* (Columbia: A. H. Pemberton, 1839), sec. 18, 92.

27. North Carolina: see, for example, "An Act to incorporate the town of Weldon, in the County of Halifax, and for the regulation thereof," chap. XXVIII, sec. 8, 150 (1842); Virginia: "An Act Concerning Patrols," chap. XXI, 1832, in *Acts Passed at a General Assembly of the Commonwealth of Virginia, Begun and Held at the Capitol, in the City of Richmond, on Monday, the fifth day of December, in the year of our Lord, one thousand eight hundred and thirty-one, and of the commonwealth the fifty-sixth* (Richmond: Ritchie, 1832). Well before the 1830s, cities in all three states had appointed patrols, but these new laws legitimately gave this authority to all cities.

28. Edgecombe County required only owners and overseers to serve as patrollers after 1819, but this was an exceptional practice until the 1850s, when a few North Carolina Piedmont counties also limited patrolling to slaveholders. Charles C. Bolton, *Poor Whites of the Antebellum South: Tenants and Laborers in Central North Carolina and Northern Mississippi* (Durham: Duke University Press, 1994), 45.

29. See, for example, petitions from fire companies asking for exemptions, December 5, 1810, and November 29, 1819, S.C. General Assembly papers, Index numbers 0010 003 1810 00167 00, 0010 004 1810 00170 00, 0010 003 1810 00168 00, and 0010 004 1819 00160 00, SCDAH, in which the Committee on Incorporations agreed to incorporate the Charleston Vigilant Fire Company and exempt them from ordinary patrol and militia duties during times of fire. See also the Petition of Hamburg Fire Engine Company, December 9, 1850, S.C. General Assembly papers, Index number 0010 003 1850 00055 00, SCDAH; Town of Lexington, December 17, 1827, Rockbridge County legislative petitions, LV.

30. Petition from Officers and members of the Vigilant Fire Company of Charleston to be incorporated and exempted from militia duty, undated, S.C. General Assembly papers, Index number 0010 003 ND00 02114 00, SCDAH.

31. Petition from People of Camden, 1829, S.C. General Assembly papers, Index number 0010 003 1829 00021 00, SCDAH. See also Julian A. Selby,

Memorabilia and Anecdotal Reminiscences of Columbia, S.C. (Columbia: R. L. Bryan, 1905), 128, on exemptions for firemen.

32. Memorial of the Intendent and members of the Town Council of Hamburg, 1859, S.C. General Assembly papers, Index number 0010 003 1859 00100 00, SCDAH.

33. Petition of the Intendent and wardens of Moultrieville, 1819, S.C. General Assembly papers, Index number 0010 003 1819 00029 00, SCDAH.

34. Report of the Committee of Incorporations, December 3, 1819, S.C. General Assembly papers, Index number 0010 004 1819 00057 00, SCDAH.

35. Copy of an 1828 patrol summons, David Doar, *A Sketch of the Agricultural Society of St. James, Santee, South Carolina, and an Address on the Traditions and Reminiscences of the Parish* (Charleston: Calder-Fladger, 1908), 23.

36. Patroller's oath in Henry Potter, ed., *The Office and Duty of a Justice of the Peace, and A Guide to Sheriffs, Coroners, Clerks, Constables, and other civil officers. According to the laws of North-carolina, with an appendix . . .* , 2d ed. (Raleigh: J. Gales and Son, 1828), 246.

37. Miscellaneous Records P-W, List of Patrols and Patrol Regulations, 1814–1845, Warren County, NCDAH; Rules for the Government of the Patrols, 1846, Miscellaneous Slave Records, Chowan County, NCDAH.

38. The justice might charge a fee for this warrant. In Richland County, records show that antebellum patrollers paid 43 cents each to receive warrants from the local magistrate. Patroller's warrant fee, undated entry, Richland County Magistrates' Docket, 1847–1850, SCDAH.

39. If charged with assault and battery on a slave, the defendant had to produce an appointment slip to avoid conviction on the grounds that he was a patroller. *State v. Atkinson,* 51 N.C. (6 Jones) 65 (1858).

40. James L. Petigru to M. M. Johnson, May 5, 1854, Petigru & King letterbooks, SCL.

41. See *State v. William Galloway and James Galloway,* indicted but not convicted, 1857, Sessions Journal, Barnwell District, South Carolina, 1857–1871, 12, 44, transcribed by Kate Woodward, WPA project, 1936, SCL. H. M. Henry alleged that courts rarely convicted men tried for resisting patrols. *The Police Control of the Slave in South Carolina* (Emory, Va.: n.p., 1914), 41.

42. Patrollers enjoyed great discretion in administering punishments, particularly since there were rarely witnesses who could testify against them in court. Aside from the absolute number of stripes a patroller could inflict, one of the few limits imposed on patrols by the North Carolina Supreme Court was that a slave could not be punished merely to gratify malice against the slave's master. *Tate v. O'Neal,* 8 N.C. (1 Hawks) 419 (1821).

43. "An act to prevent the owners of slaves from hiring to them their own time, to make compensation to Patrolls, and to restrain the abuses com-

mitted by free negroes and mulattoes," North Carolina state session laws, chap. 4, secs. IV–V (1794).

44. *Richardson v. Saltar,* 4 N.C. (Taylor) 505 (1817).

45. Clause 4, *Patrol Regulations for the County of Rowan* (Salisbury, N.C.: Philo White, 1825), NCC. South Carolina citizens also knew the number of men required to constitute a lawful patrol. See C. W. Jones to Louis Manigault, December 17, 1855, in James M. Clifton, ed., *Life and Labor on Argyle Island: Letters and Documents of a Savannah River Rice Plantation, 1833–1867* (Savannah: Beehive Press, 1978), 202.

46. William K. Scarborough, *The Overseer: Plantation Management in the Old South* (1966; reprint, Athens, Ga.: University of Georgia Press, 1984), 91.

47. Jacob Stroyer, *My Life in the South* (1879; reprint, enl. ed., Salem, Mass.: Newcomb & Gauss, 1898), 62.

48. Stampp, *Peculiar Institution,* 153.

49. Stampp notes that one professional slave catcher made $600 per year capturing runaway slaves, ibid., 189.

50. For records of slaves being captured by private citizens in the early eighteenth century, see William L. Hopkins, *Middlesex County, Virginia: Wills and Inventories 1673–1812 and other Court Papers* (Richmond: n.p., 1989), 232, 234, 244, 249, 254, 268, 273–274, 277.

51. Example: "Giles Harnes of the county aforesaid [Chesterfield] hath this day made oath before me that Foster a negro man Slave whom he hath now brought before [me] is a runaway as he believes and that he has Just cuse [cause] to believe he is the property or in the employ of Henry Heth of the county aforesaid that he was taken up on the Turnpike road near Morains shop in the county aforesaid this day and the distance in my opinion betwen where he was taken up & the residence of the aforesaid Heth is six & a half miles" and so Harnes received "For taking up five dollars[,] 10 cents per mile for taking Home which is $5.65." Haley Cole, certificate for apprehending runaway slave, June 7, 1821, Heth Family papers (MSS 10986), UVA. See also Richard Thornton, Justice of the Peace, affidavit of December 21, 1848, Halifax County, Virginia Justices of the Peace, VHS.

52. Letter no. 745, John Boswell to Richd. Morris, May 27, 1773, Morris Papers (indexed as part of the Eighteenth Century collection, MSS 38-79), UVA. See also letter no. 1249, J. Will, August 1, 1799, UVA. For other examples of certificates for runaways, see Deposition of Justice of the Peace Hudgins, May 28, 1803, in Richard Foster papers (MSS 3523), UVA.

53. See payments of "apprehending fee" in City Sergeant Register 1841–1846, Richmond, VHS.

54. For printed advertisements published in local newspapers, see Lathan A. Windley, comp., *Runaway Slave Advertisements,* 4 vols. (Westport, Conn.:

Greenwood, 1983). An owner might send private letters to circulate in a particular region if he thought he knew where a runaway was going. See George N. Thrift to unknown correspondent, December 15, 1846, Thrift Family papers (MSS 9153), UVA.

55. This did not apply to patrollers in South Carolina rural areas, who were not paid.

56. Phillips, *American Negro Slavery,* 274.

57. For a general list of the methods overseers used to control slaves, see Stampp, *Peculiar Institution,* 149–150.

58. Overseers were often paid for capturing runaway slaves, while the loss of a slave and the cost of its retrieval might well be deducted from an overseer's salary. For a slave captured while staying at another plantation, see John Hartwell Cocke, Sr., to Joseph C. Cabell, October 29, 1831, Cabell Family papers (MSS 38-111), UVA. Some overseers, like Thomas Finklea, organized patrols to recapture runaways. Mark S. Schantz, " 'A Very Serious Business': Managerial Relationships on the Ball Plantations, 1800–1835," *SCHM* 88 (1987): 15–16.

59. Scarborough, *The Overseer,* 67.

60. April 1771 and April 1775, tax accounts of John Lyon and William Campbell, sheriffs, New Hanover County court minutes, 1771–1779, NCDAH. Alan Watson, "The Constable in Colonial North Carolina," *NCHR* 68 (1991): 1–16.

61. Michael W. Hancock to Benjamin Oliver, July 29, 1813, Thomas Chrystie papers, VHS.

62. October 11, 1782, 312–315, and January 24, 1787, 140, Richmond City Common Hall Records, No. 1, LV.

63. George Teamoh, *God Made Man, Man Made the Slave: The Autobiography of George Teamoh,* ed. Nash Boney, Rafia Zafar, and Richard Hume (Macon, Ga.: Mercer University Press, 1990), 175–176n20.

64. Ibid., 74.

65. Other scholars have tangentially noted the unique role Southern police assumed in restricting slave movement, but the strongest description linking police to racial control is Dennis Rousey, *Policing the Southern City: New Orleans, 1805–1889* (Baton Rouge: Louisiana State University Press, 1996), who explores this phenomenon in New Orleans. See also Eric Monkkonen, *Police in Urban America, 1860–1920* (Cambridge: Cambridge University Press, 1981), 163. Compare Edward L. Ayers, *Vengeance and Justice: Crime and Punishment in the Nineteenth-Century American South* (New York: Oxford University Press, 1984), 83.

66. Louis Cei, "Law Enforcement in Richmond: A History of Police-Community Relations, 1737–1974" (Ph.D. diss., Florida State University, 1975), 43.

67. J. W. Tompkins address to "Brother officers," undated (c. 1859), Tompkins Family papers, SCL.

68. Rawick, ed., *American Slave,* vol. 8(1), 104. One Texas slave interviewed went so far as to say that patrols were like policemen of the twentieth century. Ibid., vol. 4(2), 183.

69. Town of Danville, Minutes 1854–68, July 4, 1854, LV; see also the reassignment of city guards as police officers to catch slaves suspected in the Vesey conspiracy, *Negro Plot: An Account of the late intended insurrection among a portion of the blacks of the City of Charleston, South Carolina* (Boston: J. W. Ingraham, 1822), 12.

70. "An Act for the Better Establishing and Regulating Patrols," in Cooper and McCord, eds., *SC Statutes,* vol. 3, 569, sec. I (1740).

71. Gladys-Marie Fry, *Night Riders in Black Folk History* (1975; reprint, Athens, Ga.: University of Georgia, Brown Thrasher Books, 1991), 44.

72. Robert M. Weir, " 'The Harmony We Were Famous for': An Interpretation of Pre-Revolutionary South Carolina Politics," *WMQ,* 3d ser., 26 (1969): 483.

73. John Blassingame, ed., *Slave Testimony: Two Centuries of Letters, Speeches, Interviews, and Autobiographies* (Baton Rouge: Louisiana State University Press, 1977), 267.

74. "An Act for the Better Establishing and Regulating Patrols," in Cooper and McCord, eds., *SC Statutes,* vol. 3, 573, sec. X (1740).

75. August 27, October 9, 11, 1860, Lemuel Reid diary, SCL; November 29, 30, 1851, Richard Eppes diary, 1851–1852, VHS.

76. C. L. Burn to "My dear Brother," November 11, 1860, Burn Family papers, SCL.

77. The claim may have failed because the patrolling (and eating) took place near Jeter's own tavern. Amelia County legislative petitions, November 30, 1810, LV, described in H. J. Eckenrode, ed., *Fifth Annual Report of the Library Board of the Virginia State Library, 1907–1908* under the title of *A Calendar of Legislative Petitions Arranged by Counties: Accomac-Bedford* (Richmond: Superintendent of Public Printing, 1908), 101.

78. Elliott J. Gorn, " 'Gouge and Bite, Pull Hair and Scratch': The Social Significance of Fighting in the Southern Backcountry," *AHR* 90 (1985): 27. That torturing others could provide a socializing bond is a recurrent theme in literature on the Ku Klux Klan and on fraternity hazing.

79. Being the captain of a patrol group was an honorific title, not on a par with being elected captain of a militia unit. The captaincy expired at the end of the patrol group's term of service.

80. Diary format patrol slips in Jones-Watt-Davis Family papers, SCL. For analysis of patrol activity based on these diaries, see Chapter 4 and Hadden, "Colonial and Revolutionary Era Slave Patrols of Virginia," in *Lethal*

Imagination: Violence and Brutality in American History, ed. Michael Bellesiles (New York: New York University Press, 1999).

81. This conclusion has been suggested elsewhere. "The larger number of slaves owned by a captain would make it appear that men of such means were appointed in districts with the larger slave concentrations." E. Russ Williams, "Slave Patrol Ordinances of St. Tammany Parish, Louisiana, 1835–1838," *Louisiana History* 13 (1972): 403.

82. John Tayloe to Landon Carter, Mount Airy, "Easter Sunday," March 21, 1771, Wellford Papers, UVA, cited in Gerald W. Mullin, *Flight and Rebellion: Slave Resistance in Eighteenth-Century Virginia* (London: Oxford University Press, 1972), 56.

83. See, for example, grand jury presentment, April 17, 1769, Charleston Court of General Sessions Journal, SCDAH.

84. Aiken Town Council Patrol Book, 1839–1859, SCDAH.

85. Records for the 2nd Beat, 2nd Battalion, 4th Regiment of South Carolina Militia, 1851–1863, Norris and Thomson Families papers, SCL.

86. See the earlier discussion of *Richardson v. Saltar* at note 44.

87. *State v. Hailey,* 28 N.C. (6 Iredell) 11 (1845).

88. The laws creating patrollers clearly envisioned this possibility: patrollers had authority to enter any building where slaves congregated (which could include white homes) or where they illegally sold goods (which could include white-run grog shops).

89. J. H. Easterby, ed., *The South Carolina Rice Plantation as Revealed in the Papers of Robert F. W. Allston* (Chicago: University of Chicago Press, 1945), 165.

90. Belton O. Townsend ["A South Carolinian," pseud.], "South Carolina Morals," *Atlantic Monthly* 39 (1877): 472.

91. John Hammond Moore, *Columbia and Richland County: A South Carolina Community, 1740–1990* (Columbia: University of South Carolina Press, 1993), 129. Although historians have hinted at this use of patrols to achieve social dominance, or their instrumental efforts in class warfare, Townsend's statement remains the clearest evidence I have found that supports this theory.

92. Genovese, *Roll, Jordan, Roll,* 22–23, 417–418. This is an interpretation shared by scholars in other fields, not just historians, including Fry, *Night Riders,* 98, and W. Marvin Dulaney, *Black Police in America* (Bloomington: Indiana University Press, 1996), 2. Morgan suggests that lower-class whites were sometimes reluctant to patrol, *Slave Counterpoint: Black Culture in the Eighteenth-Century Chesapeake and Lowcountry* (Chapel Hill: University of North Carolina Press, 1998), 307–308.

93. Genovese, *Roll, Jordan, Roll,* 22.

94. Collectively reprinted in Rawick, ed., *American Slave;* George P. Rawick,

ed., *The American Slave: A Composite Autobiography: Supplement Series 1,* 12 vols. (Westport, Conn.: Greenwood, 1977); and George P. Rawick, ed., *The American Slave: A Composite Autobiography: Supplement Series 2,* 10 vols. (Westport, Conn.: Greenwood, 1979). For examples of slave contempt, see Rawick, ed., *American Slave Series 1,* vol. 2(1), 68, 251–252. I have supplemented the WPA accounts with fugitive slave narratives published in the nineteenth century. On the utility of the WPA narratives as fact and fiction, see Peter Kolchin, "The Process of Confrontation: Patterns of Resistance to Bondage in Nineteenth-Century Russia and the United States," *Journal of Social History* 11 (1977–78): 467.

95. Originals of the Amelia County tithable lists are housed at the Library of Virginia, Richmond (LV), and have been microfilmed, reels R-55 and R-56. The Norfolk County tithables are in such a poorly preserved state that the originals have been sealed by the Norfolk County court to prevent damage by the general public. The noted Virginia genealogist Elizabeth Wingo received authorization to publish transcriptions of the tithables. Her work is available in three indexed volumes: Elizabeth B. Wingo and W. Bruce Wingo, comps., *Norfolk County, Virginia, Tithables, 1730–1750* (Norfolk: n.p., 1979); *Norfolk County, Virginia, Tithables, 1751–1765* (Norfolk: n.p., 1981); and *Norfolk County, Virginia, Tithables, 1766–1780* (Norfolk: n.p., 1985).

96. Parish levies began in 1629, and county levies probably were not assessed until the 1650s. Tithes were usually from 10 to 20 pounds of tobacco per year, although special expenses (like building a new church) could drive the rate much higher. Precisely when the tax year ended varied by county. For an excellent introduction to the tax system in Virginia generally, see Peter V. Bergstrom, "Nothing So Certain: Taxes in Colonial Virginia" (Williamsburg: Colonial Williamsburg Foundation, Dept. of Historical Research, 1984), microfiche. See also Peter V. Bergstrom, "A Glossary for Virginia's Colonial Economy" (Williamsburg: Colonial Williamsburg Foundation, Dept. of Historical Research, 1983), microfiche.

97. To figure out the amount of taxes that a given household owed, the county and parish would total their expenses, then add up all the persons who counted as tithables, and divide the number of tithes into the expenses to figure out how much each person owed for a given year.

98. Charles Irby, for example, was responsible for making out tithe lists every year from 1743 to 1756. The men chosen to list the tithes were often the wealthiest in the county, holding positions of authority such as constable, sheriff, and justice of the peace. Comparison of large landowners and tithe takers based on Kathleen Hadfield, ed., *Historical Notes on Amelia County* (Amelia, Va.: Amelia County Historical Committee, 1982), 58–59. Continuity in the tithe takers meant that they were less likely to omit someone

from their lists, and they were more likely to be consistent in making notations about men serving as patrollers. Amelia and Norfolk counties have
also been the subject of excellent local histories: Hadfield, ed., *Amelia
County,* and Thomas J. Wertenbaker, *Norfolk: Historic Southern Port,* 2d ed.
(Durham: Duke University Press, 1962).

99. Patrollers mentioned in Eastern Shore, Tidewater, Northern Neck, and
Southside County court minute books from the 1750s to 1800. They are
easist to locate in the county's annual tax accounting. Some tithe takers
failed to make notations about *any* holder of local office. This would indicate that the tithe exemptions for all officeholders (patrollers included)
were kept in separate records, or their tithes were reduced by the court and
not by the individual tithe taker.

100. Norfolk had inhabitants as early as the 1630s. See Morgan P. Robinson,
"Virginia Counties: Those Resulting from Virginia Legislation," *Bulletin
of the Virginia State Library* (Richmond: Superintendant of Public Printing, 1916), vol. 9, 124. Norfolk's population boomed from 1750 to 1775,
and the town became the largest eighteenth-century population center
on Chesapeake Bay. Brent Tarter, ed., *The Order Book and Related Papers
of the Common Hall of the Borough of Norfolk, Virginia, 1736–1798* (Richmond: Virginia State Library, 1979), 3–12; Peter J. Albert, "The Protean
Institution: The Geography, Economy, and Ideology of Slavery in Post-
Revolutionary Virginia" (Ph.D. diss., University of Maryland, 1976), 48–
49.

101. David Cecelski, "The Shores of Freedom: The Maritime Underground Rail-
road in North Carolina, 1800–1861," *NCHR* 71 (1994): 180–184; Tommy
Bogger, "Maroons and Laborers in the Great Dismal Swamp," in Jane H.
Kobelski, ed., *Readings in Black and White: Lower Tidewater Virginia*
(Portsmouth, Va.: Portsmouth Public Library, 1982), 1–8.

102. Paula J. Martinac, " 'An Unsettled Disposition': Social Structure and Geo-
graphic Mobility in Amelia County, Virginia, 1768–1794" (master's thesis,
College of William and Mary, 1979), 18. On the white settlement of Southside counties, see Richard L. Morton, *Colonial Virginia,* vol. II, *Westward
Expansion and Prelude to Revolution 1710–1763* (Chapel Hill: University of
North Carolina Press, 1960), 552–564. On the definition of "Southside,"
see Michael L. Nicholls, "Origins of the Virginia Southside, 1703–1753: A
Social and Economic Study" (Ph.D. diss., College of William and Mary,
1972).

103. Albert, "The Protean Institution," 57–58.

104. Philip D. Morgan and Michael L. Nicholls, "Slaves in Piedmont Virginia,
1720–1790," *WMQ,* 3d ser., 40 (1989): 218, table II; U.S. Bureau of the
Census, *Historical Statistics of the United States: Colonial Times to 1970,* 2
vols. (Washington: Bureau of the Census, 1975), vol. 2, series Z 1–19,

1168. If anything, the number of slaves is probably underestimated, since tithable records only noted slaves above age sixteen.

105. Albert, "The Protean Institution," 107–108.

106. Evarts B. Greene and Virginia D. Harrington, *American Population before the Federal Census of 1790* (1932; reprint, Gloucester, Mass.: P. Smith, 1966), 152–153; Richard Dunn, "Black Society in the Chesapeake, 1776–1810," in Ira Berlin and Ronald Hoffman, eds., *Slavery and Freedom in the Age of the American Revolution* (Chicago: University of Illinois Press, 1986), 61, 69.

107. The Amelia County data is missing tithe lists from 1772 to 1777, hence the total number of patrollers appointed in those years is lower than average.

108. Prince Edward County was formed in 1754 with land taken from Amelia County.

109. The 43 men served a total of 137 year-long appointments in patrol duty, out of 185 year-long appointments made. Goochland County in the 1760s–1780s also reappointed men repeatedly. J. Michael Crane, "Twenty Lashes 'Well Laid On': Slave Patrols in Colonial Virginia" (seminar paper, Purdue University, 1998), 26. I am indebted to Michael Crane for sharing his research with me.

110. Sikes served in 1750, 1751, 1753, 1754, 1757, 1759, 1761, and 1766.

111. Rawick, ed., *American Slave,* vol. 2(2), 101.

112. Ibid., vol. 15(2), 330. Wording of quote rendered in standard English.

113. Ibid., vol. 2(2), 101, 240.

114. Charles L. Perdue, Thomas E. Barden, and Robert K. Phillips, eds., *Weevils in the Wheat: Interviews with Virginia Ex-Slaves* (Charlottesville: University Press of Virginia, 1976), 52–53.

115. Exceptions: James and John Chappell, James and William Crenshaw, Anthony and Charles Hundley, Peter and Abraham Jones.

116. Crane has discovered a similar familial appointment pattern for Sussex County for 1763–1775. His study comparing Sussex County (not repetitive) and Goochland County (repetitive) in this period reveals appointment patterns that mirror Amelia and Norfolk counties. "Twenty Lashes 'Well Laid On,' " 20–21, 26.

117. In Norfolk County, John Boggus (1765, 1766, 1768), Thomas Holstead (1753), Jonathan Mercer (1766), and John Williams (1751, 1754, 1757, 1766, 1774) worked as patrollers with their sons. In Amelia County, John Chappell (1749), John Willson (1752), John Cook (1755), John Deaton (1766), and Moses Morris (1767) all had sons who served with them on patrols.

118. In Norfolk County, Josiah Ives, living in the home of his father, James Ives, was a patroller in 1770. In Amelia County, only John Booth and James

Crenshaw were patrollers while living with their fathers (Booth in 1752 and 1753, Crenshaw in 1766).

119. For example, patroller Charles Anderson had two land grants for 400 and 3,000 acres, and Thomas Ellis had a grant for 275 acres. The grants came only four or five years before Anderson and Ellis served as patrollers. A series of three associated maps re-create early settlement patterns by compiling all land patents made in Amelia County from original surveyors' records covering Amelia (1717–65), Nottoway (1728–60), and Prince Edward (1737–1823) counties. Robert Brumfield, "A Plat of the Land Patents in Amelia County, Virginia," 3 maps (Amelia, Va.: Amelia Historical Committee, 1987), LV.

120. Like other Southside counties, Amelia County experienced a large influx of enslaved African children in this period. Because they were omitted from tithable lists (being under the age of sixteen), the total number of slaves and slave-owning households in the community was higher than the numbers recorded here. However, this should not introduce a significant skew to the data recorded, because patrollers and nonpatrollers were equally likely to have African slave children in their households.

121. The rising percentage of slaveholders was linked to the decline in Amelia County's white population toward the end of the eighteenth century from a large outmigration of non–slave-holding whites, which shrank the total white population in the county. Martinac, "Social Structure and Geographic Mobility in Amelia County," 3, 39.

122. Hadfield, ed., *Amelia County,* 58–59.

123. For example, these are two typical years:

Type of household	Number (%)
1767	
No slaves	707 (53.0)
1 slave	224 (16.8)
2–5 slaves	278 (20.8)
6–9 slaves	84 (6.3)
10 or more slaves	41 (3.1)
1771	
No slaves	725 (51.0)
1 slave	261 (18.4)
2–5 slaves	303 (21.3)
6–9 slaves	94 (6.6)
10 or more slaves	38 (2.7)

Source: Data compiled from Wingo and Wingo, comps., *Norfolk County, Virginia, Tithables, 1766–1780.*

The relative wealth of patrollers in Norfolk County based upon landholdings also supports these conclusions. When acreage began to be noted by tithe takers in Norfolk in the 1765, most patrollers owned anywhere from 100 to 300 acres of land, with a few men listed as having no land. In Norfolk in 1776, the area was so thoroughly settled that 90 percent was owned by people in tracts of less than 500 acres. Almost 80 percent of the landowners had plots of less than 300 acres. Therefore, ownership of plots varying from 100 to 300 acres in size, with occasional larger and smaller ones, suggests that patrollers were among the "middling sort" of their communities, not at the bottom. Adele Hast, *Loyalism in Revolutionary Virginia: The Norfolk Area and the Eastern Shore* (Ann Arbor: UMI Research Press, 1982), 173.

124. However, it should be noted that the majority of Amelia County patrollers who owned slaves only owned one slave, thus putting them near the bottom of the *slaveholding* portion of Amelia's community.

125. Landowning data comparable to Norfolk County's suggests that Amelia patrollers were also among the majority group of landowners in their county. Most patrollers owned 100 to 300 acres of land at the time of their appointment. In 1782, the following landholding patterns prevailed in Amelia County:

Land owned	No. of persons owning (%)
Less than 100 acres	104 (10.1)
100–299 acres	523 (50.9)
300–499 acres	185 (18.0)
500–999 acres	156 (15.1)
1,000–2,999 acres	57 (5.5)
3,000–4,999 acres	2 (0.2)
5,000+ acres	2 (0.2)

Source: Table transcribed from Martinac, "Social Structure and Geographic Mobility in Amelia County," 24. Compare data on other Virginia counties in Morgan, *Slave Counterpoint*, 43–44.

126. Roughly two-thirds of white Amelia County residents were slave owners.

	Number of slaves (%)	
	1768	1788
No slaves	265 (30.4)	457 (36.2)
1–5 slaves	443 (51.0)	540 (42.7)
6–15 slaves	147 (17.0)	224 (17.7)
16 or more slaves	14 (1.6)	43 (3.4)

Source: Table transcribed from Martinac, "Social Structure and Geographic Mobility in Amelia County," 39.

127. These conclusions also apply to early South Carolina. In 1721, the South Carolina legislature complained that the patrols were generally composed of "the choicest and best men" because by serving in the patrols at that time, they were then exempt from serving in the militia. As a result, the South Carolina legislature merged the militia and patrol formally in 1721 to prevent the social separation between the militia and patrol. "An Act for the Better Settling and Regulating the Militia," in Cooper and McCord, eds., *SC Statutes*, vol. 9, 639 (1721).

128. Crane found a similar pattern in Sussex County for 1763–1775. "Twenty Lashes 'Well Laid On,' " 22.

129. Hadfield, ed., *Amelia County*, 484, 489.

130. Morgan and Nicholls, "Slaves in Piedmont Virginia," 218, table II. It can be seen from the table that the majority of Virginia's slave population shifted from the Tidewater to the Piedmont region in the period 1755 to 1782:

Area	1755	1782
Tidewater	66%	46%
Piedmont	33%	51%
Shenandoah	1%	3%

131. Even as late as the 1850s, patrols in Piedmont North Carolina were still not the domain of poor whites. See Bolton, *Poor Whites of the Antebellum South*, 45–46. For longtitudinal studies of slave patrols in two nineteenth-century communities, see Hadden, "Patrol Membership in a Southern City: Aiken, South Carolina" and "Danger at the Margins: Slave Patrollers in Perquimans County and the Dismal Swamp Effect" (unpublished papers).

132. Comparisons of Perquimans County, North Carolina, patrol data, county tax, and federal census materials show that in 1810, patrollers typically owned 2–10 slaves, while most county residents did not own any. The largest slave owners, however, did not get appointed to patrol work.

Number of slaves	Households with slaves (%)	Patrollers with slaves (%)
None	419 (52.0)	8 (27.6)
1	85 (10.6)	5 (17.2)
2–5	117 (14.5)	12 (41.4)
6–10	65 (8.1)	3 (10.3)
11–25	107 (13.3)	1 (3.4)
26+	12 (1.5)	0 (0.0)

By 1860 both patterns had altered, as the number of total slave owners declined, many masters owned much larger groups of slaves, and the men appointed as patrollers had risen in status.

Number of slaves	Households with slaves (%)	Patrollers with slaves (%)
None	740 (73.6)	10 (29.4)
1	47 (4.7)	1 (2.9)
2–5	81 (8.1)	1 (2.9)
6–25	102 (10.1)	9 (26.5)
26+	35 (3.5)	9 (26.5)

Note: Patrollers not identified in tax records: 4

Source: Perquimans County Tax Returns, 1810–1811 and 1860–1861, and Patrols 1810 and 1847–1865, Perquimans County–Miscellaneous Records 1710–1933, NCDAH; Perquimans County, Population of the United States in 1810, Third Census, United States Census Office (microfilm); Perquimans County, Population of the United States in 1860, Eighth Census, United States Census Office (microfilm).

Although far larger numbers of men were appointed as patrols from higher-status groups, many of these individuals employed overseers, which suggests that they very likely intended for their overseers to serve as patrollers in their place. However, the total number of patrollers who owned no slaves held relatively constant from 1810 to 1860, indicating a continuing disinclination to appoint men as patrollers who owned no slaves of their own. For a full analysis of this data, see Hadden, "Danger at the Margins."

133. C. W. Jones to Louis Manigault, December 17, 1855, and January 4, 1856, Charles Manigault to "Mon Cher Louis" [Louis Manigault], December 27, 1855, Louis Manigault papers, DU. This episode is further explored in William Dusinberre, *Them Dark Days: Slavery in the American Rice Swamps* (Oxford: Oxford University Press, 1996), 132–133 and n. 22.

134. Governors' messages to the South Carolina General Assembly, no. 921, Paul Hamilton, November 25, 1806, S.C. General Assembly papers, SCDAH.

135. Grand jury presentment, Georgetown District, November 9, 1829, S.C. General Assembly papers, Index number 0010 015 1829 00003 00, SCDAH.

136. Governors' messages to the South Carolina General Assembly, no. 768, enclosed letter of William Hayne to John Drayton, October 20, 1800, S.C. General Assembly papers, SCDAH.

137. See, for example, grand jury presentment, January 20, 1794, S.C. General Assembly papers, Index number 0010 015 1794 00006 00, SCDAH.

138. *Winyah Observer* (Georgetown, S.C.), September 6, 1845. This observation has been made by earlier historians. See Stampp, *Peculiar Institution*, 214.

139. Charles Manigault to "Mon Cher Louis" [Louis Manigault], January 4, 1856, Louis Manigault papers, DU.

140. "An Act for the regulation of the Militia of this state," in Cooper and McCord, eds., *SC Statutes,* vol. 9, 686, sec. XIII (1782); "An Act requiring the Major-Generals of the Militia of this state to cause one uniform system of evolutions to be adopted by the cavalry, within their respective divisions; for perfecting the several officers of the militia throughout this state, in their military duties; and for other purposes therein mentioned," ibid., vol. 8, 513, sec. V (1808). Fines did not increase after 1809. "An Act to amend and explain the militia laws of this state," ibid., vol. 8, 517, sec. IX (1809).

141. Fines were twenty shillings in the colonial and early national period, then they were converted to three dollars. See, for example, "An act for amending the several laws for regulating and disciplining the militia, and guarding against invasions and insurrections," in Hening, ed., *VA Statutes,* vol. XI, 489, sec. VIII (1784); "An Act for regulating the militia of this Commonwealth," ibid., vol. XIII, 351, sec. 32 (1792); "An Act, to amend and reduce into one, the several acts of the General Assembly, for regulating the Militia of this Commonwealth," in *Acts Passed at a General Assembly of the Commonwealth of Virginia: Begun and held at the Capitol, in the City of Richmond, on Monday, the Fifth Day of December, One Thousand Eight Hundred and Three* (Richmond: Meriwether Jones, 1804), chap. I, sec. 46, 14 (1804).

142. Patrol fine, 1860, Daniel W. Jordan papers, DU.

143. Multiple court fine entries for neglect of patrol duty showing fines received (ranging from two to twelve dollars), Aiken Municipal Court Docket, 1839–1849, SCDAH. For a full analysis of Aiken's patrol system, see Hadden, "Patrol Membership in a Southern City."

144. Grand jury presentment, November 18, 1817, S.C. General Assembly papers, Index number 0010 015 1817 00008 00, SCDAH.

145. See *Tate v. O'Neal* 8 N.C. (1 Hawks) 418 (1821).

146. Nat Whitaker was a patroller, according to one former Wake County slave. Rawick, ed., *American Slave,* vol. 15(2), 402.

147. Willis Whitaker owned 1,410 acres in Panther Branch and 27 slaves, Thomas Whitaker owned 1,200 acres and 7 slaves. Panther Branch District, Wake County Tax Returns, 1856, NCDAH.

148. Of the landowners taxed in Panther Branch District, Wake County, sixty owned more than 200 acres, and sixty owned less than 200 acres. Nineteen men appeared to own no land at all. The men appointed as patrollers were the following: Seth Jewel, no slaves, no land; Orrin Williams, no slaves, no land; Addison King, no slaves, 100 acres; Hugh Blalock, 3 slaves, 130

acres; Benjamin Walton, 1 slave, 200 acres; Calvin Baugh, 1 slave, 250 acres.

149. Grand jury presentment, Abbeville, S.C. General Assembly papers, Index number 0010 015 1853 00001 00, SCDAH.

150. Dulaney, *Black Police in America*, 8–10.

151. Bolton, *Poor Whites of the Antebellum South*, 45–46.

152. Wyatt-Brown has unearthed similar information about Southern mob brutality: community leaders intermittently supervised mob violence against social outcasts. Bertram Wyatt-Brown, *Southern Honor: Ethics and Behavior in the Old South* (Oxford: Oxford University Press, 1982), 435–493.

4. In Times of Tranquility

1. Epigraph: Edward Cantwell, *The Practice of Law in North Carolina*, vol. 1, *Legislative and Executive Powers* (Raleigh: Strother and Marcum, 1860), 377.

2. One clear exception to this trend among recent historians is Charles C. Bolton, *Poor Whites of the Antebellum South: Tenants and Laborers in Central North Carolina and Northern Mississippi* (Durham: Duke University Press, 1994).

3. George P. Rawick, ed., *The American Slave: A Composite Autobiography*, 19 vols. (Westport, Conn.: Greenwood, 1973–1976), vol. 15(2), 321.

4. Petition of Citizens of York District, November 18, 1830, S.C. General Assembly papers, Index number 0010 003 1830 00123 00, SCDAH.

5. Rawick, ed., *American Slave*, vol. 17(1), 14; George P. Rawick, ed., *The American Slave: A Composite Autobiography: Supplement Series 1*, 12 vols. (Westport, Conn.: Greenwood, 1977), vol. S1–7(2), 742–743. On slave folktales about tricks and flight, see Lawrence Levine, *Black Culture and Black Consciousness: Afro-American Folk Thought from Slavery to Freedom* (Oxford: Oxford University Press, 1977), esp. 121–133.

6. Joseph Brooks, box 1, folder 9 (Slave Life no. 111), WPA Folklore papers (MSS 1547), UVA.

7. Governors' messages to the South Carolina General Assembly, no. 650, A. Vanderhorst, enclosed affidavit of William Ellison, November 24, 1795, and Peter Ryan, November 24, 1795, S.C. General Assembly papers, SCDAH.

8. George P. Rawick, ed., *The American Slave: A Composite Autobiography: Supplement Series 2*, 10 vols. (Westport, Conn.: Greenwood, 1979), vol. S2–4(3), 1115.

9. Rawick, ed., *American Slave*, vol. 3(4), 58.

10. Ibid., vol. 15(2), 338.

11. James L. Smith, *Autobiography of James L. Smith, Including, Also, Reminiscences of Slave Life, Recollections of the War, Education of freedmen, Causes of the Exodus, Etc.* (Norwich: Press of the Bulletin Co., 1881), 33–34.

12. Peter Randolph, *Sketches of Slave Life: or, Illustrations of the 'Peculiar Institution,'* 2d ed. (Boston: n.p., 1855), 68.

13. Fisk University, *Unwritten History of Slavery: Autobiographical Accounts of Negro Ex-Slaves* (Nashville: Social Science Institute, Fisk University, 1945), 124–125.

14. Rawick, ed., *American Slave,* vol. 16(5), 11–13.

15. Ibid., vol. 15(2), 132; ibid., vol. 14(1), 121–122; Rawick, ed., *American Slave Series 1,* vol. 11(1), 9–10.

16. Rawick, ed., *American Slave,* vol. 14(1), 424–425.

17. Charles L. Perdue, Thomas E. Barden, and Robert K. Phillips, eds., *Weevils in the Wheat: Interviews with Virginia Ex-Slaves* (Charlottesville: University Press of Virginia, 1976), 52–53.

18. Austin Steward, *Twenty-Two Years a Slave, and Forty Years a Freeman: Embracing a Correspondence of Several Years, While President of Wilberforce Colony, London, Canada West* (Rochester: Alling, 1857), repr. in *Four Fugitive Slave Narratives* (Reading, Mass.: Addison-Wesley, 1969), 22.

19. Rawick, ed., *American Slave,* vol. 2(1), 251–252.

20. H. Milton Blake to Samuel McGowan, December 1, 1860, Samuel McGowan papers, SCL.

21. See, e.g., "An act to restrain negroes and mulattoes from behaving disorderly and for other purposes," [undated act], 64, Town of Abingdon Trustee & Council Minutes 1778–1803, LV.

22. October 26, 1793, cited in Philip D. Morgan, *Slave Counterpoint: Black Culture in the Eighteenth-Century Chesapeake and Lowcountry* (Chapel Hill: University of North Carolina Press, 1998), 374. The *South-Carolina Weekly Gazette* similarly noted that patrols had taken "a bright bay HORSE" from a slave they encountered near Dorchester. October 31, 1783. Patrols in Union District confiscated a gun. *Rice v. Parham,* Sessions Journal, Union District, S.C. (1838), SCL.

23. *South-Carolina and American General Gazette,* November 1, 1780.

24. Specific passes for Ann from J. B. Jones and Samuel Jones, October 14, 1858, and December 23, 1853, Jones Family papers, VHS. On slaves' use of passes, language, and appearance to self-fashion new identities, see David Waldstreicher, "Reading the Runaways: Self-Fashioning, Print Culture, and Confidence in Slavery in the Eighteenth-Century Mid-Atlantic," *WMQ,* 3d ser., 54 (1999): 243–272.

25. Owners who regularly gave passes: Rawick, ed., *American Slave,* vol. 2(1), 304; ibid., vol. 14(1), 83, 200. Owners who rarely gave passes: ibid., vol. 14(1), 396.

26. "Rules for the Government and Management of Plantations," *DeBow's Review* 22 (January 1857): 38.

27. Randolph, *Sketches of Slave Life,* 67.

28. Pass for Ben from Larkin Hundley, February 8, 1857, Hundley Family papers, section 4, VHS.

29. Petition of Inhabitants of Saint Georges Dorchester, undated, S.C. General Assembly papers, Index number 0010 003 ND00 01573 00, SCDAH; Petition of Citizens of York District, November 18, 1830, S.C. General Assembly papers, Index number 0010 003 1830 00123 00, SCDAH.

30. Memorial of the City Council of Charleston, undated, S.C. General Assembly papers, Index number 0010 003 ND00 01799 00, SCDAH.

31. Petition, undated, S.C. General Assembly papers, Index number 0010 003 ND00 02812 00, SCDAH.

32. Ibid.

33. Ibid. Petition of Citizens of York District, November 18, 1830, S.C. General Assembly papers, Index number 0010 003 1830 00123 00, SCDAH; Petition of Citizens of Orangeburgh District, October 15, 1854, S.C. General Assembly papers, Index number 0010 003 1854 00048 00, SCDAH. In response, the legislature said that existing patrol laws should remedy the problems and that no new legislation was necessary. Report of the Committee on Colored Population, December 2, 1854, S.C. General Assembly papers, Index number 0010 004 1854 00043 00, SCDAH.

34. Isaac D. Williams, *Sunshine and Shadow of Slave Life* (1885; reprint, New York: AMS Press, 1975), 28.

35. Perdue, Barden, and Phillips, eds., *Weevils in the Wheat,* 47.

36. Slave pass, original c. 1820, Slavery–Miscellaneous Papers, SHC. "Bull" is an archaic word for the dregs of a whiskey barrel.

37. Moses Roper, *A Narrative of the Adventures and Escape of Moses Roper, from American Slavery* (1837; reprint, Philadelphia: Rhistoric Publications, 1976), 51; Rawick, ed., *American Slave,* vol. 3(3), 187, 220.

38. Moses Grandy, *Narrative of the Life of Moses Grandy* (Boston: Oliver Johnson, 1844), republished in *Five Slave Narratives: A Compendium* (New York: Arno Press and the New York Times, 1968), 38.

39. Grand jury presentment, January 20, 1772, Charleston Court of General Sessions Journal, 1769–1776, SCDAH.

40. Ibid. See also *South Carolina Gazette,* January 25, 1772.

41. *Southern Patriot,* February 2, 1826. Patrols were looking for suspicious

materials following a string of fires that had started two months earlier. Ibid., December 24, 1825, January 11, 1826; *Charleston Mercury,* December 30, 1825.

42. Memorial to the City Council of Charleston, undated, S.C. General Assembly papers, Index number 0010 003 ND00 01799 00, SCDAH.

43. Conversation between Governor Edward Dudley and Jack recorded in Moses Ashley Curtis diary, October 23, 1830, SHC.

44. Rawick, ed., *American Slave,* vol. 3(3), 152; Rawick, ed., *American Slave Series 2,* vol. S2–1(15), 387. The use of badges lapsed prior to 1860, when the law became strictly enforced again. Michael P. Johnson and James L. Roark, *Black Masters: A Free Family of Color in the Old South* (New York: W. W. Norton, 1984), 241–242.

45. Olaudah Equiano, *The Life of Olaudah Equiano, or Gustavus Vassa the African,* ed. Paul Edwards (1814; reprint, Hong Kong: Longman Group, 1989), 116–117.

46. Tommy Lee Bogger, "The Slave and Free Black Community in Norfolk, 1775–1865" (Ph.D. diss., University of Virginia, 1976), 150, cited in Gary Collison, *Shadrach Minkins: From Fugitive Slave to Citizen* (Cambridge, Mass.: Harvard University Press, 1997), 20. See also Loren Schweninger, "Prosperous Blacks in the South, 1790–1880," *AHR* 95 (1990): 31–56, esp. 33.

47. Benjamin Drew, *A North-Side View of Slavery; The Refugee, or the Narratives of Fugitive Slaves in Canada* (Boston: John P. Jewett, 1856), republished in *Four Fugitive Slave Narratives,* 182.

48. Ira Berlin, *Slaves without Masters: The Free Negro in the Antebellum South* (New York: Pantheon, 1974), 270–271; recognizance bond of William Kees, Criminal Actions Concerning Slaves and Free Persons of Color, 1856–1859, Craven County, NCDAH. See also *State v. James Allen,* Miscellaneous Records of Slaves and Free Persons of Color, 1755–1871, Granville County, NCDAH.

49. John Thompson, *The Life of John Thompson, A Fugitive Slave; Containing his History of 25 Years in Bondage, and His Providential Escape* (Worcester: John Thompson, 1856), 67–74.

50. Ethan Allen Andrews, *Slavery and the Domestic Slave-Trade in the United States* (Boston: Light and Stearns, 1836), 102; Rawick, ed., *American Slave,* vol. 3(3), 25; ibid., vol. 3(4), 51.

51. Rawick, ed., *American Slave,* vol. 3(3), 277; Perdue, Barden, and Phillips, eds., *Weevils in the Wheat,* 294.

52. *Carolina Centinel,* June 16, 1821.

53. Rawick, ed., *American Slave,* vol. 15(2), 218.

54. Ibid., vol. 14(1), 243; ibid., vol. 3(4), 10.
55. Leonora Herron, "Conjuring and Conjure-Doctors," *Southern Workman* 24 (1895): 117–118.
56. Georgia Writers' Project, Savannah Unit, Work Projects Administration, *Drums and Shadows: Survival Studies among the Georgia Coastal Negroes* (Athens, Ga.: University of Georgia Press, Brown Thrasher Books, 1986), 7.
57. Levine, *Black Culture and Black Consciousness,* 72.
58. Many WPA interviewees, when asked if they knew about patrollers, remembered that they had the power to whip slaves, even if they knew nothing else about them. See, e.g., Rawick, ed., *American Slave,* vol. 2(1), 101; ibid., vol. 2(2), 15, 328–329; ibid., vol. 3(3), 57, 89, 173, 220, 252; ibid., vol. 7(1), 210; ibid., vol. 15(2), 314, 365, 383; Rawick, ed., *American Slave Series 2,* vol. S2–7(6), 2501.
59. Margaret Walker, *Jubilee* (Boston: Houghton Mifflin, 1966), 168–170.
60. Rawick, ed., *American Slave,* vol. 2(1), 241.
61. Ibid., vol. 2(1), 301; ibid., vol. 3(3), 25; ibid., vol. 3(4), 96, 248–249; ibid., vol. 4(2), 25; ibid., vol. 9(3), 63–64; ibid., vol. 15(2), 218; Rawick, ed., *American Slave Series 1,* vol. S1–12(1), 271.
62. J. Blair to Miss Blair, June 29, 1783, James Iredell papers, DU, cited in Morgan, *Slave Counterpoint,* 308.
63. Orville Elder, *Samuel Hall: 47 Years a Slave* (Washington, Iowa: Journal Print, 1912), n.p.
64. How male and female slaves engaged in different kinds of absenteeism, and may have had dissimilar relationships with patrols, is explored by Stephanie Camp in "Viragos: Slave Women's Everyday Politics in the Old South" (Ph.D. diss., University of Pennsylvania, 1998). See also Rawick, ed., *American Slave,* vol. 14(1), 141, and Leslie Schwalm, *Hard Fight for We: Women's Transition from Slavery to Freedom in South Carolina* (Urbana: University of Illinois Press, 1997), 41.
65. Peter to James C. Johnston, November 6, 1849, Hayes Collection, reel 13, SHC.
66. Rawick, ed., *American Slave,* vol. 15(2), 416–417.
67. Ibid.
68. Ibid., vol. 15(2), 430.
69. Ibid., vol. 3(4), 1.
70. Rawick, ed., *American Slave Series 1,* vol. S1–11(1), 9–10.
71. Lucille B. Jayne, box 1, folder 10, WPA Folklore papers (MSS 1547), UVA.
72. Rawick, ed., *American Slave,* vol. 14(1), 64.
73. See the Alan Lomax cassette tape collection of slave songs, SCL.
74. A shorter version first appeared in William F. Allen, *Slave Songs of the United States* (New York: A. Simpson, 1867), 89. The longer version appears in "Collection of Negro Melodies," folder E, Charles M. Wallace pa-

pers, LV. Wallace began collecting songs and fragments systematically in 1896, and "by far the greater part of the work was simply the recalling of what I had heard in childhood." A North Carolina version of this song can be found in Henry M. Belden and Arthur P. Hudson, *Folk Songs from North Carolina* (Durham: Duke University Press, 1952), vol. 3, 531–533.

75. Mrs. Goldie Hamilton and J. B. Hamilton, Box 30, folder 1228, WPA Folklore papers (MSS 1547), UVA. Two other Virginia versions of this song are in folder 1228, interviews with Burma Bowie and Susan R. Morton, WPA Folklore papers (MSS 1547), UVA. The Virginia version of this song is also included in Bruce Rosenberg's *Folksongs of Virginia: A Checklist of the WPA Holdings in the University of Virginia Library* (Charlottesville: University Press of Virginia, 1969). See also Cecil J. Sharp, comp., *English Folk Songs from the Southern Appalachians,* 2 vols. (London: Oxford University Press, 1932), vol. 2, 359. Modern commercial recordings have been made of this song by Southern artists, including Gid Tanner & His Skillet Lickers (Rounder Records 1005), Moses Platt (AFS L4), and others, all available at SHC. See also Rawick, ed., *American Slave,* vol. 3(3), 152; ibid., vol. 14(1), 424–425; and Rawick, ed., *American Slave Series 2,* vol. S2–1(15), 387 for other versions. See Rawick, ed., *American Slave,* vol. 3(4), 238 for a different, less common, patroller song. The enduring popularity of this song among African Americans may have contributed the title to Chester Himes's twentieth-century novel about the pursuit of a black man by the police, *Run Man Run* (New York: G. P. Putnam, 1966).

76. Grandy, *Life of Moses Grandy,* 38.

77. Whether their horseback chases gained them honor or dishonor has been explored by Kenneth S. Greenberg, *Honor and Slavery: Lies, Duels, Noses, Masks, Dressing as a Woman, Gifts, Strangers, Humanitarianism, Death, Slave Rebellions, the Proslavery Argument, Baseball, Hunting, and Gambling in the Old South* (Princeton: Princeton University Press, 1996), 128–130.

78. Charles Ball, *Slavery in the United States: A Narrative of the Life and Adventures of Charles Ball, A Black Man . . .* (1837; reprint, Detroit: Negro History Press, 1970), 312, 331.

79. See Gladys-Marie Fry, *Night Riders in Black Folk History* (1975; reprint, Athens, Ga.: University of Georgia, Brown Thrasher Books, 1991), 59–81, on slave owners' use of supernatural beliefs and fears to frighten slaves.

80. In addition to the diaries Eppes kept on a daily basis for over forty years, housed at the VHS, more biographical information about Richard Eppes can be found in Philip A. Bruce, *Virginia: Rebirth of the Old Dominion,* 5 vols. (Chicago: Lewis Publishing, 1929), vol. 5, 144–145; Michael L. Nicholls, " 'In the Light of Human Beings': Richard Eppes and His Island Code of Laws," *VMHB* 89 (1981): 67–78; Shearer D. Bowman, "Conditional Unionism and Slavery in Virginia, 1860–1861: The Case of Dr. Rich-

ard Eppes," *VMHB* 96 (1988): 31–54. Eppes owned more than fifty slaves, although he was listed as having no slaves at his Prince George County home. Stephen E. Bradley, Jr., abstr., *The 1850 Federal Census, Prince George County, Virginia* (Keysville, Va.: n.p., 1990), 21. Eppes Island and Bermuda Hundred constituted his main land holdings. His home at City Point became Ulysses Grant's command headquarters during the Virginia campaign, and is now part of the National Park system.

81. November 29 and 30, 1851, Richard Eppes diary, 1851–1852, VHS. The records for Prince George County court, where Mrs. Penny would have been prosecuted, are not extant. This episode was first described in Philip J. Schwarz, *Twice Condemned: Slaves and the Criminal Law of Virginia, 1705–1865* (Baton Rouge: Louisiana State University Press, 1988), 300.

82. Petitions, Legislative Papers, 1859–1860, NCDAH, cited in Bolton, *Poor Whites of the Antebellum South,* 46.

83. Perdue, Barden, and Phillips, eds., *Weevils in the Wheat,* 82.

84. J. D. Green, *Narrative of the Life of J. D. Green, A Runaway Slave, From Kentucky, Containing an Account of His Three Escapes, in 1839, 1846, and 1848* (Huddersfield, England: Henry Fielding, 1864), 23.

85. Rawick, ed., *American Slave,* vol. 3(4), 63.

86. R. Nicholas Olsberg, ed., *The Journal of the Commons House of Assembly, 23 April 1750–31 August 1751* (Columbia: University of South Carolina Press, 1974), 375.

87. Rawick, ed., *American Slave,* vol. 2(1), 197; ibid., vol. 3(4), 55; ibid., vol. 14(1), 29–30; Rawick, ed., *American Slave Series 1,* vol. S1–12(1), 271; ibid., vol. S1–5(1), 161.

88. Rawick, ed., *American Slave,* vol. 5(3), 111; ibid., vol. 7(1), 210; ibid., vol. 14(1), 141; Rawick, ed., *American Slave Series 2,* vol. S2–7(6), 2712.

89. Rawick, ed., *American Slave,* vol. 15(2), 321; ibid., vol. 14(1), 264; Rawick, ed., *American Slave Series 1,* vol. S1–4(2), 345; ibid., vol. S1–12(1), 271.

90. Richmond County restricted patrollers to fifteen lashes, Miscellaneous Officials' Bonds and Records, Patrol 1826, NCDAH.

91. Rawick, ed., *American Slave Series 1,* vol. S1–4(2), 576.

92. A similarly detailed series of reports exists for several counties in eighteenth-century Virginia, and replicates the Panther Branch material in many details. Sally Hadden, "Colonial and Revolutionary Era Slave Patrols of Virginia," in *Lethal Imagination: Violence and Brutality in American History,* ed. Michael Bellesiles (New York: New York University Press, 1999).

93. Records of Slaves and Free Negroes, n.d. and 1788–1829, Miscellaneous Records 1772–1952, Wake County, NCDAH.

94. The patrollers' report lists the names of the owners' houses according to the night patrols visited them: 5 houses, April 12; 7 houses, April 14; 7 houses, April 25; 7 houses, May 2.

95. Number of homes visited per night of patrolling: 7 houses (3 nights); 5 houses (3 nights); 4 houses (4 nights); 3 houses (10 nights); 2 houses (6 nights); 1 house (6 nights); 0 houses (2 nights).

96. The group went on patrol throughout the week, but some evenings were more heavily patrolled than others. Rides by specific night of the week: Sunday, 13 rides; Monday, 3 rides; Tuesday, 2 rides; Wednesday, 3 rides; Thursday, 2 rides; Friday, 1 ride; Saturday, 10 rides. In order, the patrol rode on the following nights: Sunday, Tuesday, Saturday, Saturday, Thursday, Saturday, Sunday, Wednesday, Saturday, Sunday, Sunday, Sunday, Saturday, Sunday, Sunday, Thursday, Friday, Monday, Saturday, Sunday, Monday, Saturday, Sunday, Monday, Saturday, Sunday, Sunday, Tuesday, Saturday, Wednesday, Sunday, Sunday, Wednesday, Saturday.

97. Nights when slaves were whipped: Sunday 4/12/1857 (1); Saturday 5/2/57 (2); Saturday 5/16/57 (1); Sunday 5/24/57 (2); Saturday 6/13/57 (1); Sunday 7/12/57 (1); Sunday 8/9/57 (3); Friday 8/28/57 (1); Sunday 10/11/57 (2); Sunday 11/8/57 (2); Monday 11/9/57 (1); Wednesday 12/23/57 (1).

98. Grand jury presentment, York District, 1807, S.C. General Assembly papers, Index number 0010 015 1807 00012 00, SCDAH (slaves attending services at night); grand jury presentment, Georgetown District, November 6, 1799, S.C. General Assembly papers, Index number 0010 015 1799 00004 00, SCDAH (slaves pretending to attend church but actually getting drunk).

99. Orville V. Burton, *In My Father's House Are Many Mansions: Family and Community in Edgefield, South Carolina* (Chapel Hill: University of North Carolina Press, 1985), 156.

100. Rawick, ed., *American Slave,* vol. 16(5), 29.

101. Ibid., vol. 16(6), 14.

102. Ibid., vol. 3(3), 89, 173; ibid., vol. 3(4), 5; ibid., vol. 14(1), 67–69; ibid., vol. 16(5), 9, 11–13; ibid., vol. 16(6), 14; Drew, *A North-Side View of Slavery,* 232, 249.

103. Charles Stevens, *Anthony Burns: A History* (Boston: J. P. Jewett, 1856), 166.

104. James Ireland, *The Life of the Rev. James Ireland, who was, for many years, pastor of the Baptist church at Buck Marsh, Waterlick and Happy Creek, in Frederick and Shenandoah counties, Virginia* (Winchester: J. Foster, 1819), 135.

105. September 5, 1789, Executive Papers, LV, reprinted in James H. Johnston, "The Participation of White Men in Virginia Negro Insurrections," *JNH* 16 (1931): 159–160; Luther P. Jackson, "Religious Development of the Negro in Virginia from 1760 to 1860," *JNH* 16 (1931): 173. For patrols breaking up a Methodist gathering in South Carolina, see *Bell ads. Graham* S.C. 1 (Nott and McCord) 278 (1818).

106. See, e.g., Charles City County petitions, December 6, 1776, cited in

George M. Brydon, *Virginia's Mother Church: and the Political Conditions Under Which It Grew,* 2 vols. (Richmond: Virginia Historical Society, 1947–52), vol. 2, 567–569, complaining that dissenters subverted slaves at night meetings; Cumberland County Legislative Petitions, May 21, 1777, and November 6, 1777, LV, cited in Brydon, *Virginia's Mother Church,* vol.2, 573–575. On other unidentified whites who obstructed the work of patrollers, see Chowan County court minutes, July 1758, NCDAH.

107. Samuel Wells Leland diary, July 9, 1853, SCL.

108. Field slaves tended to run away either during or after harvest season in eighteenth-century North Carolina. Marvin L. Michael Kay and Lorin Lee Cary, *Slavery in North Carolina, 1748–1775* (Chapel Hill: University of North Carolina Press, 1995), 134. However, eighteenth-century Virginia and South Carolina slaves apparently ran away during all seasons but winter, and were more likely to abscond in summer. Gerald W. Mullin, *Flight and Rebellion: Slave Resistance in Eighteenth-Century Virginia* (London: Oxford University Press, 1972), 192n84; Morgan, *Slave Counterpoint,* 152.

109. They rode on January 3 and 10 in 1858.

110. Panther Branch patrols active on Easter Sunday, April 12, and December 19 and 23, 1857. Similar data on harvest and holiday patrolling in Patrol Records, 1830–1831, Gates County, NCDAH.

111. Examination of the tax lists for Panther Branch shows that they did not visit all houses that owned slaves. Panther Branch District, 1856–1860, Wake County Tax Returns, NCDAH.

112. They visited all houses that had more than five slaves in their portion of the district during the course of the year. Houses visited four times or more:

Name	Number of visits	Number of slaves in household
Susan Banks	7	17
Plyer Barber	6 (twice one evening)	5
John Jones	18 (twice on four evenings)	3
Penny Jones	4	9
Willis Jones	5	2
Nathan J. Myatt	7	8
Hardy Penny	5	5
Simon Smith	6	3*
Simon Turner	6	13
Ezekiel Young	7 (twice one evening)	10

*Simon Smith's other slaves were taxed in Raleigh, which suggests that they hired their time in the city.

113. The Panther Branch patrollers' report is in Orrin Williams's handwriting.

114. June 13 and November 9.

115. Egerton suggests that when slaves knew patrollers were active, they avoided the main roads and stuck to wooded trails. The Eppes diary indicates that patrollers knew this trick and sometimes counteracted it. Douglas Egerton, *Gabriel's Rebellion: The Virginia Slave Conspiracies of 1800 and 1802* (Chapel Hill: University of North Carolina Press, 1993), 53.

116. Green, *Narrative of the Life of J. D. Green,* 23–24; Rawick, ed., *American Slave,* vol. 3(4), 42.

117. Rawick, ed., *American Slave,* vol. 2(1), 319–320.

118. Ball, *Slavery in the United States,* 330.

119. Ibid., 329–330. Other slaves also believed that patrols worked after eight at night. Rawick, ed., *American Slave,* vol. 3(4), 248–249.

120. Rawick, ed., *American Slave,* vol. 16(3), 39. On the flurry of activity before a South Carolina "negro hunt," see Ruth Hastings to Mary Hastings, June 16, 1852, Hastings papers, Clements Library, University of Michigan.

121. Williams, *Sunshine and Shadow of Slave Life,* 28–29.

122. Rawick, ed., *American Slave,* vol. 3(4), 155.

123. Governors' messages to the South Carolina General Assembly, no. 1325, Thomas Bennett, December 9, 1822, S.C. General Assembly papers, SCDAH.

124. No evidence has been found to suggest that overseers ever prevented patrols from completing their rounds. On collaboration, see Rawick, ed., *American Slave,* vol. 2(1), 235.

125. "Plantation Management-Police," *Southern Agriculturist,* no. 4 (April 1853): 99–100; *DeBow's Review* 14 (1853): 177–178. These suggestions originated with the Virginian St. George Cocke.

126. Rawick, ed., *American Slave,* vol. 2(1), 204.

127. Ibid., vol. 15(2), 314.

128. James L. Petigru to M. M. Johnson, May 5, 1854, Petigru & King letterbooks, SCL.

129. Governors' messages to the South Carolina General Assembly, no. 650, A. Vanderhorst, enclosed affidavit of Peter Ryan, November 7, 1795, S.C. General Assembly papers, SCDAH.

130. Governors' messages to the South Carolina General Assembly, no. 650, A. Vanderhorst, enclosed affidavit of James McBride, November 7, 1795, S.C. General Assembly papers, SCDAH.

131. Rawick, ed., *American Slave,* vol. 2(1), 72, 231; ibid., vol. 2(2), 106; ibid., vol. 3(3), 285; ibid., vol. 3(4), 206; ibid., vol. 10(5), 137; ibid., vol. 14(1), 23, 458; ibid., vol. 15(2), 287; ibid., vol. 16(5), 18–19.

132. Rawick, ed., *American Slave Series 1,* vol. S1–4(2), 576.

133. Rawick, ed., *American Slave*, vol. 3(3), 285; ibid., vol. 3(4), 114, 170–171; Rawick, ed., *American Slave Series 1*, vol. S1–4(2), 576.
134. Rawick, ed., *American Slave*, vol. 18(1), 4; Rawick, ed., *American Slave Series 1*, vol. S1–4(2), 576; Rawick, ed., *American Slave Series 2*, vol. S2–4(3), 1318.
135. Rawick, ed., *American Slave Series 1*, vol. S1–4(2), 576.
136. Rawick, ed., *American Slave*, vol. 14(1), 458.
137. Ibid., vol. 15(2), 96.
138. "Mother" to "Uncle John," September 4 [1849?], folder 8, Frank Nash papers, SHC.
139. Rawick, ed., *American Slave*, vol. 3(4), 248–249; Rawick, ed., *American Slave Series 1*, vol. S1–3(1), 171; ibid., vol. S1–11(2), 133.
140. Rawick, ed., *American Slave*, vol. 3(4), 206; ibid., vol. 2(1), 262; ibid., vol. 3(4), 248–249.
141. Ibid., vol. 2(1), 319–320.
142. Ibid., vol. 8(2), 181–182.
143. Ibid., vol. 14(1), 67–69; ibid., vol. 16(5), 11–13.
144. Ibid., vol. 10(6), 188–189.
145. *State v. Duke, Cuff and Arthur,* Slave Papers, 1796–1800, Bertie County, NCDAH. The men received thirty-nine lashes each.
146. *Spirit of the Age* (Raleigh), May 27, 1857.
147. Legislative papers, 1830, NCDAH, cited in James Brewer, "An Account of Negro Slavery in the Cape Fear Region prior to 1860" (Ph.D. diss., University of Pittsburgh, 1949), 77–78.
148. Steward, *Twenty-Two Years a Slave*, 24.
149. This George Mason (1797–1870) was descended from the more famous Revolutionary era George Mason (1725–1792). As the sixth George Mason to bear the name, he distinguished himself from all others by adding "of Hollin Hall" to his correspondence. Pamela Copeland and Richard Mac-Master, *The Five George Masons: Patriots and Planters of Virginia and Maryland* (Charlottesville: University of Virginia Press, 1975).
150. All materials for the preceding paragraphs found in the correspondence of Governor Thomas W. Gilmer, 1840, Executive Papers, LV. The valuation of the slaves is found in the Auditor of Public Accounts (no. 756), Condemned Slaves Executed or Transported, 1833–1846, LV. Alfred, aged twenty-eight, was valued at $900 and sold on September 16, 1840, to R. Littlejohn in a group with twenty-seven other slaves. He was one of twelve bondsmen valued as high as $900 in the group. Condemned slaves might wait as much as a year before being bought from the state (and in some cases they died, and the state made no profit from them). Slave traders typically bought groups of slaves (at least five) at the

penitentiary and presumably took them to the Deep South or out of the country.

5. In Times of Crisis

1. Epigraphs: [Janet Schaw], *Journal of a Lady of Quality; being the Narrative of a Journey from Scotland to the West Indies, North Carolina, and Portugal, in the years 1774 to 1776*, ed. Evangeline Walker Andrews and Charles McLean Andrews (New Haven: Yale University Press, 1923), 199–200, and Angelina Grimké, "Appeal to the Christian Women of the South," *Anti-Slavery Examiner* 1 (1836): 24.

2. I wish to distinguish between slave insurrections, threatened or real, and individual acts of slave unrest, such as arson or theft. Theft or arson with no further intent of obtaining a slave's freedom I have considered under the rubric of everyday behavior in Chapter 4. In this chapter, I am concerned with slave insurrections that had the potential for disrupting Southern society, as well as the resulting permanent loss to white citizens of their slave property.

3. In 1800 the Virginia rebels began with few bloodletting objectives and little intention of leaving the state. See Douglas Egerton, *Gabriel's Rebellion: The Virginia Slave Conspiracies of 1800 and 1802* (Chapel Hill: University of North Carolina Press, 1993), 48–49, 64–65.

4. See, e.g., Eugene Genovese, *Roll, Jordan, Roll: The World the Slaves Made* (New York: Vintage Books, 1976), 588–595; Carl N. Degler, "Slavery in Brazil and the U.S.: An Essay in Comparative History," *AHR* 75 (1970): 1013–1016; Degler, *Neither Black nor White: Slavery and Race Relations in Brazil and the United States* (New York: Macmillan, 1971); Kenneth Stampp, "Rebels and Sambos: The Search for the Negro's Personality in Slavery," *JSH* 37 (1971): 387n53.

5. Charles Ball, *Slavery in the United States: A Narrative of the Life and Adventures of Charles Ball, A Black Man . . .* (1837; reprint, Detroit: Negro History Press, 1970), 331.

6. See the comments of Charles Steuart to Walter Tullideph, September 23, 1751, microfilm, Colonial Williamsburg ("the country is under so proper regulation that we have no apprehension of an Insurrection").

7. Wyatt-Brown convincingly describes this dichotomous state of affairs. Bertram Wyatt-Brown, *Southern Honor: Ethics and Behavior in the Old South* (Oxford: Oxford University Press, 1982), 405–406.

8. Colonel Spotswood, Lieutenant Governor of Virginia, to the Lords Commissioners for Trade and Plantations, October 15, 1712, PRO C. O. 5/1316 fols. 384–385, *VCRP* reel 40.

9. Bull to Earl of Hillsborough, November 30, 1770, in K. G. Davies, ed., *Documents of the American Revolution, 1770–1783,* 21 vols. (Shannon: Irish University Press, 1972–1981), vol. 2, 272.

10. Grand jury presentment, *South Carolina Gazette,* no. 1140, May 1, 1756, for March 17, 1756; June 2, 1766, for October 16, 1765.

11. Wm. Campbell to Col. Baldwin, September 4, 1831, William Campbell papers (MSS 1441), UVA.

12. *Negro Plot: An Account of the late intended insurrection among a portion of the blacks of the City of Charleston, South Carolina* (Boston: J. W. Ingraham, 1822), 35.

13. Ibid., 39.

14. Shauna Bigham and Robert May, "The Time O' All Times? Masters, Slaves, and Christmas in the Old South," *Journal of the Early Republic* 18 (1998): 282–284. In North Carolina, the annual Jonkonnu festival could also be appropriated by slaves for planning rebellions. Elizabeth Fenn, " 'A Perfect Equality Seemed to Reign': Slave Society and Jonkonnu," *NCHR* 65 (1988): 134–135. These mainland practices may have derived from Caribbean roots: British West Indian slave revolts occurred more frequently in festive December. Robert Dirks, *Black Saturnalia: Conflict and its ritual expression on British West Indian slave plantations* (Gainesville: University Presses of Florida, 1987), 167–190.

15. Bull to the Lords Commissioners for Trade and Plantations, January 20, 1766, Records in the British Public Record Office Relating to South Carolina, 1663–1782 (microfilm), vol. 31, 20.

16. Report of Charleston slave revolt, *Massachusetts Spy, or Worcester Gazette,* December 20, 1797, Slave Conspiracy Papers, SCL. For a humorous patroller's report of a Christmas revolt that never occurred, see A. M. Kirkland to Catherine Ruffin, January 10, 1831, Ruffin, Rouhlac and Hamilton papers, SHC.

17. Robert T. Scott to Fanny S. C. Scott, December 31, 1856, Keith Family papers, box 4, VHS.

18. William Gooch, Lieutenant Governor, to the Lords Commissioners for Trade and Plantations, June 29, 1729, PRO C. O. 5/1322, fols.10–13, VCRP reel 42.

19. J. F. D. Smyth, *A Tour in the United States of America,* 2 vols. (Dublin: Price, Moncrieffe, 1784), vol. 2, 101; Sylvia Frey, *Water from the Rock: Black Resistance in a Revolutionary Age* (Princeton: Princeton University Press, 1991), 51.

20. Bull to Lords Commissioners for Trade and Plantations, January 20, 1766, Records in the British Public Record Office Relating to South Carolina, 1663–1782 (microfilm), vol. 31, 20. Relations between runaways and Native Americans fluctuated and were not always hostile. See Philip D. Mor-

gan, *Slave Counterpoint: Black Culture in the Eighteenth-Century Chesapeake and Lowcountry* (Chapel Hill: University of North Carolina Press, 1998), 478–484.

21. For one such order concerning a South Carolina swamp and its runaway inhabitants, see Governors' messages to the South Carolina General Assembly, no. 1191, David R. Williams, 1816, S.C. General Assembly papers, SCDAH.

22. *Wilmington Chronicle,* July 3, 10, 17, 1795; Jeffrey J. Crow, "Slave Rebelliousness and Social Conflict in North Carolina, 1775 to 1802," *WMQ,* 3d ser., 37 (1980): 94.

23. Johnston County: Guion G. Johnson, *Ante-Bellum North Carolina: A Social History* (Chapel Hill: University of North Carolina Press, 1937), 514; Wake County: Herbert Aptheker, *American Negro Slave Revolts* (New York: Columbia University Press, 1943), 262–263.

24. Militia Records during the Nat Turner Revolt, 1831, Gates County Miscellaneous Records, NCDAH; *Raleigh Register,* September 29, 1831, cited in Charles E. Morris, "Panic and Reprisal: Reaction in North Carolina to the Nat Turner Insurrection, 1831," *NCHR* 62 (1985): 37. Swamps also served as way stations for flight out of the South. See David Cecelski, "The Shores of Freedom: The Maritime Underground Railroad in North Carolina, 1800–1861," *NCHR* 71 (1994): 177–181.

25. John Thornton, "African Dimensions of the Stono Rebellion," *AHR* 96 (1991): 1101–1113.

26. Hugh Drysdale, Lieutenant Governor of Virginia, to the Lords Commissioners for Trade and Plantations, December 20, 1722, PRO C. O. 5/1319 fols. 82–84, *VCRP* reel 41.

27. Hugh Drysdale, Lieutenant Governor, to the House of Burgesses, May 10, 1723, PRO C. O. 5/1319 fols. 107–108, *VCRP* reel 41. As a result, the colony enacted an "Act directing the Tryall of Slaves comitting Capitall crimes, and for the more effectuall punishing of Conspiracies and Insurrections," discussed in Drysdale's next letter to the Lords Commissioners for Trade and Plantations, June 29, 1723, PRO C. O. 5/1319 fols. 114, *VCRP* reel 41.

28. In 1730, only a few years later, Drysdale's successor, Lieutenant Governor Gooch, reported that slaves had again agitated to obtain their freedom. William Gooch, Lieutenant Governor of Virginia, to the Lords Commissioners for Trade and Plantations, September 14, 1730, PRO C. O. 5/1322 fols.158–159, *VCRP* reel 42.

29. Patrols attacked a woman who tried to shield William Pollock's slave during the 1802 revolt's aftermath, Joseph Skinner to James Johnston, June 10, 1802, Hayes Collection, reel 5, SHC.

30. Wm. Campbell to Col. Baldwin, September 4, 1831, William Campbell pa-

pers (MSS 1441), UVA, in which a young slave was threatened by an overseer that "if he did not disclose *something*" he would be punished, and so he accused eleven other men of planning an insurrection in Norfolk.

31. Joseph Skinner to James C. Johnston, June 10, 1802, Hayes Collection, reel 5, SHC.

32. Stephen Channing, *Crisis of Fear: Secession in South Carolina* (New York: W. W. Norton, 1974), 21–23. At the highest levels, repeatedly unsubstantiated rumors could lead to a reluctance to believe true insurrectionary activity was taking place. For example, in 1800, Virginia governor James Monroe chose to do nothing at the beginning of Gabriel's rebellion, while Richmond mayor James McClurg automatically strengthened local patrols. Egerton, *Gabriel's Rebellion*, 67, 127.

33. For more on the 1802 rebellion, see Egerton, *Gabriel's Rebellion,* esp. 144.

34. Morris, "Panic and Reprisal," 35.

35. On the comparative use of transportation versus execution, see Philip J. Schwarz, *Twice Condemned: Slaves and the Criminal Law of Virginia, 1705–1865* (Baton Rouge: Louisiana State University Press, 1988).

36. Patrollers' Account, June 9, 1810, Free Negro and Slave Records, Chesterfield County, LV; Jno. Tyler to Cmd. of the 1st Batt., 40th Reg., Louisa County, January 10, 1811, NYHS; Edward Pearson, ed., *Designs against Charleston: The Trial Record of the Denmark Vesey Slave Conspiracy of 1822* (Chapel Hill: University of North Carolina Press, 1999), 106.

37. Patrollers' Claims, 1760–1862, Free Negro and Slave Records, Chesterfield County, LV; "A Journal of the proceedings of Matthew Wynne and his company of Patrolers," "Johan Smith . . . list of Patroling," and "June 25, 1769 Chris'n Rives . . . Patrold," Sussex County papers, 1769–1770, LV; J. Michael Crane, "Twenty Lashes 'Well Laid On': Slave Patrols in Colonial Virginia" (seminar paper, Purdue University, 1998), 17.

38. Egerton, *Gabriel's Rebellion*, 132–134.

39. To prevent clashes over the authority of these overlapping groups, some commanders had the foresight to designate different areas that each patrol or militia group would supervise. Thomas Bennett to Colonel [George Warren] Cross, June 17, 1822, Thomas Bennett papers, SCL.

40. October 1831 court patrol appointments, Miscellaneous Records 1775–1900, P-W, Caswell County, NCDAH.

41. Joseph C. Cabell to John Hartwell Cocke, October 4, 1831, and October 12, 1831, Cabell Family papers (MSS 38-111), UVA.

42. John Hartwell Cocke to Joseph C. Cabell, October 7, 1831, Cabell Family papers (MSS 38-111), UVA. Ad hoc patrol groups also appeared in Norfolk following news of Gabriel's revolt. Egerton, *Gabriel's Rebellion*, 99. False rumors could also spur the formation of impromptu patrol groups. Thomas Davis daybook, September 10, 1835, DU.

43. Benjamin Williams to William L. Davies, February 16, 1802, Davies to Williams, February 17, 19, 1802, and Williams to Davies, February 22, 1802, Governors' Letter Books, vol. 14(2), NCDAH.

44. Crow, "Slave Rebelliousness," 100; Bertie County Slave papers, 1744–1815, NCDAH; *Raleigh Register,* July 6, 1802; Johnson, *Ante-Bellum North Carolina,* 510–513.

45. Morris, "Panic and Reprisal," 49.

46. [Charlotte Hooper] to William De Berniere Hooper, September 20, 1831, John De Berniere Hooper papers, SHC.

47. Rachel Blanding to Hannah Lewis, July 4, 1816, William Blanding papers, SCL. See also Mary Lamboll to Elizabeth Gilchrist, July 25, 1822, Beach Letters, SCHS.

48. V. J. Trist to Nicholas Trist, September 25, 1831, Nicholas Philip Trist papers, SHC.

49. Adelaide Fries et al., eds., *Records of the Moravians in North Carolina,* 11 vols. (Raleigh: North Carolina Historical Commission, 1922–1969), vol. 8, 3972, 4006.

50. Pearson, ed., *Designs against Charleston,* 185, 188.

51. E. M. Starr to Zalmon Wildman, July 19, 1822, Zalmon Wildman papers, SCL.

52. James Allen to John James Allen, Allen Family papers, September 6, 1831, and undated, VHS; Wm. Campbell to Col. Baldwin, September 4, 1831, William Campbell papers (MSS 1441), UVA.

53. Mary McPhail to Mary Venable Carrington Grigsby, September 30, 1831, Carrington Family papers, section 26, VHS.

54. Harriet Jacobs, *Incidents in the Life of a Slave Girl, Written by Herself* (1861; reprint, New York: Oxford University Press, 1988), 97–103; Negro Congregational Diary, September 25, 1831, Moravian Archives, Winston-Salem, N.C., cited in Jon Sensbach, "Culture and Conflict in the Early Black Church: A Moravian Mission Congregation in Antebellum North Carolina," *NCHR* 71 (1994): 424. On weapons found in subsequent patrol searches, see Pearson, ed., *Designs against Charleston,* 114.

55. Charles Lyell, *A Second Visit to the United States of North America,* 2 vols. (New York: Harper, 1849), vol. 1, 219.

56. V. J. Trist to Nicholas Trist, September 25, 1831, Nicholas Philip Trist papers, SHC.

57. John Cowper to James Monroe, April 17, 1802, Executive Papers, LV, cited in Douglas Egerton, " 'Fly across the River': The Easter Slave Conspiracy of 1802," *NCHR* 68 (1991): 103. Details on Monroe's reactions in Egerton, *Gabriel's Rebellion,* 135–138. Similar reaction by South Carolina's governor, ordering patrols to duty for two weeks after learning of an intended 1793

rebellion, William Moultrie to James Wood, August 29, 1793, William Moultrie papers, SCL.

58. Richard C. Wade, "The Vesey Plot: A Reconsideration," *JSH* 30 (1964): 142, 144.

59. *Negro Plot*, 7.

60. Ibid., 10. Similar quick action by Virginia ad hoc patrols helped stymie Gabriel's revolt in 1800. Egerton, *Gabriel's Rebellion*, 72–73.

61. Rules and Regulations for the government of the Patroll of New Hanover County, June 16, 1831, New Hanover County Court of Pleas and Quarter Sessions, 365–366, NCDAH.

62. William Gooch, Lieutenant Governor, to the Lords Commissioners for Trade and Plantations, September 14, 1730, PRO C. O. 5/1322 fols. 158–159, *VCRP* reel 42; Gooch to the Lords Commissioners for Trade and Plantations, February 12, 1730/31, PRO C. O. 5/1322 fols. 161–163, *VCRP* reel 42. But even though he also gave special orders that all men should carry guns to church, he was compelled to say after a few weeks that the practice had been "intirely dropt." Gooch to Bishop of London, May 28, 1731, Lambeth Palace Library, Fulham Palace papers, letter no. 111, *VCRP* reel 591.

63. William Byrd Harrison to Ann Byrd, undated, Byrd Family papers, section 15, VHS.

64. "Permanent Order," July 18, 1822, William Yeadon papers, SCL.

65. *Norfolk American Beacon*, August 26, 1831, cited in Gary Collison, *Shadrach Minkins: From Fugitive Slave to Citizen* (Cambridge, Mass.: Harvard University Press, 1997), 19.

66. William Byrd Harrison to Ann Byrd, undated, Byrd Family papers, section 15, VHS.

67. The Hertford County Court of Pleas and Quarter Sessions ordered the Murfreesboro militia to assist in suppressing the Turner insurgents and to protect the county. Rumors spread through twenty-one North Carolina counties. Morris, "Panic and Reprisal," 31–32.

68. Clippings from Richmond newspaper on slavery in Virginia, 100–105, William Price Palmer scrapbook, VHS.

69. Howard Ohline, "Georgetown, South Carolina: Racial Anxieties and Militant Behavior, 1802," *SCHM* 73 (1972): 130–134.

70. Mary Pinckney to Mrs. Manigault, February 5, 1798, Ralph Izard Family papers, SCL; Alfred Hunt, *Haiti's Influence on Antebellum America: Slumbering Volcano in the Caribbean* (Baton Rouge: Louisiana State University Press, 1988), chap. 4; James Sidbury, *Ploughshares into Swords: Race, Rebellion, and Identity in Gabriel's Virginia, 1730–1810* (Cambridge: Cambridge University Press, 1997), prologue.

71. *Charleston Courier,* October 4, 1831; Lieutenant Governor James Wood (Virginia) to Governor William Moultrie (South Carolina), August 14, 1793, Governors' messages to the South Carolina General Assembly, SCDAH; William Moultrie to James Wood, August 29, 1793, William Moultrie papers, SCL. Such coordination might seem excessive except that slaves planned rebellions which readily crossed government boundaries. Morgan, *Slave Counterpoint,* 667.

72. Charles Pinckney to Colonel Vanderhorst, May 28, 1792, Charles C. Pinckney papers, SCL.

73. Governors' messages to the South Carolina General Assembly, no. 768, John Drayton, September 27, 1800, S.C. General Assembly papers, SCDAH. Ironically, Drayton had received only secondhand information in September about the revolt. Not until October did Virginia's governor, James Monroe, confirm that there had been a rebellion, and that the leaders had been executed. Monroe to Drayton, October 21, 1800, in Governors' messages to the South Carolina General Assembly, no. 768, John Drayton, S.C. General Assembly papers, SCDAH.

74. Robert Pringle to Andrew Pringle, December 27, 1739, in Walter B. Edgar, ed., *The Letterbook of Robert Pringle,* vol. 1: *April 2, 1737–September 25, 1742,* 2 vols. (Columbia: University of South Carolina Press, 1972), vol. 1, 163. Similar reports surfaced after the Turner revolt. *Charleston Mercury,* September 14, 1831, *Norfolk Southern Argus,* September 30, 1831, cited in Collison, *Shadrach Minkins,* 19.

75. Douglas R. Egerton, "Gabriel's Conspiracy and the Election of 1800," *JSH* 56 (1990): 192, 208.

76. Frederick L. Olmsted, *A Journey in the Seaboard Slave States in the years 1853–1854, with remarks on their economy,* 2 vols. (1856; reprint, New York: G. P. Putnam's Sons, 1904), vol. 1, 22. The same increased vigilance swept through Richmond following the Nat Turner revolt in 1831. Patrols roamed through the city every night. *Richmond Enquirer,* September 13, 1831.

77. Colonel Benjamin Watson to Governor Stokes, September 25, 1831, Governor's Papers, vol.62, NCDAH, cited in Aptheker, *Slave Revolts,* 304.

78. George P. Rawick, ed., *The American Slave: A Composite Autobiography,* 19 vols. (Westport, Conn.: Greenwood, 1973–1976), vol. 9(3), 145.

79. *Charleston Mercury and Morning Advertiser,* August 9, 19, 20, October 30, 1822. Laws might try to prevent contact between slaves and free blacks, or target specific areas for increased patrolling. Philip Hamer, "Great Britain, the United States, and the Negro Seaman Acts, 1822–1848," *JSH* 1 (1935): 3–28; "An Act to Regulate the Performance of Patrol Duty on Charleston Neck, 20 December 1823," Benjamin Elliott and Martin Stroebel, eds., *The*

Militia System of South-Carolina, Being a Digest of the Acts of Congress Concerning the Militia, Likewise the Militia Laws of This State (Charleston: Miller, 1835), 45. One suggestion called for altering the number of whites and blacks resident in Charleston by promoting white European emigration while removing slaves from the city, indirectly reducing the need for patrols. [Thomas Pinckney], "Reflections, Occasioned by the Late Disturbances in Charleston, by Achates" (Charleston: Miller, 1822), 23, repr. Paul Finkelman, ed., *Slave Rebels, Abolitionists, and Southern Courts,* ser. IV, 2 vols. (New York: Garland, 1988), vol. 1, 185.

80. Hertford County officials printed copies of patrol regulations, Hertford County court minutes May 1832, Minute Docket 1830–1868, NCDAH, broadside in Charles Vann papers 1739–1880, NCDAH.

81. Petition from residents of Richland county, undated, no. 373, S.C. General Assembly papers, SCDAH.

82. J. H. Easterby, ed., *Journal of the Commons House of Assembly, September 12, 1739–March 26, 1741* (Columbia: Historical Commission of South Carolina, 1952), 242; *South Carolina Gazette* May 17, 1740, cited in Darold Wax, " 'The Great Risque We Run': The Aftermath of Slave Rebellion at Stono, South Carolina, 1739–1745," *JNH* 67 (1982): 139.

83. *Washington Gazette,* August 22, 1823, citing text from the *Charleston City Gazette,* August 14, 1823.

84. Wyatt-Brown, *Southern Honor,* 72–73, 371.

85. Richmond: the Public Guard formed in 1802, see Egerton, *Gabriel's Rebellion,* 164; Charleston: *Acts and Resolutions of the General Assembly of the State of South-Carolina passed in December 1822* (Columbia, 1822), 9–11; Cooper and McCord, eds., *SC Statutes,* vol., 6, 179, 220.

86. Hunt, *Haiti's Influence,* chap. 4; Peter Hinks, *To Awaken My Afflicted Brethren: David Walker and the Problem of Antebellum Slave Resistance* (University Park, Penn.: Pennsylvania State University Press, 1997), 134–140; Joe Wilkins, "Window on Freedom: South Carolina's Response to British West Indian Slave Emancipation, 1833–1834," *SCHM* 85 (1984): 135–144.

87. William Gooch, Lieutenant Governor, to Bishop of London, May 28, 1731, letter no. 111, Lambeth Palace Library, Fulham Palace Papers, *VCRP* reel 591. Despite the new laws, masters continued to let slaves assemble on plantations without supervision, leading the governor to issue a special proclamation allowing militia commanders to appoint patrols for Christmas, Easter, and Whitsuntide holidays, when slaves were most active. Proclamation of William Gooch, Lieutenant Governor, October 28, 1730, copy sent in a letter to the Secretary of State and others, July 19, 1731, PRO C. O. 5/1377 fols. 153–154, *VCRP* reel 47, also in PRO C. O. 5/1322 fols. 212–213, *VCRP* reel 42.

88. Thomas Broughton to Lords Commissioners for Trade and Plantations,

Feburary 1737, Original Correspondence, Secretary of State, PRO C. O. 5/388, cited in Edward Pearson, " 'A Countryside Full of Flames': A Reconsideration of the Stono Rebellion and Slave Rebelliousness in the Early Eighteenth-Century South Carolina Lowcountry," *Slavery and Abolition* 17 (1996): 37.

89. Philip A. Bruce, *Institutional History of Virginia in the Seventeenth Century; an Inquiry into the Religious, Moral and Educational, Legal, Military, and Political Condition of the People Based on Original and Contemporaneous Records,* 2 vols. (New York: G. P. Putnam's Sons, 1910), vol. 2, 199–200.

90. Ruth A. Hudnut and Hayes Baker-Crothers, "Acadian Transients in South Carolina," *AHR* 43 (1938): 500–503.

91. Robert Dinwiddie, *The Official Records of Robert Dinwiddie, Lieutenant-Governor of the Colony of Virginia, 1751–1758, Now First Printed from the Manuscript in the collections of the Virginia Historical Society,* 2 vols. (1883; reprint, New York: AMS Press, 1971), vol. 2, 102.

92. Hill & Guerard to James Pierce, June 16, 1743, Hill & Guerard papers, SCL.

93. William Fleming to Lieutenant Governor Francis Fauquier, July 26, 1763, in George Reese, ed., *The Official Papers of Francis Fauquier, Lieutenant Governor of Virginia, 1758–1768,* 3 vols. (Charlottesville: University Press of Virginia, 1980–1983), vol. 2, 998; Woody Holton, " 'Rebel against Rebel': Enslaved Virginians and the Coming of the American Revolution," *VMHB* 105 (1997): 164.

94. Henry Laurens to John Lewis Gervais, January 29, 1766, in Philip Hamer et al., eds., *Papers of Henry Laurens,* 14 vols. (Columbia: University of South Carolina Press, 1967–1976), vol. 5, 53.

95. Christopher Gadsden to William Samuel Johnson, April 16, 1766, in Richard Walsh, ed., *The Writings of Christopher Gadsden, 1746–1805* (Columbia: University of South Carolina Press, 1966), 72. Gadsden expressed similar sentiments in his letter to Samuel Adams, May 23, 1774, ibid., 93.

96. Sylvia R. Frey, "Between Slavery and Freedom: Virginia Blacks in the American Revolution," *JSH* 49 (1983): 375.

97. On slaves' response to the Revolution, see Frey, *Water from the Rock,* and Peter H. Wood, " 'The Dream Deferred': Black Freedom Struggles on the Eve of White Independence," in Gary Okihiro, ed., *In Resistance: Studies in African, Caribbean, and Afro-American History* (Amherst: University of Massachusetts Press, 1986), 166–187.

98. Holton, "Rebel against Rebel," 166.

99. Extract of a letter from London, *South Carolina Gazette,* May 29, 1775.

100. Robert Olwell, " 'Domestick Enemies': Slavery and Political Independence in South Carolina, May 1775–March 1776," *JSH* 55 (1989): 30–31.

101. John R. Alden, "John Stuart Accuses William Bull," *WMQ,* 3d ser., 2

(1945): 318; Frey, *Water from the Rock,* 57. See reports of other rebellion rumors in June investigated by the Council of Safety. M. Foster Farley, "The South Carolina Negro in the American Revolution, 1775–1783," *SCHM* 79 (1978): 76.

102. Governor Lord William Campbell to Earl of Dartmouth, August 31 [1775], in Davies, ed., *Documents of the American Revolution,* vol. 11, 94–95.

103. Governor Josiah Martin to Earl of Dartmouth, June 30 [1775], ibid., vol. 9, 211. Pitt County's Committee of Safety responded with heightened patrol activity in July. Saunders, ed., *CRNC,* vol. 10, 61–64. Alan Watson has shown that Martin, while denying he made any threat, implied that insurrection was not an unreasonable method to force the colonists into submission. "Impulse toward Independence: Resistance and Rebellion among North Carolina Slaves, 1750–1775," *JNH* 63 (1978): 324–325.

104. Alden, "John Stuart Accuses William Bull," 318–319, citing a letter from General Gage to John Stuart, March 1775; similar comments in letter from Alexander Innes to Earl of Dartmouth, May 16, 1775, B. D. Bargar, "Charles Town Loyalism in 1775: The Secret Reports of Alexander Innes," *SCHM* 63 (1962): 128; on the events of May and June 1775 generally, see Peter H. Wood, " 'Taking Care of Business' in Revolutionary South Carolina: Republicanism and the Slave Society," in Jeffrey J. Crow and Larry E. Tise, eds., *The Southern Experience in the American Revolution* (Chapel Hill: University of North Carolina Press, 1978), 280–282n39.

105. Grand jury presentment, Beaufort District, *South-Carolina and American General Gazette,* January 16, 1777, for November 30, 1776; grand jury presentment, Beaufort District, *Gazette of South Carolina,* May 12, 1777, for April 30, 1777.

106. In South Carolina, overseers were not exempt from militia and patrol duty during peacetime. In Virginia, overseers were exempt from militia and patrol duty except during times of war or insurrection.

107. Grand jury presentment, Ninety Six District, *South-Carolina and American General Gazette,* December 12, 1776, for November 15, 1776.

108. Amelia County legislative petition, 1775, LV, H. J. Eckenrode, ed., *Fifth Annual Report of the Library Board of the Virginia State Library, 1907–1908,* under the title of *A Calendar of Legislative Petitions Arranged by Counties: Accomac-Bedford* (Richmond: Superintendent of Public Printing, 1908), 107, reprinted in *VMHB* 15 (1907): 19. Citizens of other Virginia counties also protested this exemption given to overseers: citizens of Chesterfield County, May 10, 1776, Randolph W. Church, comp., *Virginia Legislative Petitions: Bibliography, Calendar, and Abstracts from Original Sources, 6 May 1776–21 June 1782* (Richmond: Virginia State Library, 1984), 4; citizens

of Lunenburg County, May 11, 1776, in Church, *Petitions,* 4; citizens of Mecklenburg County, May 20, 1776, in Church, *Petitions,* 9; citizens and militia of Amelia County, June 4, 1776, in Church, *Petitions,* 17; citizens of Caroline County, June 12, 1776, in Church, *Petitions,* 24.

109. See, for example, grand jury presentment, Ninety Six District, *South-Carolina and American General Gazette,* December 12, 1776, for November 15, 1776; grand jury presentment, *South-Carolina Gazette and Country Journal,* June 20, 1775, for May 16, 1775.

110. "In the Committee at Newbern," May 31, 1775, in Fries et al., eds., *Records of the Moravians in North Carolina,* vol. 2, 929.

111. Jon Sensbach, *A Separate Canaan: The Making of an Afro-Moravian World in North Carolina, 1763–1840* (Chapel Hill: University of North Carolina Press, 1998), 208.

112. Proceedings of the Pitt County Safety Committee, July 8, 1775, Saunders, ed., *CRNC,* vol. 10, 87; Colonel John Simpson to Colonel Richard Cogdell, July 15, 1775, ibid., vol. 10, 94–95.

113. Robert Smith to [Joseph Hewes?], May 23, 1775, reel 3, Hayes Collection, SHC.

114. Jeffrey Crow, "Tory Plots and Anglican Loyalty: The Llewelyn Conspiracy of 1777," *NCHR* 55 (1978): 10–11.

115. June 21, 1775, July 13, 1775, July 21, 1775, Wilmington, North Carolina Safety Committee, *Wilmington-New Hanover Safety Committee Minutes, 1774–1776,* ed. Leora H. McEachern and Isabel M. Williams (Wilmington, N.C.: Wilmington-New Hanover County American Revolution Bi-centennial Association, 1974), 30, 43, 45, 47.

116. [Schaw], *Journal of a Lady of Quality,* 200–201.

117. Paul D. Escott and Jeffrey J. Crow, "The Social Order and Violent Disorder: An Analysis of North Carolina in the Revolution and the Civil War," *JSH* 52 (1986): 399.

118. Crow, "Slave Rebelliousness," 85.

119. November 8, 1774, Richmond County court order book 1773–1776, December 3, 1776, November 4, 1777, and November 5, 1781, Richmond County court order book 1776–1784, LV. Although Princess Anne County officials paid their patrollers considerably less than their Richmond counterparts, patrols suddenly appeared as part of the county budget in 1776, where they had been absent in 1775. January 24, 1775, December 23, 1776, Princess Anne County court minute book 1773–1782, LV.

120. Norfolk Borough Committee to Peyton Randolph, July 31, 1775, in Robert L. Scribner and Brent Tarter, eds., *Revolutionary Virginia: The Road to Independence,* 7 vols. (Charlottesville: University Press of Virginia, 1973–1983), vol. 3, 378.

121. Wood, "Taking Care of Business," 284.

122. Scribner and Tarter, eds., *Revolutionary Virginia,* vol. 3, 83.

123. Broadside, October 14, 1775, Williamsburg, Va., from the committee of Safety to the commanding officer of the Militia of Westmoreland county, UVA. Text of circular discussed in Edmund Berkeley, Jr., comp., *Revolutionary America, 1763–1783: An Exhibit of a Number of Curious and Valuable Letters and Documents in Which May be Discovered the Sentiments of the Period . . .* (Charlottesville: University Press of Virginia, 1977), 27–28.

124. Broadside, 1775, sent to the "The County Lieutenant of Westmoreland," William Augustine Washington papers, DU, reprinted in Scribner and Tarter, eds., *Revolutionary Virginia,* vol. 4, 435–436.

125. Governor Earl of Dunmore to Earl of Dartmouth, March 1 [1775], PRO C. O. 5/1373, and Davies, ed., *Documents of the American Revolution,* vol. 9, 109.

126. Benjamin Quarles, "Lord Dunmore as Liberator," *WMQ,* 3d ser., 15 (1958): 495, 497.

127. Frey, "Between Slavery and Freedom," 378.

128. Crow, "Slave Rebelliousness," 87.

129. William Hutchinson et al., eds., *Papers of James Madison,* 17 vols. to date (Chicago: University of Chicago Press, 1962–), vol. 1, 153.

130. Michael A. McDonnell, "Popular Mobilization and Political Culture in Revolutionary Virginia: The Failure of the Minutemen and the Revolution from Below," *JAH* 85 (1998): 952–962.

131. Frey, *Water from the Rock,* 155.

132. Printed broadside, October 14, 1775, reprinted in Berkeley, comp., *Revolutionary Virginia,* 27–28; Proclamation, November 7, 1775, Scribner and Tarter, eds., *Revolutionary Virginia,* vol. 4, 334.

133. Governor Earl of Dunmore to Earl of Dartmouth, June 25 [1775], in Davies, ed., *Documents of the American Revolution,* vol. 9, 204. Frey believes that Dunmore did not intend to start a general rebellion, but only to encourage enough slave defections to hamper the rebel war effort. Frey, "Between Slavery and Freedom," 378, 389.

134. Olwell, "Domestick Enemies," 42, 47–48.

135. Samuel Johnston to Joseph Hewes, November 26, 1775, in Original Correspondence, Secretary of State, Admiralty, PRO C. O. 5/123 fols. 623–625, VCRP reel 66.

136. The order to double patrols came from the Virginia Revolutionary Convention, acting as the new Virginia legislature. Scribner and Tarter, eds., *Revolutionary Virginia,* vol. 5, 199; Holton, "Rebel against Rebel," 171; Quarles, "Lord Dunmore as Liberator," 498.

137. Matthew Pope to John Jacob, 1775, British Library, Additional Ms. 34813, VCRP reel 549.

138. John Banister to "Dear Sir," May 11, 1781, John Banister papers, VHS.

139. Julian Boyd, ed., *Papers of Thomas Jefferson,* 27 vols. (Princeton: Princeton University Press, 1950), vol. 1, 267.

140. Bedford County legislative petitions, November 16, 1777, Edmund Ruffin, Jr., LV, described in Eckenrode, *Calendar,* 210; petition of Samuel and Goodrich Boush, Norfolk County, May 9, 1776, LV, described in Church, *Petitions,* 3; petition of Bennett Tompkins, York County, May 27, 1776, in Church, *Petitions,* 11; petition of Christopher Calvert, unknown county, May 29, 1776, in Church, *Petitions,* 14; petition of Thomas Hughes, unknown county, June 22, 1776, in Church, *Petitions,* 32; petition of Thomas Jacobs and Edmund Bailey, Accomack County, October 14, 1776, in Church, *Petitions,* 41.

141. Petition of John Willoughby, Jr., Norfolk County, June 3, 1777, LV, described in Church, *Petitions,* 112.

142. Edmund Pendleton to James Mercer, March 19, 1776, Robert Williams Daniel papers, VHS.

143. Allan Kulikoff, *Tobacco and Slaves: The Development of Southern Cultures in the Chesapeake, 1680–1800* (Chapel Hill: University of North Carolina Press, 1986), 418n75.

144. Quarles, "Lord Dunmore as Liberator," 501. This was also the case when South Carolina slaves near Charleston ran off to join the royal governor on his ships. Robert Olwell, *Masters, Slaves, and Subjects: The Culture of Power in the South Carolina Low Country, 1740–1790* (Ithaca, N.Y.: Cornell University Press, 1998), 237–241.

145. Quarles, "Lord Dunmore as Liberator," 506. The owners at least cherished the hope that any slaves who ran away to the British might be returned as "wandering property," but the British proved unwilling to return bondsmen who sought shelter within their lines.

146. Benjamin Quarles, *The Negro in the American Revolution* (Chapel Hill: University of North Carolina Press, 1961), 138, 149.

147. Crow, "Slave Rebelliousness," 87.

148. Frey, *Water from the Rock,* 65, 165. Slaves escaped patrols during the war by crossing the river at will, ibid., 88.

149. Robert Simons, "Regimental Book of Captain James Bentham, 1778–1780," *SCHM* 53 (1952): 16, 111, 232; Frey, *Water from the Rock,* 120–121.

150. Frey, *Water from the Rock,* 142, 174, 177, 179; Crow, "Slave Rebelliousness," 89; John Hope Franklin and Alfred A. Moss, *From Slavery to Freedom: A History of African Americans,* 8th ed. (New York: Knopf, 2000), 87.

151. Clark, ed., *SRNC,* vol. 24, 725–730. Whether these laws were actually enforced remains an open question, but their creation certainly reflected a perceived problem by white Carolinians.

152. Michael Mullin, "British Caribbean and North American Slaves in the Era

of War and Revolution, 1775–1807," in Crow and Tise, eds., *Southern Experience in the American Revolution,* 240–241; on wartime maroonage along the Savannah River, John Duncan, "Servitude and Slavery in Colonial South Carolina 1670–1776" (Ph.D. diss., Emory University, 1972), 600–611; "Expedition against Negroes," March 1787, South Carolina Treasury Ledgers and Journals 1783–1791, reel 4, SCDAH.

153. Insurrection rumors abounded, and even Moravian brethren appointed extra patrollers. Fries et al., eds., *Records of the Moravians in North Carolina,* vol. 7, 3169, 3177, 3236.

154. Walter Jones to James Monroe, December 20, 1814, James Monroe papers, LC, cited in Aptheker, *Slave Revolts,* 27.

155. *Richmond Enquirer,* July 2, 1814.

156. John Randolph to Josiah Quincy, July 4, 1813, Edmund Quincy, *Life of Josiah Quincy of Massachusetts* (Boston: Fields, Osgood, 1869), 333; William P. Palmer, ed., *Calendar of Virginia State Papers and Other Manuscripts, 1652–1781, Preserved in the Capitol at Richmond,* 11 vols. (1875–1893; reprint, New York: Kraus, 1968), vol. 10, 267, 388.

157. Diary entry for summer 1813, in Claude G. Bowers, ed., *The Diary of Elbridge Gerry, Jr.* (New York: Brentano's, 1927), 198–199.

158. St. George Tucker to Joseph C. Cabell, April 27, 1814, Cabell Family papers (MSS 38-111), UVA.

159. *Richmond Enquirer,* October 8, 1813.

160. May 1813, June 1814, June 1815 county levies, Accomack County court order books, 1812–1814, 1815–1817, LV. Not surprisingly, patrollers made up a growing proportion of county expenses (as they had done in Richmond County during the Revolution), accounting for one-third of the county's total budget in 1813.

161. Patrollers' Claims, 1760–1862, Free Negro and Slave Records, Chesterfield County, LV.

162. Frank Cassell, "Slaves of the Chesapeake Bay Area and the War of 1812," *JNH* 57 (1972): 147–148.

163. Return of James Martin, Captain of Patrol, 1813, William Martin papers, Private papers collection, LV; Accomack County court order books, 1809–1811, 1812–1814, 1815–1817, LV.

164. Petition, 1814, S.C. General Assembly papers, Index number 0010 003 1814 00039 00, SCDAH.

165. Rules for Patrollers (August 1814), List of Patrols and Patrol Regulations 1814–1845, Miscellaneous Records, Warren County, NCDAH.

166. Orders for August 26, 1812, and June 21, 1814, Bright Williamson collection, also in the Third Regiment, South Carolina State Troops collection, SCL.

167. H. C. Roberts to Henry Burn, February 24, 1861, Burn Family papers, SCL.
168. Ironically, the slave made this comment before the November 1860 election. South Carolina Abbeville District Military Vigilance Poliece [sic], October 11, 1860, Fouche Family papers, SCL.

6. Patrollers No More

1. Epigraph: *Camden (S.C.) Confederate,* October 30, 1862. I am indebted to John Hammond Moore for this reference.
2. North Carolina: Wayne Durrill, *War of Another Kind: A Southern Community in the Great Rebellion* (New York: Oxford University Press, 1990), 44–45; South Carolina: Walter Edgar, *South Carolina: A History* (Columbia: University of South Carolina Press, 1998), 360.
3. *Murfreesboro Citizen,* November 30, 1859, cited in Victor Howard, "John Brown's Raid at Harpers Ferry and the Sectional Crisis in North Carolina," *NCHR* 55 (1978): 410–411; *Wilmington Journal,* October 28, 1859; *New Bern Daily Progress,* October 29, 1859. Washington County residents also considered setting up additional patrols, Caroline Pettigrew to Charles Pettigrew, October 30, 1859, Pettigrew Family papers, SHC.
4. Stephen Channing, *Crisis of Fear: Secession in South Carolina* (New York: W. W. Norton, 1974), 28.
5. Steven Tripp, *Yankee Town, Southern City: Race and Class Relations in Civil War Lynchburg* (New York: New York University Press, 1997), 81.
6. David Gavin diary, December 17, 1859, SHC; "Mother" to "Darling Child," December 9, 1860, deRosset Family papers, SHC.
7. The antebellum patrol had focused its attention on slaves and free blacks, although it could also inquire at "suspicious houses" where slaves gathered. In the colonial period, predecessors of patrols were directed to confront servants or slaves, black or white.
8. Channing, *Crisis of Fear,* 27.
9. "True Vigilance," *Beaufort (S.C.) Enterprise,* September 26, 1860.
10. Rev. C. C. Jones to Lt. Charles C. Jones, Jr., July 10, 1862, in Robert M. Myers, ed., *The Children of Pride: A True Story of Georgia and the Civil War* (New Haven: Yale University Press, 1972), 929.
11. *Charleston Mercury,* November 11, 1859; *Anderson (S.C.) Intelligencer,* September 11, 1860.
12. Channing, *Crisis of Fear,* 265–266 and n. 27.
13. Charles L. Pettigrew to Caroline Pettigrew, November 14, 1860, Pettigrew Family papers, SHC, cited in Durrill, *War of Another Kind,* 20. Durrill suspects that poor whites supported area slaves in wartime attempts to harass local planters, 59–60.

14. *Charlotte Western Democrat,* April 2, 1861.

15. Channing, *Crisis of Fear,* 267 and n. 30.

16. James Johnson to Henry Ellison, August 20, 1860, in Michael P. Johnson and James L. Roark, eds., *No Chariot Let Down: Charleston's Free People of Color on the Eve of the Civil War* (Chapel Hill: University of North Carolina Press, 1984), 85, 87.

17. All excerpts from "The Journal of the Proceedings of the Beech Island Agricultural Club, 1856–1862, and Journal of the Proceedings of the Beech Island Agricultural and Police Society 1851," WPA transcription by Lula McNinch, 142–145, SCL (last quote emphasis added).

18. Ibid., 185–186. The discussions of these well-to-do gentlemen about patrol work are at variance with Durrill's analysis of patrolling as the work of lower-class whites harassing planters. *War of Another Kind,* 21.

19. Rachel N. Klein, *Unification of a Slave State: The Rise of the Planter Class in the South Carolina Backcountry, 1760–1808* (Chapel Hill: University of North Carolina Press, 1990), 47.

20. Richard M. Brown, *The South Carolina Regulators* (Cambridge, Mass.: Harvard University Press, 1963), 134.

21. Channing, *Crisis of Fear,* 269–272.

22. In the case of Adams County, Mississippi, a revolt did materialize in September 1861, although white residents were careful to prevent knowledge of the event from spreading across the South. See Winthrop D. Jordan, *Tumult and Silence at Second Creek: An Inquiry into a Civil War Slave Conspiracy* (Baton Rouge: Louisiana State University Press, 1993).

23. William H. Russell, *My Diary North and South,* ed. Eugene H. Berwanger (1863; reprint, New York: Alfred A. Knopf, 1988), 98.

24. Leon F. Litwack, *Been in the Storm So Long: The Aftermath of Slavery* (New York: Vintage Books, Random House, 1980), 28.

25. Patrols 1848–1859 and 1860–1861, Miscellaneous Records of Slaves and Free Persons of Color 1755–1871, Granville County, NCDAH; *Edgefield Advertiser,* May 22, 1861.

26. "An Act to Amend and Suspend Certain Portions of the Militia and Patrol Laws of This State," *Acts of the General Assembly of the State of South Carolina, passed in December, 1861.* (Columbia: Pelham, 1862), 11–14.

27. Governor F. W. Pickens to Mayor Macbeth, April 8, 1861, Francis W. Pickens papers, SCL.

28. April 17, 1861, Town of Danville, Minutes 1854–1868, LV.

29. *Charleston Mercury,* November 27, 1861.

30. Adjutant Inspector General S. R. Gist to Brigadier General J. Simons, May 29, 1861, James Simons papers, SCL; General W. L. T. Prince to Col. I. E. Wingate, December 11, 1861, W. L. T. Prince papers, SCL.

31. Litwack, *Been in the Storm So Long,* 28.
32. Wilbur F. Davis, "Recollections of My Life—Especially during the War 1861–62—for My Children," transcribed copy in the Davis Family papers, 40–42 (MSS 7396), UVA.
33. Correspondence, Minutes of Commissioner Meetings, and Petition concerning the defense of Fayetteville, July 29, 1861, City of Fayetteville, Miscellaneous Records 1769–1917, NCDAH.
34. I disagree with historians who claim that during the Civil War slave patrols disappeared completely and were replaced by home guard units. Merton L. Dillon, *Slavery Attacked: Southern Slaves and Their Allies, 1619–1865* (Baton Rouge: Louisiana State University Press, 1990), 246. Historians like Bell Wiley and Carl Olson have suggested that patrols increased, not decreased, at the war's beginning. Wiley, *Southern Negroes, 1861–1865* (New Haven: Yale University Press, 1938), 35–36. Olson wrote that although patrolling was done about once every two weeks before the war, with the outbreak of the Civil War "once a week or oftener was considered necessary." Carl I. Olson, "The Negro and Confederate Morale" (master's thesis, University of Mississippi, 1951), 65. On vigilance society patrolling, see *Edgefield Advertiser,* November 29, 1861.
35. In Edgefield, the removal of the Riflemen Company to active duty and the diminished exercises of local vigilante associations led to renewed calls for more patrolling in winter 1861. *Edgefield Advertiser,* November 20, 1861. On the renewal of vigilance society patrolling, *Edgefield Advertiser,* November 29, 1861.
36. Appointment slips, March 1, 1862, and April 2, 1862, No. 2 Beat, 2nd Battalion, 4th Regiment, South Carolina militia, Norris and Thomson Families papers, SCL.
37. January 7, 1862, J. W. Bill, Town of Danville, Minutes 1854–1868, LV.
38. Appointments to Patrol 1838–1861, Slaves and Free Negroes Records, Miscellaneous Records, Davie County, NCDAH.
39. Adj. Gen. to Col. J. J. Rhodes, April 11, 1862, Adjutant General's Militia Letter Book, 1862–1864 (microfilm 44), NCDAH; Adj. Gen. to Col. G. C. Moses, April 15, 1862, ibid.; Adj. Gen. to Col. Walter Newton, May 8, 1862, ibid.; Adj. Gen. to Col. J. G. Moses, May 24, 1862, ibid.; Adj. Gen. to Col. D. Outlaw, May 31, 1864, ibid.
40. *Marion (S.C.) Star,* June 18, 1861, cited in Herbert Aptheker, *American Negro Slave Revolts* (New York: Columbia University Press, 1943), 360.
41. James Chesnut, Jr., Chief of the Department of the Military of South Carolina, *Report of the Chief of the Department of the Military of South Carolina, to his Excellency, Governor Pickens* (Columbia: Charles P. Pelham, 1862), 4, 5, 10.

42. William K. Scarborough, *The Overseer: Plantation Management in the Old South* (1966; reprint, Athens, Ga.: University of Georgia Press, 1984), 139.

43. Theodore L. Gourdin to W. G. DeSaussure, November 26, 1862, Theodore L. Gourdin papers, SCL.

44. Message of Jefferson Davis to the Senate and House of Representatives of the Confederate States, March 28, 1862, *Journal of the Congress of the Confederate States of America, 1861–1865,* U.S. Congress, Senate, 58th Cong., 2d sess., S. Doc. 234 (Washington, D.C.: Government Printing Office, 1904), vol. 2, 106.

45. "An act to further provide for the public defense," and "An act to exempt certain persons from enrollment for service in the armies of the Confederate States." The first act provided for no exemptions whatsoever, and the second act described the exemptions deemed valid. *Public Laws of the Confederate States of America,* 1st Cong., 1st sess., April 16, 1862, chap. 31, 29–32, and 1st Cong., 1st sess., April 21, 1862, chap. 74, 51–52. Copy consulted at Houghton Library, Harvard College, bound collectively as *Statutes at Large of the Provisional Government of the Confederate States of America,* ed. James M. Matthews (Richmond: R. M. Smith, 1862–1864). Hereafter cited as *Public Laws of the CSA.*

46. Edward H. Phillips, "The Lower Shenandoah Valley during the Civil War: The Impact of War upon the Civilian Population and upon Civil Institutions" (Ph.D. diss., University of North Carolina at Chapel Hill, 1958), 56.

47. James B. Heyward, November 12, 1861, Heyward and Ferguson Family Papers and Books, SHC.

48. The second exemption act of 1862 replaced an earlier one from April 1862. "An act to exempt certain persons from military duty and to repeal an act entitled 'An act to exempt certain persons from enrollment for service in the Army of the Confederate States,' approved 21st April, 1862," *Public Laws of the CSA,* 1st Cong., 2d sess., October 11, 1862, chap. 45, 77–79.

49. In 1863 the law was changed to allow exemption only upon payment of $500 to the government. "An act to repeal certain clauses of an act entitled 'An act to exempt certain persons from military service,' &c., approved October 11, 1862," *Public Laws of the CSA,* 1st Cong., 3d sess., May 1, 1863, chap. 80, 158–159. 1864: "An act to organize forces to serve during the war," *Public Laws of the CSA,* 1st Cong., 4th sess., February 17, 1864, chap. 65, 211–215, discussed below. In the congressional index, the law is described more generally as the "Exemption of police for the management of slaves on plantations." Ibid., viii. By 1863, only 200 overseers were ex-

empt in Virginia, 120 in North Carolina, and 301 in South Carolina. Wiley, *Southern Negroes*, 50.

50. William L. Shaw, "The Confederate Conscription and Exemption Acts," *AJLH* 6 (1962): 384–385.

51. Affidavit of R. F. W. Allston, August 26, 1863, in J. H. Easterby, ed., *The South Carolina Rice Plantation as Revealed in the Papers of F. W. Allston* (Chicago: University of Chicago Press, 1945), 277–278. Similar petition discussed by North Carolinian Thomas Ruffin and his overseer R. M. Abbot, August 15, 1863, J. G. Hamilton, ed., *Papers of Thomas Ruffin*, 4 vols. (Raleigh: Edwards and Broughton, 1920), vol. 3, 330.

52. R. F. W. Allston to the Secretary of War, January 5, 1864, in Easterby, ed., *South Carolina Rice Plantation*, 278–279.

53. Benjamin Quarles, *The Negro in the Civil War* (1953; reprint, New York: Da Capo, 1989), 165.

54. "To the voters of the 5th Congressional District of North Carolina," broadside, September 1, 1863, A. H. Arrington papers, SHC.

55. *Journal of the Senate of the General Assembly of the State of North Carolina, Second Session* (Raleigh: The Senate, 1863), 36, 43, cited in Harold Moser, "Reaction in North Carolina to the Emancipation Proclamation," *NCHR* 44 (1967): 69.

56. Emma Holmes, *Diary of Miss Emma Holmes, 1861–1866*, ed. John Marszalek (Baton Rouge: Louisiana State University Press, 1979), 203. On wartime slave insurrection rumors, see Harvey Wish, "Slave Disloyalty under the Confederacy," *JNH* 23 (1938): 443.

57. Governor Vance to Jefferson Davis, May 21, 1863, Augustus Montgomery to Major-General Foster, May 12, 1863, Jefferson Davis to Governor Zebulon Vance, *OR*, ser. 1, vol. XVIII, 1067–1069, 1077.

58. Gourdin to W. G. DeSaussure, November 26, 1862, Theodore L. Gourdin papers, SCL.

59. Wiley, *Southern Negroes*, 36.

60. George P. Rawick, ed., *The American Slave: A Composite Autobiography*, 19 vols. (Westport, Conn.: Greenwood, 1973–1976), vol. 10(5), 243.

61. Beat No. 2, 2nd Battalion, 4th Regiment, South Carolina Militia, February 21, 1863, Norris and Thomson Families papers, SCL.

62. Town of Abingdon Trustee & Council Minutes, 1830–1864, LV.

63. Henry County patrol records, 1858–1864, LV. These patterns for relatively unaffected areas of Virginia are supported by patrol evidence for some parts of South Carolina during the war. Records of Beat No. 2, 2nd Battalion, 4th Regiment, South Carolina Militia, Norris and Thomson Families papers, SCL.

64. *Camden (S.C.) Confederate,* November 21, 1862.

65. William W. Blackford to Launcelot M. Blackford, May 30, 1861, William W. Blackford papers, VHS.

66. John H. Davis to Cadet [Thomas] Anderson, February 7, 1863, Kincaid-Anderson Family papers, SCL.

67. Charles Phillips to Kemp P. Battle, April 25, 1861, Battle Family papers, SHC.

68. Jere Pearsall to President Jefferson Davis, November 25, 1863, reprinted in Ira Berlin et al., eds., *The Destruction of Slavery: Freedom, A Documentary History of Emancipation, 1861–1867,* ser. I, vol. I (Cambridge: Cambridge University Press, 1985), 94–95. See also E. G. Ashton to Governor Zebulon Vance, September 27, 1864, Governor's Papers, NCDAH, for another example of a local guard that formed to patrol during the war.

69. Charles L. Perdue, Thomas E. Barden, and Robert K. Phillips, eds., *Weevils in the Wheat: Interviews with Virginia Ex-Slaves* (Charlottesville: University Press of Virginia, 1976), 54.

70. John Blassingame, ed., *Slave Testimony: Two Centuries of Letters, Speeches, Interviews, and Autobiographies* (Baton Rouge: Louisiana State University Press, 1977), 660.

71. Rawick, ed., *American Slave,* vol. 14(1), 190–191; Olson, "The Negro and Confederate Morale," 65; Solomon Northup, *Twelve Years a Slave* (New York: Miller, Orton & Mulligan, 1855), 237.

72. George P. Rawick, ed., *The American Slave: A Composite Autobiography: Supplement Series 1,* 12 vols. (Westport, Conn.: Greenwood, 1977), vol. S1–11(2), 133.

73. Rawick, ed., *American Slave,* vol. 17(1), 289–290.

74. Inland cities like Columbia, Raleigh, and Charlotte experienced large influxes of refugees. Mary Massey, "Southern Refugee Life during the Civil War," *NCHR* 20 (1943): 6, 13–15 and William Harris, "Lincoln and Wartime Reconstruction in North Carolina, 1861–1863," *NCHR* 63 (1986): 158.

75. Adele Petigru Allston to Jesse Bellflowers, July 16, 1864, in Easterby, ed., *South Carolina Rice Plantation,* 292.

76. Albert B. Moore, *Conscription and Conflict in the Confederacy* (New York: Macmillan, 1924), 308.

77. For a brief description of the decision made by Union commanders to call slaves contraband of war, and the congressional ratification of this policy in the Confiscation Acts, see Roger L. Ransom, *Conflict and Compromise: The Political Economy of Slavery, Emancipation, and the American Civil War* (Cambridge: Cambridge University Press, 1989), 205–206.

78. William F. Messner, "Black Violence and White Response: Louisiana

1862," *JSH* 41 (1975): 20; circular from Captain Jno. O'Brien, March 23, 1863, *OR*, ser. 1, vol. XIV, 292–293.

79. Rawick, ed., *American Slave*, vol. 17(1), 289–290.

80. 1862–63 list of fugitive slaves made by Thomas C. Robins, Robins Family papers, VHS.

81. Ervin Jordan, *Black Confederates and Afro-Yankees in Civil War Virginia* (Charlottesville: University Press of Virginia, 1995), 80.

82. Leon Litwack has theorized that only a limited number of slaves actually tried to flee to the approaching Union army. He reasoned that "[t]here were mounted citizens' patrols, river patrols, and Confederate sentinels that had to be eluded, as well as pursuing bloodhounds" for any runaway slave who actually tried to reach the Northern army. Litwack, *Been in the Storm So Long*, 54. Quarles speculates that the close supervision that slaves received from patrols and other residents during the war also prevented them from rising in revolt. Quarles, *Negro in the Civil War*, 53.

83. Leslie Schwalm, *Hard Fight for We: Women's Transition from Slavery to Freedom in South Carolina* (Urbana: University of Illinois Press, 1997), 93.

84. *Richmond Enquirer*, February 9, 1864; *Richmond Examiner*, March 18, 1865.

85. Brig. Gen. N. G. Evans to Capt. T. A. Washington, January 28, 1862, *OR*, ser. 1, vol. VI, 78–81; E. Kearny to Brig. Gen. W. S. Walker, June 23, 1863, *OR*, ser. 1, vol. XXVIII, pt. ii, 158; Brig. Gen. Evans to Colonel P. F. Stevens, January 21, 1862, *OR*, ser. 1, vol. VI, 81–82; Major-General Pemberton to Major W. P. Emanuel, *OR*, ser. 1, vol. XIV, 541.

86. Schwalm, *A Hard Fight for We*, 104–105; *OR*, ser. 4, vol. II, 978–979, and ser. 1, vol. XIV, 541, 588–589, 609.

87. William F. Wickham, Diary VIII, 1862–1864, July 20, 1863, William F. Wickham diary, VHS.

88. Lynda Morgan, *Emancipation in Virginia's Tobacco Belt, 1850–1870* (Athens, Ga.: University of Georgia Press, 1992), 112.

89. *OR*, ser. 1, vol. XIV, 744.

90. Louisiana slave Octavia Albert, describing an aborted escape, wrote that as her group of fugitives was recaptured, they hoped that the men who caught them "were advanced guards of Union soldiers, but instead of that they proved to be 'Cadien patrollers watching out for runaways." Octavia V. R. Albert, *The House of Bondage, or Charlotte Brooks and Other Slaves* (1890; reprint, New York: Oxford University Press, 1988), 115.

91. Louis Manigault to "Mon Cher Papa" [Charles Manigault], November 24 and December 2, 1861, Louis Manigault papers, SCL.

92. The requirement that all residents use passes to leave a restricted area mimicked seventeenth-century laws that limited free movement for many people in society, not just slaves. See Chapter 1.

93. 1863 Charleston pass, SCL; Quarles, *Negro in the Civil War,* 44.
94. W. C. Corsan, *Two Months in the Confederate States: An Englishman's Travels through the South,* ed. Benjamin Trask (Baton Rouge: Louisiana State University Press, 1996), 72.
95. On population growth in Richmond, Raleigh, and other Southern cities, see Howard Rabinowitz, *Race Relations in the Urban South 1865–1890* (1978; reprint, Athens, Ga.: University of Georgia Press, 1996), 19.
96. Louis Cei, "Law Enforcement in Richmond: A History of Police-Community Relations, 1737–1974" (Ph.D. diss., Florida State University, 1975), 45.
97. Ibid., 56–57; Emory Thomas, *The Confederate State of Richmond* (Austin: University of Texas Press, 1971), 156.
98. General Orders No. 8, March 1, 1862, in James D. Richardson, ed., *Messages and Papers of the Confederacy,* 2 vols. (Nashville: United Printing Co., 1905), vol. 1, 220. Lynchburg took similar action in August 1862. Tripp, *Yankee Town, Southern City,* 127.
99. *Richmond Examiner,* January 13, 1865.
100. Schwalm, *A Hard Fight for We,* 106–107.
101. Special Order No. 28, August 13, 1863, Headquarters 4th Brigade, Charleston, General and Special orders issued from Headquarters, 1st military district, Department of South Carolina, Georgia, and Florida, Confederate States Army Records, microfiche no. 51–518, SCHS.
102. Special Order No. 32, August 6, 1863, ibid.
103. Rawick, ed., *American Slave,* vol. 3(3), 127; ibid., vol. 17(1), 200.
104. Ibid., vol. 14(1), 309.
105. Town of Danville, Minutes, 1854–1868, LV.
106. February 21, 1865, Town of Roxboro Minutes, 1855–1865, NCDAH.
107. John Dawson to Governor Zebulon Vance, January 13, 1865, Governor's papers, NCDAH; Litwack, *Been in the Storm So Long,* 29.
108. James Williams to W. W. Long, July 4, 1864, Slave Records, Miscellaneous Records 1852–1865, Yadkin County, NCDAH.
109. Pasquotank County court minutes, February 9, 1862, NCDAH, cited in Stephen Ash, *When the Yankees Came: Conflict and Chaos in the Occupied South, 1861–1865* (Chapel Hill: University of North Carolina Press, 1995), 22–23.
110. Francis B. Simkins and James W. Patton, *Women of the Confederacy* (Richmond: Garrett and Massie, 1936), 162.
111. Louis Manigault scrapbooks, 190, transcribed by Nora Davey of WPA, 198, SCL; Ash, *When the Yankees Came,* 95–96.
112. Phillips, "The Lower Shenandoah Valley during the Civil War," 272.

113. Quarles, *Negro in the Civil War,* 65; *OR,* ser. 1, vol. V, 431–432; *OR,* ser. 1, vol. XI, pt. 3, 364; *OR,* ser. 1, vol. II, 5, 38, 747; *OR,* ser. 1, vol. XI, pt. 1, 74.

114. David Schenck diary, February 22, 1862, SHC.

115. J. H. H. to "Dear Pat," June 5, 1865, Theodore Honour papers, SCL.

116. John F. Flintoff diary, May 27, 1865, NCDAH.

117. Charles B. Dew, *Bond of Iron: Master and Slave at Buffalo Forge* (New York: W. W. Norton, 1994), 340.

118. Schwalm, *A Hard Fight for We,* 133–135; Donald Nieman, *To Set the Law in Motion: The Freedmen's Bureau and the Legal Rights of Blacks, 1865–1868* (Millwood, N.Y.: KTO Press, 1979), 42, 122.

119. Petition to the Federal Military Command, Georgetown District, March 6, 1865, Sparkman Family papers, SHC, cited in James L. Roark, *Masters without Slaves: Southern Planters in the Civil War and Reconstruction* (New York: W. W. Norton, 1977), 84.

120. Lieut. Levi Harmon to Lieut. Greene, April 6, 1866, Levi Harmon papers, SCL.

121. In Norfolk and Portsmouth, night watches continued to work even after the towns were occupied by Northern forces. *Norfolk New Regime,* March 6, 1864, July 2, 1864.

122. Council meeting, May 19, 1864, Town of Abingdon Trustee & Council Minutes, 1830–1864, 148, LV.

123. Messner, "Black Violence and White Response," 20.

124. Holmes, *Diary of Miss Emma Holmes,* 454.

125. *Norfolk New Regime,* July 2, 1864.

126. Elias Horry Deas to daughter, July 1865, Elias Horry Deas papers, SCL.

127. Dahlgren to Captain Johnston Creighton, February 27, 1865, John A. B. Dahlgren papers, DU.

128. Litwack, *Been in the Storm So Long,* 219.

129. Elias Horry Deas to daughter Ann, July 15, 1865, Elias Horry Deas papers, SCL.

130. Eric Foner, *Reconstruction: America's Unfinished Revolution, 1863–1877* (New York: Harper and Row, 1988), 81.

131. John P. McConnell, "Negroes and Their Treatment in Virginia from 1865 to 1867" (Ph.D. diss., University of Virginia, n.d.) (Pulaski, Va.: B. D. Smith & Brothers, n.d.), 19; reprinted as McConnell, *Negroes and Their Treatment in Virginia from 1865 to 1867* (1910; reprint, New York: Negro Universities Press, 1969).

132. McConnell, *Negroes and Their Treatment in Virginia from 1865 to 1867,* 19.

133. Albemarle County court minute book, v.18, May 1, 1865, cited in Joseph

C. Vance, "The Negro in the Reconstruction of Albemarle County, Virginia" (master's thesis, University of Virginia, 1953), 4.

134. *Wilmington Herald,* July 10, 1865.

135. McConnell, *Negroes and Their Treatment in Virginia from 1865 to 1867,* 19.

136. Peter Rachleff, *Black Labor in the South, 1865–1890* (Urbana: University of Illinois Press, 1989), 35; John T. O'Brien, *From Bondage to Citizenship: The Richmond Black Community, 1865–1867* (New York: Garland, 1990), 148–149.

137. Union commanders faced a dilemma, in part because some forecast a possible famine within a few months, due to lost agricultural labor. "[M]ilitary necessity required that the blacks in conquered areas be kept at work but political and moral considerations made it impossible to hold them as slaves." William Cohen, *At Freedom's Edge: Black Mobility and the Southern White Quest for Racial Control 1861–1915* (Baton Rouge: Louisiana State University Press, 1991), 7; O'Brien, *From Bondage to Citizenship,* 122.

138. *New Bern (N.C.) Daily Progress,* July 24, 1862.

139. On provost marshals in Virginia, see William Blair, "Justice versus Law and Order: The Battles over Reconstruction of Virginia's Minor Judiciary, 1865–1870," *VMHB* 103 (1995): 165–167.

140. *Richmond Times,* May 20, 1865; O'Brien, *From Bondage to Citizenship,* 149.

141. Deposition of Albert R. Brooks, June 1865, Freedman's Bureau Records, Virginia, assistant commissioner reports, Record Group 105, box 48, National Archives. Women were taken to the city almshouse; men were taken to the Confederate Chimborazo Hospital complex. O'Brien, *From Bondage to Citizenship,* 150.

142. Tripp, *Yankee Town, Southern City,* 168, 188.

143. However, for a counterexample of the Union army's protection of blacks from abuse at the hands of Norfolk police, see George C. Rable, *But There Was No Peace: The Role of Violence in the Politics of Reconstruction* (Athens, Ga.: University of Georgia Press, 1984), 31.

144. Edward L. Ayers, *Vengeance and Justice: Crime and Punishment in the Nineteenth-century American South* (New York: Oxford University Press, 1984), 174.

145. Cei, "Law Enforcement in Richmond," 58–59; *Richmond Examiner,* November 11, 1861; Thomas, *Confederate State of Richmond,* 29.

146. John Hammond Moore, "The Norfolk Riot: 16 April 1866," *VMHB* 90 (1982): 155–164; James McDonough, "John Schofield as Military Director of Reconstruction in Virginia," *CWH* 15 (1969): 242–243.

147. *New York Tribune,* June 12, 17, 1865.

148. Ibid.

149. John O'Brien, "Factory, Church, and Community: Blacks in Antebellum

Richmond," *JSH* 4 (1978): 509; Rachleff, *Black Labor in the South*, 35–37. On the repeal of the pass laws, see General Orders No. 77, *OR*, ser. 1, vol. XLVI, pt. 3, 1293. For more on the protests in Richmond, see Foner, *Reconstruction*, 155; June P. Guild, *Black Laws of Virginia* (1936; reprint, New York: Negro Universities Press, 1969). Even after the removal of the military offenders, the provost marshal's men could continue to give offense to freedmen by roughly arresting them or denying them protection from rowdy whites. O'Brien, *From Bondage to Citizenship*, 194–195.

150. Perdue, Barden, and Phillips, eds., *Weevils in the Wheat*, 234; Blair, "Justice versus Law and Order," 166–167, 174.

151. E. Whittlesey to T. H. Ruger, February 20, 1866, and Whittlesey to James Anderson, May 14, 1866, North Carolina, Letters Sent by the Assistant Commissioner, Bureau of Refugees, Freedmen, and Abandoned Lands, Record Group 105, National Archives; William Beadle to Fred Beecher, February 12, 1866, North Carolina, Letters Sent by the Superintendent of the Southern District, Bureau of Refugees, Freedmen, and Abandoned Lands, Record Group 105, National Archives, cited in Roberta Sue Alexander, *North Carolina Faces the Freedmen: Race Relations during Presidential Reconstruction* (Durham: Duke University Press, 1985), 131; S. W. Laidler to Thaddeus Stevens, May 7, 1866, in James A. Padgett, ed., "Reconstruction Letters from North Carolina: Letters to Thaddeus Stevens," *NCHR* 18 (1941): 185–186.

152. In an 1866 altercation between soldiers, blacks, and police in Charleston, the freedmen found shelter in the bureau's offices. William McFeely, *Yankee Stepfather: General O. O. Howard and the Freedmen* (1968; reprint, New York: W. W. Norton, 1994), 274. For debate on whether bureau agents did or did not protect ex-slaves, see Foner, *Reconstruction*, and McFeely, *Yankee Stepfather*, viii–ix.

153. *Wilmington Herald*, July 17, 1865, commenting on affairs in Norfolk.

154. April 10, 1867, Special orders No. 15, South Carolina Secretary of State, Special orders of the 2nd Military District, 1867–1868, SCDAH; on Richmond police officers using excessive violence against freedmen, see Rabinowitz, *Race Relations in the Urban South*, 55.

155. July 25, 1867, Special Orders No. 108, South Carolina Secretary of State, Special orders of the 2nd Military District, 1867–1868, SCDAH; July 29, 1867, Special Orders No. 111, ibid.

156. July 29, 1867, Special Orders No. 111, ibid.

157. January 1868, Special Orders No. 1, ibid. Clous's actions are a striking contrast to the collaboration between some military officials and Southern whites, who were sometimes aided in their home invasions of freedmen by Union troops. The racial attitudes of local Union officers sometimes led to

partnerships with local whites, rather than opposition such as Clous's. See Schwalm, *A Hard Fight for We,* 218.

158. Henry William Ravenel, *The Private Journal of Henry William Ravenel, 1859–1887,* ed. Arney R. Childs (Columbia: University of South Carolina Press, 1947), 218, 223; Rable, *But There Was No Peace,* 26.

159. See, for example, Mary F. Powell to Ellen C. Janney, January 5, 1868, Janney-Leaphart Family papers, SCL.

160. Litwack, *Been in the Storm So Long,* 428.

161. W. McKee Evans, *Ballots and Fence Rails: Reconstruction on the Lower Cape Fear* (Chapel Hill: University of North Carolina, 1966), 71–75; Rable, *But There Was No Peace,* 27; Schwalm, *A Hard Fight for We,* 219–220.

162. Dan T. Carter, "The Anatomy of Fear: The Christmas Day Insurrection Scare of 1865," *JSH* 42 (1976): 347; *Wilmington Herald,* August 3, 1865.

163. Holden to Mayor and Commissioners of the Town of Wilmington, July 15, 1865, Andrew Johnson papers, LC; Mayor and Commissioners of the Town of Wilmington to Holden, August 3, 1865, Governor's Papers, NCDAH; Samuel A. Duncan to Asst. Adjutant General, July 26, 1865, Letters Received, Records of the United States Continental Command, Army of Ohio and Department of North Carolina, National Archives, cited in Alexander, *North Carolina Faces the Freedmen,* 10, 12.

164. Carter, "The Anatomy of Fear," 347.

165. W. N. H. Smith and Jesse J. Yeates to Governor Holden, July 17, 1865, Governor's Papers, NCDAH, cited in Alexander, *North Carolina Faces the Freedmen,* 124.

166. Litwack, *Been in the Storm So Long,* 428; *Anderson (S.C.) Intelligencer,* June 22, 1865.

167. Joseph G. D. Hamilton, *Reconstruction in North Carolina* (1914; reprint, Freeport, N.Y.: Books for Libraries Press, 1971), 103; Kenneth St. Clair, "Military Justice in North Carolina, 1865: A Microcosm of Reconstruction," *CWH* 11 (1965): 341–350.

168. Evans, *Ballots and Fence Rails,* 129–130, 68–70.

169. See, for example, Charles B. Foster to Governor F. H. Pierpont, December 11, 1865, in William P. Palmer, ed., *Calendar of Virginia State Papers and Other Manuscripts, 1652–1781, Preserved in the Capitol at Richmond,* 11 vols. (1875–1893; reprint, Kraus, 1968), vol. 11, 471. Pierpont was elected governor in June 1861 by the Restored (Unionist) Virginia government, active in western Virginia. His authority was recognized by many federal officials, including President Lincoln. Pierpont organized the Alexandria constitutional convention, which drafted the 1864 constitution which abolished slavery in Virginia. Richard Lowe, *Republicans and Reconstruc-*

tion in Virginia, 1856–70 (Charlottesville: University Press of Virginia, 1991), 13, 20–22.

170. "How much truth there is in the report I do not pretend to say." D. C. Ragsdale to Virginia Governor F. H. Pierpont, November 28, 1865, Palmer, ed., *Calendar of Virginia State Papers,* vol. 11, 461.

171. Susan P. Lee, *Memoirs of William Nelson Pendleton* (Philadelphia: J. B. Lippincott, 1893), 410.

172. Brigadier General George W. Giles to Colonel H. W. Smith, August 29, 1865, Records of the Bureau of Refugees, Freedmen and Abandoned Lands, South Carolina, file box 23, National Archives; Mrs. Y. B. Manning to husband, September 4, 1865, Williams-Miller-Chesnut-Manning papers, box 8, SCL, cited in Carter, "The Anatomy of Fear," 340, 353n26; *Edgefield Advertiser,* November 22, 1865.

173. Jane Pringle to Maj. Gen. D. Sickles, December 19, 1865, Letters Received, Ser. 2392, 4 Subdist., Mil. Dist. of Charleston, RG 393, pt. 2, no. 142, cited in Schwalm, *A Hard Fight for We,* 186.

174. Carter, "The Anatomy of Fear," 351; similar sentiments expressed in 1866 and 1867 by Union officers stationed in South Carolina, Lt. Col. Garrett Nagle to Maj. A. M. L. Crawford, November 30, 1867, East. Dist. of Colleton, Ser. 3353, RG 105, and Geo. A. Williams to Maj. E. Deane, December 13, 1867, Charleston, Reports of Conditions and Operations, reel 35, microfilm, 869, cited in Schwalm, *A Hard Fight for We,* 188.

175. *Edgefield Advertiser,* November 22, 1865.

176. *Anderson (S.C.) Intelligencer,* October 26, 1865, December 7, 1865; *Wilmington Herald,* August 10, 1865.

177. Carter, "The Anatomy of Fear," 362.

178. Erwin Surrency, "The Legal Effects of the Civil War," *AJLH* 5 (1961): 148.

179. "An act concerning negroes and persons of color or of mixed blood," *Public Laws of the State of North Carolina, Passed by the General Assembly at the Session of 1865* (Raleigh: Pell, 1866) chap. 40, sec. 16, 104.

180. "An Act to Amend and re-enact the 9th section of chapter 103 of the Code of Virginia for 1860, defining a Mulatto, providing for the punishment of Offences by Colored Persons, and for the admission of their Evidence in Legal Investigations; and to repeal all Laws in relation to Slaves and Slavery, and for other purposes," February 27, 1866, *Acts of the General Assembly of the State of Virginia, Passed in 1865–66* . . . (Richmond: Allegry & Goode, 1866), chap. 17, 84–85.

181. *Journal of the Convention of the People of South Carolina, held in Columbia, S.C., September, 1865* . . . (Columbia: J. A. Selby, 1865), 59–64.

182. See Theodore B. Wilson, *The Black Codes of the South* (University: Univer-

sity of Alabama Press, 1965). For a full listing of the Black Code statutes for each former Confederate state, see Cohen, *At Freedom's Edge,* 30–31, or Senate Executive Document no. 6, January 3, 1867, 39th Congress, 2d sess., no. 1276, 170–230.

183. "An act to provide for the Re-organization of the militia," *Acts of the General Assembly of the State of South Carolina, Passed at the Sessions of 1864–65* (Columbia: Julian A. Selby, printer to the State, 1866), no. 4752, 316–345.

184. The Code comprised "An Act preliminary to the legislation induced by the emancipation of slaves," "An Act to amend the Criminal Law," and "An Act to establish and regulate the domestic relations of persons of color, and to amend the law in relation to paupers and vagrancy." *Acts of the General Assembly of the State of South Carolina, Passed at the Sessions of 1864–65,* 271–304. The laws are described collectively in greater detail in Francis B. Simkins and Robert H. Woody, *South Carolina during Reconstruction* (Chapel Hill: University of North Carolina Press, 1932), 48–50.

185. E. P. Millikey to Robert Gourdin, August 14, 1865, Robert Gourdin papers, DU, cited in Joel Williamson, *After Slavery: The Negro in South Carolina during Reconstruction, 1861–1877* (Chapel Hill: University of North Carolina Press, 1965), 74.

186. *Anderson (S.C.) Intelligencer,* July 13, 1865, September 28, 1865.

187. Proclamation c. 1866, S.C. General Assembly papers, Index number 0010 016 ND00 00620 00, SCDAH.

188. Cohen, *At Freedom's Edge,* 35; Wilbert Jenkins, *Seizing the Day: African Americans in Post–Civil War Charleston* (Bloomington: Indiana University Press, 1998), 55.

189. *Richmond Times,* June 21, 1865, cited in McConnell, "Negroes and Their Treatment," 45–46; *Lynchburg Virginian,* June 12, 1865.

190. *Lynchburg Virginian,* June 12, 1865.

191. Ibid., November 4, 1865.

192. "An Act providing for the punishment of Vagrants," *Acts of the General Assembly of the State of Virginia, Passed in 1865–66 . . . ,* chap. 28, 91–93.

193. *Congressional Globe,* February 17 and March 10, 1866, 908, 1305.

194. "An act to punish vagrancy," March 2, 1866, *Public Laws of the State of North Carolina . . . 1865,* chap. 42, 111.

195. Hamilton, *Reconstruction in North Carolina,* 28.

196. "An act to provide for the more efficient Government of the Rebel States," chap. 153, sec. 3, in Richard Peters, ed., *The Public Statutes at Large of the United States of America, from the Organization of the Government in 1789, to March 3, 1845,* 17 vols. (1848; reprint, Buffalo: Dennis & Co., 1961), vol.

14, 428–429. For a fuller discussion of the Reconstruction Act and Congress's actions, see Foner, *Reconstruction*, 271–277.

197. W. J. Cash, *The Mind of the South* (1941; reprint, with an introduction by Bertram Wyatt-Brown, New York: Vintage Books, Random House, 1991), 112.

Epilogue

1. Eric Foner, *Reconstruction: America's Unfinished Revolution, 1863–1877* (New York: Harper and Row, 1988), 78.

2. Illinois and Indiana even prohibited the immigration of free African Americans into their territory. Few Northern states granted them the right to vote. Leon F. Litwack, *North of Slavery: The Negro in the Free States, 1790–1860* (Chicago: University of Chicago Press, 1961), 64–152.

3. Joel Williamson, *After Slavery: The Negro in South Carolina during Reconstruction, 1861–1877* (Chapel Hill: University of North Carolina Press, 1965), 260, 372.

4. Ibid., 261; Alrutheus Taylor, *The Negro in South Carolina during Reconstruction* (New York: Russell and Russell, 1969), 189; Foner, *Reconstruction*, 437.

5. Peter Rachleff, *Black Labor in the South, 1865–1890* (Urbana: University of Illinois Press, 1989), 40.

6. In Edgefield County, a July 1874 parade of black militia reportedly had more than a thousand armed men participating. Orville V. Burton, *In My Father's House Are Many Mansions: Family and Community in Edgefield, South Carolina* (Chapel Hill: University of North Carolina Press, 1985), 257; Julie Saville, *The Work of Reconstruction: From Slave to Wage Laborer in South Carolina, 1860–1870* (Cambridge: Cambridge University Press, 1994), 150.

7. Milledge Luke Bonham to Governor Scott, August 19, 1868, Milledge Luke Bonham papers, SCL.

8. See Chapter 6 for a full discussion of the patrolling plans made by the Beech Island Agricultural Society.

9. *Edgefield Advertiser*, November 3, December 10, 1870, cited in Orville V. Burton, "Ungrateful Servants? Edgefield's Black Reconstruction: Part 1 of the Total History of Edgefield County, South Carolina" (Ph.D. diss., Princeton University, 1976), 104–106. This may be the same planter police force described in J. C. A. Stagg, "The Problem of Klan Violence: The South Carolina Up-Country, 1868–1871," *Journal of American Studies* 8 (1974): 316.

10. Saville, *Work of Reconstruction,* 129.

11. Donald Nieman, *To Set the Law in Motion: The Freedmen's Bureau and the Legal Rights of Blacks, 1865–1868* (Millwood, N.Y.: KTO Press, 1979), 44.

12. Richard Zuczek, "The Last Campaign of the Civil War: South Carolina and the Revolution of 1876," *CWH* 42 (1996): 22.

13. Peggy Lamson, *The Glorious Failure: Black Congressman Robert Brown Elliott and the Reconstruction in South Carolina* (New York: W. W. Norton, 1973), 86; Francis B. Simkins and Robert H. Woody, *South Carolina during Reconstruction* (Chapel Hill: University of North Carolina Press, 1932), 499–504. The goals and structure of these groups can be found in ibid., "Plan of the Campaign of 1876," 564–569.

14. Melinda Hennessey, "Racial Violence during Reconstruction: The 1876 Riots in Charleston and Cainhoy," *SCHM* 86 (1985): 106.

15. In discussing the Klan, I include other contemporary vigilante groups like the Invisible Brotherhood, the White Brotherhood, and the Knights of the White Camellia. On their various names, see *KKK Hearings,* vol. 1, 22.

16. W. McKee Evans, *Ballots and Fence Rails: Reconstruction on the Lower Cape Fear* (Chapel Hill: University of North Carolina, 1966), 129–131; Burton, *In My Father's House Are Many Mansions,* 289; Herbert Shapiro, *White Violence and Black Response: From Reconstruction to Montgomery* (Amherst: University of Massachusetts Press, 1988), 8.

17. Louis Towles, ed., *A World Turned Upside Down: The Palmers of South Santee, 1818–1881* (Columbia: University of South Carolina Press, 1996), 475.

18. Nieman, *To Set the Law in Motion,* 122.

19. Richard Zuczek, *State of Rebellion: Reconstruction in South Carolina* (Columbia: University of South Carolina Press, 1996), 18.

20. Leslie Schwalm, *A Hard Fight for We: Women's Transition from Slavery to Freedom in South Carolina* (Urbana: University of Illinois Press, 1997), 133–134; Williamson, *After Slavery,* 259.

21. Report of General Carl Schurz to President Johnson, U.S. Congress, Senate, 39th Cong., 1st sess., Senate Exec. Doc. 2, cited in W. E. B. DuBois, *The Gift of Black Folk* (1924; reprint, Millwood, N.Y.: Kraus-Thomson, 1975), 201.

22. General Canby directed the military district of North and South Carolina in 1867–1868. Max Heyman, " 'The Great Reconstructor': General E. R. S. Canby and the Second Military District," *NCHR* 32 (1955): 57–58.

23. W. McKee Evans, *To Die Game: The Story of the Lowry Band, Indian Guerrillas of Reconstruction* (Baton Rouge: Louisiana State University Press, 1971), 60–61.

24. George C. Rable, *But There Was No Peace: The Role of Violence in the Politics*

of Reconstruction (Athens, Ga.: University of Georgia Press, 1984), 72; Stagg, "The Problem of Klan Violence," 316.

25. General Fessenden quoted in Carl Schurz, *Speeches, Correspondence, and Political Papers of Carl Schurz,* ed. Frederic Bancroft, 6 vols. (New York: G. P. Putnam's Sons, 1913), vol. 1, 312.

26. On the Klan, see Allen W. Trelease, *White Terror: The Ku Klux Klan Conspiracy and Southern Reconstruction* (New York: Harper and Row, 1971); David M. Chalmers, *Hooded Americanism: The First Century of the Ku Klux Klan, 1865–1965* (Garden City, N.Y.: Doubleday and Co., 1965); Stanley F. Horn, *Invisible Empire: The Story of the Ku Klux Klan, 1866–1871* (Cos Cob, Conn.: John E. Edwards, 1969).

27. John Hope Franklin, *Reconstruction: After the Civil War* (Chicago: University of Chicago Press, 1961), 154.

28. William B. Romaine, *A Story of the Original Ku Klux Klan* (Pulaski, Tenn., 1924), 13.

29. Wyn C. Wade, *The Fiery Cross: The Ku Klux Klan in America* (New York: Simon and Schuster, 1988), 18.

30. Gladys-Marie Fry, *Night Riders in Black Folk History* (1975; reprint, Athens, Ga.: University of Georgia, Brown Thrasher Books, 1991), 113.

31. Herbert Shapiro, "The Ku Klux Klan during Reconstruction: The South Carolina Episode," *JNH* 49 (1964): 49–53; *KKK Hearings,* vol. 3, 7. Earlier interpretations focused on the "poor whites" in the Klan. Francis B. Simkins, "The Ku Klux Klan in South Carolina, 1868–1871," *JNH* 12 (1927): 618–619.

32. Lamson, *Glorious Failure,* 113; *KKK Hearings,* vol. 1, 304, vol. 2, 317, vol. 4, 680–681.

33. Schurz, "Report on the Condition of the South," in *Speeches, Correspondence, and Political Papers of Carl Schurz,* vol. 1, 351.

34. Foner, *Reconstruction,* 430.

35. Evans, *Ballots and Fence Rails,* 300.

36. Edward L. Ayers, *Vengeance and Justice: Crime and Punishment in the 19th-Century American South* (New York: Oxford University Press, 1984), 161.

37. Bertram Wyatt-Brown, *Southern Honor: Ethics and Behavior in the Old South* (Oxford: Oxford University Press, 1982), 368–369; Dickson D. Bruce, *Violence and Culture in the Antebellum South* (Austin: University of Texas Press, 1979); W. J. Cash, *The Mind of the South* (1941; reprint, with an introduction by Bertram Wyatt-Brown, New York: Vintage Books, Random House, 1991), 43–44, 135.

38. Rachel Klein, "Ordering the Backcountry: The South Carolina Regulation," *WMQ,* 3d ser., 38 (1981): 661–680.

39. *KKK Hearings,* vol. 3, 44.

40. Trelease, *White Terror,* 19.

41. James L. Roark, *Masters without Slaves: Southern Planters in the Civil War and Reconstruction* (New York: W. W. Norton, 1977), 144; Leon F. Litwack, *Been in the Storm So Long: The Aftermath of Slavery* (New York: Vintage Books, Random House, 1980), 429.

42. Robert E. Shalhope, "Race, Class, Slavery, and the Antebellum Southern Mind," *JSH* 37 (1971): 571; Edmund Morgan, *American Slavery, American Freedom: The Ordeal of Colonial Virginia* (New York: W. W. Norton, 1975), 380–381.

43. See Drew Faust, ed., *The Ideology of Slavery: Proslavery Thought in the Antebellum South, 1830–1860* (Baton Rouge: Louisiana State University Press, 1981) for an overview of various pro-slavery justifications.

44. *KKK Hearings,* vol. 7, 649–650.

45. In Virginia, the Klan seemed most active in Warrenton, Lexington, and Frederick, as well as the southern Piedmont. William Blair, "Justice versus Law and Order: The Battles over Reconstruction of Virginia's Minor Judiciary, 1865–1870," *VMHB* 103 (1995): 178n51.

46. Foner, *Reconstruction,* 431; Evans, *Ballots and Fence Rails,* 135; Otto Olsen, *Carpetbagger's Crusade: The Life of Albion Winegar Tourgée* (Baltimore: Johns Hopkins University Press, 1965), 147; Lynda Morgan, *Emancipation in Virginia's Tobacco Belt, 1850–1870* (Athens, Ga.: University of Georgia Press, 1992), 270n16.

47. Otto Olsen, "The Ku Klux Klan: A Study in Reconstruction Politics and Propaganda," *NCHR* 39 (1962): 342, 345.

48. Williamson, *After Slavery,* 262, 265–266, 459.

49. Foner, *Reconstruction,* 430. Stagg first pointed out the difficulty of a simple racial calculus for determining prevalent locations of Klan activity, "The Problem of Klan Violence," 304–305. On the related question of the geography of lynching, see Edward L. Ayers, *The Promise of the New South: Life after Reconstruction* (New York: Oxford University Press, 1992), 156–157.

50. Zuczek, *State of Rebellion,* 58.

51. Evans, *To Die Game,* 97. The body count in South Carolina may never be known. Williams estimates that there were thirty-eight Klan murders in 1870–1871 alone. Lou Falkner Williams, *The Great South Carolina Ku Klux Klan Trials, 1871–1872* (Athens, Ga.: University of Georgia Press, 1996), 29.

52. Evans, *Ballots and Fence Rails,* 101–102. On the use of black mob violence in retaliation against white violence, see Steven Tripp, *Yankee Town, Southern City: Race and Class Relations in Civil War Lynchburg* (New York: New York University Press, 1997), 245.

53. John P. McConnell, *Negroes and Their Treatment in Virginia from 1865 to 1867* (1910; reprint, New York: Negro Universities Press, 1969), 72.

54. James Sefton, *The United States Army and Reconstruction, 1865–1877* (Westport: Greenwood Press, 1980), 224.

55. Tripp, *Yankee Town, Southern City,* 248.

56. Zuczek, *State of Rebellion,* 92–93; Evans, *To Die Game,* 135; Olsen, "Ku Klux Klan," 349–352.

57. The Klan has had three active periods since the Civil War's conclusion: the 1870s, the 1920s, and the modern Klan of the latter twentieth century. For an overview of these different Klans, see Carl N. Degler, "A Century of the Klans: A Review Article," *JSH* 31 (1965): 435–443.

58. George P. Rawick, ed., *The American Slave: A Composite Autobiography,* 19 vols. (Westport, Conn.: Greenwood, 1973–1976), vol. 15(2), 136.

59. *KKK Hearings,* vol. 2, 87–88.

60. Belton O. Townsend ["A South Carolinian," pseud.], "South Carolina Morals," *Atlantic Monthly* 39 (1877): 470–471.

61. Rawick, ed., *American Slave,* vol. 2(1), 204; ibid., vol. 2(2), 103.

62. Ibid., vol. 17(1), 200. For the accuracy of postwar patroller claims, see Chapter 6.

63. Ibid., vol. 10(6), 340.

64. Editor's comment in George P. Rawick, ed., *The American Slave: A Composite Autobiography: Supplement Series 1,* 12 vols. (Westport, Conn.: Greenwood, 1977), vol. S1–4(2), 391.

65. Rawick, ed., *American Slave,* vol. 2(2), 250–251.

66. Ibid., vol. 2(2), 106.

67. Rawick, ed., *American Slave Series 1,* vol. S1–4(2), 345.

68. Rawick, ed., *American Slave,* vol. 3(3), 19.

69. Trelease, *White Terror,* 57; Fry, *Night Riders,* 89, 158.

70. Rawick, ed., *American Slave,* vol. 2(1), 17, 242.

71. Ibid., vol. 14(1), 144, 200, 268.

72. Williams, *Great South Carolina Ku Klux Klan Trials.*

73. On disguised Klan attacks, see *KKK Hearings,* vol. 2, 65–66, 136, 159. Some Klan members did not disguise themselves. Shapiro, "Ku Klux Klan during Reconstruction," 36.

74. Ralph Luker, "The Crucible of Civil War and Reconstruction in the Experience of William Porcher DuBose," *SCHM* 83 (1982): 67.

75. Fry, *Night Riders,* 148. Zuczek would dispute the primacy of the Klan's role in controlling "moral abuses." *State of Rebellion,* 56.

76. Williams, *Great South Carolina Ku Klux Klan Trials,* 29.

77. *KKK Hearings,* vol. 2, 65, 136–137.

78. A. S. Wallace to Scott, October 29, 1868, box 3, folder 18, Governor Robert K. Scott papers, SCDAH, cited in Zuczek, *State of Rebellion,* 58.

79. Trelease, *White Terror,* 72, 115–116, 190–191; Shapiro, "Ku Klux Klan during Reconstruction," 36–37.

80. Evans, *Ballots and Fence Rails,* 145; *KKK Hearings,* vol. 1, 35, vol. 2, 47, 51–52, 63; Rawick, ed., *American Slave,* vol. 14(1), 425.

81. Booker T. Washington, *Up from Slavery: An Autobiography* (1901; reprint, New York: Viking, Penguin, 1986), 77–78.

82. Joseph G. D. Hamilton, *Reconstruction in North Carolina* (1914; reprint, Freeport, N.Y.: Books for Libraries Press, 1971), 453.

83. This same mentality permeated public lynch mobs and private justice. As long as local government was perceived to be in the hands of Northern interlopers and freedmen, many Southern whites believed they were justified in taking the law into their own hands. Cash, *Mind of the South,* 118–119.

84. Sefton, *United States Army and Reconstruction,* 221–222.

85. Evans, *Ballots and Fence Rails,* 131.

86. On postwar police and black-white relations, see Melinda Hennessey, "To Live and Die in Dixie: Reconstruction Race Riots in the South" (Ph.D. diss., Kent State University, 1978).

87. Dennis C. Rousey, "Yellow Fever and Black Policemen in Memphis: A Post-Reconstruction Anomaly," *JSH* 51 (1985): 359, table 1.

88. Howard Rabinowitz, *Race Relations in the Urban South, 1865–1890* (1978; reprint, Athens, Ga.: University of Georgia Press, 1996), 42.

89. Hennessey, "Racial Violence during Reconstruction," 105.

90. Bernard E. Powers, "Community Evolution and Race Relations in Reconstruction Charleston, South Carolina," *SCHM* 95 (1994): 42–43.

91. Hamilton, *Reconstruction in North Carolina,* 467.

92. Charles F. Hard reminiscences, Charles F. and Ellen W. Hard manuscripts, SCL.

93. See Maurice Halbwachs, *On Collective Memory,* trans. Lewis Coser (Chicago: University of Chicago Press, 1992), 48; Michael Kammen, *Mystic Chords of Memory: The Transformation of Tradition in American Culture* (New York: Knopf, 1991), 4–17; and the March 1989 issue of the *JAH* devoted to memory in American history.

94. Carl V. Harris, "Reforms in Government Control of Negroes in Birmingham, Alabama, 1890–1920," *JSH* 38 (1972): 567–569; Tripp, *Yankee Town, Southern City,* 232.

95. Wyatt-Brown, *Southern Honor,* 369, 436; Ayers, *Vengeance and Justice,* 26, 31–33.

96. See, for example, Fabius Busbee, *A Digest of All the Criminal Cases in North Carolina, 1789–1879* (Raleigh: Edwards, Broughton & Co., 1880), 58.

97. Joel Williamson, *The Crucible of Race: Black/White Relations in the American South since Emancipation* (New York: Oxford University Press, 1984), 19. See also Eugene J. Watts, "The Police in Atlanta, 1890–1905," *JSH* 39 (1973): 168.

98. Rawick, ed., *American Slave,* vol. 14(1), 141; ibid., vol. 10(6), 340.

Bibliography

Primary Sources: Manuscript Collections

CLEMENTS LIBRARY, UNIVERSITY OF MICHIGAN, ANN ARBOR
Hastings papers

LIBRARY OF VIRGINIA, RICHMOND
Town of Abingdon Trustee & Council Minutes, 1778–1864
Accomack County court order books
Albemarle County court minute book
Albemarle County legislative petitions
Amelia County legislative petitions
Amelia County tithable lists
Auditor of Public Accounts, Condemned Slaves transported or executed
Bedford County legislative petitions
J. Willcox Brown papers
Chesterfield County, Free Negro and Slave Records
Town of Danville, Minutes
Executive Papers, Governor Thomas W. Gilmer
Giles County legislative petitions
Henry County patrol records
Legislative petitions
William Martin papers
Norfolk County legislative petitions
Princess Anne County court minute books
Richmond City Common Hall Records
Richmond County court order book
Rockbridge County legislative petitions
Southampton County Patrol Returns and Lists
Spotsylvania County court minute books
Sussex County papers
Virginia Colonial Records Project
Charles M. Wallace papers

NEW-YORK HISTORICAL SOCIETY, NEW YORK
Jno. Tyler letter

NORTH CAROLINA COLLECTION, WILSON LIBRARY, UNIVERSITY
OF NORTH CAROLINA AT CHAPEL HILL
Patrol Regulations for the County of Rowan
Patrol Regulations for the Town of Tarborough

NORTH CAROLINA DIVISION OF ARCHIVES AND HISTORY,
RALEIGH
Adjutant General's Department, Letters, Orders, and Returns
Adjutant General's Department, Militia Letter Book
Bertie County Slave papers
Caswell County, Miscellaneous Records
Chowan County court minutes
Chowan County, Miscellaneous Slave Records
Craven County, Criminal Actions Concerning Slaves and Free Persons of Color
Craven County, Patrol Appointment
Davie County, Miscellaneous Records, Slaves and Free Negroes Records
City of Fayetteville, Miscellaneous Records
John F. Flintoff diary
Gates County, Miscellaneous Records
Gates County, Patrol Records
General Assembly Session Records
Governor's Letter Books
Governor's Papers
Granville County, Miscellaneous Records of Slaves and Free Persons of Color
Granville County, Records of the Commissioners of the Town of Oxford
Hertford County court minutes
New Hanover County court minutes
New Hanover County Court of Pleas and Quarter Sessions
Onslow County, Patrol, Officials' Bonds & Records
Pasquotank County court minutes
Perquimans County Tax Returns
Perquimans County Patrols, Miscellaneous Records
Richmond County, Patrol, Miscellaneous Officials' Bonds and Records
Town of Roxboro Minutes
Stokes County, Miscellaneous Records
Charles Vann papers
Wake County, Miscellaneous Records

Wake County Tax Returns, Panther Branch District
Warren County, Miscellaneous Records
Yadkin County, Miscellaneous Records, Slave Records

PUBLIC RECORD OFFICE, LONDON
Acts of Barbados, 1642–1692
Journal of the Barbados Assembly
Minutes of the Governor's Council, Barbados

RARE BOOK, MANUSCRIPT, AND SPECIAL COLLECTIONS LIBRARY,
DUKE UNIVERSITY, DURHAM
John A. B. Dahlgren papers
Thomas Davis daybook
Daniel W. Jordan papers
Louis Manigault papers
William Augustine Washington papers

SOUTH CAROLINA DEPARTMENT OF ARCHIVES AND HISTORY,
COLUMBIA
Aiken Municipal Court Docket
Aiken Town Council Patrol Book
Charleston Court of General Sessions Journal
Edgefield County, Sheriff, Militia & Road Duty Fines & Executions
Governor Archdale's Laws
Richland County Magistrates' Docket
South Carolina General Assembly Papers
South Carolina Secretary of State, Special Orders of the 2nd Military District
South Carolina Treasury Ledgers and Journals, 1783–1794 (microfilm)

SOUTH CAROLINA HISTORICAL SOCIETY, CHARLESTON
Beach Letters
Confederate States Army Records, General and Special orders of Headquarters,
    1st military district

SOUTH CAROLINIANA LIBRARY, UNIVERSITY OF SOUTH
CAROLINA, COLUMBIA
Thomas Bennett papers
William Blanding papers
Milledge Luke Bonham papers
Branchville Vigilant Society journal

Burn Family papers
Charleston, South Carolina, papers
Elias Horry Deas papers
Franklin William Fairey papers
Fouche Family papers
Gaston-Strait-Wylie-Baskin Family papers
Theodore L. Gourdin papers
Hampton Family papers
Charles F. and Ellen W. Hard manuscripts
Levi Harmon papers
Robert Hayne papers
Hill and Guerard papers
Theodore Honour papers
W. J. Hughes papers
Ralph Izard Family papers
Janney-Leaphart Family papers
Jones-Watts-Davis Family papers
Journal of the Proceedings of the Beech Island Agricultural Club, and Journal of
    the Proceedings of the Beech Island Agricultural and Police Society
Kincaid-Anderson Family papers
Samuel Wells Leland diary
Alan Lomax cassette collection
Rawlins Lowndes papers
Louis Manigault papers and scrapbooks
Samuel McGowan papers
William Moultrie papers
Norris and Thomson Families papers
Petigru and King letterbooks
Francis W. Pickens papers
Charles C. Pinckney papers
W. L. T. Prince papers
Lemuel Reid diary
James Simons papers
Slave Conspiracy papers
South Carolina State Troops collection
Washington Taylor diary
Tompkins Family papers
Townes Family papers
Zalmon Wildman papers
Bright Williamson collection
William Yeadon papers

SOUTHERN HISTORICAL COLLECTION AND SOUTHERN FOLKLIFE
COLLECTION, WILSON LIBRARY, UNIVERSITY OF NORTH
CAROLINA AT CHAPEL HILL
A. H. Arrington papers
Battle Family papers
Moses Ashley Curtis papers
deRosset Family papers
Edgefield Military Record, 9th Regiment, South Carolina Militia
David Gavin diary
Hayes Collection
Heyward and Ferguson Family papers
John De Berniere Hooper papers
Frank Nash papers
Pettigrew Family papers
Ruffin, Rouhlac, and Hamilton papers
David Schenck papers
Slavery—Miscellaneous papers
Nicholas Philip Trist papers

SPECIAL COLLECTIONS DEPARTMENT, UNIVERSITY OF VIRGINIA
LIBRARY, CHARLOTTESVILLE
Cabell Family papers (MSS 38-111)
William Campbell papers (MSS 1441)
Davis Family papers (MSS 7396)
Richard Foster papers (MSS 3523)
Heth Family papers (MSS 10986)
Morris papers (indexed as part of the Eighteenth Century Collection, MSS 38-
    79)
Thrift Family papers (MSS 9153)
Works Progress Administration (WPA) Folklore papers (MSS 1547)

VIRGINIA HISTORICAL SOCIETY, RICHMOND
Allen Family (of Botetourt County) papers
Aylett Family papers
John Banister papers
William W. Blackford papers
Byrd Family papers
Carrington Family papers
Thomas Chrystie papers
City Sergeant Register, Richmond
Daniel W. Cobb diary

John Parke Custis papers
Robert Williams Daniel papers
Richard Eppes diaries
Eppes Family papers
Faulkner Family papers
Hundley Family papers
Jones Family papers
Keith Family papers
William Price Palmer scrapbook
Richmond City Police Book
Robins Family papers
Virginia Justices of the Peace
William F. Wickham diary

Primary Sources: Printed Material

Acts and Resolutions of the General Assembly of the State of South-Carolina passed in December 1822. Columbia, 1822.

Acts and Resolutions of the General Assembly of the State of South Carolina, Passed in December, 1839. Columbia: A. H. Pemberton, 1839.

Acts and Statutes of the Island of Barbados. Made and Enacted since the Reducement of the Same, unto the Authority of the Common-wealth of England. London: W. Bentley, [1654].

Acts of Assembly, Passed in the Island of Barbadoes, From 1648, to 1718. London: John Baskett, 1721.

Acts of the General Assembly of the State of South Carolina, Passed at the Sessions of 1864–65. Columbia: Julian A. Selby, 1866.

Acts of the General Assembly of the State of South Carolina, passed in December, 1861. Columbia: Pelham, 1862.

Acts of the General Assembly of the State of Virginia, Passed in 1865–66 . . . Richmond: Allegry & Goode, 1866.

Acts of the General Assembly of Virginia, passed at the Session commencing 7th January, and ending 10th April, 1839, in the sixty-third year of the Commonwealth. Richmond: Shepherd, 1839.

Acts Passed at a General Assembly of the Commonwealth of Virginia, begun and held at the Capitol, in the City of Richmond, on Monday, the fifth day of December, in the Year of our Lord, one thousand eight hundred and thirty-one, and of the commonwealth the fifty-sixth. Richmond: Ritchie, 1832.

Acts Passed at a General Assembly of the Commonwealth of Virginia: Begun and held at the Capitol, in the City of Richmond, on Monday, the Fifth Day of Decem-

ber, One Thousand Eight Hundred and Three. Richmond: Meriwether Jones, 1804.

Acts Passed by the General Assembly of the State of North Carolina, at the Session of 1830–1831. Raleigh: Lawrence & Lemay, 1831.

Carrington, W. C. G. *Laws for the Government of the City of Raleigh, Containing all legislative enactments relative thereto, and the ordinances of the Board of Commissioners, now in force; from the first act of incorporation to 1838*. Raleigh: Raleigh Register, 1838.

The Charter of the Town of Aiken, with the By-Laws and Ordinances, Passed by the Town Council in June 1860. Charleston: A. J. Burke, 1860.

Davies, K. G., ed. *Documents of the American Revolution, 1770–1783*. 21 vols. Shannon: Irish University Press, 1972–1981.

De Renne, George, and Charles C. Jones, Jr. *Acts Passed by the General Assembly of the Colony of Georgia, 1755 to 1774*. Wormsloe, Ga.: n.p., 1881.

Easterby, J. H., ed. *The Journal of the Commons House of Assembly, November 10, 1736–June 7, 1739*. Columbia: Historical Commission of South Carolina, 1951.

——— *The Journal of the Commons House of Assembly, September 12, 1739–March 26, 1741*. Columbia: Historical Commission of South Carolina, 1952.

——— *The Journal of the Commons House of Assembly, May 18, 1741–July 10, 1742*. Columbia: Historical Commission of South Carolina, 1953.

Eckenrode, H. J., ed. *A Calendar of Legislative Petitions Arranged by Counties: Accomac-Bedford*. In *Fifth Annual Report of the Library Board of the Virginia State Library, 1907–1908*. Richmond: Superintendent of Public Printing, 1908.

Edwards, Alexander, comp. *Ordinances of the City Council of Charleston*. Charleston: W. P. Young, 1802.

Hall, Richard, comp. *Acts Passed in the Island of Barbados. From 1643, to 1762, inclusive*. London, 1764.

Journal of the Congress of the Confederate States of America, 58th Cong., 2d Sess., Senate doc. 234. Washington, D.C.: Government Printing Office, 1904.

Journal of the Convention of the People of South Carolina, held in Columbia, S.C., September, 1865 . . . Columbia: J. A. Selby, 1865.

Journal of the Senate of the General Assembly of the State of North Carolina, Second Session. Raleigh: The Senate, 1863.

Olsberg, R. Nicholas. *Journal of the Commons House of Assembly, 1750–1751*. Columbia: University of South Carolina Press, 1974.

Palmer, William P., ed. *Calendar of Virginia State Papers and Other Manuscripts, 1652–1781, Preserved in the Capitol at Richmond*. 11 vols. 1875–1893. Reprint, New York: Kraus, 1968.

Public Laws of the Confederate States of America. 1st Cong., 1st Sess. Richmond: R. M. Smith, 1862.

Public Laws of the Confederate States of America. 1st Cong., 2d Sess. Richmond: R. M. Smith, 1862.

Public Laws of the Confederate States of America. 1st Cong., 3d Sess. Richmond: R. M. Smith, 1863.

Public Laws of the Confederate States of America. 1st Cong., 4th Sess. Richmond: R. M. Smith, 1864.

Public Laws of the State of North Carolina, Passed by the General Assembly at the Session of 1865. Raleigh: Pell, 1866.

The Public Statutes at Large of the United States of America from the Organization of the Government in 1789, to March 3, 1845. Edited by Richard Peters. 17 vols. 1848. Reprint, Buffalo: Dennis & Co., 1961.

Rawlin, William, comp. *The Laws of Barbados, Collected in One Volume.* London: n.p., 1699.

Recopilación de leyes de los reynos de las Indias. 4 vols. 1681. Reprint, Madrid: Ediciones Cultura Hispanica, 1973.

Records in the British Public Record Office Relating to South Carolina, 1663–1782, 6 reels (microfilm).

Sainsbury, W. N., J. W. Fortescue, and Cecil Headlam, eds. *Calendar of State Papers, Colonial Series, America and West Indies.* 43 vols. 1860. Reprint, Nendeln, Liechtenstein: Kraus, 1978.

Salley, Alexander S., ed. *Journal of the Commons House of Assembly* [South Carolina]. 21 vols. Columbia, 1907–1946.

——— *Journal of the Grand Council, April 11, 1692–September 26, 1692.* Columbia: State Co., 1907.

——— *Journal of the Grand Council, August 25, 1671–June 24, 1680.* Columbia: State Co., 1907.

Statutes at Large of the Provisional Government of the Confederate States of America. Ed. James M. Matthews. Richmond: R. M. Smith, 1862–1864.

Tarter, Brent, ed. *The Order Book and Related Papers of the Common Hall of the Borough of Norfolk, Virginia, 1736–1798.* Richmond: Virginia State Library, 1979.

U.S. Bureau of the Census. *Historical Statistics of the United States: Colonial Times to 1970.* 2 vols. Washington, D.C.: Bureau of the Census, 1975.

U.S. Bureau of the Census. Population of the United States in 1810, Third Census, North Carolina, Perquimans County (microfilm).

U.S. Bureau of the Census. Population of the United States in 1860, Eighth Census, North Carolina, Perquimans County (microfilm).

U.S. Bureau of the Census. Population of the United States in 1860, Eighth Census, North Carolina, Wake County (microfilm).

Watkins, Robert, and George Watkins, eds. *Digest of the Laws of the State of Georgia . . .* Philadelphia: R. Aitken, 1800.

Wingo, Elizabeth B., and W. Bruce Wingo. *Norfolk County, Virginia, Tithables, 1730–1750.* Norfolk: n.p., 1979.

——— *Norfolk County, Virginia, Tithables, 1751–1765.* Norfolk: n.p., 1981.

——— *Norfolk County, Virginia, Tithables, 1766–1780.* Norfolk: n.p., 1985.

MAPS

Map of Wake County, Drawn from actual Surveys by Fendol Bevers, County Surveyor. Raleigh, n.d. [1871]. Map Collection, North Carolina Collection, Wilson Library, University of North Carolina at Chapel Hill.

A Plat of the Land Patents in Amelia County, Virginia, compiled by Robert Brumfield (Amelia, Va.: Amelia Historical Committee, 1987). Library of Virginia.

PERIODICALS

Anderson (S.C.) Intelligencer
Anti-Slavery Examiner
Beaufort (S.C.) Enterprise
Camden (S.C.) Confederate
Carolina Centinel
Charleston City Gazette
Charleston City Gazette & Daily Advertiser
Charleston Courier
Charleston Evening Courier
Charleston Mercury
Charleston Mercury and Morning Advertiser
Charleston Strength of the People
Charlotte Western Democrat
Congressional Globe
DeBow's Review
Edenton (N.C.) Gazette
Edgefield Advertiser
Gazette of South Carolina
Lynchburg Virginian
Marion (S.C.) Star
Murfreesboro Citizen
New Bern (N.C.) Daily Progress
New York Tribune
Norfolk American Beacon
Norfolk New Regime

Norfolk Southern Argus
North Carolina Historical & Genealogical Register
Raleigh Register
Richmond Enquirer
Richmond Examiner
Richmond Times
South-Carolina and American General Gazette
South Carolina Gazette and Country Journal
South Carolina Gazette
South-Carolina Weekly Gazette
Southern Agriculturist
Southern Patriot
Spirit of the Age
State Gazette of South Carolina
Virginia Historical Register and Literary Notebook
Washington Gazette
Wilmington Chronicle
Wilmington Herald
Wilmington Journal
Winyah Observer (Georgetown, S.C.)
Winyaw Intelligencer (Georgetown, S.C.)

COURT CASES
Bell ads. Graham S.C. 1 (Nott and McCord) 278 (1818)
Elizabeth City v. Kenedy 44 N.C. (Busbee) 89 (1852)
Rice v. Parham, Sessions Journal, Union District, 1838, SCL
Richardson v. Saltar 4 N.C. (Taylor) 505 (1817)
Somerset v. Stewart Lofft I, 98, Eng. Rep. 499 [KB. 1772]
State v. James Allen, Miscellaneous Records of Slaves and Free Persons of Color,
    1755–1871, Granville County, NCDAH
State v. Atkinson 51 N.C. (6 Jones) 65 (1858)
State v. Boozer et al. 36 S.C.L. (5 Strob.) 21 (1850)
State v. Duke, Cuff and Arthur, Slave papers, 1796–1800, Bertie County, NCDAH
State v. William Galloway and James Galloway, Sessions Journal, Barnwell District, 1857, SCL
State v. Hailey 28 N.C. (6 Iredell) 11 (1845)
Tate v. O'Neal 8 N.C. (1 Hawks) 418 (1821)

Index

restrictions on, 190, 198–202; Union army controls movement of, 191–196; violence toward, 195–197, 207–217; and weapons, 195–197, 206, 211–213; and militia, 197–202, 315n6; become politically active, 201, 204; Southern white attitudes toward, 201–204, 206–216; beliefs about freedom, 203–204; Northern attitudes toward, 203–204; white psychological dominance of, 209, 214; respond to Ku Klux Klan, 210; remember patrols, 212–213, 218–219. *See also* Black Codes; Christmas insurrection scare; Free blacks; Freedmen's Bureau; Police, African American; Slaves; Union Leagues

Freedmen's Bureau, 190, 194, 201, 204, 209, 311n152

France, 139, 153, 167

French and Indian War, 153. *See also* Native Americans

French law and slavery, 226n12

Gabriel's rebellion, 57, 61, 115, 149–150, 287n3, 290n42, 292n60. *See also* Slave revolts

Gallman, Lucy (former slave), 63, 94

Georgetown (S.C.), 100, 149, 169, 177, 184, 186; forms patrol group, 53–56; compensates patrols, 63–64, 251n67; freedmen flock to, 190

Georgia, 115–117, 153, 160–161, 169, 185

Gilmer, Thomas, 133–135

Gooch, William, 30–31, 141–142, 148

Goochland County (Va.), 144, 270nn109,116

Grand juries, 22, 62–65, 100, 102, 140, 256n117, 268n145

Grandy, Moses (former slave), 113, 120

Great Dismal Swamp, 92, 129, 142, 239n129. *See also* Norfolk (Va.); Norfolk County (Va.); North Carolina; Swamps

Grimké, Angelina, 137–138

Haiti. *See* St. Domingue

Hamburg (S.C.), 76–77

Hammond, James Henry (slave master), 6–7, 81, 171

Henry, Patrick, 158–159

Henry County (Va.), 180

Hermandad, 10, 227n14. *See also* Slave catchers

Honor, 2, 70, 111, 130–131, 151–152, 208, 218

Huckstering, 12, 15

"Hue and cry" system, 3, 25–26

Indentured servants, 25–27, 33; used in mainland colonies, 8; in Barbados, 11; conspire with slaves, 13; in militia, 13; and

patrols, 22, 301n7; in N.C., 24; in Va., 28; feared by white masters, 153; in S.C., 232n58

Indians. *See* Native Americans

Jacobs, Harriet (former slave), 146

Jamaica, 14, 141–142

Johnston, Dennis (slave master), 133–135

Justices of the peace, 144, 174; appoint patrollers, 50, 78, 263n38; permit slaves to be whipped, 61; authorize rewards for runaways, 81; serve as patrols, 98

Kemble, Fanny (foreign traveler), 57, 60–61

King, Addison (patroller), 124–125, 127–128

Kingsford, William (foreign traveler), 41, 58

King William County (Va.), 126

Ku Klux Klan, 49, 51, 166, 318n45; and slave patrols, 3–4, 211–216, 218–220; patrol methods and, 168, 202, 207, 209–210; predecessors of, 206; veterans prefer police guard to, 206; origins, 207, 210; membership in, 208–210, 317n31; areas dominated by, 210; and folktales, 213; former masters bar, 213; as white law enforcement, 216–219; socializing in, 266n79; alternate names for, 316n15; active periods of, 319n57. *See also* Vigilante groups

Ku Klux Klan Act, 211

Latin America. *See* Brazil; Mexico; Peru

Legal history: Southern, 1; English law arrives in colonies, 8; laws may not reflect actual restrictions, 12; Barbadian slave laws influence S.C., 14, 18; shift from voluntary to mandatory enforcement, 17–18; routinized legal process, 36; debate about origins of colonial law, 225n8; "borrowing" of legal conceptions, 226n10

Leland, Samuel Wells (patroller), 74, 126–127

Lide, Hugh (slave master), 112–113

Lincoln, Abraham, 172, 177, 188

Loker (fictional slave catcher), 71–72, 80

Low Country (S.C.), 62, 65, 100, 108, 210. *See also* Georgetown

Lynchburg Virginian, 200

McBride, James (patroller), 107, 130

McGowan, Samuel, 66–67

Madison, James, 154, 159

Manigault, Charles (slave master), 99–100

Manigault, Louis (slave master), 99–100, 185

Marks (fictional slave catcher), 71–72, 80

Maroons, 14, 24, 30, 141–142, 175. *See also* Slaves, runaways

Martin, Josiah, 155–156, 296n103

Mason, George (slave master), 134–135, 286n149